FIRESIDE

Simon and Schuster's

# Guide to
# SHELLS

By Bruno Sabelli

Edited by
HAROLD S. FEINBERG,
The American Museum of Natural History

A Fireside Book
Published by Simon and Schuster
New York

The publisher wishes to thank the following for having provided some of the specimens which appear in the photographs: Dr. Gianna Spada, Bologna; Mario and Kety Angioi, Rome; Dr. Louis Joannis Demay, Director of the Musée de Malacologie, Nice; Professor Jacques Arnoult, Director of the Musée Océanographique of the Principality of Monaco; the Laboratorio di Malacologia dell'Instituto e Museo di Zoologia dell' Universita di Bologna; Claudio Ebreo, Director of the Tropical Aquarium at Syracuse; Cesare Corsini, Milan.

The photographs which appear in this volume are by Giuseppe Mazza—with the following exceptions: Entries 147, 302, 345: Sidney Horenstein, New York City; entry 166, pages 467, 485: George Raeihle, West Babylon, New York; pages 469, 487, 495, 497 © American Museum of Natural History.

A Fireside Book
Published by Simon and Schuster
A Division of Gulf & Western Corporation
Simon & Schuster Building
Rockefeller Center
1230 Avenue of the Americas
New York, New York 10020

Manufactured by Officine Grafiche di Arnoldo Mondadori Editore, Verona
Printed in Italy

1  2  3  4  5  6  7  8  9  10
1  2  3  4  5  6  7  8  9  10 Pbk.

Library of Congress Cataloging in Publication Data
Main entry under title:
Simon and Schuster's guide to shells.
    (A Fireside book)
    Translation of Conchiglie by B. Sabelli.
    Includes index.
    1. Shells—Identification. I. Feinberg, Harold S.
II. Sabelli, Bruno.   Conchiglie. III. Title: Guide
to shells.
QL430.4.S54      594'.04'7      79-21463
ISBN 0-671-25319-0
ISBN 0-671-25320-4 Pbk.

English translation by Thomas Snow and Neil Stratton
Drawings by Raffaella Giacometti
Symbols created by Raffaello Segattini

# CONTENTS

INTRODUCTION                                          page      9

SOFT SURFACE MOLLUSKS
  Occurring in sand, mud,
  and aquatic vegetation                              entries   1–133

FIRM SURFACE MOLLUSKS
  Occurring in rocks, gravel,
  and oyster beds                                     entries   134–221

CORAL DWELLERS                                        entries   222–302

OTHER MARINE MOLLUSKS                                 entries   303–335

LAND AND FRESH WATER MOLLUSKS                         entries   336–357

CLASSIFICATION TABLE OF THE SPECIES
  MENTIONED IN THE TEXT                               page      465

GLOSSARY                                              page      499

INDEX OF ENTRIES                                      page      503

## Note

The text is divided into five chapters. The first deals with mollusks that live on soft surfaces, the second with those that live on firm surfaces, the third with those of the coral formations, the fourth with those living in other marine habitats, and the fifth with the land and fresh water dwellers. It must be emphasized, however, that while some species are strictly limited to specific habitats (*Tapes aureus* being found only on soft bottoms for example, and never on hard substrates), other species live in a variety of environments. Although many cones, for example, normally live under sand, they can also be collected, especially when laying their eggs, while attached to rocks or coral. The assignment of some species to a specific habitat and so to one chapter in preference to another is, therefore, to some extent arbitrary. Mollusks that inhabit coral formations are understood for our purposes to be those of the coral sands in addition to those found on or under the coral itself.

The mollusks that live in special habitats are the pelagic animals (and are therefore not included in any other chapter) and those that live on algae, plants or other organisms, no matter what the substrate.

To facilitate comparisons between species of the same genus or family, all the illustrated species, including those figuring in the introduction, are listed in systematic order at the end of the book.

We have chosen to discuss the characteristics of the operculum under the heading, "shell."

The symbols that accompany the individual articles are purely indicative and approximate. The symbol representing geographical distributions will be obvious when compared with the map of Woodward malacological provinces on pp 46–47 of the Introduction.

## Note On Geographic Symbol

The map represents shell distribution based on Woodward's system of malacological regions and does not necessarily indicate occurrence within the entire region. For specific information regarding distribution, refer to entry.

# EXPLANATION OF SYMBOLS

## DIMENSIONS

 very small to small

 middle-sized

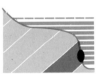 large to very large

## DISTRIBUTION

## HABITATS

 supralittoral

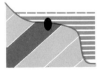 mesolittoral

 infralittoral

 circumlittoral

 aphytal or deep

 pelagic

fresh water

terrestrial

The shells that are the subject of this book are the calcareous (containing calcium carbonate) protective coverings of the various land and water animals called mollusks. The shells of animals like barnacles, crabs, et cetera, are not within our scope. Many people forget that the shell is only one part—the most obvious, of course, and the longest lasting—of an organism that is complex and interesting in itself (although some mollusks may not have a shell). Shells exhibit a wide variety of pattern and coloring that often match those of the animals that build them. So we will begin by trying to define and describe the animals themselves as precisely as possible before going on to discuss the shells.

## The phylum Mollusca

A *phylum* is a large group of living things with anatomies that are similar as a result of their common evolution. There are about thirty *phyla* in the animal kingdom. Examples are the *Porifera*, or sponges; the *Arthropoda*, or spiders, crabs, insects, et cetera; and the *Chordata*, or animals (including the vertebrates), with at least primitive forms of spinal cord.

The phylum Mollusca includes a seemingly infinite variety of forms in their evolution. Many authorities believe that the phylum comprises more than 100,000 species—only the Arthropoda include more—thus making it one of the largest and most important phyla. Its representatives have assumed a seemingly infinite variety of forms in their evolution.

## General structure

The diversity of specific shapes within the phylum Mollusca makes it impossible to define *mollusk* in terms of any distinctive trait. Structures that are prominent in some groups may be completely lacking in others. A strategy that *malacologists* (specialists in mollusks) often use to simplify definition is to imagine a theoretical animal with very general characteristics that may be individually lacking in any one or more actual classes of mollusk. This model was once thought to represent the primitive form from which all other members of the phylum are descendants. We think of it as a sort of ideal form that combines the main characteristics of the group.

The body of our theoretical mollusk will consist, then, of five fundamental parts—the "foot," the head, the visceral mass, the mantle and the shell. The *foot* is the muscular organ that the mollusk uses when he crawls from one place to another. Different mollusks have different types of foot, and its shape is determined by how the animal moves and the type of substrate the animal lives on (unless it is a swimming species). Anterior to the foot is the *head* (similar to a snail's), often with one or two pairs of tentacles with eyes at their bases or outer ends. Posterior to the foot is a kind of sac or mound, containing the digestive, excretory, circulatory, and genital organs, called the *visceral mass*. This mass is covered by a layer of integument, called the *mantle*, or *pallium*, which extends at its base into a

The generalized, "model" mollusk—(1) mouth, (2) eye, (3) tentacles, (4) salivary gland, (5) liver, (6) shell, (7) mantle, (8) crystalline style, (9) gut, (10) gonad, (11) pericardium (coelum), (12) ventricle, (13) atrium, (14) excretory organ, (15) pallial chamber, (16) anus, (17) gill, (18) asphradium, (19) visceral nervous cords, (20) pedal retractor muscle, (21) foot, (22) stomach, (23) pedal nerve cords, (24) peri-esophagal nerve ring, (25) radula.

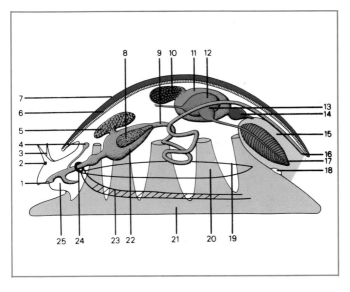

marginal fold enveloping the head and foot. The space between the mantle and the rest of the animal's body is called the *pallial chamber,* or *mantle cavity.* We shall see that most of the interactions between the mollusk and its environment are conducted by way of the pallial chamber and the organs it contains. The mantle is also the part of the body that secretes the shell.

**Anatomy**
We have been discussing the external structure of our hypothetical mollusk. Let us now take a general look at a few characteristics of its internal anatomy. We shall first distinguish the organs and organ systems that carry out the digestive functions of the mollusk from those that govern its interactions with the external environment. We will go on to consider the reproductive organs along with certain strategies that the mollusks employ to perpetuate and multiply their kind.

**Anatomic organization of hypothetical mollusks**
The *alimentary system* provides for the ingestion, digestion, absorption and assimilation of food. This system begins at the *mouth,* located anteriorly and ventrally in the head (when there is one). The mouth leads to the *buccal cavity,* the side of which may be provided with a pair of strong plates called *jaws,* separated or joined above and covered by a hard chitinous secre-

**11**

tion from the surface tissues. The jaws are reinforced by a sort of cartilaginous tissue and provided with a more or less complex musculature. Anterior to the buccal cavity is the *pharynx,* most of which is occupied by the *odontophore,* a device that can be protruded to some extent from the mouth and supports a tonguelike structure (the *radula*) equipped with rows of tiny teeth. Opening into the pharynx are ducts from one or two pairs of *salivary glands* that may in some species have been modified into organs to secrete the venom used to paralyze or kill the animal's prey. The alimentary tract continues with the *esophagus* and then expands into a *stomach,* where the food, which has been reduced to strings of particles glued together with mucus, is partly digested but mostly forced by tiny *cilia* (whiplike structures) into the ducts of two large digestive glands that occupy nearly all the space within the visceral mass. Since digestion in mollusks takes place both extracellularly (especially in the stomach) and intracellularly (especially in the hepatopancreas), the organ must both secrete digestive enzymes and absorb particles of food. The posterior part of the stomach in many mollusks is more or less conical and in bivalves contains a translucent rodlike structure, the *crystalline style,* which secretes special enzymes to digest certain carbohydrates called *glucides.* After the stomach comes the more or less convoluted *hindgut,* or intestine, which opens at the *anus* into the pallial cavity. In the diagram on page 11 the hindgut is shown crossing the pericardial cavity and the atrium of the heart. This is however a primitive characteristic that can be found only in some mollusk groups.

The *circulatory system* transports and distributes the material assimilated from the alimentary system, along with the oxygen required by the chemical processes carried out within the cells, to the various parts of the body. In the mollusks the circulatory system is "open"——the blood, or *hemolymph,* passes directly from the rather gross blood vessels into spaces or gaps between the organs. The *heart,* which pumps the blood by contracting, is a simple organ with a pair of auricles, or atria, that receive the oxygenated blood from the gills and pump it into the single ventricle, which then sends it through the immediately posterior aorta to the different regions of the body. In the mollusks, only arterial (oxygenated) blood passes through the heart. The organ is contained in the *pericardial cavity,* which fills the rest of the body cavity, the *coelum.* The blood——in contrast to that of vertebrates, which contains many different kinds of free-floating cells (red and white corpuscles, etc.)——has only a few such cells, and the respiratory pigments, the large molecules that capture and release oxygen, are suspended directly in it instead of being enclosed in cells. Mollusks have two main respiratory pigments——the red hemoglobin, which contains iron and is rarely present, and the blue, copper-containing hemocyanin.

The *excretory system* eliminates the catabolic products, materials that result from the breakdown of assimilated food, mainly nitrogenous substances (ammonia and urea). The organs that perform this function—one, two, or more "kidneys"—are quite different in the various groups of mollusks. In their most primitive form they are connected to the pericardial cavity by the *renipericardial ducts*. Often at least one of these excretory ducts will be modified to form a *gonoduct*, a passage for the transportation of the *gametes*——the spermatozoa or eggs. The gonoducts and excretory ducts open into the pallial chamber.

The *respiratory system,* which captures the oxygen required for the chemical processes within the cells, is usually represented by a pair of *gills* in the pallial chamber, but in most gastropods the right gill has disappeared. The gills in the diagram on page 11 are of what is thought to be a more primitive type. They are shaped more or less like a feather, with a central axis and two series of gill branches like the barbs of a feather on each side. The gills are the site of respiratory exchange——the exhalation of carbon dioxide and inhalation of oxygen. The gills found in different groups of mollusks may assume various forms reflecting the animals' environments and feeding habits. Land snails, of course, have no gills, but a primitive sort of lung instead. The pallial chamber is an especially important structure. It mediates between the animal and its external environment, and is found in almost all the various groups, which have "invented" novel strategies for using it in different types of water current or have modified it into special organs. Some experts even consider the chamber itself to be an organ.

### Interactions with the environment

These are handled by the *nervous system* (including the sense organs) and the *muscular system.* We will concern ourselves only with the muscles that make up the foot and those that attach the animal to its shell. Both systems, of course, have very different forms in different groups of animals. Basically there are two extreme types of neural organization (with many intermediate forms)——the cord system, in which the neural tree tapers and branches in smooth lines; and the ganglion system, which is characterized by knots of nerve cells called ganglia, bound together by nervous tissue consisting of slender elongations of the cells. In the latter, there is a pair of cerebral ganglia located in the head symmetrically with and dorsally to the alimentary canal (called the *supraesophagal ganglia*), connected to each other by a transverse band of nerve tissue called a *commissure* and to a pair of closely packed pedal ganglia (innervating the foot) below the alimentary canal by two longitudinal connectives. The supraesophagal ganglia also give rise to two nerve cords that spread throughout the body of the mollusk and come together again in the rear. Distributed along these cords are certain symmetrical pairs of ganglia, mainly the pleural (connected by commissures to the pedal), which innervates the mantle and its associated sense organs, and the parietal and visceral, which generally inner-

Top: Cord-type nervous system—(1) periesophagal nerve ring, (2) esophagus, (3) pleural cord, (4) pedal cord.
Bottom: Ganglion nervous system—(1) cerebral ganglion, (2) pleural ganglion, (3) esophagus, (4) visceral ganglion, (5) parietal ganglion, (6) pedal cord, (7) pedal ganglion.

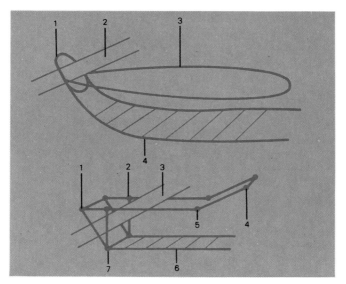

vate the organs of the visceral mass. The *sense organs* are of several types—*photoreceptors,* which may range in complexity from simple patches of photosensitive pigment, with or without lenses, to real eyes as complex as those of vertebrates; *statocysts,* organs that sense the orientation of the body in space; and *chemoreceptors,* which may range from simple cells sensitive to certain substances in the animal's environment to fully developed organs like the *asphradium,* located in the pallial chamber, where it tests the water passing over the gills. Tactile organs called tentacles may be located at the edge of the mantle or at other points on the body.

## Methods of reproduction and dispersion
All the functions we have considered so far are related to the survival of the individual animal. The *reproductive system* on the other hand relates to the survival of the species. Sexual dichotomy is not as clearly defined among the mollusks as it is among many other animals. Some groups are *dioecious* (that is, its individuals are entirely male or female), while others are *hermaphroditic* (that is, individuals combine the characteristics of both sexes). Hermaphroditism in the mollusk is usually of the type in which the gametes of the different sexes do not mature at the same time, and there is evidence of the existence, in most species, of mechanisms to inhibit self-impregnation, so that reproduction requires two partners. This means that the individual heredities will be combined, and different

Top: The tentacles that can be seen emerging from between the two valves of this *Pectin jacobaeus* have both tactile and chemoreceptive functions.
Bottom: Even the edges of the mantle on this file shell are abundantly provided with sensory tentacles.

Top: *Buccinulum corneum* depositing egg cases.
Bottom: *Phalium granulatum* above newly deposited egg cases.

Left: Spermatozeugma of *Cerithiopsis tubercularis*——(1) sperm.
Right: Spermatophore of the cephalopod *Loligo*——(1) hood, (2) ejaculatory organ,
(3) cement gland, (4) external tunica, (5) sperm mass, (6) tunicary filament.

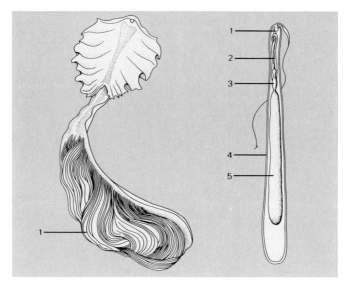

characteristics can be acquired more easily. It is evident that even hermaphroditism is more advantageous than dioecism, because at least a hermaphroditic animal can always mate with any other animal of the same species and thus has a much higher chance of ensuring successful impregnation. Whether male or female, dioecious or hermaphroditic, each animal will be provided with a reproductive organ (*gonad*) to produce the gametes. In one kind of fertilization, called external, both eggs and sperm are released into the water, and fertilization takes place there. This results in an enormous waste of germ cells, and the phylum has, over the course of its evolution, developed several mechanisms for internal fertilization. Male individuals or those functioning as males may have a copulatory organ, or penis, for introducing the spermatozoa directly into the genital tract of the female. Some groups carry their sperm in special packets called *spermatophores* or in a modified body part called a *spermatozeugma*. Mollusks——except for a few groups in which the animals incubate their eggs within the female genital tract——deposit them in the environment, so another advantage of internal fertilization is that membranes or shells can be formed around the fertilized eggs during their descent along the genital tract to protect them from various environmental agents. In addition to being protected by their individual shells, groups of eggs may be enclosed in egg cases or deposited in specially sheltered locations. The embryo usually develops into a larval form that hatches and is carried

Egg-laying and the successive stages in embryonic development in Lymnaea.

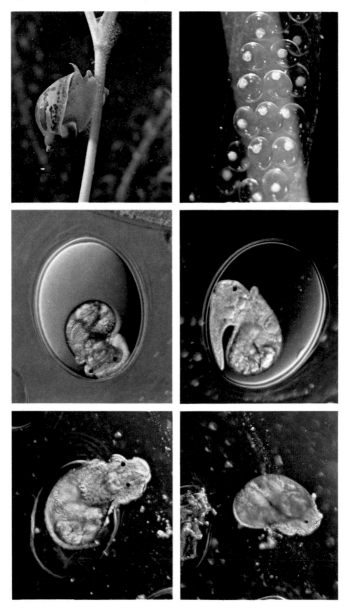

Trocophore of *Patella*——(1) apical ciliary tuft, (2) double ring of cilia, (3) larval mouth.

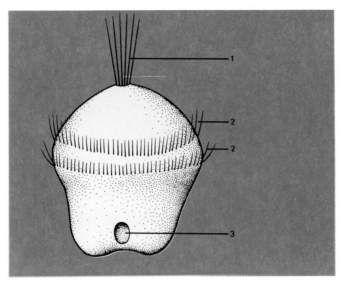

far away by the water, ensuring the dispersion of the various species, most of which occupy vast geographical areas. There are two main types of larva. The form thought to be the most primitive is the *trochophore,* which is shaped like a toy top with cilia in a ring around its widest part and in a tuft on top. Often the trochophore will develop while still within the egg into a second larval stage called a *veliger.* This stage is characterized by an enlarged ciliar ring called the *velum.* The veliger already has certain body parts found in the adult——the foot, the mantle, a larval shell formed from a gland called the shell gland, and a sort of head divided into two or more wide lobes provided with tiny cilia that propel the larva through the water and convey suspended food particles to the mouth. Both larval forms are found mainly in salt-water mollusks and rarely among the fresh-water types. Like the trochophore, the veliger is carried by currents of water to places far from its place of origin. It has recently been shown that some veligers can travel from one coast of the Atlantic to the other, while others last only a few hours. Near the end of the larval stage the animal begins to reabsorb the velum and descends to the bottom of the sea, undergoing a metamorphosis to an adult form if it finds a suitable substrate, and dying if it does not. We can often draw conclusions about an animal's larval stage by examining the traces of its development left in the well-preserved adult shell. With some mollusks it is even possible to make out the different sculpturing (surface marking) of the larval shell at the

**19**

Veliger of a prosobranch gastropod.
Left: Ventral view.
Right: Lateral view—(1) velum, (2) larval shell, (3) foot, (4) operculum, (5) mouth,
(6) eye, (7) pallial chamber.

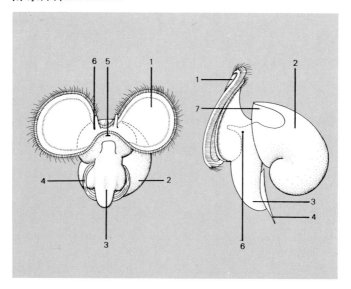

apex of the adult structure, and we can sometimes distinguish another, more remote stage with different ornamentation, which represents the remains of the shell formed by the embryo within the egg.

## CLASSIFICATION
We will now discuss some actual versions of the hypothetical generalized molluscan structure described above as they occur among different groups and see how they have become diversified during the evolution of the phylum.

### Biological classification
The problem of just what to call a particular organism has always been significant. What the English call a robin is a very different bird from the American. On the other hand the same animal may have different names—"mountain lion" and "cougar," for instance—even in different regions of one country. Biologists have had to overcome these ambiguities to keep from communicating at cross purposes, and the result is the binomial system of nomenclature.

Just as the animal and other kingdoms of living organisms are broken down into phyla, each phylum in turn is subdivided into lower-ranking groups that have similar characteristics. This process is known as *classification*, and the branch of biology that deals with such problems is called *systematics*, or *taxon-*

Apical whorls on a turris shell, showing different types of sculpturing. The first whorl represents the embryonic shell, the second and third the larval shell, and the fourth is the primary whorl of the teloconch—the adult shell.

omy. The scientific theory behind it we owe to the eighteenth-century Swedish botanist Carl von Linné (whose name is more familiar in its Latinized form Linnaeus). He had the idea of compiling a uniform, hierarchical system, a "system of nature," so that every animal or plant could be referred to without ambiguity. The basis of his system is a two-word expression—in Latin, of course, since it was the official language of science in Linnaeus' time—for every type of plant or, later, animal: *"Cymatium femorale."* The first word, regularly capitalized, is the name of the *genus,* the group of all organisms that share certain characteristics, and the second is the name of the *species,* a group of organisms that are different in some particular way from all others in the genus. Members of the doglike genus, for instance, all share the generic name *Canis* (Latin for "dog"); the wolf members are called *Canis lupus* ("wolf dog"); the domesticated dog is known as *Canis familiaris* ("domestic dog"); the jackal as *Canis aureus* ("golden dog"); and the coyote as *Canis latrans* ("barking dog").

The binomial name sometimes is followed by the proper name of a person and a date—*"Pinctada radiata* (Leach, 1814)." The name is that of the scientist who first described or named the species, and the four-digit number signifies the year in which he did so. If the species remains in the original genus, then there are no parentheses around the author's name and date. If, however, a subsequent worker changes the generic name by assigning the species to another genus, then the original author's name and date are placed within parentheses. The initial "L." always stands for *Linnaeus* (or Linné). The parentheses in this case mean that even though the author did name the species *"radiata,"* he attributed it to a different genus and it was later reassigned to the *Pinctada* by another authority.

The binomial, or Linnaean, method of nomenclature is still in use today, although genus and species are not the only *taxa,* or categories, recognized. Related genera are placed within a *family,* families within an *order,* orders within a *class,* classes within a *phylum,* and phyla finally within a *kingdom.* These are the main taxa, and taxonomists have adopted many intermediate groups. They are listed in the table below. Next to some of the terms are parentheses containing standardized or conventional endings, developed from Latin endings, which the International Commission for Zoological Nomenclature (ICZN) has adopted for names referring to groups of that particular rank. The name *Canidae,* for example, which refers to the family that comprises the genus *Canis* and the foxes, the African hunting dog, et cetera, necessarily refers to a family, because all family names and only family names end in -dae. These names are obligatory for the lower taxa and are recommended for superclasses, classes, subclasses, orders, and suborders. The taxonomic categories in italics and underscored in the table are the main ones.

*Kingdom*
  Subkingdom
    *Phylum*
      Subphylum
        Superclass ( -a)
          *Class* ( -ea)
            Subclass ( -ia)
            Infraclass
              Superorder
                *Order* ( -ida)
                  Suborder ( -ina)
                  Infraorder
                    Superfamily ( -oidea or -acea)
                      *Family* ( -dae)
                        Subfamily ( -inae)
                        Tribe ( -ini)
                        *Genus*
                          Subgenus
                          *Species*
                            Subspecies

An organism can be assigned to a kingdom or phylum by relatively objective criteria of similarity in structure or characteristics. Assignments to other taxa are more subjective. To distinguish and define the different orders of the class of insects, for example, one of the characteristics is wing structure. The Hymenoptera (ants, wasps, bees, etc.) have membranous wings; the Lepidoptera (butterflies and moths) have scaly wings; and so forth. In the mammalian class, on the other hand, we use completely different criteria, like the number and type of teeth, in assigning an animal to a particular order. If two organisms can mate and produce *fertile* young, the parents by definition belong to the same species. Since the young produced by mating two animals of different species will be sterile, it may be said that the two species exist in reproductive isolation from each other. This is the classical biological definition. It implies that a species is to be defined, not by exclusively morphological criteria, but by a number of morphological and functional characteristics that are the results of evolution. The concept is quite different from that adopted in the early 1900s and still in use for practical identification. The latter, the typological definition of species, derives from certain theories of the Platonic philosophers that the world of our experience is nothing but a reflection of an ontologically higher world made up of ideal forms and that the various members of a species are therefore nothing but imperfect manifestations of the form or "idea" implicit in the genus. The task of systematics, then, is to identify both the ideal essence of the animal or plant as represented by the genus and the specific *differentiae* that made the individual an imperfect copy. Such an attitude does not lead to mere illogical pigeonholing, since it has been refined by inductive studies of the major and minor relationships and differences among countless individuals since the time of Aristotle. As a result, certain characteristics take precedence over others that are regarded as only accidental. We do not class birds and bats together because they both have wings, and we no longer call whales or porpoises fish because they live in the water. The characteristics that we do employ are derived from the more modern evolutionary and functional taxonomy in that they are the results of more or less demonstrable evolutionary histories. It should also be stressed that taxonomy is not immutable; it advances with our knowledge of science, so that species are assigned to new groups and new taxa are occasionally described.

### Molluscan subphyla and classes

According to the most recent classification, the phylum Mollusca is divided into two subphyla: (1) the *Aculifera*, characterized by spicules, spikelike structures, of various kinds on the mantle and either by the absence of a shell or by a shell divided into eight plates; and (2) the *Conchifera*, characterized by shells except for cases where the shell is vestigial or has disappeared over the course of evolution.

The classes *Aplacophora* (solenogasters), *Caudofoveata* and *Polyplacophora* (chitons) are closely related. The first two were formerly regarded as the single class *Aplacophora*, because they have no shells. They are strange, wormlike mol-

Left: *Chaetoderma nitidulum,* mollusk of the class Caudofoveata—(1) mouth, (2) anus, (3) ctenidia.
Right: *Dondersia festiva,* representative of the class Aplacorphora—(1) mouth, (2) pedal furrow.

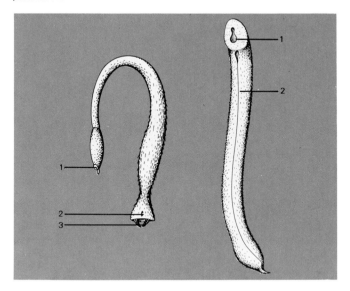

lusks with a body covered by a cuticulated mantle armed with chitinous spicules. The foot is reduced to a shieldlike append-age (in the Caudofoveata) or limited to a ventral furrow. They have no definite head or true pallial chamber. They are all ma-rine animals. There are 120 species of Aplacophora ranging in size from 2 to 100 millimeters. The Caudofoveata are repre-sented by sixty species ranging from 5 to 140 millimeters in size. The Polyplacophora are bilaterally symmetrical mollusks with shells that in their present-day forms are divided into eight overlapping articulated plates (or valves). This series of plates is bordered by a mantle covered with different kinds of spic-ules and is called the *girdle.* They have a soled foot, an only slightly differentiated head, and a pallial chamber that sur-rounds practically the whole body. The gills occur in various numbers and are posterior. There is a mouth at one end and an anus at the other. The nervous system is of the cord type. There are two sexes, and the egg develops into a trochophore. There are about a thousand living species, all marine.

The extant classes—*Monoplacophora, Gastropoda* (snails, slugs, limpets and conchs), *Bivalvia* (clams, oysters, etc.), *Scaphopoda* (tusk shells), and *Cephalopods* (squids, octo-puses and nautiluses) and the extinct †*Rostroconchia,* †*Sten-othecoida* and †*Mattheva*—have an evolutionary affinity.

Malacologists used to think that the Monoplacophora had be-come extinct in the Devonian Period, 350 million years ago, until a scientific journal reported in 1957 that ten living speci-mens and three shells of a species of this class had been dis-

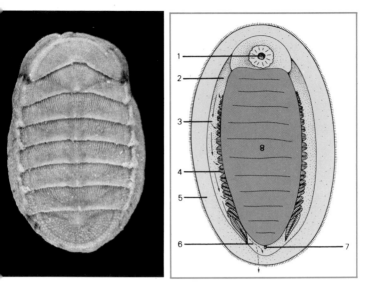

Left: The chiton *Ischnochiton rissoi,* clearly showing the eight valves and the girdle.
Right: Ventral view of the chiton *Lepidochitona cinerea*—(1) mouth, (2) inhalant current, (3) pallial chamber, (4) gills, (5) girdle, (6) exhalant current, (7) anus, (8) foot.

covered five years previously at a depth of 3,570 meters off Costa Rica. The species was named *Neopilina galatheae* (*neo-* meaning "new," *Pilina* being a related fossil genus, and *Galathea* the Danish ship that had dredged up the shell). Since then, other species have been collected in various parts of the world and in shallower waters (a little over 100 meters). The Monoplacophora have more or less flattened conical shells and exhibit partial *metamerism,* a segmental body structure with certain organs repeated in each segment rather than with one organ serving the whole body. These animals have five series of gills in the pallial chamber between the circular foot and the margin of the shell, which is light and fragile. Among other anatomical peculiarities are the mouth at the anterior end (with the anus at the opposite end), the eight paris of foot-retractor muscles, the six pairs of *nephridia* (excretory organs), the two pairs of gonads, and the nervous system, which is basically of the çord type and, so, rather primitive.

The Gastropoda, with more than 80,000 species, constitute the most numerous class and the only one adapted for life on land as well as in water. More than 60 percent of the species are marine however. The foot is usually highly developed and well suited for crawling (a "soled foot"), and the head is usually distinct. Sometimes the posterior dorsal part of the foot is provided with a horny or calcareous structure called the *operculum,* which can be drawn in against the mouth of the shell to stop it up when the animal has retreated inside.

Shell of the monoplacophore *Neopilina galathea*. Dorsal (A) and lateral (B) views and ventral view of the morphology of the soft parts (C)—(1) mouth, (2) velum, (3) gills, (4) foot, (5) edge of mantle, (6) anus, (7) shell.

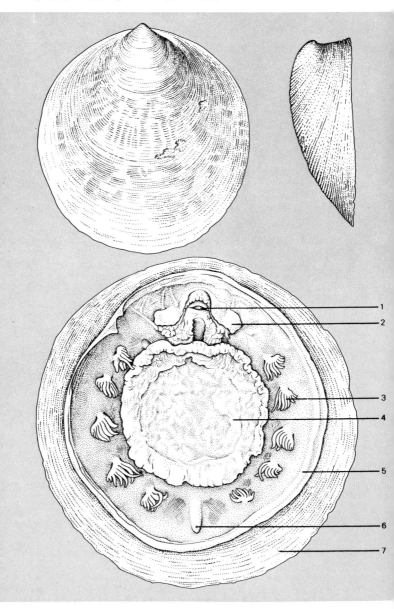

Top: *Hexaplex trunculus*. Note the operculum on the dorsal surface of the foot.
Bottom: *Ocenebra erinacea*. The operculum neatly seals off the aperture with the soft parts retracted.

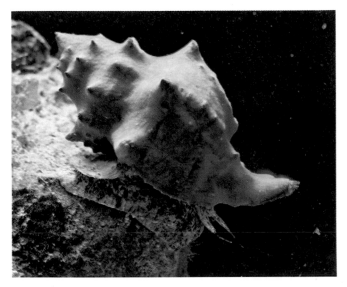

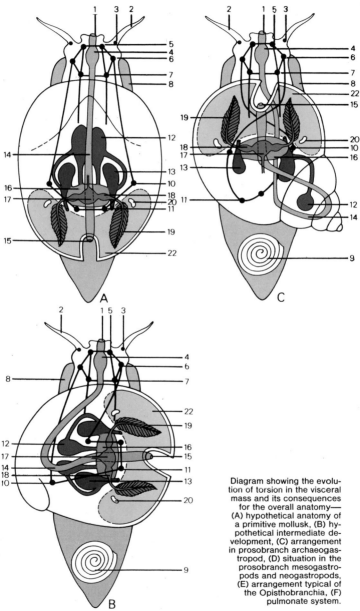

Diagram showing the evolution of torsion in the visceral mass and its consequences for the overall anatomy— (A) hypothetical anatomy of a primitive mollusk, (B) hypothetical intermediate development, (C) arrangement in prosobranch archaeogastropod, (D) situation in the prosobranch mesogastropods and neogastropods, (E) arrangement typical of the Opisthobranchia, (F) pulmonate system.

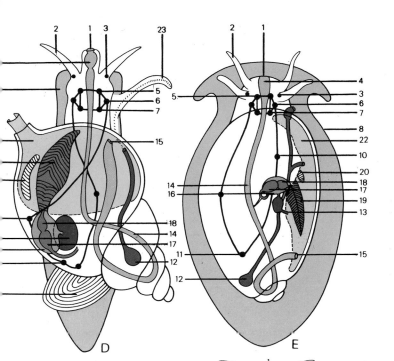

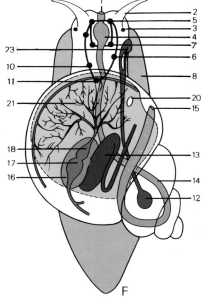

(1) mouth, (2) tentacles, (3) eyes, (4) radula, (5) cerebral ganglion, (6) pleural ganglion, (7) pedal ganglion, (8) foot, (9) operculum, (10) parietal ganglion, (11) visceral ganglion, (12) gonad, (13) excretory organ, (14) gut, (15) anus, (16) pericardium, (17) ventricle, (18) atrium, (19) gill, (20) asphradium, (21) lung, (22) pallial chamber, (23) copulatory organ.

*Charonia nodifera,* a prosobranch gastropod.

The gastropod body goes through a complicated and much disputed process called *torsion,* which is already evident in the trochophore in more primitive forms and in the veliger in more advanced forms. Torsion means that the visceral mass is twisted through a 90-degree angle and, together with the shell that covers it, takes on a spiral shape. This twisting shifts the pallial chamber to the anterior end of the animal, and one member of each of the organs that occur in pairs is reduced in size (except in the most primitive forms), so that there is only one kidney, for instance, while the heart has only one atrium, which receives the oxygenated blood from a single gill. Even the gonads are of different sizes. The nervous system is ganglionic, and there is a marked tendency for the ganglia to be concentrated in the head (*cephalization*). In many species torsion also forces the pleuroparietal connectives to cross each other in a figure eight.

The class *Gastropoda* is nowadays divided into three subclasses—the *Prosobranchia* ("front gills," so called because the gill or gills are in front of the heart); the *Opisthobranchia* ("rear gills"), or sea slugs; and the land snails, the *Pulmonata* ("lunged," with, instead of gills, the pallial chamber modified into a sort of lung, well supplied with blood vessels, called the pulmonary sac). The latter two classes are also collectively called *Euthyneura* ("straight nerves") because the neural connectives are not crossed. Whereas the Prosobranchia and Opisthobranchia are almost exclusively marine, almost all the

Top: an opisthobranch (nudibranch) gastropod.
Bottom: a pulmonate gastropod. Note the pneumostome, the opening in the pallial chamber through which the lung makes contact with the air.

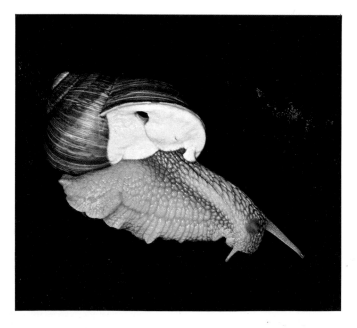

Top: the anatomy of a bivalve—(1) umbo, (2) hinge, (3) liver, (4) stomach, (5) anterior abductor muscle, (6) mouth, (7) labial palp, (8) periesophagal cingulum, (9) cerebropleural ganglion, (10) pedal ganglion, (11) foot, (12) gut, (13) gonad, (14) genital pore, (15) shell, (16) edge of mantle, (17) gill, (18) excretory organ, (19) visceral ganglion, (20) inhalant siphon, (21) exhalant siphon, (22) anus, (23) posterior abductor muscle, (24) posterior aorta, (25) pericardium, (26) heart.

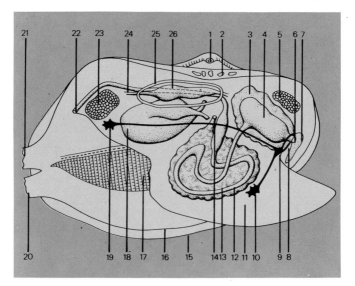

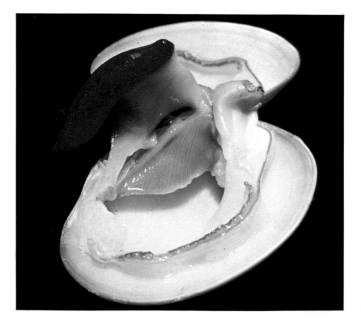

Opposite page, bottom: *Callista chione* opened to reveal the anatomy.
Top: various types of bivalve gills (in transverse section)—(A) protobranch, (B) filibranch, (C) eulamellibranch, (D) septibranch. (1) foot, (2) ctenidium, (3) branchial
filaments, (4) suprabranchial chamber, (5) septum.

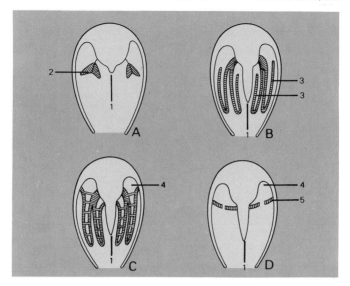

Pulmonata live in fresh water or on land.

The *Bivalvia,* so called because their shells are divided into two hinged-together parts called "valves," are also called *Pelecypoda,* because many species have a foot shaped like a battle-ax (*Greek pelekys*), a form well adapted for digging in sand or mud. The mouth and anus are at opposite ends of the animal, and the hindgut crosses the pericardium and ventricle. There is no radula. The gills are highly developed and modified for filtering out particles of food suspended in the water as well as for respiration. The pallial chamber, which completely surrounds the body, is bordered by two mantle lobes that secrete the valves of the shell. The margins of these lobes tend to stick together or even become fused, leaving two apertures, one ventral, which draws in currents of water to be circulated within the pallial chamber, and one dorsal, through which the water is expelled. In some species the mantle is elongated at these apertures and forms tubelike structures called *siphons.* The nervous system is ganglionic. There is a veliger stage of development. Some fresh-water species have a special larval form called a *glochidium* that is parasitic on the gills or other parts of fish or salamander. There are about 20,000 living species of bivalves, most of which are marine. Most of the mollusks in this class live on the loose bottoms of bodies of water, where they burrow in the sand or mud.

The *Scaphopoda,* or tusk shells, all exclusively marine, comprise about a thousand species that are characterized by a tu-

Bottom: The arrows indicate the directions of water currents into and out of the siphons in various types of bivalves.
Opposite page, top: the anatomy of a scaphopod—(1) captacula, (2) mouth, (3) proboscis, (4) cerebral ganglion, (5) pleural ganglion, (6) visceral ganglion, (7) esophagus, (8) excretory organ, (9) liver, (10) gonad, (11) posterior aperture, (12) mantle, (13) shell, (14) anus, (15) gut, (16) radula, (17) pedal ganglion, (18) foot.

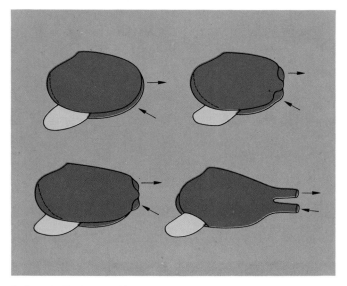

bular shell shaped like an elephant's tusk and open at both ends. Tusk shells live partly buried in the mud or sand, with the smaller posterior end protruding to allow the escape of catabolites, feces and gametes. The conical foot emerges from the anterior end. The head, also anterior, is reduced to a simple proboscis, a tubular organ ending in the mouth. Special sense organs, slender tentacles called *captacula,* also serve to collect particles of food from the water. As for the interior anatomy, the heart lacks both auricles and atria, there are no differentiated respiratory organs (respiration taking place through the surface of the body), the gonads emit gametes through the excretory system, and the nervous system is ganglionic. The larva is a trochophore.

The class *Cephalopoda,* which numbers about seven hundred living and more than ten thousand fossil species, consists of marine species exclusively. Only one of the two subclasses, the *Nautiloida,* has an external shell. The other subclass, the *Coleoidea,* has an internal, almost always reduced, shell or often none at all. The name of the class (''head-foot'') comes from the foot and head being shifted to the anterior end and modified into a series of arms that surround the mouth and are armed with rows of suckers on the inner side. This cephalopod carries a ventrally located structure in the form of a truncated cone called the *funnel,* that can expel water from the pallial chamber like the jet on an airplane to propel the animal through the water. The head is well developed and the mantle more or less covers the visceral mass and secretes the materi-

Bottom: the anatomy of a cephalopod—(1) oral arm, (2) tentacular arm, (3) sucker, (4) mouth, (5) mandible, (6) radula, (7) eye, (8) brain, (9) cartilaginous capsule, (10) salivary gland, (11) esophagus, (12) liver, (13) shell, (14) stomach, (15) pericardium, (16) ventricle, (17) gonad, (18) gonadal coelum, (19) ink sac, (20) vena cava, (21) branchial heart, (22) atrium, (23) gill, (24) pallial chamber, (25) excretory organ, (26) genital aperture, (27) excretory aperture, (28) anus, (29) funnel, (30) valvular limbus.

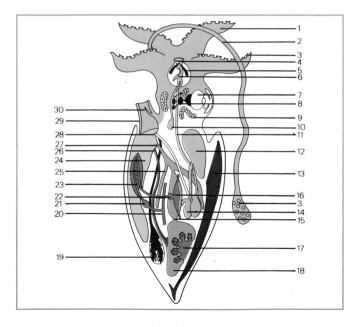

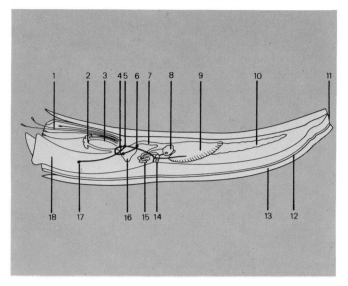

Top: brood shell of *Argonauta nodosa*.
Bottom: Male and female of *Argonauta argo*. The female, much larger than the male, is partly concealed by the brood shell. The male has a well-developed hectocotylus.

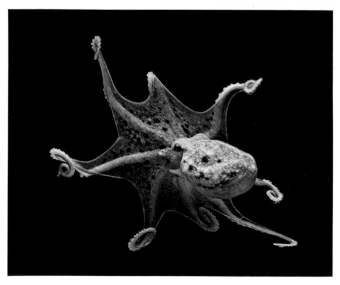

als that form the shell (when present), which is contained in a special internal dorsal pouch. The mouth is provided with two robust jaws shaped like a parrot's beak. The intestine is folded so that the anal aperture faces forward. The heart is assisted in pumping by two supplementary so-called branchial hearts that force blood into the gills. The nautiloid heart has two pairs of auricles that receive the blood from two pairs of gills, which is why the subclass is also called *Tetrabranchia* ("four gills"), while the *Coleoidea* and *Dibranchia* have only one pair of each. The ganglionic nervous system, highly developed and cephalized, is enclosed in a cartilaginous capsule. The eyes are almost as complex as the eyes of vertebrates. The genital system has only one gonad. The sperm is contained in spermatophores that are conveyed to the female by a modified arm called the *hectocotylus*. In some species this structure may even become detached and float along in the water until it encounters a female. Special glands in the female secrete capsules around the eggs, which are deposited in clusters on the bottom of the sea or kept in a special egg pouch formed of two modified arms. Development is direct, with no larval forms, and the embryos are nourished from a yolk sac, an exceptional characteristic among the invertebrates. While the nautiloid subclass has few living species, the coleoids have many, divided into the orders *Decapoda*, with ten arms (two of them elongated, called the tentacles) and an external shell, and *Octopoda*, with eight arms and no shell.

The prosobranch gastropod *Monodonta turbinata* with the radula extroflexed.

## TWO IMPORTANT TAXONOMIC CRITERIA

We will now discuss in greater detail the morphology of two structures that are of particular interest because they are characteristic of each species and therefore important bases for classification—the radula and the shell.

### The radula

This apparatus, also called the tongue, is supported on a structure called the *odontophore*. The radula is a ribbonlike membrane with transverse rows of *denticles,* or "teeth," on the top. Each row may consist of from one to many denticles, and the number of rows varies. The odontophore is a muscular cushion reinforced with what are called *cartilages* because of their resemblance to vertebrate hyaline cartilage. The more primitive animals usually have more cartilages. There is a *cuticle,* or elastic membrane, in the alimentary tract between the radula and the odontophore. The radula is open and flattened toward the front of the odontophore and is maintained in position by tensor muscles. Posteriorly, the edges of the rádular ribbon curve up to form a tube called the *radular sheath*.

The radular sheath lies in a furrow along the middle of the back of the odontophore and protrudes posteriorly into a body cavity that is closed at the other end, called the *radular sac*. The membranes of the radula and the denticles are formed from

Diagrams showing the relations between the radula and various parts of the anterior section of the digestive tract—(A) the radula as seen from above resting on the odontophore (anterior) and the radular pouch (posterior); (B) Transverse section of the radula in retraction—(1) mouth, (2) radular teeth, (3) cartilage, (4) musculature, (5) elastic membrane, (6) subradular membrane, (7) radular pouch, (8) esophagus, (9) pharynx.

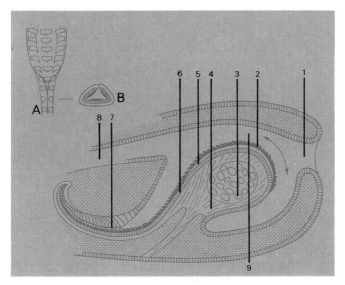

special cells called *odontoblasts* at the base of the radular sac. The pharyngeal cavity often extends along the bottom of the radular apparatus to form the *subradular pouch*. These structures are quite similar in all mollusks except the bivalves, where they are completely lacking.

**The shell**
As mentioned above, the mantle secretes the materials that build up the shell, the outer layer, or *periostracum* (which can be added to only at its outer margin), and the inner layer, or *nacre* (mother-of-pearl). The periostracum, which covers the whole surface of the shell, is organic, having a protein base, and starts out as a single homogenous layer, differentiating later into two or more layers. The remainder of the shell is formed mainly of calcium carbonate. Calcium ions from the environment (fresh or salt water or land) are transported in the molluscan bloodstream to the mantle and then excreted into a fluid between the mantle and the shell. Here is produced the calcium carbonate that is absorbed by the *conchiolin*, the protein matrix that is also secreted by the mantle. The composition of this extrapallial fluid, which depends on the concentration of various substances in the blood and tissues, determines the chemical nature and the conformation of the matrix of conchiolin and the growth rate of the calcium carbonate crystals. This mineral crytallizes in various forms (systems), two of which are utilized in shells—*calcite,* made up of

Arrangement of the layers of a bivalve shell and their relation to the mantle that secretes them—(1) periostracum, (2) layer with calcite prisms, (3) layer with aragonite lamellae, (4) external pallial epithelium, (5) internal pallial epithelium, (6) retractor muscle controlling the edge of the mantle, (7) internal pallial fold, (8) median pallial fold, (9) periostracal furrow, (10) external pallial fold, (11) edge of the shell.

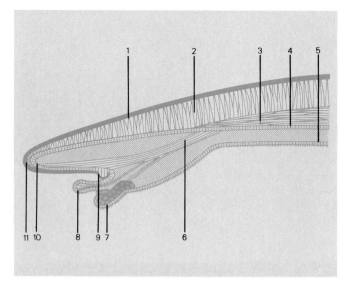

rhombohedral, scalenohedral, or prismatic crystals in the trigonal system, and *aragonite,* with elongated prismatic crystals in the rhombic system. Shell structure is dictated in part by the calcitic or aragonitic nature and the type of aggregation of these crystals. Today we recognize eight different types of crystalline shell structure, and we usually find two or three different types in the same shell.

In many mollusks (especially bivalves) the middle layer of the shell, between the periostracum and the nacre layer, is built up out of a *prismatic structure*—calcite, or in rare cases (freshwater mussels and trygonids) aragonite, prisms of various patterns oriented perpendicular to the surface.

*Crossed-lamellar structure* is undoubtedly the most frequent. It is found in many marine bivalves and in marine and fresh-water gastropods. It consits mainly of aragonite, although some cases of crossed-lamellar calcite (crossed foliaceous structure in the ancylids, oysters and limpets) do occur. It consists of overlapping primary lamellae composed of secondary lamellae that are made up in turn of tertiary crystals fused together. Since the primary lamellae overlap the secondary at an angle of approximately 45 degrees, the structure is exceptionally strong.

The *nacre structure* forms the innermost layer of the shell of many mollusk families and is not found outside the phylum. Among bivalves it is found in the Mytilidae, pearl oysters, Pinnidae, fresh-water mussels, and Trygonidae, and among the

gastropods in the abalones, Stomatiidae, top shells, Umbonidae, and Angariidae. In the cephalopods it makes up the internal layer of the dividing walls in the shells of Nautilus and Spirula. Nacre is composed of superimposed flakes of aragonite parallel to the internal surface of the shell. In shells with a nacreous layer, the area where the muscle is inserted, called the *myostracum*, has a special structure of flakes of aragonite modified so that their prisms are perpendicular to the surface, lending additional strength.

In some bivalves (oysters, scallops, spiny oysters and saddle oysters) and some other mollusks there is an innermost layer called the *pseudonacre* because of its resemblance to real mother-of-pearl. This layer has a *foliaceous structure* made up of more or less parallel flakes of calcite, which may be oriented parallel, oblique or perpendicular to the internal surface of the shell.

*Granular structure* is rather rare in the molluscan shell. It is composed of irregular grains of aragonite (in the cuttlefish) or calcite (in the brood shell of Argonauta).

*Homogeneous structure* is so called because it looks amorphous under the electron-scanning microscope, although actually made up of minuscule grains of aragonite. This structure is typical of the pteropods and heteropods.

*Complex crossed-lamellar structure*, consisting of aragonite, is present in the innermost layer of the shell of certain Nerita, for example. It is made up of prisms of polygonal section comparable to the primary lamellae of the crossed-lamellar structure. These prisms are in turn composed of superimposed elementary cones 1 micron thick (secondary lamellae) that are made up in turn of a large number of (tertiary) crystals radiating from the apex of the cone toward the edge.

Many shells have only two layers— the periostracum and the inner layer. The periostracum may have either a prismatic or a crossed-lamellar structure, whereas the structure of the inner layer will be a combination of nacre, myostracum and foliaceous. The other structures are much rarer. They may form other intermediate layers or take the place of one of the basic types.

## HABITAT

We have already seen that mollusks may live in either fresh or salt water or on land. The vast majority, however, live in the sea, and since it is these animals that will be the main subject of this book, we will confine most of our discussion to that environment.

Marine mollusks may be *benthic* or *pelagic*. Benthic organisms, which make up the largest proportion, live on or near the bottom of the sea. Pelagic plants and animals live free in the water. Since they are in the minority they will be treated individually in the articles concerned with mollusks living in special environments. Most marine mollusks are members of *biotic communities,* populations of different plant and animal species that always live together in a particular habitat. Although space does not permit us to discuss the different marine biotic communities that are known throughout the world (even though the subject would be useful in making a collection of specimens that would be more than a mere assemblage), it will be worthwhile to mention at least some of the major divisions of the *benthic dominion.* We will be dealing both with hard substrates (rocky surfaces that the animals crawl over as they feed) and loose (muddy or sandy) substrates.

The benthic dominion can be divided into two general zones—the *littoral* and the *deep.* The former extends as far down as algae can survive, which is the farthest depth at which the light that these plants utilize in photosynthesis extends. The second zone extends from the lower limit at which plant life can survive to the depths of the sea. Since this boundary depends to a certain extent on the transparency of the water, it is impossible to assign a precisely measured depth to it. Very turbid water filters out more light than does calm sea, so that photosynthesis can occur in the former only to comparatively moderate depths. Because the littoral zone is more accessible to the amateur collector either directly (going under the water) or indirectly (by dredging) the examples discussed in the book entries refer mostly to mollusks from this region. Mention is also made, however, of certain mollusks that live in the deep

Diagram showing the arrangement of the crystals of calcium carbonate in a crossed lamellar structure—(A) primary lamellae, (B) individual primary lamella, (C) secondary lamella, (D) tertiary lamella.

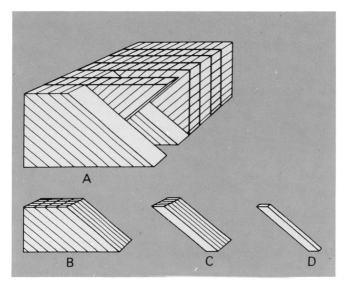

zone and may be found occasionally in the nets of deep-sea fishermen.

The littoral zone may be divided into *planes*, regions within which the environmental conditions (which depend on the height of the plane above sea level) are constant or change only gradually.

The highest plane is the *supralittoral*, which covers the strip of beach above the high-tide level. This area is submerged only occasionally, in areas where the tide is especially strong and during the great equinoctial tides. Where the tide is weak, as in the Mediterranean, the supralittoral plane is wetted only by the spray that results from the combined actions of waves and wind. It is a transitional environment between water and land, which the sea can only keep moist.

The next plane is the *mesolittoral,* known also as the intertidal zone. It extends from the high-tide mark to the normal low-tide mark.

In tropical regions (between the Tropic of Cancer and the Tropic of Capricorn), where fine and colloidal sedimentation (mud and clay) predominates, there occur mangrove swamps. These are forests of shrubs and trees that, although they are of different species, resemble each other structurally and are found in similar environments. They are also adapted to salt water. There are two mangrove *floras*—the occidental (in tropical America and western Africa); and the oriental, or Indopacific (in eastern Africa, the Indian Ocean, and the western Pacific). The latter has many more species. Although many types of animal live in association with the mangrove, the plants are represented by few species, all of which can tolerate salt water and wide ranges of temperature. Most of these animals live on the trunks or roots of the mangrove (a hard substrate). Some belong to the mesolittoral plane, some to the supralittoral, and some to the infralittoral.

The *infralittoral plane* extends from the lower limit of the mesolittoral to the lowest depths at which a certain family of plants. called the *Zosteraceae* can survive. It is the region of the water that is most accessible to man and, hence, the most studied. The biotic communities, typified at this level by both flowering plants (Poseidonia, eelgrass and turtle grass) and green algae, are found most frequently on loose substrates. Some of the populations that exist on hard substrates are characterized by algae and others by the Anthozoa (coral, sea pens, and sea anemones), especially the hard coral. The latter animals are responsible, of course, for the formation of reefs and atolls that are found only within an intertropical zone between 35 degrees north latitude and 25 degrees south latitude and are especially highly developed in the Indopacific region. Reefs support not one but a number of biotic communities. Barrier reef and atoll communities can be analyzed into three complexes, proceeding from the open sea toward the coast or interior of the lagoon: the seaward slope; the shelf (with populations that live among the dead coral skeletons of the upper reaches of the reef); and the landward, or lagoon, slope (with populations living on hard substrates composed of living coral animals or on loose substrates made up of a more or less coarse detritus formed from the disintegration of the coral or other calcareous organisms that inhabit the reef). When we speak of reef-dwelling mollusks, we will be dealing with those that live on both hard and loose bottoms.

The *circumlittoral plane* extends down to the lowest level at which green algae can survive. One of its characteristics is the calcareous remains of both animals and plants, particularly impressive in the neighborhoods of reefs, which form a transition between a loose substrate and a hard one.

The environments we have so briefly discussed provide homes for a tremendous variety of mollusks. None of these animals, however, can be found in every ocean or sea. The most cursory interest in conchology is enough to demonstrate that the most showy shells are the products of warm seas, while the more colorless come from colder waters. Many, including the most impressive, can be found only in very restricted habitats, where environmental conditions are particularly suited to their specific requirements. The giant clams that used to be made into holy-water founts are found only in the Indian and Pacific oceans, although the reef formations they inhabit are very similar to those of the warmer Atlantic waters. Many mollusks can

Pages 46 and 47: Map of the malacological provinces—(1) Arctic, (2) Boreal, (3) Aleutian, (4) Lusitanian, (5) Celtic, (6) Carolinian, (7) Oregonian, (8) Californian, (9) Japonic, (10) Indopacific, (11) Panamic, (12) Caribbean, (13) Senegalese, (14) South African, (15) Australian, (16) New Zealand, (17) Peruvian, (18) Argentinian, (19) Magellanic, (20) Antarctic.

reproduce only in water that remains above a certain temperature, so that they cannot be found in cooler areas. The nineteenth-century conchologist Woodward studied these worldwide variations and concluded that certain areas he called *provinces,* characterized by large numbers of species lacking in neighboring provinces, could be distinguished. There were, of course—instead of sharp boundaries between provinces—transitional zones in which it was possible to find species from neighboring provinces, but still it was possible to say that more than 50 percent of the species found in one province could not be found in its neighbor. Woodward's classification is still in use today. The oceans are divided into eighteen malacological provinces as shown in the map on pages 46–47.

## WHERE AND HOW TO COLLECT

Anyone walking along a beach can observe and collect seashells. That is how almost all collections start. Beach shells, however, are only simple husks, lacking the softer parts, and often worn by the action of water and sand. Bivalves are often missing a valve. Anyone who wants to devote himself seriously to collecting soon begins to search for living specimens, the intact shells and soft parts of which will permit a more accurate identification of their species. Although it is easy to find shells along the beach, it is difficult at first to come upon living specimens. Almost all mollusks live their lives in hiding; and only with patience can one learn how and where to look. The individual entries will often supply details on the habitats of the various species, so that one can gain some idea of where to find a particular species.

When collecting terrestrial species it is best to look in damp areas—under rocks, for instance, or in cracks in cliffs and stone walls, under the bark of logs, in or under moss, under beds of fallen leaves, and even between the leaves of lettuce in the garden or kitchen. Collecting is usually more successful after a rain, when higher humidity induces the mollusks to leave their hiding places. Watch for the shiny slime trails that the animals leave in their wake. If you follow them in the right direction they will often lead you to where the animals are hiding. Holes in leaves or chewed-off edges will often betray the presence of a snail.

Marine and fresh-water mollusks can usually be found by a little digging in a muddy or sandy bottom. Sometimes you only have to follow the trail that many mollusks leave as they crawl under the sand. The prey will turn up at one end or the other. A trowel is always handy for removing the first few inches of the bottom to get at the animals. Many bivalves betray their presence by the "eyes," the two holes made in the sand by the water flowing in and out of the siphons. Finding mollusks on rocky bottoms is more complicated. Look in rock clefts and under stones. To obtain small species pull up bunches of sea-

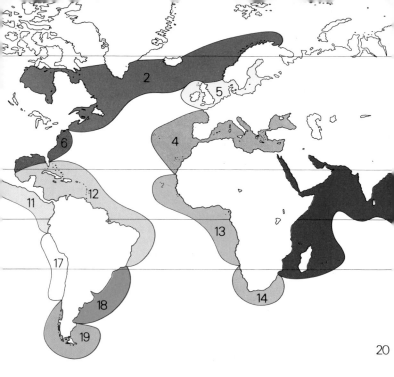

weed and shake them out under the water over a fine-meshed sieve or in a bucket of fresh water. Still other, rock-boring species can be found by breaking apart rocks or pieces of wood that have been in the water a long time. Obviously these methods work only in shallower waters.

At greater depths you will have to use a dredge or even visit fishing boats in the hope that their decks and nets have not been cleaned too thoroughly. Often it is worthwhile to gather *detritus,* the coarse sand that covers large areas of the ocean bottom. Detritus should be washed well in fresh water, allowed to dry, and carefully searched with a magnifying glass. You will soon discover that this sediment is made up of fragments of the animals and plants that build skeletons or calcareous shells. Among these fragments you will find unbroken shells that are too small to be recovered by other means. Another trick is to look in the stomachs of fish or starfish that feed on mollusks. Some rare cowries are often collected in this way.

For a collection to have significance and not just be a bunch of pretty shells, each specimen must be carefully labeled with the data pertaining to its discovery——information as to the date, site, and depth of collection, the type of substrate and bottom, the geography and name of the collector, whether the animal was alive or dead, et cetera. It is a good idea to write everything down right away and not trust to memory. Otherwise a fine collection may be compromised.

Before we leave the subject of collecting and collections, an

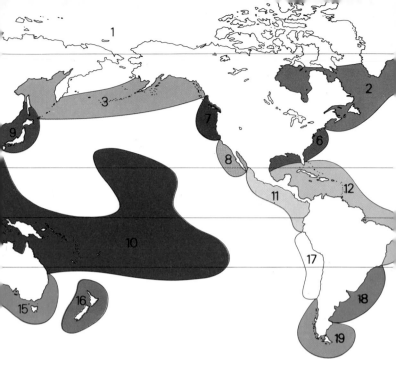

important word on conservation is in order. Many species have become rare or potentially endangered, due to pollution, over-collecting, land clearance, and various other kinds of human interference with the environment. Therefore a good collector is a conservationist and never takes more than he needs. It is good practice to disturb the environment as little as possible.

## PRESERVING THE ANIMAL AS A WHOLE

Once the animal has been collected, measures must be taken to preserve it. If the whole animal and not just the shell is of interest, you will have problems. Living mollusks retreat into their shells when caught and must be induced to come out again before they can be killed.

With terrestrial mollusks the simplest procedure is to place the animal in a jar of fresh water and screw on the lid. In probably less than twenty-four hours the mollusk will come out of its shell in search of oxygen and will die in this position. Open the jar and nudge the animal on the head with a stick to see if it is dead yet. If there is no reaction replace the water with 70-percent alcohol. The specimen will keep for many years. The same method can be tried with marine mollusks, although it rarely works. There are other procedures to get the animals to die outside of their shells. They include dropping crystals of menthol into the jar, which is this case is filled with water from the animal's habitat, adding Epsom salts over several hours, or adding other substances that may be difficult for the amateur to obtain. If you have a lot of patience you might try suspending ice wrapped in cheesecloth over a jar of sea water containing the animal. As the ice melts, the fresh water will gradually mix in with the salt water and kill the animal. These methods, however, as well as others that are even longer and more complicated, are never completely reliable. You will often end up with the animal closed up in its shell. Put it in 70-percent alcohol to preserve it for a fairly long time. Formalin in a 4-percent solution with sea water has been used, but it is not advisable, first because it tends in time to leach the calcium out of the shell, but even more because it hardens the soft parts and make them difficult to extract.

## CLEANING

Once the specimens have been obtained, labeled and put in alcohol, they will keep until you have time to "clean" them, to extract the soft parts. Open each specimen jar in turn, pour off the alcohol, and put the specimen in a container of fresh water. Then get a good hold on the interior parts with a crochet needle, tongs, or one of the many instruments that every malacologist invents for himself, and pull the animal out of the shell. If the gastropod has an aperculum, it should be detached from the foot and preserved, usually attached to a piece of cotton inserted in the mouth of the shell. Gastropods also have a liver, which can be especially objectionable when it rots; so, you should be very careful to scrape it out completely. A handy tool for this is an old screen-door spring. Insert one end in the shell and twist the spring back and forth within the *columella,* the central column of the shell, until you can get a grip on the organ and induce it to come out. If this doesn't work, it often helps to pour in a little hydrogen peroxide or a 50-percent chlorine solution. In a few hours the chemicals will dissolve all the remaining organic material. Wash the shell carefully. Handle the chemicals with caution, because they can burn both your skin and your clothing. If you don't have the time or the inclination for such complicated procedures, you may find it simple to soak the shell, with whatever fragments you can't scrape out, in 70-percent alcohol for a while and let it dry. It will still be putrid for a while, but will eventually stop smelling. If you want to preserve the soft parts of the mollusk as well, put them in a container with 70-percent alcohol, being sure to label them with the date of collection and a number or code corresponding to that of the shell itself, so that it will always be possible to tell which go with which. If you are not interested in dissection (which may, however, be indispensable in certain cases for correct identification), just throw the soft parts away. Put the shell, together with its label, in a box or plastic bag. Be sure to write all the data on the label itself, and label the shells with code numbers referring to a notebook or file of the complete information. If the shell is too small to label, put the label in the box or bag along with the shell.

Section of a piece of wood infested with shipworms.

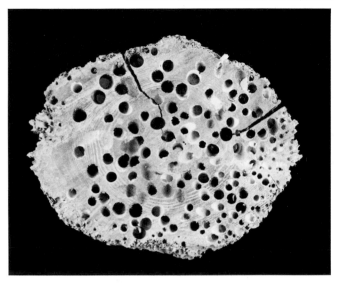

Section of a piece of wood infested with shipworms.

## WHERE TO KEEP YOUR SHELLS

Most beginning collectors just keep their specimens in any kind of box. Showier shells are often kept in transparent plastic boxes. After a while, however, if you become more serious, you will want to find a better way to organize and maintain your collection. You can construct, or have someone make, a cabinet with drawers of different sizes to put the individual boxes in. Keep in mind that drawers on the large side, say about 20 by 20 inches (interior) will be more useful. The drawers should be of different heights—most of them 2 to 2 1/2 inches deep, some 4, a few 6, and perhaps one 8 inches deep for the largest shells. The specimens themselves will go into cardboard or plastic boxes measuring, say 2 by 2 inches, 2 by 3, 3 by 4, 4 by 5, and 5 by 7, probably no larger, made to fit snugly inside the drawers. The shells may be put into plastic bags provided with the code number and label before going into the boxes. Make every effort to prevent returning the specimens into the wrong boxes after study, something that has spoiled many a fine collection. Very tiny shells should be kept in plastic or glass tubes, like those used by watchmakers for replacement parts, inside the larger boxes. Once the storage cabinet is ready, the specimens must be classified, their binomial names and code numbers written on the labels, and the specimens put away.

Try to be as orderly as possible. Always keep your collection neat, with every specimen clean and accompanied by its relevant data and code number. Remember that one shell containing the remains of the liver may be a little smelly, but a hundred thousand will stink worse than anything that even the most fanatic collector can stand.

The need for careful record keeping will soon become obvious. It is a good idea to start keeping files as soon as possible. File cards are much more practical than a bunch of notebooks. One useful arrangement is by the site where the shells were found. Another is by species. Do not be afraid of keeping too many data—you will soon discover the advantages of complete records. So start while your collection is still small. It will be more difficult when it has attained respectable proportions.

## CLASSIFYING YOUR SPECIMENS

Molluscan taxonomy in the sense of an attempt to reconstruct the phylogeny of the animals is based not on a small number of characteristics but on all the morphological or more general biological peculiarities of the phylum. Since it is difficult to discuss these traits exhaustively in our limited space, we will not go into any greater detail on the characteristics we outlined above. We will confine ourselves to the examples of the radula and the alimentary system in general as their structures vary within a subclass, that of the prosobranch gastropods, to form a basis for a natural classification.

In each row of denticles on the radula of the Prosobranchia there is a middle, or *rachidian, tooth,* one or more *lateral* denticles to the right and left of the central, and farther out on both sides, one or more *marginal* denticles. The denticles often have one or more *cusps,* or points. If there are more than one, the middle cusp, which is usually more highly developed, is called the *mesoconum,* while the others are called *endocona* if they are nearer the midline of the radula, and ectocona if they are nearer the edge. Although the pattern of denticles varies from species to species there are certain definite types of radula—basically seven. The *hystricoglossate* radula has one central and many not very distinct lateral and marginal denticles. Some of the marginals have bands of bristles, which is how this type got its name (Greek for "porcupine tongue"). The *rhipidoglossate* radula has one central and usually five lateral and several marginal teeth on each side. Malacologists have developed a system of representing the denticular pattern by formulas. A rhipidoglossate system is represented by the formula

$$\infty + 5 + R + 5 + \infty$$

where R stands for the single central or rachidian denticle, 5 for the number of lateral and $\infty$ for the large and indeterminate number of the marginal denticles. Sometimes the outermost lateral denticle is larger than the others. It is called the *dominant* denticle, and the formula becomes

$$\infty + D + 4 + R + 4 + D + \infty$$

On the *docoglossate* radula the central denticle is very small or even absent, and there are three laterals (with the outside lateral dominant) and three marginals on each side. The formula is

$$3 + D + 2 + R + 2 + D + 3$$

or sometimes

$$3 + D + 2 + 0 + 2 + D + 3.$$

The *taenioglossate* radula has seven denticles in each row—one central and one lateral and two marginals on each side. The formula is

$$2 + 1 + R + 1 + 2.$$

There are, however, variations on the basic pattern. The radula may have no marginal denticles at all. The *ptenoglossate* radula is thought to derive from the preceding type. It has no central denticle, and the other teeth are almost identical and vary in number, so that the formula is

$$n + 0 + n.$$

The formula for the *rachiglossate* radula, which has three teeth in each row (one central and one on each side), is

$$1 + R + 1$$

or, in some cases where the laterals are also missing—

$$0 + R + 0.$$

Finally, the *toxoglossate* radula has only two lateral teeth in each row—

$$1 + 0 + 1.$$

We have gone into such detail with respect to these formulas, even though the characteristics involved are microscopic and not easily accessible to the amateur, because they are the basis for classifying certain important groups of gastropods with names derived from the radular type, like the Taenioglossa, Stenoglossa, Toxoglossa, et cetera.

The evolutionary history of the subclass Prosobranchia involves the gradual transition from a herbivorous feeding habit to a carnivorous (predatory) pattern. This dietary change is evidenced by the slow evolutionary changes of the radula itself, which begins to have fewer denticles, especially marginal and lateral, in the carnivorous species. The hystricoglossate or rhipidoglossate radula or the primitive order Archaeogastropoda, with its large number of denticles used to scrape algae off the rocks on which the animals graze, has evolved into a docoglossate form with only three pairs of laterals and marginals. The taenioglossate radula of the order Pectinibranchia or Mesogastropoda, which is partly herbivorous and partly carnivorous, retains not only the central, but also one lateral and two marginal denticles. The Neogastropoda or Stenoglossa, typically predators, have either a rachiglossate radula from which the marginal denticles have completely disappeared or a toxoglossate radula, which also lacks the central,

Different types of radula——(A) hystricoglossate radula of an archaeogastropod; (B) rhipidoglossate radula of a trochid (archaeogastropod); (C) docoglossan radula of Patella (archaeogastropod); (D) ptenoglossate radula of an epitonid (mesogastropod); (E) taenioglossate radula of a mesogastropod; (F) rachiglossate radula of a muricid (neogastropod); (G) toxoglossate radula of a turrid (neogastropod); (H) radular apparatus of the Conidae (neogastropod), showing one tooth (harpoon) in the process of seizing the prey.

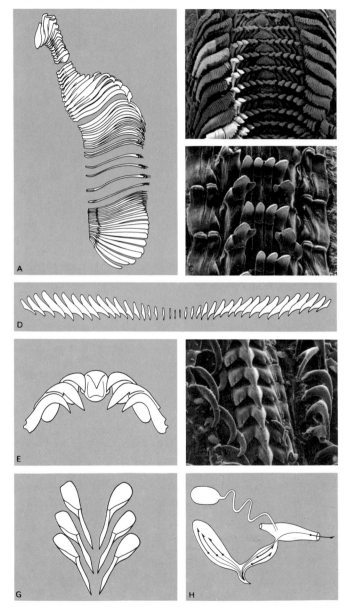

the two remaining laterals in each row being used in succession like harpoons to capture and poison the prey. Only the Opisthobranchia do not fit into the pattern. The radula is ptenoglossate. Many of these animals have adapted to parasitism on polyps (sea anemones, coral, etc.).

Evolutionary modifications can be found in other structures as well as the radula, and all of these differences help to demonstrate evolutionary relationships among the taxa of lower rank than the order, all the way down to the species. Although all of these characteristics are important to the malacologist, other biologists and naturalists and collectors will find it much more practical to rely on more obvious structures like the shell as criteria of classification. Although this structure is not always a dependable clue to the animal's descent and cannot support a really scientific classification, it is of great practical importance for identification. But, as we have said (and as is often not very well understood by biologists themselves), classification, the systematic study of all the traits that contribute to the reconstruction of an evolutionary history is one thing, and identification is another. Identification has little to do with systematics and is concerned only with traits that, although phylogenetically uninteresting, are useful in identifying an organism and assigning it a name from the binomial nomenclature in order to communicate this fact to others.

Finally, then, we must look at the shell and discuss the various types that occur in the most important classes and how we can use them in identifying our specimens, bearing in mind that the shell by itself may not be a sufficient criterion in identifying either the species or its higher classification.

The shell of the order *Polyplacophora,* or chitons, consists of eight flexibly attached overlapping calcareous plates, or valves. The anterior plate (I) which overhangs the mouth, and the posterior plate (VIII), which overhangs the anal aperture, are usually semicircular, while the six intermediate plates (II–VII) are roughly rectangular. A transverse section of one of the plates will reveal several layers, perhaps five in the more evolved forms, two of which are of special taxonomic interest. These are the *tegmentum,* or outer layer, which may be differently colored and sculptured in various species, and the whitish innermost *articulamentum,* the surface of muscular attachment. If you examine the tegmentum of any of these plates you will usually see two diagonal lines that divide up the surface in one of two different patterns.

In the *lepidopleuride* type the anterior plate has only one anterior region, the intermediate plates have one median and two lateral, and the posterior plate one median and one posterior region. The *acanthochitonide* type has an anterior plate with one anterior region, intermediate plates with one *jugal* and two *lateropleural* regions, and a posterior plate with one jugal region adjacent to two pleural and one posterior region. The posterior plate often has a raised apex, the *mucro*. Its position on

Diagram of various types of sculpturing in different areas on the valves of a chiton and of various types of girdle structures——(1) cephalic plate, (2) radial ribs, (3) longitudinal ribs, (4) radially distributed granulation, (5) radial ribs, (6) median (central) region, (7) lateral region, (8) posterior plate, (9) mucro, (10) granulation, (11) jugum, (12) scale, (13) spicules, (14) bristle tufts, (15) girdle.

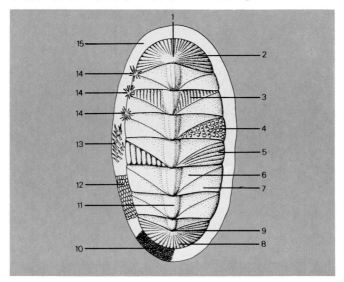

the median axis varies from species to species, so that it is important in identification. These regions may be completely smooth or sculptured quite differently from species to species. Looking at the inside of the shell, you can see how the articulamentum of each intermediate or posterior plate extends forward in two processes to articulate with the plate that is next anterior. The space between two of these *apophyses* is called the *jugal sinus*.

Below the two lateral regions the articulamentum divides into thin *sutural laminae* at the girdle that may be divided into two or more *slit teeth*. The slits continue as radial furrows up to the posterior median apex of the plate. The anterior and posterior plates have a single sutural lamina at the girdle, and this lamina is frequently serrated into *insertion teeth* that help fix the shell to the girdle. The larger kinds of plates are riddled with pores of two sizes——*micropores* and *macropores*——full of sensory cells. The number and distribution of sensory cells around a *macroesthacyte* varies from species to species. The girdle is divided into superior and inferior bands that have projections of various shapes and sizes, and that originate in one or more mantle cells. These may be spicules, scales or bristles, and there are usually more than one (with a maximum of nine) type on the girdle. Sometimes the two bands of girdle are separated by a fringe of spicules. In the genus *Acanthochitona* there are eighteen tufts of needlelike spicules on the dorsal band that are distributed as follows: four in front of the anterior plate and

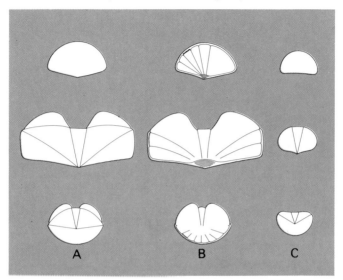

seven on each side between two contiguous intermediate plates.

The gastropod shell usually spirals around an axis called the *columella*. There is often a small depression called the *umbilicus* in the base of the columella. The body of the animal, attached to the columella by the columellar muscle, protrudes from a large opening in the shell called the *aperture*. The outer edge of the aperture is called the *peristome,* or lip. There are two basic types of gastropod shell, *homostomatous* and *siphonostomatous.* In the latter type the surface of the peristome is interrupted by a notch that sometimes extends into the siphonal canal. In the former type there is no such notch, and the lip is continuous. The spiral begins at the apex of the shell, which corresponds to the embryonic, or larval, whorl. The successive whorls of the shell around the columella are almost always cemented together along lines called sutures. Usually the spiral runs clockwise, or *dextrally,* although some species twist in the opposite direction, or *sinistrally.* Hold the shell with the apex up and the aperture facing you, and the shell will be dextral if the aperture is on the right and sinistral if it is on the left. There are many other characteristics that help to identify the species of a shell: the presence or absence of spines, ridges or sculpture, as well as the overall shape—conic; biconic (like two cones with their bases together); fusiform (long and thick in the middle); or discoidal (like a plate, with all the coils lying in one plane). Space does not permit us to discuss

Schematic drawing of a generalized gastropod shell showing structures of taxonomic significance——(A) posterior, (B) anterior, (C) length, (D) spire, (E) body whorl—(1) spire angle, (2) apex, (3) mammillary sculpturing, (4) spiral stripes, (5) shoulder, (6) axial ribs, (7) columella, (8) columellar fold, (9) spiral ribs, (10) spine,

all the terminology in use. The less obvious terms are discussed in the individual book entries.

Bivalve shells may have valves that are symmetrical and equal (equivalve) or different (inequivalve). The dorsal edge, or margin, of a valve is the one with the beak, or *umbo,* and the opposite edge is the ventral margin. If a line traced from the umbo perpendicular to the ventral margin divides the shell into two roughly equal parts the valves are called equilateral, otherwise nonequilateral. Dorsal and anterior to the umbo there is a moon-shaped depression called the *lunule.* Posteriorly there is another, shallower depression called the *escutcheon,* or the *ligament,* the cartilaginous "hinge" of the shell in those that have one on the outside. The ligament has an elastic action that holds the shell open, and it is only the tension of the two large adductor muscles that closes the shell and keeps it closed. Inside the shell, underneath the umbo, there is a series of alternating grooves and ridges on each valve, the *hinge teeth,* which mesh together with the teeth on the opposite valve to ensure that the two will fit together snugly when the shell is closed. There are six basic types of hinge teeth, and they are taxonomically significant with groups named after the pattern of teeth. The *taxodont* hinge has a large number of similar small teeth. The *actinodont* hinge has two single teeth or two series of teeth radiating out from a point beneath the umbo, one series facing anteriorly and the other posteriorly. The teeth of the *heterodont* hinge are small and of different size——one or more called *cardinal* under, and others called lateral, anterior and posterior to the umbo. Those on the *pachydont* hinge are few, large, and not well defined. They are considered cardinal teeth. The *isodont* type is symmetrical. Each valve has one tooth and one groove to the right and left of the midline. The *edentulous* hinge has only very rudimentary teeth.

The general form and sculpture of the valve can also provide clues to identification of the bivalve. Still another indication is supplied by the marks left on the inside of the shell by certain organic structures. The most important of these marks are the *scars,* where the adductor muscles attach to the shell. Usually there is one anterior and one posterior (*dimyarian* bivalves) scar, but sometimes the anterior adductor is lacking (*monomyarian*) so that there is only one scar. In dimyarian mollusks the two scars may be equal (*isomyarian*), or the anterior may be smaller than the posterior (*anisomyarian*). Another significant mark on the inside of the shell is a line called the pallial line, which runs parallel to the ventral margin of the shell from one muscle scar to the other and indicates the attachment of the muscles that anchor the mantle to the shell. When this line is continuous, the vivalve is called *integripalliate.* In the other, *sinopalliate,* type of shell the line forms a posterior bay or *sinus* where the mantle is loose, to make room for the siphons. The scaphopod shell is, as we have seen on page 63, shaped like an elephant's tusk. The concave side is the dorsal, and the convex the ventral. The anterior aperture, the one the foot pro-

(11) posterior sinus, (12) labial tooth, (13) external lip, (14) lip tooth, (15) siphon, (16) siphonal canal, (17) pseudoumbilicus, (18) siphonal fasciole, (19) columellar folds, (20) labial folds, (21) umbilicus, (22) internal (columellar) lip, (23) callus, (24) varix, (25) tubercle, (26) whorl, (27) sutures, (28) carina (keel), (29) cancellate sculpturing.

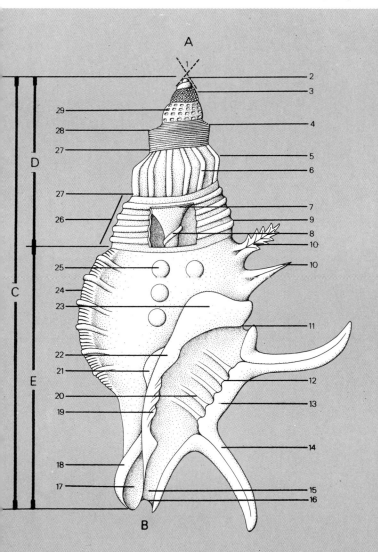

Top left: Section of mesogastropod shell showing the axis (columella) of spiral.
Top right: different types of gastropod opercula—(1) multispiral with central nucleus, (2) paucispiral with subcentral nucleus, (3) with apical nucleus, (4) with marginal nucleus.
Bottom: Some characteristic types of gastropod shells—(1) conical, (2) biconical, (3) obconic, (4) turreted, (5) fusiform, (6) patelliform, (7) spherical.

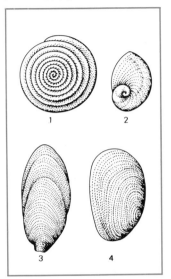

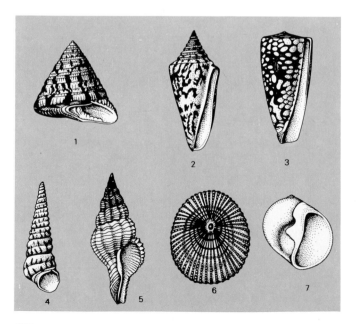

Shells of the pulmonate *Helix aspersa*. Right: Dextral form. Left: Sinistral form.

trudes from, is the ventral. In some species, especially of the family *Siphonodentallidae*, however, this aperture is contracted; its diameter is less than the widest part of the shell. There are other ways of identifying the species of the animal. If the shell has longitudinal ridges, count them and note their shape. Are there one or more furrows with U- or V-shaped profiles? Does the shell have slits or notches at the *apical* ("narrower") end, or a small calcareous siphon extending beyond the apical margin?

The various types of modern cephalopod shells are described and illustrated in the book entries on *Nautilus pompilius*, *Spirula spirula*, *Sepia officinalis*, and *Loligo vulgaris*.

Upper figure: Left valve of a bivalve (interior view). Lower figure: The two valves (dorsal view)—(A) dorsal edge, (B) ventral side, (C) width, (D) length, (E) depth, (F) posterior edge, (G) anterior edge, (H) left valve, (I) right valve—(1) umbo, (2) muscle scar, (3) pallial line, (4) pallial sinus, (5) hinge, (6) ligament, (7) escutcheon, (8) lunule.

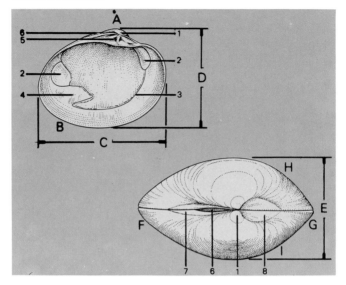

Photo, top: Actinodont (and schizodont) hinge.
Bottom: (A) taxodont hinge, (B) heterodont hinge, (C) isodont hinge.

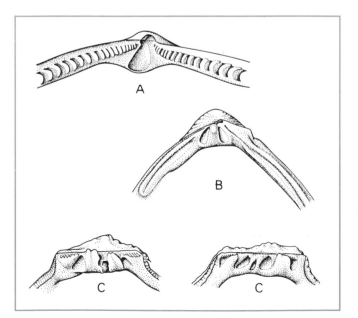

A

B

C

C

Different types of muscle scars and pallial lines in bivalves—(A) taxodont, integropalliate, isomyarian, and dimyarian; (B) sinopalliate, anisomyarian, and dimyarian; (C) monomyarian; (D) sinopalliate, isomyarian, dimyarian, and heterodont—(1) ligament, (2) hinge, (3) adductor muscles, (4) pallial line, (5) anterior adductor muscle, (6) posterior adductor muscle, (7) pallial sinus.

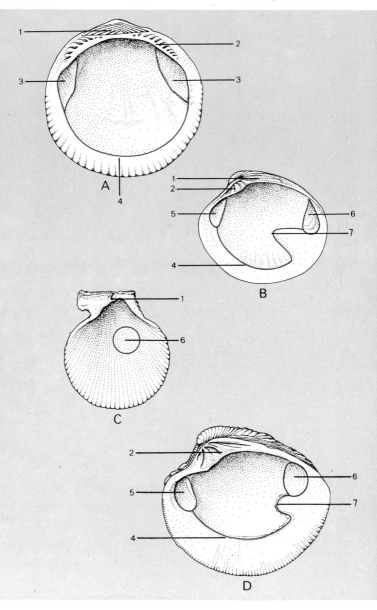

Top: Scaphopod shell—(A) posterior, (B) anterior, (C) dorsal side, (D) ventral side.
Bottom: Two different types of posterior—(1) apical notch, (2) terminal siphon.

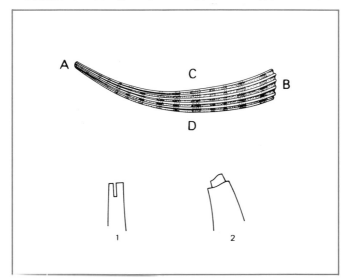

# SOFT SURFACE
# MOLLUSKS

# 1 ACANTHOCARDIA ACULEATA
## Spiny Cockle

**Family** Cardiidae

**Shell** Medium-large (3 to 4 inches), solid, convex valves equivalve and inequilateral, roughly oval in shape. In color, uniformly deep yellow brown. The sculpture consists of 20 to 22 well-developed ribs, which have almost triangular spikes along the mid-line. Between the ribs are very marked concentric grooves. In examples that are not fresh, the spines that normally cover the whole shell are almost everywhere missing, except on the rear edge of the valves (shown in the photograph). The external ligament is behind the umbones, the hinge is heterodont. Inside the valves are two identical scars (dimyarian and isomyarian), joined by a continuous pallial line, lacking a sinus.

**Body** As in all *Cardiidae*, the foot, roughly cylindrical, is well developed and is used by the mollusk for leaping, rather than for digging in the sand. In this species, as in the others, the distal extremity of the foot is a bright red.

**Habitat** This species is quite tolerant of its environment, living on sand, muddy sand and the coarse detritus of the infralittoral zone.

**Distribution** Celtic and Lusitanian provinces, extending into the Mediterranean.

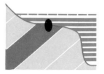

---

# 2 ACTEON TORNATILIS
## Linnes Baby-Bubble

**Family** Acteonidae

**Shell** Of small size (approximately ¼ inch), quite thick, fairly short, conical spire with slightly convex whorls, impressed suture, elongated oval in shape. The first turns of the shell are heterostrophe—that is, their axis of coiling forms an angle to the adult shell's columella. The aperture is a very elongated oval; has a thin, sharp outer lip; and the columellar lip has a light callus and a deep fold at the base. The sculpture consists of thin spiral grooves more marked toward the posterior and anterior edges of the whorls. Pink hazel in color, with one or two whitish spiral bands. The operculum is horny, pale yellow and transparent.

**Body** The foot is very wide, differentiated anteriorly into a podium. The head broadens into a cephalic disc that has two lateroposterior lobes, incorrectly called tentacles. The eyes are sessile. Inside the mantle cavity there is the gill, the osphradium and the penis. The species is hermaphrodite. The radula lacks rachidial teeth and has a very large number of lateral teeth.

**Habitat** Lives on sandy or sandy-muddy bottoms in the infralittoral zone.

**Distribution** Celtic and Lusitanian provinces.

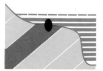

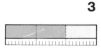

## 3   AMUSSIUM JAPONICUM
### Sun-and-Moon Scallop

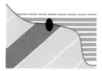

**Family**   Pectinidae
**Shell**   Medium size (3 to 4 inches), very thin, slightly inequi-valved and equilateral. Unlike the other pectins discussed, the two "ears" are equal and symmetrical on both the sides. The coloration of this species is distinctive, the right valve is white and the left valve is reddish with lighter concentric lines. It is likely that this coloration is for camouflage—the right (white) valve facing downward. The coloration of the left valve (red), as a whole, is more like the substratum, and so the bivalve is less visible to predators. The outer surface is completely smooth and glossy, while the inner has thin radial ridges that extend over more than half the surface and stop flush with the margin of the valve. The hinge lacks teeth, but has two pairs of sym-metrical thickenings, or crura; one pair along the cardinal line (cardinal crura) and one pair underneath the junction of the ears and the main body of the valve (auricular crura).
**Body**   See the descriptions of the species of Chlamys.
**Habitat**   Lives on sandy or muddy bottoms of the infralittoral zone.
**Distribution**   Characteristic of the Japonic Province; related species are found elsewhere in the Pacific.

## 4   ANCILLA
### Ancillas

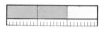

**Family**   Olividae
**Shell**   Medium to medium-small in size (1½ to 3½ inches) thin and light, not fragile, high spire, siphonal canal short and wide, vaguely similar to an olive in shape, from which the name of the family derives. The whorls are moderately convex, and the suture is scarcely incised. However, they are almost always covered by a large callus, except the body whorl. The aperture is oval and elongated, with a thin outer lip—sometimes sharp—and an inner lip with a light callus that extends pos-teriorly. The sculpture usually consists of two or three spiral furrows in the anterior part of the body whorl. The color is vari-able; usually hazel or chestnut with whitish or darker-brown spiral bands. The operculum is horny, thin and yellowish, sometimes smaller than the aperture. The illustration shows *Ancilla urasima* (Lischke) on the left and *Ancilla albacallosa* (Lischke) to the right.
**Body**   The foot is so developed it covers the shell. The head has two thin tentacles, with the eyes on the proximal third. The mantle siphon is very long. The radula is rachiglossan.
**Habitat**   The species of the genus Ancilla normally live in the sand during the day and above it at night, usually in the upper regions of the infralittoral zone.
**Distribution**   This genus lives mainly in the Japonic and Indo-Pacific provinces; also in other provinces.

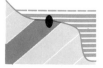

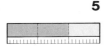

## 5  APORRHAIS OCCIDENTALIS
### American Pelican's Foot

**Family**  Aporrhaidae

**Shell**  Medium size (2 to 2½ inches), high conical spire, rather thick and solid, with swollen whorls and very impressed sutures. The outer lip is broadened and forms a large unfingered expansion, unlike all the other aporrhaids. Both outer and columellar lips are strongly thickened. The sculpture consists of a score of strong well-spaced axial ribs, usually curving, also a spiral ornament of thin, deeply incised grooves, especially marked on the body whorl. Whitish cream or grayish in color. The operculum is very small, horny and ellipsoidal, with smooth edges.

**Body**  Similar to the strombids, especially in the structure of the long and narrow foot with a smaller anterior lobe and a large posterior one that bears the operculum and enables the mollusk to leap. The eyes are not pedunculated, but are at the base of the tentacles. As in all Mesogastropods the mantle cavity contains only one gill, the osphradium and in males, the copulatory organ. The radula is taenioglossan.

**Habitat**  Lives on sandy or muddy bottoms from depths of a few meters (a few yards) to several hundreds. Therefore it is an infralittoral, circalittoral and even an aphytal species.

**Distribution**  A cold-water species found in the Arctic, Boreal (Western) and Carolinan provinces.

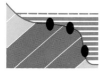

## 6  APORRHAIS PESPELECANI
### Pelican's Foot

**Family**  Aporrhaidae

**Shell**  Medium size (2 inches), quite high conical spire, with an outer lip characteristically broadened and fingered, looking like a bird's foot (hence its specific name). The whorls are angular with a nodular median keel (two in the body whorl); the suture is hardly incised. The outer lip of the aperture is thickened, and the inner lip produces a marked columellar callus. In this species, as in the rest of the superfamily Strombacae, the development of the external fingers marks the attainment of sexual maturity. The sculpture consists of the nodular keel and thin spiral grooves that extend over the whole surface. The coloration is very variable—white, beige, darkish chestnut, reddish brown or patched, axially flamed with darker shades than the base color. The operculum is horny, ellipsoidal, with a terminal nucleus.

**Body**  Quite like the Strombidae, it is pink or reddish with whitish spots, the foot is very long and narrow, the eyes sessile, set at the bases of the long tentacles. The mantle cavity has one gill, the osphradium and, in males, the penis. The radula is taenioglossan.

**Habitat**  Typically soft bottoms in the infralittoral zone.

**Distribution**  Lusitanian, Celtic and a small part of the Boreal provinces.

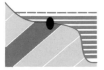

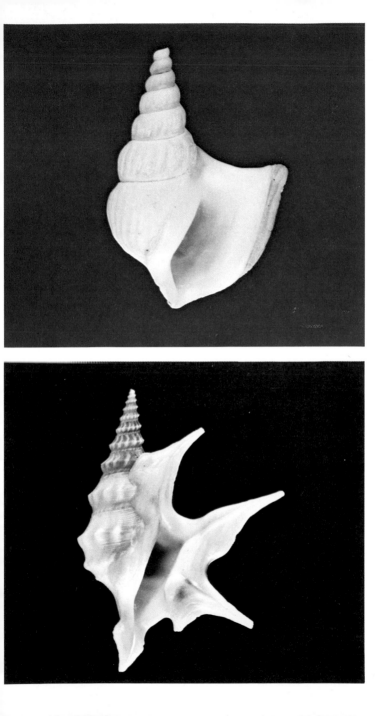

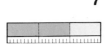

## 7 ARCHITECTONICA PERSPECTIVA
### Sundial

**Family** Architectonicidae

**Shell** Medium size (1 ½ inches), thin and strong, low spire, breadth more than double the height, the whorls are only slightly convex, almost flat, sutures deeply incised. The flat base has a fairly wide and deep umbilicus surrounded by a nodular swelling. The thin aperture lip is nearly square in shape. The sculpture of the body whorl consists of a broad and slightly raised band running below the suture and two narrower and more raised bands at the periphery, with another three on the basal side. All these bands can be quite granular as they intersect with the growth lines, which are fairly incised. The coloration is light brown on either side of white stripes, following the bands of the sculpture. The operculum is horny, dark brown, slightly spiral, a roughly central nucleus and with a tubercle on the inner surface.

**Body** It has some anatomical characteristics intermediate between the Prosobranchs and the Opisthobranchs; these have led some authors to classify the Architectonicidae as a family of a new transitional order, the Heterogastropods. The radula is ptenoglossan, without a rachidial tooth and with fourteen pairs of lateral teeth.

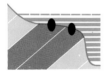

**Habitat** Fine sandy bottoms in the infralittoral zone and sometimes in the circalittoral.

**Distribution** A fairly common species throughout the Indo-Pacific provinces.

## 8 ARCINELLA ARCINELLA
### True Spiny Jewel Box

**Family** Chamidae

**Shell** Medium size (1 to 2 inches), convex valves, slightly inequivalved and inequilateral. The coloration is cream or delicately pink. The sculpture consists of a score of radial ribs decorated with spines whose breadth progressively increases from the umbo to the ventral margin of the valve. Between the ribs there are small granulations, irregularly arranged. The lunule is very differentiated and heart-shaped. The ligament is external, the hinge is pachyodont. As in all Chamidae, there are two large muscle scars; in this case, the posterior is bigger than the anterior (dimyarian, anisomyarian), the pallial line is continuous, with no sinus.

**Body** The foot is rather reduced, in keeping with its sedentary life; the mantle cavity has a pair of gills, each consisting of two series of lamellae, extensively fused by interlamellar junctions (eulamellibranch).

**Habitat** Unlike other Chamidae, this species and others of the genus live on coarse, soft substrata or even on sandy or muddy bottoms; only the juvenile stages can adhere, with the right valve, to a fragment of shell or some other rigid substratum, while the adults live unattached on the bottom.

**Distribution** Typical of the Caribbean Province, extending from Florida to Brazil.

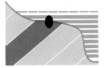

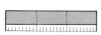

## 9 ARCTICA ISLANDICA
### Ocean Quahog

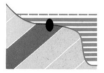

**Family** Arcticidae

**Shell** Large size (3 to 5 inches), moderately swollen, thick and robust valves, almost circular, equivalved and inequilateral. It has a thick dark brown to blackish periostracum. The only sculpture consists of thin concentric grooves. The external ligament is well developed, reaching the end of the posterior margin of the valve, and is posterior to the umbones. The hinge is heterodont, the right valve has three cardinal teeth one anterior lateral tooth and one posterior lateral tooth, while the left valve also has three cardinal teeth but only one lateral tooth, the posterior. Inside the valves the two slightly different muscle scars are very noticeable (dimyarian, anisomyarian) linked by a continuous pallial line (integropalliate), without a sinus. The shell has a crossed-lamellae structure.

**Body** A pair of gills each consisting of two series of lamellae extensively linked by interlamellar junctions (eulamellibranch). The foot is large and the two mantle lobes fuse to form two stout siphons.

**Habitat** Essentially infralittoral, even though it can be found in the circalittoral zone. Prefers sandy or sandy-muddy bottoms of cold seas.

**Distribution** Typically boreal, can extend as far as the Celtic and Carolinan provinces.

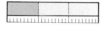

## 10 ARCULARIA GIBBOSULA
### Southern Mediterranean Nassa

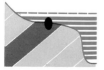

**Family** Nassariidae

**Shell** Small size (approximately ½ inch), quite thick and strong, a rather high conical spire, short siphonal canal, open and twisted as in all the Nassariidae. The body whorl is very large, spherical, covering much of the preceding one, involute and the suture is hardly incised. The aperture is ovoidal, the outer lip has an external thickening and thin internal folds. The columellar lip, in adults, forms a large callus that completely covers the ventral surfaces of the body whorl. There is no sculpture except for a rib with one, two or three hardly visible blunt nodules, and this is on the periphery of the dorsal surface of the body whorl. The color is yellowish or yellow brown, except for the callus and lips, which are white. The operculum is horny, yellowish, has an apical nucleus, is roughly triangular and has fringed inner and outer margins.

**Body** The rather wide triangular foot has, as in very many nassariids, two appendices at the posterior end. The mantle siphon is very long. The radula is rachiglossan.

**Habitat** Lives hidden under the sand with just its mantle siphon protruding. In the infralittoral zone.

**Distribution** An uncommon species that lives on the southern shores of the Mediterranean.

## 11 ASPRELLA
## Cone Shells (recurved and southern)

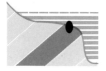

**Family**  Conidae

**Shell**  Large size (2 to 3 inches), rather thin, light, quite fragile, tall conical spire; the keeled body whorl usually enfolds the preceding one up to the shoulder; marked suture, decidedly biconical in shape, with a stepped spire. The aperture is very narrow, with almost parallel margins; the outer lip is thin, sharp and fragile. The sculpture usually consists of flattened spiral bands, which are of similar sizes and are separated by fairly deep furrows. In many species the keel of the whorls is crowned. The coloration is often light brown, with darker brown spots on the bands of the sculpture, tending to form stripes, interrupted axially. The periostracum is thin and transparent. The operculum is small, about a fifth of the size of the aperture, horny, dark chestnut with an apical nucleus. In the illustration are *Asprella arcuata* (Gray, 1838) on the left, and *Asprella australis* on the right.

**Body**  There is no morphological or anatomical information, even approximate, about the species of this genus. According to some malacologists it is a subgenus of *Conus*. The radula is toxoglossan.

**Habitat**  The species of the genus Asprella live on the muddy bottoms of the circalittoral zone.

**Distribution**  The genus *Asprella* is found in many tropical provinces throughout the world.

---

## 12 ASTARTE BOREALIS
## Boreal Astarte

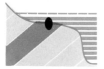

**Family**  Astartidae

**Shell**  Medium small in size (1 to 2 inches), solid, moderately convex valves equivalved and almost equilateral, circular or oval in shape, with the umbones frequently eroded. The thick periostracum is yellowish in color in young individuals, darkish brown to blackish in adults. The shell is cream in color. The sculpture consists of incised concentric lines, or sometimes toward the umbo, slightly raised ribs. The external ligament takes over half the area posterior to the umbones. The hinge is heterodont, with two cardinal teeth on the right valve and three on the left. The outer margin of the valve is smooth. The two equal muscle scars (dimyarian, isomyarian) are joined by a continuous pallial line (integropalliate) without a sinus. The shell has a crossed-lamellae structure.

**Body**  A pair of gills each made of two series of lamellae, extensively fused by interlamellar junctions (eulamellibranch). The foot is moderately developed.

**Habitat**  Sand in the infralittoral zone.

**Distribution**  Very wide, almost all the cold seas of the Northern Hemisphere. Found in the Arctic, Boreal, Celtic and North Pacific Boreal provinces, the coasts of Europe, North America as far as Massachusetts Bay and Asia as far as northern Japan.

## 13 BABYLONIA FORMOSAE
### Formosan Babylon

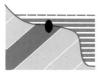

**Family** Buccinidae
**Shell** Medium size (2 inches), rather thin, light, but not very fragile, spire, moderately high, elongated oval in appearance, convex whorls, with markedly caniculated suture. The swelling at the base of the shell around the umbilicus is distinctive. The oval aperture has a tapered outer lip and an inner lip that has a callus confined to the posterior half, which covers part of the ventral surface of the last whorl. There is no sculpture, and the surface is smooth and glossy. The base color is cream, with darkish-brown spots in spiral rows and arranged as axially broken bands. The surface is covered by a thin dark-brown periostracum. The operculum is horny, light chestnut with an apical nucleus.
**Body** As in all buccinids the foot is well developed, the head has two tentacles with an eye at the base of each and one long retractile proboscis. The mantle has a very long siphon. The mantle cavity contains the gill, osphradium and, in males, behind the right tentacle, the penis. The radula is rachiglossan.
**Habitat** As with very many buccinids, it lives on sandy or muddy bottoms in the infralittoral zone.
**Distribution** Found in the Indo-Pacific Province, confined to the western Pacific.

## 14 BASSINA DISJECTA
### Tasmania Venus Clam

**Family** Veneridae
**Shell** Medium size (2 inches), delicate, moderately swollen, equivalve and inequilateral, yellowish-white in color except for the lamellae of the sculpture, which have a pinkish hue. The sculpture consists of thin concentric lamellae, well-spaced, curved, grooved on the outer surface and prolonged posteriorly to form a spoutlike process. Between these lamellae thin growth lines can be seen. The ligament, deeply set in the dorsal margin, is very long, running from the umbones to the end of the hinge, which is typically heterodont with only the three cardinal teeth on each valve. The muscle scars are almost equal (dimyarian, isomyarian) and the Pallial line has a shallow sinus (sinopalliate).
**Body** A pair of gills each consisting of two series of lamellae extensively fused in interlamellar junctions (eulamellibranch). The foot and siphon are moderately developed.
**Habitat** Sand or muddy sand in the infralittoral zone.
**Distribution** Fairly restricted, found only in Southern Australia and Tasmania. The range of the genus *Bassina* extends from there to New Zealand.

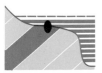

## 15 BATHYBEMBIX ARGENTEONITENS
### Silvery Trochus

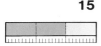

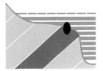

**Family**   Trochidae
**Shell**   Medium size (2 inches), light and fragile, a regular conical spire, fairly high, convex whorls, impressed suture, convex base. Shell lacks an umbilicus, and aperture has a thin sharp outer lip. The sculpture consists of a series of large nodules, which are quite numerous, situated about halfway up the whorls; these nodules tend to disappear on the apical whorls. There are other granular ridges that cover the whorls of the spire, on the body whorl. One rib is subsutural, and one immediately above the attachment of the lip, with four or five others on the base. The lines of growth are almost invisible. The shell is exclusively mother-of-pearl (very rare) and is covered by a thin periostracum, which is not resistant, chestnut in color. The operculum is horny, thin, yellowish, with a central nucleus.
**Body**   No information on this species; as it is placed in the subfamily Monodontinae, one should refer to *Monodonta turbinata* as a rough guide. The radula is rhipidiglossan.
**Habitat**   Although it is a common species, no author gives precise indications of the type of bottom on which it lives; possibly it lives on soft bottoms in the circalittoral, perhaps even bathyal zones.
**Distribution**   Appears to be limited to the Japonic Province.

## 16 BUCCINUM UNDATUM
### Common Northern Buccinum

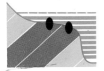

**Family**   Buccinidae
**Shell**   Medium large in size (2 to 4 inches), not very thick, solid, conical spire, generally high, but sometimes with rather flattened spires, very convex whorls and markedly impressed suture. The aperture is ovoidal, and the outer lip is not thickened or toothed, and it lacks inner folds; the columellar lip has a fairly striking callus, which partly adheres to the ventral surface of the body whorl. The sculpture consists of almost equidistant spiral grooves and quite big axial ribs that tend to fade at the edge of the body whorl and are generally sinuous. The color is yellowish white or light hazel; the periostracum is light chestnut and not very resistant. The operculum is horny, smaller than the aperture and has a central nucleus.
**Body**   A large foot, whole body cream with blackish patches. The head has a pair of tentacles with an eye at the base of each, and a very long proboscis. The siphon is also well developed. The females gather in groups to deposit their eggs in a communal mass of egg capsules, inside which the veligers develop and metamorphose into the young individuals that hatch out. The radula is rachiglossan.
**Habitat**   *Buccinum undatum* lives on sandy or muddy bottoms in the infralittoral or even circalittoral zones.
**Distribution**   It is found around the Atlantic in the Lusitanian (the northern zone), Celtic, Boreal and Arctic provinces.

## 17 BURSA DUNKERI
### Japanese Frog Shell

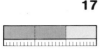

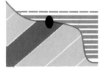

**Family** Bursidae
**Shell** Medium size (2 inches), very solid, thick elongated spherical, quite high spire, very swollen whorls, impressed suture. It is characterized, as are the other bursids, by a pair of large symmetrical varices on the lateral margin of each whorl. The aperture is round, with a short anterior siphonal canal and a longer posterior one which is attached for almost all its length to the varix of the preceding whorl. The outer lip is thickened and bears some strong teeth (8 to 10), which are much narrower than the spaces between them. The columellar lip, which has a thin callus that covers part of the ventral surface of the body whorls, has many teeth that are continued as grooves inside the aperture. The sculpture consists of large tubercles arranged on strong spiral ribs; between these are thin ridges that tend to disappear. It is hazel in color, with brownish patches of broken lines. The aperture is yellowish varying from light to orange-yellow. The operculum is horny, with an almost central nucleus.
**Body** There is no literature on this species. The radula is taenioglossan.
**Habitat** The author of the species did not specify the type of substrate, but by comparison with related species the substrate it lives on would be rocks of the infralittoral zone.
**Distribution** Seems to be restricted to the Japonic Province.

## 18 CADULUS JEFFREYSI
### Jeffrey's Cadulus

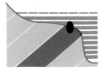

**Family** Siphonodentaliidae
**Shell** Very small in size (approximately ¼ inch), rather thin, light, quite fragile, slightly similar in shape to an elephant's tusk, as are almost all scaphopods but with an anterior portion that tends to contract so that the anterior aperture is only slightly larger than the posterior one. The distal extremity lacks both holes and lobes for the calcareous siphon. The surface is smooth and glossy, a translucent white in color.
**Body** No literature on this species, and so one is limited to outlining the known anatomical and morphological characteristics of the family Siphonodentaliidae. The foot is tubular and long, and it ends in a fringed anterior disc, which anchors the animal to the substratum. The radula is highly developed, formed by a row of rachidials and by a row of lateral and marginal teeth per side. The mantle cavity, as in all scaphopods, lacks gills. The water enters and leaves through the anterior aperture and carries the oxygen to the mantle, which takes over the respiratory function.
**Habitat** *Cadulus jeffreysi* lives in the circalittoral zone on soft bottoms, usually muddy.
**Distribution** A widely distributed species, found in the Boreal (Eastern), Celtic and Lusitanian provinces.

## 19 CANCELLARIA CANCELLATA
### Cancelled Nutmeg

**Family** Cancellariidae
**Shell** Medium size (1 ½ to 2 inches), fairly thick and robust conical spire not very high, spherical in shape, swollen whorls and a deeply impressed suture. The aperture is wide, and the edge of its outer lip is thin and sharp, and it is folded internally the callused columellar lip has large folds. The sculpture consists of sharp spiral ribs that cross similar axial ribs, forming a network of rectangles. Cream in color, with a spiral chestnut band (two on the last whorl). The periostracum is thin and lacks an operculum.
**Body** The foot is not very thick, but it is very long; the distinct head has a pair of tentacles, and at the base of each, on a swelling, is an eye; the proboscis, thin at its anterior end, is swollen posteriorly and is covered by a membrane. The mantle siphon is rather short. In the mantle cavity there is the gill, the osphradium and, in males, a very large penis, situated behind the right tentacle. The radula is a very special type of rachiglossan, made up of a single series of very long, thin rachidian teeth.
**Habitat** It lives on detrital or muddy bottoms in the infralittoral and circalittoral zones.
**Distribution** Lusitanian, restricted to the Western Zone and West African provinces.

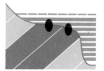

## 20 CARDITAMERA FLORIDANA
### Broad-ribbed Cardita

**Family** Carditidae
**Shell** Medium size (1 to 1 ½ inches), robust, roughly rectangular in shape, equivalved and inequilateral. It has a rather thick gray periostracum which hides the underlying coloration. The color of the outer surface is a grayish-white with chestnut dashes arranged concentrically on the ribs. On the inside there are two small brown patches above the two muscle scars. The sculpture consists of a score of radial ribs that are broader than the spaces between them and have stubby tubercules all along their length. The external ligament is posterior to the umbones, the hinge is heterodont, with strong cardinal teeth and well-defined lateral teeth. There are two conspicuous muscle scars, of different size, on the inside of the valves (dimyarian and anisomyarian), and the pallial line is continuous (integropalliate) without a sinus. The hinge has a crossed-lamellae structure.
**Body** A moderately developed foot and a pair of gills each of which consists of two series of lamellae extensively fused by interlamellar junctions (eulamellibranchs). As with other Carditidae, it has a byssus by means of which it is attached to the substratum.
**Habitat** This species (very common) lives on fairly coarse soft bottoms in the infralittoral zone.
**Distribution** *Carditamera floridana* found in the Caribbean Province, southern half of Florida and Mexico.

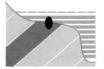

## 21 CARDITES ANTIQUATA
### Old Cardita

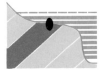

**Family** Carditidae

**Shell** Medium size (1 to 1 ½ inches), robust, equivalved and inequilateral, rather swollen valves. It has a persistent periostracum, rather thick, varying in color from hazel to dark chestnut. The color of the valves is cream, with irregular pinkish- or darkish-chestnut patches, on the sculpture, which consists of thick radial ribs, wider than the spaces between them; these are granular, due to intersecting with the concentric growth lines. The lunule is very small and impressed. The ligament is external and posterior to the umbones. The hinge is heterodont, with one cardinal tooth on the right valve, while there is a small anterior cardinal tooth on the left valve and an elongated posterior cardinal tooth. The two muscle scars are roughly equal (dimyarian, isomyarian) and are linked by a continuous pallial line (integropalliate) without a sinus. The hinge has a crossed-lamellae structure.

**Body** A moderately developed foot, a pair of gills each of which consists of two series of lamellae extensively fused by interlamellar junctions (eulamellibranch).

**Habitat** A characteristic species of the coarse sands and fine gravels, subject to bottom currents in the infralittoral zone.

**Distribution** Confined to the Lusitanian Province.

## 22 CARDIUM COSTATUM
### Ribbed Cockle

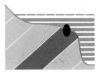

**Family** Cardiidae

**Shell** Large (4 inches), very fragile, light, full swollen valves, equivalve and inequilateral, roughly round in shape. It has a thin but very resistant chestnut periostracum that often persists between the large radial ribs that characterize the sculpture. These ribs are rather pronounced and in section have the shape of an elongated isosceles triangle. Another peculiarity of these ribs is that they are hollow, as is apparent if the ventral border of the valves is examined for places where they are broken. Pure white in color. The hinge is heterodont, the external ligament is posterior to the umbones. In this species, as in all Cardiidae, the two muscle scars are equal (dimyarian, isomyarian), and they are linked by a continuous pallial line (integropalliate) without a sinus.

**Body** No precise information about the morphology of *Cardium costatum*. Presumably the shape of the foot and the type of gills do not differ substantially from the other Cardiidae.

**Habitat** Circalittoral bottoms, coarse sand, perhaps also fine sand or even muddy bottoms.

**Distribution** Rather restricted, the Atlantic coasts of Morocco to Angola.

## 23 CASSIDARIA ECHINOPHORA
### Spiny Helmet

**Family** Cassidae
**Shell** Medium-large in size (2 to 3½ inches), rather thin, light but not very fragile. The spire is conical of rather variable height so its shape can vary from spherical to elongated-spherical. The whorls are convex, the suture is impressed. The aperture is wide, slightly half-moon in shape, it has a dorsally curved siphon, the outer lip is bent backward, sometimes it has a slight external varix, irregularly and bluntly toothed. The columellar lip has a wide, rather thin callus that covers part of the ventral surface of the body whorl and is expanded laterally. The sculpture consists of irregular ridges that are much wider than the intervening spaces and which sometimes are fused. Some individuals have a variable number (from 1 to 5) of bluntly gnarled spiral ribs. The periostracum is thin, light hazel in color except for the aperture and the columellar callus, which are a porcelainlike white. The operculum is ovoidal; it has a marginal nucleus.
**Body** The foot is very developed and so is the head, which has two fairly large and long tentacles. The mantle has a long siphon. The mantle cavity contains one gill, a bipectinate osphradium and, in males, behind the right tentacle, the penis. The radula is taenioglossan.
**Habitat** It lives on fairly coarse detrital bottoms or on sand in the circalittoral zone and deeper.
**Distribution** Lusitanian, particularly common in the Mediterranean.

## 24 CASSIS FIMBRIATA
### Fimbriate Helmet

**Family** Cassidae
**Shell** Fairly large in size (4 inches), rather light, not very thick, robust, short spire, and the body whorl covers a large part of the preceding one (involute), very impressed suture, spherical in shape. The elongated aperture is pear-shaped and is not very wide, its outer lip is almost without teeth internally, and it is bordered by a conspicuous varix externally. The columellar lip has a thin callus that covers almost the whole of the ventral surface of the body whorl. The siphon is short and curved dorsally. The sculpture consists of thin axial ridges, which intersect with three nodular spiral ribs, slightly raised. There are also strong varices. The color is grayish yellow with axial chestnut spotting and eight dark-chestnut spiral lines, twelve on the last whorl. The parietal callus is a darkish cream. The operculum is thin, horny and yellow.
**Body** The foot is rather large and is rounded both anteriorly and posteriorly, whitish with a marginal chestnut band. The distinct head has two short pointed tentacles, which are white at the base and tip. The eyes are about halfway along the tentacles on the outer edge of them. The radula is taenioglossan.
**Habitat** The species lives on the sand from the mesolittoral to the circalittoral zone, but it is commonest in the upper levels of the infralittoral zone.
**Distribution** Found only in the Australian Province.

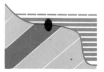

## 25 CASSIS MADAGASCARIENSIS
## Queen Helmet

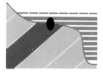

**Family** Cassidae
**Shell** Very large in size (4 to 9 inches), thick, spire very low
the body whorl covers a large part of the preceding whorl (i
volute). The aperture is rather narrow, the outer lip is thickene
by a strong callus turned back outward and bordered by
varix. The inner lip is also callused. In adults the lower surfac
of the body whorl extends over its margins. The outer lip ha
strong teeth, the central ones are much bigger and broade
than the gaps between them. The columellar lip has muc
smaller teeth, and they extend over a large part of the length o
the callus. It is cream in color, with irregular dark-chestnu
patches. The callus of the aperture is light chestnut or crean
the teeth are white, and the intervening spaces are generall
chestnut. The sculpture consists of raised spiral ridges, excep
for three that are very large and nodular. The growth lines giv
a slightly netlike appearance to the surface. The operculum i
horny, almost rectangular, and has a marginal nucleus.
**Body** The foot and head are very large and well developed
The two tentacles are dark chestnut with orange ends. Th
eggs are deposited in masses of capsules. The radula i
taenioglossan.
**Habitat** Lives on the sandy bottoms of the infralittoral zone.
digs into the sand to find the echinoderms on which it feeds.
**Distribution** Found in Caribbean and Carolinian Province.

---

## 26 CERASTODERMA GLAUCUM
## Greenish Edible Cockle

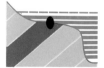

**Family** Cardiidae
**Shell** Fairly thin, medium in size (1 ½ inches), very conve
valves, equivalved and inequilateral. The periostracum is thi
and varies in color from hazel to dark chestnut. The coloratio
of the shell also varies, but most individuals are yellowish wit
the posterior portion of the valves a fairly deep green. Th
sculpture consists of 22 to 28 radial ribs crossed by wea
growth lines, which create scales on the ribs. However, thes
scales are easily lost in individuals that are not fresh. The ex
ternal ligament is posterior to the umbones, and the inner sur
face has two equal muscle scars (dimyarian, isomyarian) joine
by a continuous pallial line (integropalliate) without a sinus. Th
hinge is heterodont.
**Body** As in all cardiids, there are a pair of gills, each made u
of two series of lamellae extensively fused by interlamella
junctions (eulamellibranch).
**Habitat** An infralittoral species that lives at moderate depth
on sand or muddy sand, tolerating large fluctuations in salinit
while the related *Cerastoderma edule* is much less toleran
Because of this, *Cerastoderma glaucum* is also found in al
most-fresh water—that is, estuaries and river deltas.
**Distribution** The Celtic and Lusitanian provinces, but be
cause of its frequent confusion with the related *Cerastoderm
edule* its actual distribution should be reconsidered.

## 27 CERITHIUM
## Horn Shells

**Family** Cerithiidae
**Shell** Medium to large size (1 to 4 inches), usually rather thick and robust, almost flat to fairly convex whorls, incised suture, very high regular conical spire. The sculpture is usually both spiral and axial; the first consists of thin grooves, sometimes disappearing, not always regularly spaced; the latter consist of nodules, tubercles and spiny ribs, which are usually very prominent, mainly on the median portion of the whorls. There are often also large axial varices. The aperture is thin but never sharp, is slightly spread out, and at the anterior has a siphon that is usually rather short. The coloration is very variable, frequently a light chestnut with darker flaming patches, sometimes of white or other patterning. Other species have grayish or dark-chestnut shells. There is always a horny pauci-spiral operculum with an almost central nucleus. The illustration shows *Cerithium adustum* (Kiener, 1842), on the left, and *Cerithium nodulosum* (Bruguière, 1792), on the right.
**Body** It has a modestly developed foot, distinct head with two tentacles at the base of which are joined the ocular peduncles. The males lack a copulatory organ. The taenioglossan radula has lateral teeth with a lateral extension.
**Habitat** The species of this genus usually live on soft bottoms of the infralittoral zone, but there are also species that live on firm substrates and also circalittoral species.
**Distribution** Restricted to the warm and temperate seas of the world.

## 28 CERVICORNIS MUREX
## Deer-horn Murex

**Family** Muricidae
**Shell** Medium in size (2 to 2½ inches), fairly thin, not fragile except for the long spines that decorate the surface. The spire is quite high, so it has a tapered overall shape. The whorls are convex and the suture is deeply impressed. The aperture is ornate, the outer lip is weakly crenellated internally and the columellar lip has a thick callus, but it doesn't extend on to the ventral part of the body whorl. The siphonal canal is almost as long as the rest of the shell. The spiral sculpture consists of bands of various thicknesses, slightly raised. The axial sculpture consists of three large varices on each whorl and between them some (3 to 5) axial ribs, rounded, slightly raised, almost disappearing. The varices bear very long spines, which fork sharply about halfway along their length. The horny operculum is chestnut, very dark, with an apical nucleus.
**Body** The foot is rather developed, truncated anteriorly, rounded at the posterior. The head has a retractile proboscis and a pair of tentacles with an eye at the base of each. In the male, the penis is behind the right tentacle in the mantle cavity and is rather thick and long. The radula is rachiglossan.
**Habitat** Lives on muddy bottoms from the mesolittoral to the circalittoral zones and even deeper. It is often found on the pearl oysters on which it feeds.
**Distribution** Found on all Australian coasts.

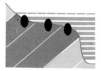

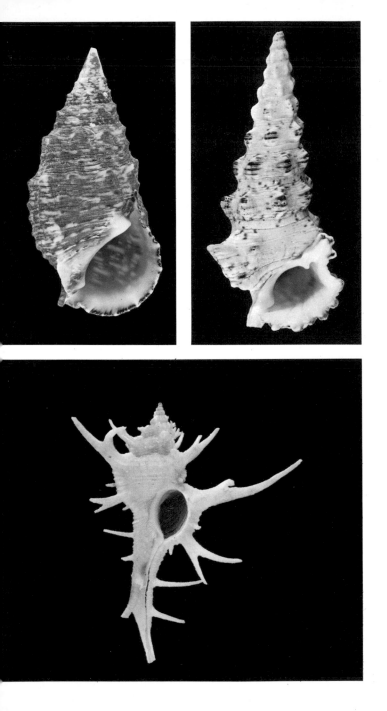

## 29 CHICOREUS SPECTRUM
### Ghost Murex

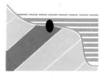

**Family** Muricidae

**Shell** Large size (3½ to 4½ inches), fairly thick, solid, high spire, giving an elongated-spindle shape. The whorls are convex, separated by a deeply impressed suture. The aperture is ovoidal, the outer lip lacks internal teeth, and the inner lip has a fairly thick but not extensive callus. The shell canal is rather long, about a third of the total height of the shell. The spiral sculpture consists of alternating thicker and thinner bands; axially it has three varices that bear some large quite branched spines on each whorl and from four to six blunt ribs between adjacent varices. Quite dark-yellow in color, with the spiral band, which is brown, covering a large part of the base color. The operculum is horny, brown, multispiral, and has an almost apical nucleus.

**Body** The foot is well developed, truncated anteriorly. A distinct head, two long tentacles with an eye at the base of each. The mantle cavity contains the gill; the osphradium; in males, the penis; and a very well-developed hypobranchial gland. The radula is rachiglossan.

**Habitat** According to the literature, this species lives on both sandy and rocky bottoms in the infralittoral zone.

**Distribution** Exclusively in the Caribbean Province.

## 30 CHLAMYS FLABELLUM
### Fan Scallop

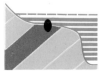

**Family** Pectinidae

**Shell** Modest size (2½ to 3½ inches), quite robust, inequivalve and inequilateral. Both the valves are moderately convex. The periostracum is very thin, chestnut in color and is not very resistant. The shell is highly colored and can vary from white to yellow, red, orange, pale violet; these colorations can be uniform or patchy, usually whitish, often with a dark edging. The sculpture consists of large radial ribs crossed by thin concentric lamellae, which derive from the growth lines of the shell. Completely without hinge teeth; these are supplanted by special thickenings called crura. The ligament is carried by a chondrophore, internal and triangular in section. There is only one muscle scar (monomyarian) and the pallial line is continuous (integropalliate).

**Body** Similar to other (illustrated) species of its genus. It swims, as do all scallops not fixed to the substratum, by rapidly opening and closing the valves.

**Habitat** It lives on sandy bottoms in the infralittoral zone resting on its right valves as all pectinids do.

**Distribution** It is found on the Atlantic coast of Africa, in both the Lusitanian and West African provinces.

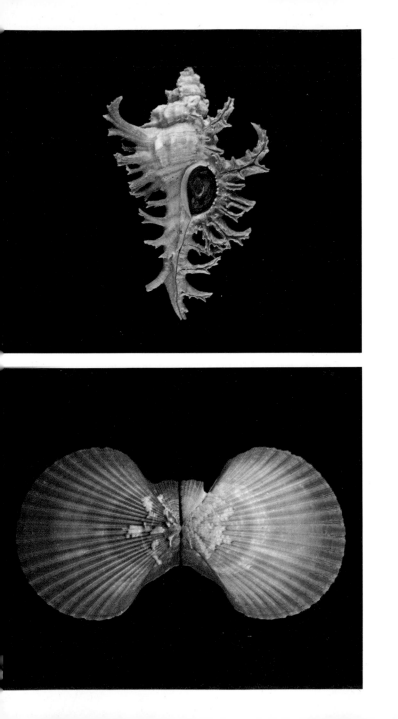

## 31 CHLAMYS MAGELLANICUS (PLACOPECTEN)
### Atlantic Deepsea Scallop

**Family** Pectinidae
**Shell** Large size (5 to 8 inches), not very thick, almost flat o slightly convex valves, inequivalved and inequilateral. The righ valve has two ears (this is quite accentuated in all pectinids lateral to the umbones, differing in shape in that the anterio one is continuous with the margin of the shell forming a deep notch through which the byssus emerges, while the posterio one doesn't have this byssal notch. The color varies from dirty white to grayish yellow or reddish gray. The sculpture consists of fine radial grooves while it lacks the ribbing typical of many of the scallops. The hinge lacks teeth (edentulous); the liga ment, reduced to a small body, triangular in section, is interna and is carried by a chondrophore. There is only a single muscle scar, and the pallial line is continuous.
**Body** It has all the characteristics of the family: a flattened circular foot, a pair of gills, each consisting of two series of fila ments, extensively connected to form four series of lamellae The mantle edge has sensitive fingers and eyes.

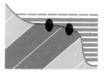

**Habitat** It is dredged from soft bottoms, mainly circalittoral also infralittoral. It is heavily fished and sold for food.
**Distribution** Mainly from the North American Arctic and Bo real provinces. Labrador to Cape Hatteras, North Carolina.

## 32 CHLAMYS SENATORIA
### Old Scallop

**Family** Pectinidae
**Shell** Fairly large and thin (2½ to 3½ inches), inequivalved and inequilateral as are all its fellow species. Its valves are moderately convex and very variable in color: yellow, orange red, violet, sometimes spotted with white. The sculpture con sists of radial ribs, raised and rounded, that have scales. al most perpendicular, arranged in concentric fashion. Because of wear on the shell, these scales can often be seen only at the margin of the valve. Between-the-ribs spaces, which are a wide as the ribs themselves, are only slightly grooved by growth lines. The ligament is internal, triangular in section and carried by a chondrophore. There is a single muscle scar (monomyarian), and the pallial line is continuous (integro palliate).
**Body** The foot is circular in shape, very flattened; the two gills are each made up of two series of lamellae (filibranch) The margin of the mantle is richly endowed with sensory elements.

**Habitat** Lives on moderately deep water on sandy bottoms in the infralittoral zone.
**Distribution** Found in the Indo-Pacific Province, restricted to the Pacific Ocean. It is found from Japan to New Caledonia and eastward to the Tonga Islands.

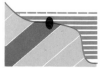

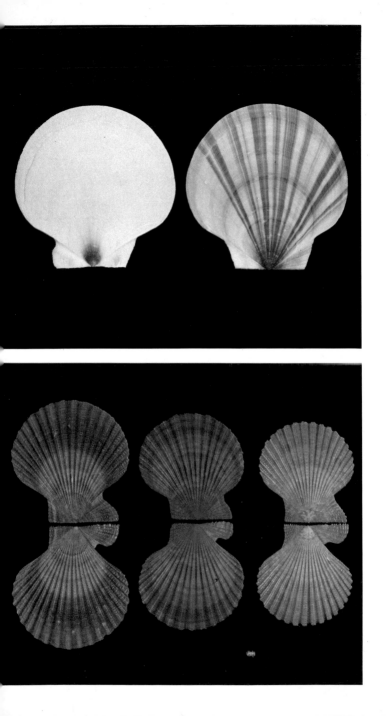

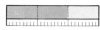

## 33 COLUMBARIUM PAGODA
### Pagoda Shell

**Family** Columbariidae

**Shell** Medium size (2½ inches), rather thin, light and fragile, high spire and distinctive siphonal canal that is bigger than the rest of the shell. The whorls are convex, keeled, and have an incised suture. The apex is rather large and nipple-shaped. The aperture is ovoidal, with a thin outer lip and a columellar lip that has a callus in part attached to a small area of the ventral surface of the body whorl. The sculpture consists almost exclusively of spiral elements; the surface of the whorls is smooth above the keel, this keel has long, flattened triangular spikes, and below it well-spaced scaly ridges that extend on to the siphon. The color is hazel or light chestnut.

**Body** A large and rather stout foot. The head has two tentacles with an eye at the base of each. The gill, osphradium and, in males, the penis are in the mantle cavity. The radula is rachiglossan.

**Habitat** Soft bottoms in the circalittoral zone.

**Distribution** Found in the Japonic Province

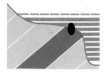

---

## 34 COLUS
### Colus

**Family** Buccinidae

**Shell** Medium or medium-large in size (2 to 5 inches), not very thick, light, fairly fragile, very high spire and fairly long siphonal canal; hence, overall appearance is spindle-shaped. The whorls are fairly convex, and the suture is always impressed. The aperture is always ovoidal, with a thin and fragile outer lip, and the inner lip often has a callus. The spiral sculpture consists of almost equidistant and similar thin bands. There may be no axial sculpture, or in some species it consists of blunt, thick, often winding ribs. The color is always yellowish white, hidden by a thin fairly reddish-chestnut periostracum. The operculum is horny, dark chestnut, and has an apical nucleus. The illustration shows *Colus gracilis* (Da Costa 1778) on the left, and *Colus islandicus* (Gmelin 1971) on the right.

**Body** It has the same characteristics described for other buccinids—i.e., well-developed foot, head with a very long proboscis, mantle with a very long siphon and, in males, a thick and long penis situated in the mantle cavity behind the right tentacle.

**Habitat** The genus *Colus* includes species that live on the sandy or muddy bottoms of the circalittoral and aphytal zones.

**Distribution** Species of this genus are found in all cold seas.

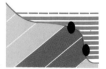

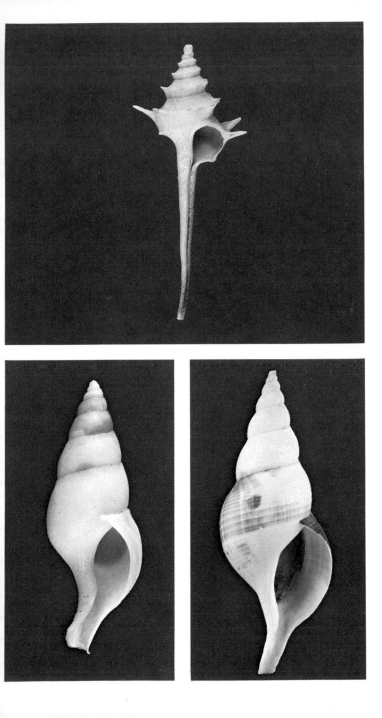

## 35 CONUS BENGALENSIS
### Bengal Cone

**Family**   Conidae

**Shell**   Large size (2½ to 4½ inches), moderately thick, fairly light, spire rather high, with the body whorl encircling the preceding one up to just below the shoulder. The whorls are slightly concave above the shoulder, which is sharp in the body whorl and rounded in the others. The aperture is very narrow and long, and has an outer lip that has a thin, sharp edge and no trace of sculpture. The patterning is formed by roughly triangular patches of varying size, white on a chestnut background. The periostracum is thin and transparent, the operculum is horny, small in size, and chestnut in color, with an apical nucleus.

**Body**   No morphological or anatomical information, even approximate, concerning this rare species. Presumably it has the same general characteristics as the other Conidae. The radula is toxoglossan.

**Habitat**   No information about either the type of bottom on which it lives or the depth at which *Conus bengalensis* can be found.

**Distribution**   The few known examples of this species came from the Gulf of Bengal, hence the specific name of this rare *Conus*.

## 36 CONUS subgenus CLEOBULA
### Cones

**Family**   Conidae

**Shell**   Medium-large to fairly large in size (1½ to 4 inches), very thick and heavy, so stout that its breadth almost equals its length. Biconical or obconical, the body whorl has a regularly rounded shoulder. The suture is deeply incised. The aperture is long, narrow, with almost parallel sides. There may be no sculpture, or there may be thin, flat ridges on the anterior part of the body whorl. In some species, the growth lines are particularly incised. Usually yellow in color, sometimes chestnut or grayish, decorated by spiral stripes or rows of patches that are arranged spirally and are brown in color. The periostracum is often thin and transparent. The operculum is horny. In the illustration are *Conus figulinus* L.1758 (on the left) and *Conus genuanus* L.1758 (on the right).

**Body**   It has the same characteristics as those already described for other species of this genus. It differs in that *C. figulinus* does not deposit the egg capsules singly on solid objects, but in a fairly branched chain, with the proximal end under the sand, which acts as an anchor for the whole.

**Habitat**   The species of this subgenus live on coral and sandy bottoms in the infralittoral zone or more rarely on sandy or muddy bottoms of the circalittoral zone.

**Distribution**   The subgenus *Cleobula* can be found in all warm tropical seas.

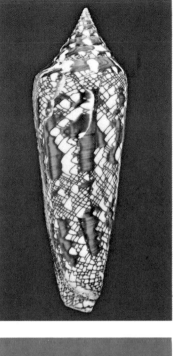

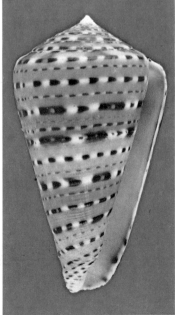

## 37 CONUS MERCATOR
### Dealer's Cone

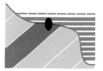

**Family** Conidae
**Shell** Small size (½ to 1½ inches), low spire. The body who
which has a very rounded shoulder, covers part of the poster
surface of the preceding whorl; is biconical in shape; has ve
incised suture. The aperture is elongated and rather narro
with a thin outer lip. The sculpture consists of thin grooves
the anterior part of the body whorl. The rather varied colorati
is distinctive: the base color is yellow; on the body whorl the
are two prominent bands, one subsutural and one media
chestnut in color with whitish rhomboidal patches. The peri
tracum is thin and transparent. The operculum is horny a
chestnut in color, is much smaller than the aperture, and h
an apical nucleus.
**Body** An elongated foot, roughly rectangular in shape, broa
ened and truncated anteriorly. The head has two long tentacl
with the eyes halfway along their length. In the mantle cav
are the gill, osphradium and, in males, the penis situated b
hind the right tentacle. The radula is, as in all Con
toxoglossan.
**Habitat** It lives on sandy bottoms probably in the infralitto
zone, but the literature contains no precise information on th
**Distribution** *C. mercator* is found only in the West Afric
Province.

---

## 38 CORBULA GIBBA
### Common Basket-shell

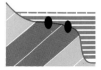

**Family** Corbulidar
**Shell** Small (½ inch), robust, very swollen, inequivalved,
the right valve is much larger than the left, inequilateral a
roughly triangular in shape. It has a persistent grayish-brov
periostracum. The shell is whitish, yellow or even reddish;
also has dark-red radial stripes. The sculpture consists of th
growth lines partially interrupted by half a dozen radial ri
present only on the left valve. The internal ligament is carri
by a triangular chondrophore. The hinge lacks teeth on the l
valve and has a small cardinal tooth and two lateral (anter
and posterior) teeth on the right valve. The two muscle sca
are almost equal (dimyarian, isomyarian) and are joined by
pallial line that has a shallow sinus (sinopalliate).
**Body** The foot is modestly developed, as is the siphon. It h
a pair of gills each of which consists of two series of lamell
extensively fused by interlamellar junctions (eulamellibranc
**Habitat** Found on sandy or muddy sandy bottoms in th
intra- and circalittoral zones.
**Distribution** Distributed through the Boreal, Celtic Lusitani
and part of the West African provinces northward to the No
wegian coast.

## 39 CUSPIDARIA CUSPIDATA
### Common Cuspidaria

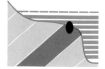

**Family** Cuspidariidae

**Shell** Small size (⅝ inch), thin, not very fragile, very swollen, almost triangular, with the posterior end prolonged into a sort of siphon that remains open at its distal extremity, equivalve and inequilateral. The periostracum is reddish brown, fairly thick, sometimes encrusted with granules of sand; the shell is whitish. The sculpture consists only of the thin concentric growth lines, the ligament is internal, carried by a small chondrophore situated immediately underneath the umbones. The hinge is a rather modified heterodont, there is only one lateral posterior tooth, very elongated, on the right valve. The two thick muscle scars are not equal, and in this case the anterior adductor muscle is larger. The pallial line has a shallow sinus (sinopalliate).

**Body** It is a septibranch—i.e., the gills are transformed into a muscular septum with numerous perforations (branchial septum) that extends from the mantle to the foot, so separating off a suprabranchial cavity.

**Habitat** The species lives on muddy or fairly coarse sandy bottoms, usually in the circalittoral zone, but it can be found at greater depths.

**Distribution** Fairly widespread, found in the Boreal, Celtic, Lusitanian and West African provinces.

## 40 CUSPIDARIA ROSTRATA
### Rostrate Cuspidaria

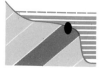

**Family** Cuspidariidae

**Shell** Medium-small in size (½ to 1 inch), rather thin and fragile, swollen ovoidal, beaked posteriorly (hence its specific name) due to a gaping tubular extension that has the siphons inside, equivalved and equilateral. White in color, obscured by a thin cream or hazel periostracum. Except for very thin, barely incised growth lines, the surface is smooth. The ligament is internal, carried by a small triangular chondrophore, which is immediately underneath the umbones. The hinge consists of a single posterior lateral tooth, rather elongated, on the right valve. The adductor muscle scars are almost equal (dimyarian, isomyarian) and the pallial line has only a shallow sinus (sinopalliate).

**Body** The foot is developed as a good digging instrument. The gills have transformed into a muscular septum that has numerous perforations (branchial septum) and extends from the mantle to the foot, so separating a superbranchial cavity (one per side) from the rest of the mantle.

**Habitat** An uncommon species that lives on sandy, muddy or fairly fine detrital bottoms in the circalittoral zone or deeper (to more than 1,600 fathoms).

**Distribution** *Cuspidaria rostrata* is widely distributed in the Arctic, Boreal, Celtic, Lusitanian, Carolinian and Caribbean provinces.

## 41 CYCLOPE NERITAEUS
### Nerite Mud-Snail

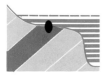

**Family** Nassariidae
**Shell** Small size (½ inch), moderately thick, robust, fairly low conical spire, covered by the body whorl, which is so wide as to almost completely enfold the preceding ones (involute). The overall shape, characteristic of the genus, is lenticular (lens-shaped). The aperture is round and has an outer lip that does not taper to its edge but is bordered by a small, external swelling and has very small internal folds. The columellar lip has a thick callus that almost completely covers the base of the shell. There is no sculpture, except for the growth lines, which are usually weakly incised. The coloring is yellowish or sometimes darkish chestnut, with darker flaming or spotting; there is often a thin subsutural band, which is also chestnut. The operculum is horny and yellowish.
**Body** Fairly wide triangular foot, with two short pointed processes at the posterior end. The mantle siphon is very long, and the only part of the mollusk visible under normal circumstances—i.e., when buried under the sand. The radula is rachiglossan.
**Habitat** Sandy or muddy-sandy bottoms, buried under the substratum, in the upper levels of the infralittoral zone.
**Distribution** It is confined to the Mediterranean.

## 42 CYMATIUM FEMORALE
### Angular Triton

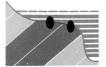

**Family** Cymatiidae
**Shell** Large size (3 to 8 inch), not very thick, robust, fairly light compared to other species of the genus, fairly high spire, angular whorls with incised suture. The aperture is an elongated oval, with a thickened outer lip, turned inward, edged by a varix with the posterior part angular, pointed, almost without teeth. The inner lip lacks teeth and has a not very thick or extensive callus. The canal is fairly long. The sculpture consists of spiral ribs, six on the last whorl, with blunt nodules, fairly developed and projecting, both these ribs and the spaces between them have deeply scored spiral grooves. In some cymatiids there are also prominent varices. The operculum is horny.
**Body** As in all cymatiids the foot is rather developed, truncated anteriorly; the head is distinct, with two moderately long tentacles, each with an eye at its base; the retractile proboscis is quite thick and long. Inside the mantle cavity there is one gill, one osphradium and, in males, a large penis. The radula is taenioglossan, with long and narrow marginals.
**Habitat** Lives on sandy bottoms with a cover of seaweed in the infralittoral and circalittoral zone.
**Distribution** A species typical of the Caribbean Province, southeastern Florida, West Indies, Bermuda and Brazil.

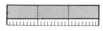

## 43 SUBFAMILY CYMBIINAE
### Volutes (some large ones called Bailer Shells)

**Family** Volutidae

**Shell** Large or very large in size (14 inches or more), usually thin and not very heavy but fairly robust, very low spire; the body whorl is large, spherical or more rarely roughly cylindrical and almost completely enfolds the preceding whorls (involute). The shoulder, sometimes hidden by a callus, is incised or caniculate. The aperture is very wide, the outer lip is thin and sharp in some species; the columellar lip has two or three strong folds and a callus that can be small or can extend over a large part of the ventral surface of the body whorl. The protoconch is very large and spherical. The sculpture is restricted to the crown of spines on the keel of the whorl's shoulder. The color is some shade of brown. The two species illustrated are *Cymbium glans* (Gmelin 1791) on the left and *Melo amphora* (Lightfoot 1786) on the right.

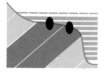

**Body** The foot is very large, round, very thick and fleshy, and it can envelop part of the shell. The tentacles, which have the eyes at their base, are short and squat. The siphon is rather short ahd thick. The females are oviparous or sometimes ovoviviparous. It has a modified rachiglossan radula—i.e., radula made up of one row of tricuspidate rachidials.

**Habitat** The species of the subfamily Cymbiinae live on sandy or muddy bottoms in the infralittoral and circalittoral zones.

**Distribution** Live in tropical waters of Indo-Pacific Province.

## 44 CYMBIOLACCA PERISTICTA
### McMichael's Volute

**Family** Volutidae

**Shell** Medium size (2 to 3 inches), not very thick, solid, moderately high, conical spire, the body whorl rather wide, a longish oval in shape. The whorls are slightly convex below the shoulder and flat above it. The broad aperture has a thin outer lip and a columellar lip with four strong folds, and is almost lacking a callus. The sculpture of the embryonic whorls is faintly grill-like, while the rest of the shell is smooth, except for a row of broad, spiny tubercles, slightly raised, curving toward the apex, situated on the shoulder. The base color is pinkish-white, which is covered by dark-chestnut spots of varying size and irregular arrangement. It lacks both operculum and periostracum.

**Body** Similar to the other volutids. The foot is rather bulky, the head small, with two lobes lateral to the tentacles, which bear the eyes. The mantle siphon is fairly long, and it has at its base two appendices of equal length. The penis is flattened, broad and situated behind the right tentacle in the mantle cavity. The modified rachiglossan radula has only a series of tricuspidate rachidians.

**Habitat** Lives on sandy bottoms at moderate depths in the infralittoral zone.

**Distribution** Lives in the Indopacific Province, limited to the seas of northern Australia.

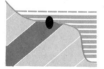

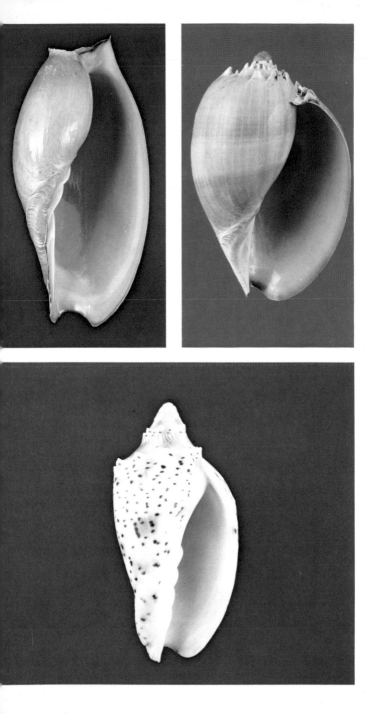

## 45 CYRTOPLEURA COSTATA
### Angel Wing

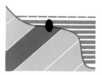

**Family** Pholadidae
**Shell** Large (4 to 7 inches), fragile, thin, swollen valve equivalved and inequilateral, elongated-ovoidal in shape. The shell is pure white in color, masked by the grayish periostracum. The sculpture consists of thirty radial ribs—hence specific name—which become almost spiny at the anterior edge. The ligament is internal, there is no hinge. The anterior adductor muscle is attached dorsally to two accessory calcareous plates, as in many Pholadidae. Inside each valve there is a prominent small calcareous process called the apophysis, to which the muscles of the foot are attached. There is a deep sinus in the pallial line.
**Body** The foot is cylindrical, short and stout. There is a pair of gills, each consisting of two series of lamellae, extensively fused by interlamellar junctions (eulamellibranch). The two siphons are fused.
**Habitat** This species lives on mud or sandy mud in the infralittoral zone. It digs with its strong foot and by movements of the valves; the long siphons allow it to burrow up to a depth of about 50 centimeters (almost 20 inches).
**Distribution** Found in the Carolinan and Caribbean provinces, southern Massachusetts to Texas and Brazil.

---

## 46 DENTALIUM INAEQUICOSTATUM
### Unequal-Ribbed Tusk

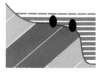

**Family** Dentaliidae
**Shell** Medium size (about 2 inches), in the shape of an elephant's tusk, as in all dentaliids, fairly thick and robust, moderately curved, opaque, and it lacks apical notch or fissure. There is often a small posterior tubular appendix in adults. The aperture is circular or polygonal in section and is thin and sharp. The sculpture consists of 9 to 12 principal longitudinal ribs, narrower than the spaces between them, which running from the apex toward the aperture alternate with thinner secondary and tertiary ribs. All the ribs tend to disappear toward the anterior end. Transverse furrows along the shell, marks of old apertures or mended fractures. The coloration is variable, rarely whitish, more often pinkish, with patches of fairly deep color, sometimes yellowish.
**Body** The cylindrical foot has at the anterior two lateral expansions that help the animal to burrow into the substratum. The head is indistinct and bears long capitate filaments, the captacula.
**Habitat** A species found on muddy or sandy or even detrital bottoms in the infra- and circalittoral zones.
**Distribution** D. inaequicostatum is a Lusitanian species fairly common in the Mediterranean.

## 47 DISTORSIO CLATHRATA
### Atlantic Distorsio

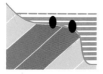

**Family** Cymatiidae

**Shell** Medium size (¾ to 3½ inches), as in all species of this genus, the axis of coiling of the individual whorls alters between them, thus giving the shell a rather crooked appearance. The whorls are regularly convex, with an incised suture. The aperture is rather small, with an irregular outline. The outer lip is strongly thickened and has strong teeth, one of which is more developed about two thirds of the way along. The upper parts of these teeth extend on to the body of the lip and form thin bands. The inner lip has a deep medioposterior indentation, is toothed, and has a light callus that covers only part of the ventral portion of the body whorl, without obscuring the underlying sculpture. Varices and thin spiral ridges, much narrower than the intervening spaces, intersect with axial ones producing small pointed nodules, make up the sculpture. It is yellowish or fairly deep hazel. The operculum is small, horny and rather thick.

**Body** The foot is moderately developed, anteriorly truncated. The head has a large proboscis, rather long, a short siphon and two tentacles that have an eye at the base of each. The radula is taenioglossan.

**Habitat** Soft bottoms in the infralittoral and circalittoral zones.

**Distribution** North Carolina to Texas and the Caribbean and Brazil.

## 48 DONAX VARIABILIS
### Coquina Shell

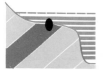

**Family** Donacidae

**Shell** Medium-small size (½ to ¾ inches), robust, roughly trapezoidal, quite convex, equivalve and inequilateral. The thin transparent periostracum gives a gloss to the valves. The coloration is extremely variable, white, yellow, pink, reddish, violet, usually with rays of deeper color. The inner surface shows the same range of color as the outer surface. The sculpture consists of thin radial grooves, which are visible on the posterior half of the valve and whose interspaces progressively increase toward the posterior margin. The heterodont hinge consists of two cardinal teeth and anterior and posterior lateral one on each valve. The two adductor-muscle scars are almost equal (dimyarian, isomyarian) and the pallial line has a sinus (sinopalliate).

**Body** A well-developed mobile foot, a good digger. The two lobes of the mantle are fused, leaving an aperture at the anterior for the foot, and at the posterior they are extended, forming two very long siphons. Each gill consists of two series of lamellae extensively fused by interlamellar junctions (eulamellibranch).

**Habitat** Soft bottoms, usually sandy in the infralittoral zone.

**Distribution** From the Carolinan and Caribbean provinces, New York to Florida and Texas. Very common.

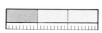

## 49  DONAX VARIEGATUS
### Common Coquina

**Family**  Donacidae
**Shell**  Medium-small size (1 ⅛ inches), fairly robust, roughly
rhomboidal in shape, moderately convex, equivalve and inequilateral. It has a thin, smooth periostracum, which is glossy
and transparent. The shell has variable base and pattern coloration, as in many donacids. It has, on both valves, a broad
white ray, that, starting from the apex and widening as it goes,
runs to the ventral border. As the extraordinary glossiness of
the valves shows, it is completely lacking in any sculpture. The
inner margin is smooth. The ligament is external, posterior to
the umbones, which are turned backward. The two muscle
scars are almost equal (dimyarian, isomyarian) and are linked
by a pallial line that has a deep sinus (sinopalliate). The shell
has a mainly crossed-lamellae structure.
**Body**  It has a pair of gills, each formed by two series of lamellae extensively fused by interlamellar junctions (eulamellibranch). The foot is good for digging, the two long siphons
allow the animal to burrow deeply into the substrate.
**Habitat**  Sand, in the infralittoral zone.

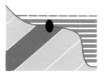

**Distribution**  Typically Lusitanian, with some populations
edging into the Celtic and West African Provinces. From
Southern British Isles south.

---

## 50  EROSARIA LAMARCKI
### Lamarck's Cowrie

**Family**  Cypraeidae
**Shell**  Medium or medium-small size (1 ¼ to 2 inches), rather
robust, a moderately high conical spire. The body whorl covers
the preceding ones (convolute), completely hiding them. It is
pear-shaped and smooth, as are all cowries, except for a series of radial ridges placed above the two slightly protruding
ends. The base is slightly convex and has a callus that extends
up to the periphery of the shell, forming a slight marginal callus.
Its aperture, only slightly curved at the rear, has narrow margins with some well-defined teeth, narrower than the intervening spaces; those on the columellar lip are fairly extensive,
while those on the outer lip are not. The dorsal base color is
hazel with round whitish patches, often with a blue-gray spot at
their centers. The radial ridges are chestnut, the base is white.
**Body**  Light brown in color, the lobes of the mantle, which can
enfold the shell when fully extended, have long, branched papillae. The radula is taenioglossan.
**Habitat**  Unlike other cypraeids, *E. lamarcki* lives on muddy
bottoms in the mesolittoral and infralittoral zones. It has sometimes been found among the roots of mangroves.

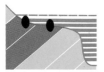

**Distribution**  From the Indo-Pacific Province, limited to the
Indian Ocean.

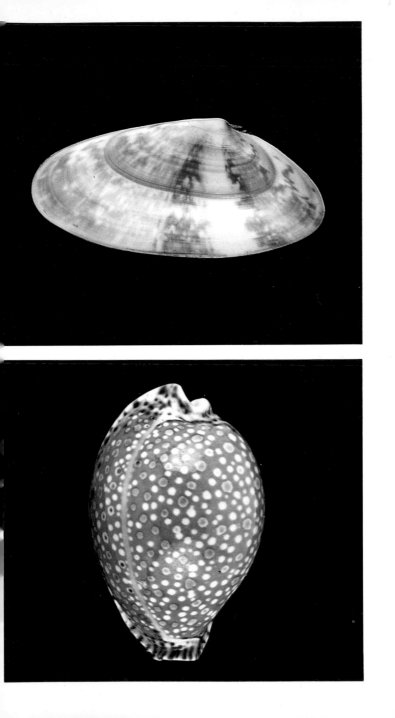

## 51 FAMILY EULIMIDAE
### (No common names, but sometimes called Parasitic Snails.)

**Shell** Small or very small in size (1/5 to ½ inches), usually rather thin, light, transparent, fairly fragile, very high conical spire, flat whorls, hardly incised suture, sometimes almost invisible. The aperture is rather elongated and ovoidal, with a thin outer lip, which is sharp and often has a convex margin. The surface is always smooth and glossy and lacks any trace of sculpture. In some species there are fairly deep axial furrows marking previous apertures. Almost always translucent, white, some species have spots or spiral stripes of darkish chestnut. The operculum is horny and yellowish. In the illustration *Eulima polita* (L.1758), on the left, and *Leiostraca subulata* (Donovan 1804), on the right.

**Body** The foot is moderately developed, rather elongated, pointed posteriorly. The head has two fairly long tentacles, each with an eye at its base. Inside the mantle cavity there is a gill, an osphradium and, in males, a penis, placed behind the right tentacle. Lacks a radula and jaws.

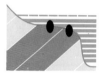

**Habitat** Usually the soft bottoms of the infralittoral and circalittoral zones. Some species are parasitic, especially on echinoderms.

**Distribution** The family Eulimidae is widely distributed in all seas.

---

## 52 SUBFAMILY FASCIOLARIINAE
### Tulip Shells

**Family** Fasciolariidae

**Shell** Medium or large in size (3 inches to 2 feet), thin or thick, never fragile, very high spire and a long or very long siphonal canal, spindle-shaped. The whorls are regularly convex, sometimes keeled, and the suture is usually impressed. The aperture is elongated, ovoidal, and with a thin or thickened outer lip always with slight internal ridges. The columellar lip can form a callus that sometimes has teeth toward the anterior end. The sculpture, rarely absent, is usually of coarse axial ribs and spiral bands that extend over the whole surface. The coloration varies greatly. The operculum is horny, chestnut in color, almond-shaped with an apical nucleus. The illustration shows *Fasciolaria tulipa* (L.1758), on the left, and *Latirus infundibulum* (Gmelin 1791), on the right. *Latirus* is sometimes placed in the subfamily Peristerniinae.

**Body** The foot is well developed, truncated anteriorly usually reddish or blackish in color, with lighter patches. The head has two not very long tentacles each with an eye at its base. The females deposit the eggs en masse in conical oviger capsules. The radula is rachiglossan.

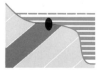

**Habitat** The species of this subfamily live on sandy-detrital or even rocky bottoms in the infralittoral zone.

**Distribution** Both illustrated species live in the Caribbean Province.

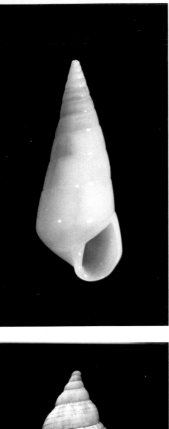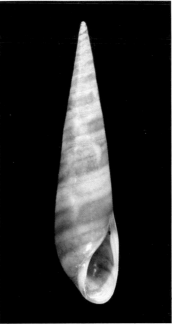

## 53 FAMILY FICIDAE
### Fig Shell

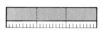

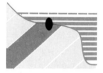

**Shell** Medium-large in size (3 to 5 inches), rather thin, fragile and light, elongated, pear-shaped, like a fig (hence the family name), low spire, with a very large body whorl, which covers a large part of the preceding one (involute). The suture is incised, the aperture is wide, smoothly curving to the end of the canal, the outer lip is thin. The sculpture can consist of either small spiral ridges or thin axial ribs; when both of these are present the surface is finely reticulated. The color varies from species to species, usually the base color is whitish or yellowish chestnut or light hazel; the patterning can consist of flaming axial lines or irregular patches darker than the background in color. They all lack an operculum. The illustration shows *Ficus communis* on the left and *Ficus filosa* on the right.

**Body** Very large foot, anteriorly truncated, angular laterally and pointed at the rear. The head is well developed, extending beyond the anterior margin of the foot, and carries two long tentacles. The mantle has two lobes that can partly cover the shell. The siphon and the proboscis are very long. The radula is taenioglossan.

**Habitat** All the species of this family live under the sand or mud in the infralittoral or, more rarely, circalittoral zones.

**Distribution** The Ficidae are found only in the warm seas of the world.

## 54 FULGORIA CLARA
### Clear Volute

**Family** Volutidae

**Shell** Medium size (2 to 4 inches), rather thin and light, but fairly robust, a rather high conical spire, tapered shape, the whorls are very convex below the shoulder and slightly concave above it, with very incised suture. The aperture is an elongated oval, with a wide sinus notch for the mantle siphon. The embryo shell is very large. The outer lip is thin, the inner has a light callus, which is extended, especially at the anterior, and covers a large part of the body whorl. The sculpture consists of fifteen well-spaced, thin axial ribs and very thin spiral grooves, extending over the whole surface. The color is uniformly yellowish or pinkish brown. It has no operculum.

**Body** Though it is not a rare species, there is little information on the morphology of this species. The foot is large, the head has two tentacles each with an eye at its base. The mantle siphon has two holes at its base. Inside the mantle cavity is the gill, the osphradium and, in males, the penis, situated behind the right tentacle. It has a modified rachiglossan radula, which has one row of rachidial teeth.

**Habitat** Soft bottoms in the circalittoral or even the aphytal zone.

**Distribution** Limited to a small zone of the Japonic Province.

## 55 FUSINUS LONGICAUDATUS
### Long-Tailed Spindle

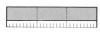

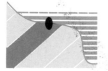

**Family** Fasciolariidae

**Shell** Medium-large in size (5½ inches), not very thick, very high spire and a siphonal canal that is almost as long as the rest of the shell, very elongated, spindle-shaped. The whorls are regularly convex and the suture is deeply impressed. The aperture is almond-shaped with a moderately thin outer lip that has weak internal folds. The columellar lip has a light callus that is slightly pushed up by the ventral surface of the body whorl. The sculpture consists of spiral ribs, which on the periphery of the whorls are alternately thicker and thinner. The axial sculpture consists of blunt ribs that are more marked on the first turns and fade on the later ones. Hazel or light chestnut in color. The operculum is horny, brownish, and has an apical nucleus.

**Body** Fairly thick but rather squat foot; the head is distinct and has two tentacles, each with an eye at its base. The mantle siphon is very long. Inside the mantle cavity there is a gill, an osphradium and, in males, the penis situated behind the right tentacle. The radula is rachiglossan.

**Habitat** Presumably it lives on soft bottoms in the infralittoral zone, though the literature is not definite.

**Distribution** It lives in the Japonic Province.

---

## 56 GARI COSTULATA
### Ribbed Sunset Clam

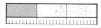

**Family** Psammobiidae

**Shell** Of medium-small size (¾ to 1 inch), thin, fragile and light, slightly inequivalve, inequilateral; an elongated oval in shape. The periostracum is thin, yellowish, glassy, and the shell varies from white to pink or violet, often with patches or rays of a darker shade. The sculpture consists of thin incised concentric grooves and more than a score posterior of radial ribs. The ligament is external and posterior to the umbones. The hinge is heterodont, lacks teeth, and has two forked cardinal teeth on the right valve and two cardinal teeth on the left valve, of which only the anterior is bifid. The muscle scars are almost equal (dimyarian, isomyarian), and the pallial line has a very deep sinus (sinopalliate).

**Body** A well-developed very mobile foot for digging. The edges of the mantle are extensively fused, leaving an anterior aperture free for the foot and two elongated posterior apertures forming the two long siphons. It has a pair of gills, each consisting of two series of lamellae extensively fused by interlamellar junctions (eulamellibranch).

**Habitat** Lives on fairly coarse sandy or muddy bottoms in the infralittoral and sometimes the circalittoral zone.

**Distribution** Found on all the Eastern Atlantic coasts and in the Mediterranean—i.e., the Boreal, Celtic Lusitanian, West African and Western South African provinces.

## 57 GLOSSUS HUMANUS
### Heart Cockle

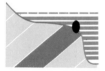

**Family** Glossidae
**Shell** Large size (3 inches), swollen valves, spherical wit█ very pronounced and partly spiraled umbones, equivalved an█ inequilateral. The periostracum is dark, variable in color fro█ hazel to a very dark reddish brown. The shell is cream in colo█ The sculpture consists of concentric lines and of very thin ra█ dial grooves. The ligament is external, fairly well developed an█ is posterior to the umbones. The hinge is heterodont and ha█ three cardinal teeth and one posterior lateral tooth on eac█ valve. The two muscle scars differ, the posterior adductor █ more developed. The pallial line is continuous (integropalliate █
**Body** It has a pair of gills, each of which consists of two se█ ries of lamellae extensively fused by interlamellar junction█ (eulamellibranch). The foot is moderately developed; the tw█ edges of the mantle are fused at the posterior to form two stou█ siphons that control the circulation of water in the mantl█ cavity.
**Habitat** This species is really circalittoral although it ha█ been found from depths of 7 meters (20 feet) to more tha█ 3,500 meters (12,000 feet). It lives on muddy sand, sandy o█ muddy bottoms.
**Distribution** G. humanus is widespread, found in the Bore█ (Western), Celtic and Lusitanian provinces.

---

## 58 GONILIA CALLIGLYPTA
### Flamed Astarte

**Family** Astartidae
**Shell** Very small size (less than ¼ inch), rather flattened wit█ solid valves, equivalve and almost equilateral, roughly triang█ lar in shape with the basal angles rounded off. Has a persister█ reddish periostracum, while the shell varies from hazel to rec█ dish in color. The sculpture, of raised, rounded, concentric rib█ forming along the median zone of the valves, an angle with th█ vertex pointing toward the umbones, is distinctive. The umbc█ small and blunt, is turned forward.

The ligament is internal and posterior to the umbo. The hing█ is heterodont, the right valve has one cardinal and one anteri█ lateral tooth, the left has two cardinal teeth and a posterior la█ eral tooth. The two muscle scars are almost equal (limyaria█ isomyarian) and are joined by a continuous pallial line (integr█ palliate). The shell has a crossed-lamellae structure.
**Body** There is no information on the morphological charac█ teristics of this rare mollusk. As in all astarids, it presumabl█ has a pair of gills, each of which has two series of lamellae ex█ tensively fused by interlamellar junctions (eulamellibranch).
**Habitat** Found on detrital or fairly coarse sandy bottoms █ the circalittoral zone.
**Distribution** It is a rather small, rare species, thus there is li█ tle precise information on its distribution. It is certainly found █ the Mediterranean and perhaps in the Lusitanian Province.

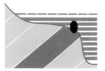

## 59 GUILDFORDIA TRIUMPHANS
### Victorious Turban

**Family** Turbinidae
**Shell** Medium size (1½ inches), rather light, not thick, with flattish, conical spire, its breadth is about double its height, with convex whorls, slightly incised suture, moderately convex base, with an umbilicus surrounded by a swelling and covered by a callus. The aperture is turned toward the back. The outer lip, thin and sharp, sinuous in shape, with a strong protuberance halfway along its dorsal margin. The sculpture consists of spiral granular lines slightly closer together in the upper part of the whorls. The body whorl has a lateral ventral keel bearing thin moderately developed spines. The lower surface has the same sculpture, except for the central area, which is covered with a thin pink mother-of-pearl callus. The coloring is pinkish with metallic highlights. The base is yellowish white. The operculum is calcareous, ovoidal, paucispiral, white, and has a smooth outer surface.
**Body** It has a large foot with an epipodium that has long tentacles, a very distinct head, only one gill and an osphradium. A rhipidoglossan radula.
**Habitat** Soft bottoms in the circalittoral zone.
**Distribution** This species and its relative *G. yoka* live in the Japonic Province.

---

## 60 HARPA COSTATA
### Ribbed Harp

**Family** Harpidae
**Shell** Medium large (3½ inches), rather thin, strengthened by numerous ribs, low spire, with a large and spherical body whorl that almost completely enfolds the preceding one (involute). The suture is very impressed. The aperture is very wide, with a broad, deep notch at the anterior for the mantle siphon. The outer lip, which has a sharp edge, is broadened externally by a robust rib. The columellar lip has a thin callus, which covers a large part of the ventral surface of the body whorl. The sculpture consists, as in all species of the genus *Harpa*, of strong, tightly packed ribs (from which it gets its specific name) that end at sharp angles. In the interspaces, the surface of the shell is finely scored by thin grooves. The base color is pinkish chestnut, and it is crossed by darker or lighter bands or stripes. It has no periostracum or operculum.
**Body** It has a very large foot, pointed posteriorly and with a semicircular expansion at the anterior. Because of its large volume it cannot be completely retraced inside the shell. The radula is rachiglossan.
**Habitat** A very rare species that lives on soft bottoms, presumably in the circalittoral zone.
**Distribution** Indo-Pacific Province—confined to the waters of the island of Mauritius.

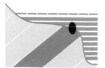

## 61 HARPULINA ARAUSIACA
### Gold-Banded Volute

**Family** Volutidae
**Shell** Medium large (3 to 4 inches), fairly thick and solid, low conical spire, pointed, faintly spherical in shape, the body whorl almost completely covering the preceding one (involute). The body whorl is weakly convex below the shoulder and almost flat above it. The aperture is broadened at the anterior and has a sharp-edged outer lip and an inner one with a light callus and three or four thin folds halfway along its length followed by three or four larger folds. The sculpture consists of axial ribs on the first whorls and a series of nodular tubercles on the body whorl. The coloration is distinctive, the base is cream, with spiral orange lines. It lacks an operculum.
**Body** There is no information, even approximate, on the morphology and anatomy of either of the two known species of the genus *Harpulina*. The characteristics of the subfamily Zidoninae, to which they belong, include the two short identical lobes at the base of the mantle siphon, the particular structure of the salivary glands, and the modified rachiglossan radula, constituted from only a series of tricuspidate rachidial teeth.
**Habitat** *H. arausiaca* lives on sandy bottoms in the lower levels of the intralittoral shore.
**Distribution** An Indo-Pacific species, known only from the northern waters of Ceylon.

## 62 HOMALOCANTHA OXYACANTHA
### Broderip's Homalocantha

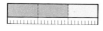

**Family** Muricidae
**Shell** Medium size (2 inches), fairly thick and robust, low spire, spindle-shaped. The body whorl has a long and broad canal. The whorls are convex and the suture is almost caniculated. The aperture is ovoidal, with an outer lip that has internal and thin folds and a columellar with a callus fully attached to a small ventral area of the body whorl. It does not have an anal furrow (i.e., the slight notching at the rear of the aperture) as other muricids do. The axial sculpture consists of from six to eight varices, furnished with longish spines on each whorl; the spiral sculpture is made up of alternating broad and thin ribs which are more prominent between the varices. Whitish in color, except the varices and spines, which are dark chestnut. The operculum is horny, chestnut in color, with a lateral nucleus, situated toward the outer margin.
**Body** A well-developed foot, as in all muricids, truncated at the front, rounded at the rear. The head has an evaginated proboscis and two tentacles, each with an eye at its base. The rachiglossan radula has rachidial teeth with five short, stout cusps.
**Habitat** No precise information in the literature, but by analogy with related species, it would live on sandy bottoms in the infralittoral zone.
**Distribution** Limited to the Panamic Province.

## 63 LAEVICARDIUM CRASSUM
### Common Egg Cockle

**Family** Cardiidae

**Shell** Medium size (2 to 3 inches), not very solid, equivalve and inequilateral, obliquely oval, with only moderately convex valves. A grayish-brown periostracum that is thin and fairly persistent. The color is usually a fairly deep cream, but there are examples that are pink, or at least they often have irregular pink spots on the umbones. The sculpture consists of fifteen slightly raised ribs, noticeable only on the median part of the valves, while they are invisible on the anterior, umbonal and posterior parts of the valves. The external ligament is posterior to the umbo. The hinge is heterodont, the two muscle scars are equal (dimyarian, isomyarian) and are linked by a continuous pallial line (integropalliate).

**Body** Whitish in color, the posterior edges of the mantle are fused and slightly extended, so forming two very short and stout siphons (inhalant, exhalant). In the region of the siphons the mantle has large umbones of finger- and even threadlike extensions.

**Habitat** Fairly coarse detrital bottoms in the circalittoral zone in which they are partly buried, leaving part of the rear of the valves and the two siphons projecting.

**Distribution** Rather widespread, the Boreal, Celtic, Lusitanian and West African provinces. From the Norwegian Sea south to Senegal and Cape Verde Islands.

---

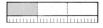

## 64 MACOMA BALTHICA
### Balthica Macoma

**Family** Tellinidae

**Shell** Medium-small (½ to 1½ inches), moderately thick and robust, oval in shape, slightly swollen equivalved and inequilateral, with a slight posterior ventral curve. The color varies from white to yellow, pale pink with the apexes more strongly colored and sometimes with slightly darker concentric bands. The periostracum, which is easily detached, is transparent. The surface is almost smooth, and the only sculpture consists of concentric growth lines. The ligament is external and posterior to the umbones. The hinge is heterodont, the two valves have two cardinal teeth, the anterior one of the right valve and the posterior of the left valve is bifid; there are no lateral teeth. The two muscle scars are equal (dimyarian, isomyarian), and the pallial line has a fairly deep sinus (sinopalliate).

**Body** It has a thin, well-developed foot, used for digging deeply into the substrate. Each gill consists of two series of lamellae extensively fused by interlamellar junctions (eulamellibranch). Water circulation through the mantle cavity is ensured by two very long siphons.

**Habitat** Muddy or sandy mud in the mesolittoral and infralittoral zones. It is very tolerant of salinity variations and is common near estuaries.

**Distribution** Widely distributed in the Arctic, Boreal, Celtic, Lusitanian (not the Mediterranean) and Carolinan provinces.

## 65 MACOMA MELO
### Mediterranean Macoma

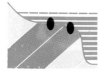

**Family** Tellinidae

**Shell** Medium in size (2½ inches), moderately swollen valves, fairly thick, almost triangular in shape, equivalve and inequilateral as in many tellinids, the rear part of the shell is slightly angled to the right. The periostracum is thin, hazel in color, and it usually persists on the margins of the valves. The shell is a beautiful pinkish red, which becomes paler from the umbones until it shades into the white at the margins of the valve. The sculpture consists of slight growth lines. The hinge is external and posterior to the umbones, which are pointed backward. The hinge is heterodont but, as is characteristic in the subfamily Macominae, lacks lateral teeth. The inner surface of the valve is also pinkish in part and has two equal muscle scars (dimyarian, isomyarian) and a pallial line with a deep sinus (sinopalliate).

**Body** As in all tellinids it has a pair of gills, each of which consists of two series of lamellae extensively fused by interlamellar junctions (eulamellibranch). The foot is thin and mobile; the siphons are very long.

**Habitat** Muddy bottoms in the infralittoral and especially in the circalittoral zones.

**Distribution** *M. melo* lives in a small area of the Lusitanian Province and extends into the Mediterranean, confined to the Sea of Alboran.

---

## 66 MACTRA GLAUCA
### Gleaming Mactra

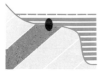

**Family** Mactridae

**Shell** Large (4 inches), moderately fragile, flattened valves, equivalve and slightly inequilateral, oval to almost triangular in shape. The periostracum is yellowish or hazel, the shell is white or cream, with irregular, reddish-brown radial stripes. The ligament is partly external and partly internal, carried by a triangular chondrophore under and to the rear of the umbones. The sculpture consists of fine concentric growth lines. The hinge is heterodont; on the right valve there are two separate cardinal teeth, two lateral anterior and two lateral posterior; on the left valve there are three cardinal teeth, one lateral anterior and one lateral posterior. There are two almost-equal muscle scars (dimyarian, isomyarian) linked by a pallial line with a posterior sinus (sinopalliate). The shell has a crossed-lamellae structure.

**Body** It has a dark moderately developed foot, a pair of gills, each of which consists of two series of lamellae extensively fused by interlamellar junctions (eulamellibranch).

**Habitat** Coarse sand or fine gravels in the upper levels of the infralittoral zone; it lives moderately buried.

**Distribution** *M. glauca* is a typically Lusitanian species from the English Channel to the Mediterranean and the North Atlantic coast of Morocco.

## 67 MALEA RINGENS
### Gaping Tun

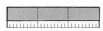

**Family** Tonnidae

**Shell** Very large (4 inches), fairly thick, robust with a flattish spire, spherical whorls. Markedly impressed suture, breadth less than height. The aperture is slightly semicircular, the outer lip is bent back and toothed on the outside. The columellar lip has a thick callus, which covers part of the body whorl and is raised to form a few slight folds situated to the side of a deep columellar furrow. The sculpture consists of broad spiral ribs rather flattened and only slightly raised, as broad as the spaces between them. Whitish in color, with light-yellow patches. There is a thin, glassy periostracum. As all tonnids, it lacks an operculum, though the larval forms have one.

**Body** A very large foot, short and broad. A distinct head with two short tentacles that bear the eyes. The proboscis is retractile and very developed. The mantle cavity has only one gill and osphradium; males have a large, flattened penis situated behind the right tentacle. The radula is taenioglossan.

**Habitat** The young live on sand, while the adults are often found under rocky projections in the infralittoral zone.

**Distribution** The Panamic Province.

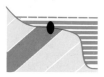

---

## 68 MALLEUS ALBUS
### White Hammer Oyster

**Family** Malleidae

**Shell** Inequivalve and inequilateral of large dimensions (4 to 7 inches), with a characteristic hammer shape (hence the name of the genus; in Latin *malleus* means "hammer"). White in color, hence its specific name. The sculpture consists of rough concentric-growth lamellae. The ligament is external. The hinge is edentulous. The inner surface has only one muscle scar (monomyarian), and the pallial line is continuous (integropalliate). The inner layer of the shell is mother-of-pearl.

**Body** It has a pair of gills each consisting of two series of filaments widely connected to form in all four series of lamellae (filibranch). The foot is reduced as in the great majority of sessile forms.

**Habitat** Oddly, this species, which lacks a byssus (the byssus is usually used to anchor to a rigid substratum) are found on sandy or muddy infralittoral zones. In *M. malleus* the byssus is widely branched, so as to form a wide area of anchorage on a loose surface.

**Distribution** An Indo-Pacific species found in the area between Northern Australia and Japan. It is most common in the southern part of the range.

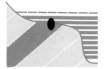

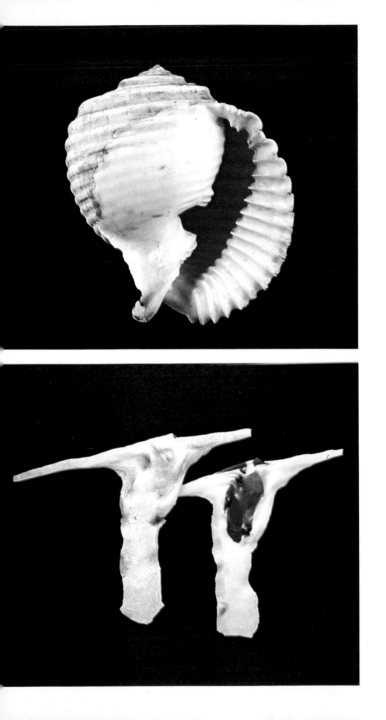

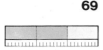

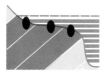

## 69 FAMILY MARGINELLIDAE
### Marginellas

**Shell**  Generally small, sometimes medium-small (¼ to more than 2 inches), rarely medium or large, fairly thick and robust, low conical spire, sometimes flattened. Hence, as the last whorl, which enfolds completely or in large part the preceding whorls (involute or convolute), it has a spherical or elongated spherical shape. The aperture is narrow, often with roughly parallel margins; the outer lip has an external thickening and sometimes is finely toothed internally. The columellar lip almost always has a few very strong folds, and sometimes a greater number of folds, which are always prominent. The sculpture is almost always absent. In some species, there are axial ribs, fairly coarse, that form blunt nodules on the shoulder. The coloration is variable. The base color varies from white, yellowish, cream, chestnut or gray, with flamings, tesselations, lines, spiral or axial bands or patches of various colors. They never have an operculum or a periostracum. The illustration shows *Marginella pseudofaba* (top left), *Bullata elegans* (top right), *Marginella goodalli* (bottom left) and *Marginella hematita* (bottom right).

**Body**  The foot is well developed, posteriorly elongated. The head is distinct and has two very long tentacles with eyes in proximal position. The mantle siphon is very developed. The mantle can be extended to cover almost the whole of the shell. The mantle cavity contains the gill, osphradium and, in males, the penis, situated behind the right tentacle. The females lay the eggs, each enclosed in a domed capsule. It has a modified rachiglossan radula, with only a row of rachidian teeth.

**Habitat**  Rather varied, found on sandy, muddy-detrital or rocky bottoms. The species of this family live in the meso- infra- and circalittoral zones. They are all predators.

**Distribution**  Marginellid species usually live in warm seas or in lesser numbers in temperate seas.

**FAMILY MELONGENIDAE**
**Whelks or Crown Shells (Melongena)**

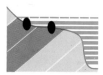

**Shell**  Varies from medium to very large in size (2½ to 2
inches), thin or thick, always rather robust, the spire can be
flattish or very high. The overall appearance is spindle- or
sometimes pear-shaped. The whorls are often very convex,
frequently keeled. Generally the suture is incised. The siphonal
canal, rather stout in the genus *Melongena*, is well developed
and long in the genus *Syrinx*. Some species of *Busycon* are
sinistral. The juvenile shell of *Syrinx aruanus* is distinctive, with
a cylindrical outline. The sculpture is spiral, usually with fairly
marked ridges, sometimes nodules or triangular spines on the
keels of the whorls. The aperture is an elongated oval, and the
outer lip is thin, with thin folds on the inner surface. The columellar lip has a callus that can extend to cover a fairly large
part of the ventral surface of the body whorl. The coloration
varies greatly from species to species, a few examples are illustrated here. The periostracum can be thin or fairly thick, yellowish or dark chestnut in color. The calcareous operculum
has an apical nucleus. The illustration shows *Melongena
corona* (top), *Busycon contrarium* (lower right), and *Syrinx
aruanus* (lower left). The latter species is the biggest gastropod
on the earth.
**Body**  The foot is fairly bulky, elongated posteriorly. The head
is distinct, and the eyes are placed at the bases of the tentacles. The mantle siphon is fairly long. The mantle cavity contains the gill, the osphradium and, in males, the penis situated
behind the right tentacle. The females deposit the eggs inside
discoidal oviger capsules, which are attached to objects underwater, in long horizontal groups.
**Habitat**  The members of this family live on muddy bottoms,
often near mangroves, in the meso-, the infra- and, rarely, the
circalittoral zones.
**Distribution**  Of the three illustrated species, the two on the
left live in the Caribbean Province and the one on the right lives
in the Australian.

## 71 MODIOLULA PHASEOLINA
### Bean Horse-Mussel

**Family** Mytilidae
**Shell** Slightly triangular in shape, size ¾ inch, equivalve, inequilateral, rounded umbones. It has a characteristic and hairy brown periostracum—i.e., bristles that are quite often fringed. The shell is yellow brown in color, no traces of sculpture at all. The ligament is external, behind the umbones. It lacks a true hinge, but in the area underneath the umbones the margin of the valve is crenulated, resembling small teeth. It is a strongly anisomyarian, dimyarian species, the anterior muscle scar being almost invisible. The pallial line is smoothly curved (integropalliate).
**Body** It has two gills each made up of two series of filaments widely connected, forming in all four series of lamellae (filibranch). As in all mytilids, the foot is reduced and there is a strong byssus. The edges of the mantle are not fused, and they extend, at the rear, just out of the valves, forming two apertures, inhalant and exhalant, allowing the circulation of water in the mantle cavity.
**Habitat** It lives on muddy and muddy-detrital bottoms in the infralittoral and, especially, the circalittoral zone to which it is confined in the Mediterranean.
**Distribution** The Boreal and Lusitanian provinces, from the coasts of Norway to Morocco and into the Mediterranean.

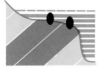

---

## 72 MYA ARENARIA
### Soft-Shell Clam, Large-Neck Clam, Steamers

**Family** Myidae
**Shell** Solid, moderately swollen, size 1 to 6 inches, rather oval in shape, inequivalve, the right valve slightly more convex than the left, inequilateral. The periostracum is a grayish brown, but the shell is a milky white. The sculpture consists of numerous concentric-growth lines and a few thin radial grooves. The ligament is partly internal and partly external, carried by a chondrophore that projects from the left valve to underneath the umbone of the right valve. The hinge is edentulous (without teeth). The muscle scars differ (dimyarian, anisomyarian). The pallial line has a deep posterior sinus (sinopalliate). The shell has a basically crossed-lamellae structure.
**Body** A pair of gills, each consisting of two series of lamellae extensively fused by interlamellar junctions (eulamellibranch). A very large and well-developed foot, and two very long siphons, which are covered by the periostracum.
**Habitat** Very tolerant of salinity variations (euryhaline), it lives on sandy, sandy-muddy, muddy or even detrital bottoms in the meso- and infralittoral zones.
**Distribution** Very widespread, the Arctic, Boreal, Celtic, Carolinan and North Pacific Boreal and Californian provinces. An important food species.

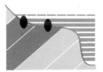

## 73 MYRTEA SPINIFERA
### Spiny Myrtea

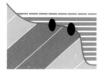

**Family** Lucinidae
**Shell** Small size (1 inch), rounded, rather flattened, characterized by the spiny posterior dorsal margin of the valves. Equivalve and inequilateral. A light-yellowish periostracum. The shell is white or cream. The sculpture consists of concentric ribs, which are regularly spaced, and, at the posterior, produce the characteristic spiny margin. The ligament is external, but it is so embedded in the region behind the umbones that it appears to be internal. The hinge is heterodont; it has one cardinal tooth on the right valve, two on the left and one anterior and one posterior lateral tooth on each valve. The two muscle scars are of different sizes (dimyarian, anisomyarian). The pallial line is smoothly curved (integropalliate).
**Body** A pair of gills, each consisting of two series of lamellae extensively fused by interlamellar junctions (eulamellibranch). The foot is well developed, good for digging, even if the species does not bury itself deeply into the substratum.
**Habitat** Muddy, sandy-muddy or gravelly muddy bottoms in the infralittoral and, especially, the circalittoral zone.
**Distribution** Rather unusual, the normal range of the species appears to be Boreal-Lusitanian, but some authors hold that examples have also been found in the gulfs of Oman and Ceylon.

---

## 74 NATICA CANRENA
### Colorful Atlantic Natica

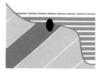

**Family** Naticidae
**Shell** Medium size (1 to 2 inches), fairly thick, robust, spherical flattish spire, the body whorl extensively covers the preceding one (involute). Its height almost equals its breadth. It lacks sculpture, if a few weak subsutural furrows of little extent are disregarded. The base has an umbilicus, and the umbilicus has a median cord that almost completely fills it. The outer lip is thin, and the inner one has a callus that covers part of the body whorl. The coloration is variable, generally consisting of chestnut lines, axial, and angled sharply along four spiral white bands; the rest of the shell is yellowish or hazel, except for the basal area, which is white. The operculum (to the left in the photograph) is calcareous, white, paucispiral, with an almost central, laterally placed nucleus. The outer surface is covered by lamellae parallel to the outer margin.
**Body** The foot and head are cream or hazel, with thin reddish-brown flamings that tend to fragment into spots. The head has two quite long tentacles. The mantle cavity has only one gill, one osphradium and, in males, a penis. The radula is taenioglossan.
**Habitat** It lives on sandy bottoms in the infralittoral zone.
**Distribution** It lives in the Carolinan or Caribbean provinces—North Carolina to Key West, West Indies, Bermuda and Brazil.

## 75 NATICARIUS HEBRAEUS
### Hebrew Moon Snail

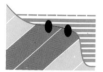

**Family** Naticidae

**Shell** Medium large (2½ inches), not very thick, robust, spherical, flattish spire, breadth usually greater than its height, with the body whorl extensively covering the preceding one (involute). The suture is barely incised. The surface is smooth, lacking any sculpture apart from some marked growth lines. The base has a rather wide and deep umbilicus. The aperture is semicircular with a thin outer lip and a light callus on the inner lip that partly covers the body whorl, and a columellar callus that continues as a cord in the umbilicus. The base color is whitish, the whole surface is decorated by small chestnut patches of different sizes, often coalescing to form irregular patches usually arranged as three stripes, one subsutural, one median and one on the lower part of the body whorl. The umbilicus is hazel in color. The operculum is calcareous, white, paucispiral, with an almost central nucleus and decorated on the outside by lamellae parallel to the outer margin.

**Body** Similar to *Naticarius millepunctatus*. A taenioglossan radula.

**Habitat** It lives on sandy, sandy-muddy or fairly coarse detrital bottoms in the infralittoral and circalittoral zones.

**Distribution** Lusitanian.

---

## 76 NATICARIUS MILLEPUNCTATUS
### Many-Spotted Moon Shell

**Family** Naticidae

**Shell** Medium size (2 inches), fairly thick, solid, spherical. The body whorl covers a large part of the preceding ones (involute). The suture is barely incised. The surface is smooth and shiny. It has no trace of sculpture, and growth lines are almost invisible. The base has a deep umbilicus; the aperture is semicircular, the outer lip is thin, and the inner lip has a columellar callus that continues into the umbilicus as a cord. Yellowish or orange in color, with a very large number of small spots (hence its specific name) of equal size and brown in color. The inner lip and the area around the umbilicus are white, while the inside of the umbilicus, including the cord, is hazel. The operculum is calcareous, white, and has a nucleus displaced toward the columellar side, paucispiral, decorated on the outer surface with lamellae parallel to the outer lip.

**Body** As in all naticids, the foot is very well developed, completely retractable into the shell, and can, when completely extended, cover a large part of the shell. The head has two rather short tentacles. The mantle cavity contains one gill, one osphradium and, in the male, the penis. The radula is taenioglossan.

**Habitat** Sandy or fairly coarse detrital bottoms in the infralittoral and circalittoral zones.

**Distribution** Lusitanian.

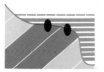

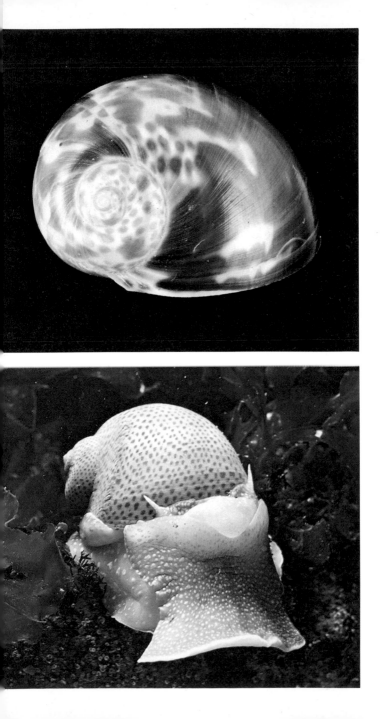

## 77 NEMOCARDIUM LYRATUM
### Lyrate Cockle

**Family**   Cardiidae
**Shell**   Medium size (2 inches), rather rounded, fragile, ver
convex valves, equivalve and almost equilateral. A fairly stron
pink color, sometimes with slightly lighter patches, irregula
both in shape and distribution. The shell color is partly hidde
by a thin grayish-brown periostracum. The sculpture is distin
tive; the posterior part of the valve has thin radial ribs and th
anterior and median parts have broad and flattened ribs tha
are obliquely arranged. The ligament is external and posterio
to the umbones. The hinge is a typical heterodont, with cardina
and lateral teeth on each valve. The inner surface, which i
pink, sometimes quite intense, bears two almost identical mus
cle scars (dimyarian, isomyarian) linked by a smoothly curve
pallial line (integropalliate). The shell has a crossed-lamella
structure.
**Body**   Like all cardiids, it has a well-developed foot, and th
posterior edges of the mantle fuse to form two slightly protrud
ing apertures (inhalant and exhalant) becoming two short, sto
siphons.
**Habitat**   An uncommon species that burrows only shallow
into the soft bottoms of the infralittoral and perhaps also th
circalittoral zone.
**Distribution**   Though there is no exact information about it
distribution, it is thought that the species is distributed in all th
tropical waters of the Indo-Pacific Province.

## 78 NEOTRIGONIA MARGARITACEA
### Pearl-Bearing Trigonia

**Family**   Trigoniidae
**Shell**   Medium size (2 inches), rather thick, triangular i
shape, equivalve and inequilateral. The umbones are directe
backward. There is a thin hazel periostracum, while the shell i
a violet brown. The sculpture consists of large radial ribs with a
granular or, rarely, lamellar surface. The ligament is external
and the hinge is unique among living bivalves in being schizo
dont, a special modification of the actinodont (isodont) type
The left valve has a pair of teeth pointing forward and a pai
pointing backward, and in the spaces between them the ante
rior and posterior teeth of the right valve fit. The inner surfac
has two adductor-muscle scars (dimyarian) and a continuou
pallial line, which has no sinus (integropalliate). The shell is a
most wholly nacreous (mother-of-pearl).
**Body**   It has a pair of gills, each of which consists of two se
ries of filaments widely connected to form in all four series o
lamellae (filibranch). The foot is well developed and bent, an
is used for making big leaps of more than 10 centimeters (
inches) in height. The body in preserved examples must be re
moved with care to avoid breaking the teeth of the hinge.
**Habitat**   Mainly from soft bottoms in the infralittoral or eve
circalittoral zones.
**Distribution**   Confined to Southeastern Australia.

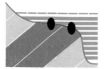

## 79 NEPTUNEA
## Neptune Shells

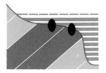

**Family** Buccinidae
**Shell** Usually of large size (2 to 5 inches), not very thick, fairly robust, high spire, rather short and slightly twisted siphonal canal, spindle-shaped or tapered-spherical in shape. The whorls are very convex, sometimes keeled, and the suture is always impressed; in some species it is almost caniculated. The aperture is ovoidal with a tapered outer lip and a slightly callused inner lip. There may be no spiral sculpture, but in the majority of species it consists of ridges or even rather broad bands; the axial sculpture is confined to growth lines. The color is variable, usually shades of light chestnut or hazel, and sometimes the spiral ribs are darker. The periostracum is thin. The operculum is horny, dark chestnut and has an apical nucleus. The illustration shows *Neptunea contraria,* which is sinistral, on the left, and *Neptunea lyrata decemcostata,* on the right.
**Body** The foot is large, well developed, as in all buccinids. The head has two tentacles and at the base of each a swelling with an eye set in it. The proboscis is retractile and very long as is the mantle siphon. The mantle cavity contains the gill, the osphradium and, in males, the penis. The radula is rachiglossan.
**Habitat** The species of the genus *Neptunea* are all found on sandy or muddy bottoms in the infralittoral and circalittoral zones.
**Distribution** The genus *Neptunea* lives in all northern cold seas.

## 80 NEPTUNEOPSIS GILCHRISTI
## Gilchrist's Volute

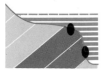

**Family** Voluntidae
**Shell** Large size (4½ to 8 inches), rather thin, light, very high conical spire and short siphonal canal, regularly convex whorls and a very impressed suture, tapered in shape, a large, bulbous protochonch. The aperture is ovoidal and very elongated, the outer lip is bent back, and the columellar lip lacks folds but has a large callus that extends to cover part of the ventral surface of the body whorl. The sculpture consists of very fine spiral grooves. A uniform pinkish cream in color, masked by a very thin olive-brown periostracum. The operculum is horny, dark chestnut, with an apical nucleus, and is much smaller than the aperture of the shell.
**Body** The foot is rather broad, the head has two well-spaced conical tentacles that carry eyes on protuberances on their outer margins. The mantle siphon is well developed. The mantle cavity contains the gill, osphradium and, in males, the penis. The radula is rachiglossan with tricuspidate rachidials and lateral teeth lacking cusps.
**Habitat** Presumed to live on soft bottoms in the circalittoral and aphytal zones.
**Distribution** Confined to the South African Province, where is rare.

## 81 NERITINA VIRGINEA
### Virgin Nerite

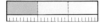

**Family** Neritidae
**Shell** Small size (½ inch), fairly thin and light but not fragile, flattish spire, spherical, the body whorl enfolds a large part of the preceding ones (involute). The suture is barely incised. The surface is smooth and glossy; it has no sculpture. The columellar area, at the base of the shell, is flattened and covered by the inner lip's callus. The aperture is semicircular, has a thin outer lip and a thick callused and finely toothed columellar lip. The coloration varies enormously both as to base color—whitish, grayish, dark red—and in the patterning—spiral bands, radial flames, largish patches. The operculum is calcareous and black.
**Body** Like all Nerites, it has some primitive characteristics: the heart has two auricles, and the ventricle is crossed by the posterior portion of the intestine. The radula is rachiglossan and it has two Nephridia, side by side, with more advanced characteristics such as having only one gill, one osphradium, no epipodium, a penis in males, internal fertilization.
**Habitat** A brackish water species, it lives in the mesolittoral zone.
**Distribution** *N. virginea* is rather common throughout the Caribbean Province, from Florida to Texas and the West Indies.

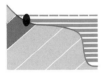

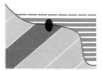

## 82 NUCULA NUCLEUS
### Common Nut Clam

**Family** Nuculidae
**Shell** Small (⅜ inch), equivalve and inequilateral, roughly triangular in shape, it has a thickish periostracum varying in coloration from yellowish to chestnut; beneath it the shell is a yellowish white. Apart from the rather faint growth lines the sculpture consists of fine radial grooves. The hinge, arranged in a reversed V is taxodont and is broken immediately underneath the umbones by the ligament, which is internal. It is a dimyarian, isomyarian species, with a smoothly curved pallial line. The ventral margin is finely toothed. The inner surface is shiny and has a thick layer of mother-of-pearl.
**Body** It has a specialized soled foot, more adapted for use as an anchor than for digging. The gills are of primitive type and the Nuculids are classified as protobranchs.
**Habitat** This mollusk lives buried moderately deep in coarse bottoms, muddy gravels or coarse sands. Though really an infralittoral species, it can be found at depths of up to 150 meters (almost 500 feet).
**Distribution** It extends from Norway to the Cape of Good Hope and then as far as Natal in the Indian Ocean.

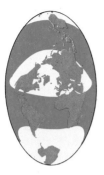

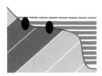

# 83

# OLIVA
## Olive Shells

**Family**  Olividae

**Shell**  Usually of medium size (1 ½ to 5 inches), but sometimes large, flattish spire, with a body whorl that enfolds the preceding whorl (involute). The suture is incised or caniculated. The aperture is narrow and long, and has a wide, deep notch for the mantle siphon. The outer lip is sharp and smooth while the columellar lip has a callus that has folds or large teeth along its whole length. No sculpture; the surface is smooth and glossy. Extremely variable in color both from species to species and within the same species. Albino, melanistic and completely orange examples are fairly common. The aperture is whitish or sometimes uniformly brightly colored. The illustration shows *Oliva porphyria* (top left), *Oliva incrassata* (top right), and *Oliva sayana* (bottom).

**Body**  The foot is very large, fairly long, and almost completely enfolds the shell. The distinct head has two long thin tentacles. The eyes are placed about a third of the way along the tentacles. The mantle siphon is very long. The mantle cavity contains a very long gill, a narrow osphradium and, in males, a long, thin penis. The radula is rachiglossan.

**Habitat**  All the species of the genus *Oliva* usually lie buried beneath the sand or mud during the day, and at night they search for food, which they seize with the foot and drag it underneath the sand to eat. They usually live in the infralittoral, but sometimes also in the mesolittoral zone.

**Distribution**  Confined to warm seas, often coral sands.

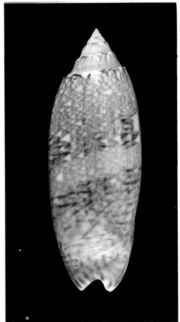

# 84

# OLIVANCILLARIA URCEUS
## Pitcher Olive

**Family**  Olividae

**Shell**  Medium size (2 inches), moderately thick and robust, flattened spire, truncated conical in shape. The body whorl almost completely enfolds the preceding one (involute). The suture is caniculated. The aperture is ogival with a wide siphonal notch. It has a thin, sharp outer lip, and the inner lip has a strong callus that extends to cover almost all the ventral surface of the body whorl and the spire; only the shell apex is left free. Apart from this furrow in the anterior region of the body whorl, there is almost no sculpture. Grayish in color, with chestnut zigzagging, axial flaming, particularly prominent near the suture. In front of the spiral furrow it is a medium-brown chestnut color. The callus is light hazel.

**Body**  As in all olives, it has a well-developed foot that, when completely extended, can enfold the shell. The very differentiated head has a pair of thin tentacles with the eyes in their proximal third. The mantle cavity contains the gill, the osphradium and, in males, a long, thin penis. The mantle siphon is very long. The radula is rachiglossan.

**Habitat**  Buried in the sand of the infralittoral zone.

**Distribution**  Caribbean Province, confined to Brazil, where it is endemic.

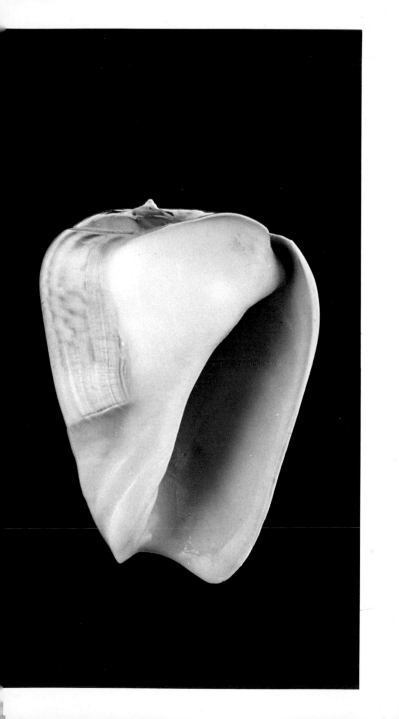

## 85 OLIVELLA
### Dwarf Olive

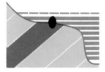

**Family** Olividae
**Shell** Small or very small in size (¼ to 1¼ inches), not very thin, fairly robust, moderately high conical spire, the body whorl enfolds almost all of the preceding one (involute), producing the shape of a small elongated olive, hence the generic name. The suture is incised, sometimes almost caniculate. The aperture is usually narrow, faintly triangular, the inner lip is thin and sharp and has weak internal folds. In some species, the columellar lip has a thin callus extending a little on to the ventral surface of the body whorl. The sculpture consists of a furrow that divides the anterior portion of the body whorl from the rest of the shell, which is smooth, the front portion having fairly prominent spiral ridges. Usually grayish, hazel or yellowish with the anterior portion being darker. The horny operculum is yellowish and normally smaller than the aperture. The illustration shows *Olivella biplicata* (left) and *Olivella voluntella* (right)
**Body** Its morphological characteristics are the same as those described for other olivids. The radula is rachiglossan.
**Habitat** This genus lives in sand or mud in the infralittoral zone.
**Distribution** The genus Olivella is widely distributed in all warm seas.

---

## 86 PALLIUM INCOMPARABILIS
### Incomparable Scallop

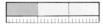

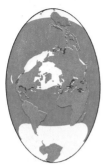

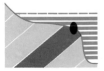

**Family** Pectinidae
**Shell** Small (1 inch), light, thin and fragile, inequivalved and inequilateral. Almost round, with two prominent triangular areas (ears) to the sides of the umbones. Its coloration is very variable: yellow, orange, red violet, chestnut or white; often these colors are broken by white or darker lines arranged in zigzags or on the right valve by whitish dashes that intersect forming a delicate reticulation. The surface, which appears smooth and glossy, is weakly scored by radial grooves, visible only under high magnification, crossed by still thinner concentric growth lines. The anterior ear of the right valve usually has six radiating and overlapping ribs. The ligament is internal, triangular in section and carried by a chondrophore. There is one muscle scar (monomyarian) and a smoothly curved pallial line (integropalliate).
**Body** No specific information concerning this species, but presumably has all the characteristics listed for other scallops.
**Habitat** Confined to muddy detrital bottoms in the circalittoral zone. It can be found attached by its thin byssus to large objects collected from these bottoms.
**Distribution** Lusitanian, limited to the Mediterranean.

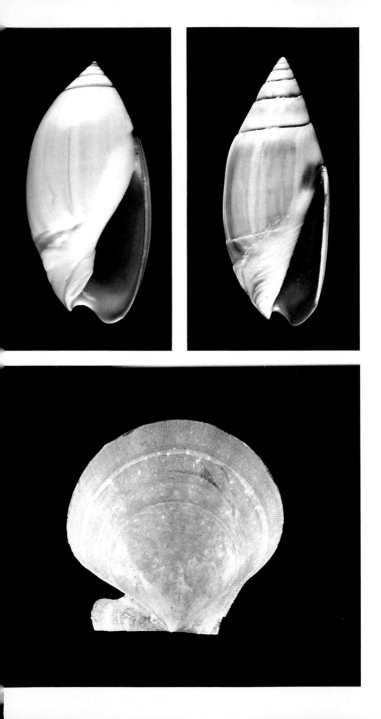

**PENICILLUS AUSTRALIS**
**Southern Watering Pot**

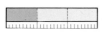

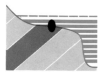

**Family**   Clavagellidae

**Shell**   The actual bivalve shell is very small (less than ½ inch) and confined to two small gaping valves, positioned dorsally almost at the anterior end of the calcareous structure (photograph top right). The large body of the mollusk, which is obviously not contained in these valves, forms a broad, long tubular calcareous shell to which fragments of the substratum are often bound. The siphons emerge from the posterior aperture of the tubular structure, which in its terminal region has several successive rows of leaved lamellae. The anterior end of the tube is closed by a slightly convex calcareous disc that has short open tubules arranged in a roughly concentric fashion. The ligament of the valves is external, the hinge lacks teeth. The shell has a nacreous structure, at least the inner part.

**Body**   As has already been said the body of the mollusk is much larger than the shell, the foot is short and stout, while the siphons are very developed. There are a pair of gills each consisting of two series of lamellae extensively fused by interlamellar junctions (eulamellibranch).

**Habitat**   *P. australis* lies buried in sand, gravel or mud in the infralittoral zone.

**Distribution**   Found in the Southeastern part of the Indo-Pacific Province.

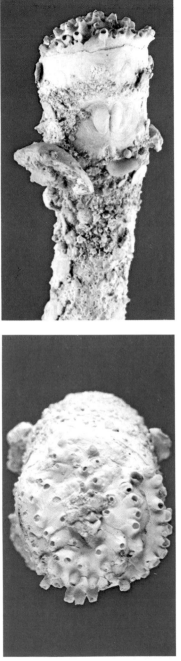

## 88 PETRICOLA PHOLADIFORMIS
### False Angel Wing

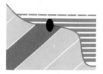

**Family** Petricolidae

**Shell** Medium size (2 inches), thin and fragile, equivalve and inequilateral. The umbones placed forward and directed down and inward. Elongated oval in shape; a dark-chestnut, not very persistent periostracum covers the white or yellowish brown of the shell. The ornament consists of fifteen radial ribs, the anterior ones being larger and carrying some spiny spatulalike processes; and the hinge is heterodont, no lateral teeth, with two cardinal teeth on the right valve, the posterior one being bifid and three on the left valve, the middle one being bifid. The muscle scars are almost equal (dimyarian, isomyarian), the pallial line has a deep sinus (sinopalliate).

**Body** It has a rather thick and stout foot as do many boring bivalves. It has a pair of gills each consisting of two series of lamellae extensively fused by interlamellar junctions (eulamellibranch).

**Habitat** *P. pholadiformis* owes its specific name to the similarity of its shell to that of the Pholadidae (convergent evolution), and like them it mechanically bores into the substratum, mud or rather compact clay. Found in the infralittoral zone.

**Distribution** Widely distributed in the Boreal, Celtic, Lusitanian (not the Mediterranean), West African, Carolinan, Caribbean and probably the Californian provinces.

## 89 PHALIUM LABIATUM
### Lipped Cask Shell

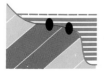

**Family** Cassidae

**Shell** Medium size (1⅓ to 3¼ inches), generally thin, light but not fragile, spherical, moderately high spire with the body whorl covering a large part of the preceding one. The suture is slightly impressed. The aperture is fairly wide, with a moderately broad canal, short and curved dorsally. The outer lip can be smooth or, more commonly, have about a score of small teeth. It also has on the outer side a moderately depressed varix. The inner lip has a thin, rather extensive callus, which covers a large part of the ventral surface of the body whorl. The sculpture is almost nonexistent. In some forms there is a keel, usually nodular on the shoulder of the body whorl; still more rarely, there can be two parallel rows of nodules. There is a narrow umbilicus, usually hidden by the columellar callus. Creamy yellow, with chestnut crescent-shaped specks, sometimes with a whitish patch in the hollow, arranged in spiral rows. The operculum is horny, dark chestnut, with fine teeth on the outer side, about two thirds the size of the aperture.

**Body** Cream in color. The foot has orange margins and the yellowish tentacles have two dark longitudinal lines. The radula is taenioglossan.

**Habitat** Infralittoral or circalittoral on sandy bottoms.

**Distribution** Confined to the Southern Hemisphere, found in the Australian, South African and Patagonian provinces.

## 90 PHARUS LEGUMEN
### Legume Pharus

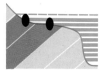

**Family** Solecurtidae
**Shell** Thin, fragile, glossy, 5 inches in size, an elongated rectangle with rounded corners, equivalve and almost equilatera. The anterior and posterior margins gape. The periostracum is greenish yellow and glossy. The shell is whitish or hazel. The sculpture is restricted to concentric lines. The ligament is external and posterior to the umbones. The hinge is heterodont the right valve has one cardinal tooth, one anterior and on posterior lateral tooth while the left valve has two cardinal teeth and one anterior and one posterior lateral tooth. The two muscle scars, visible on the inner surface, differ greatly, the anterior adductor scar being larger than the posterior adductor's (dimyarian, anisomyarian). The pallial line has a sinu (sinopalliate).
**Body** It has a very mobile digitiform foot, a pair of gills, each consisting of two series of lamellae extensively fused by inter lamellar junctions (eulamellibranch). It has two long siphons, as do all bivalves that live deeply buried beneath the surface.
**Habitat** It lives on fine and clean sands from the lower meso littoral levels to the upper infralittoral levels.
**Distribution** *P. legumen* is typically Lusitanian; in the Atlantic it ranges from southern Brittany to northern Morocco, and extends into the Mediterranean.

---

## 91 PINNA RUDIS
### *Rude Pen Shell*

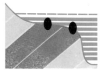

**Family** Pinnidae
**Shell** Medium-large in size (7 to 22 inches), equivalve an inequilateral, rather elongated triangular, its coloration con sists of various shades of darkish chestnut, the inside tends t orange, with a fairly extensive nacreous region in the apica portion. The sculpture consists of well-spaced concentri growth lines, which cross blunt radial ribs; at their point of in tersection, rather long, spiny and spoutlike processes are formed. It lacks a hinge, the ligament is very long occupying over half the dorsal posterior margin. There are two very dissimilar muscle scars (dimyarian, anisomyarian). The pallial line is not visible. The valves gape ventrally. Inside there is a laye of mother-of-pearl in two lobes, dorsal and ventral.
**Body** The foot is very reduced in keeping with its sessile life while the byssal (pedal) gland is highly developed; the byssus in all pinnids is secreted as rather long filaments and these were even used, in the past, as a textile fiber for making gloves The two gills each consist of two series of lamellae extensively fused by interlamellar junctions (eulamellibranch).
**Habitat** This species lives attached to loose substrates usually coarse sands, down to great depths in the infralittora and sometimes the circalittoral zones.
**Distribution** Found on both sides of the Atlantic in the Lusi tanian and Caribbean provinces.

## 92  PITAR LUPANARIUS
### Comb Venus

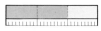

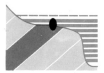

**Family**  Veneridae

**Shell**  Medium size (1 to 2 inches), moderately swollen, valves, thick, roughly triangular, equivalve and inequilateral; the sculpture consists of numerous sharp concentric lamellae which, toward the rear, are replaced by two radial rows of spines, often very long. Whitish in color, while the lamellae and the base of the spines are speckled with a fairly intense violet. The ligament is external posterior to the umbones. The hinge is typically heterodont, with three cardinal teeth and one well-developed lateral posterior tooth on each valve, two anterior lateral teeth on the right valve and one on the left. The two muscle scars are similar (dimyarian, isomyarian), and the pallial line has a deep sinus.

**Body**  It has a pair of gills each consisting of two series of lamellae extensively fused by interlamellar junctions (eulamellibranch). As with all venerids the foot and siphons are well developed.

**Habitat**  Infralittoral sands down to about twenty meters (66 feet) in depth.

**Distribution**  Rather widespread. The Californian (Southern Province, Panamic and Northern Peruvian provinces. A closely related species, *P. dione* (L. 1758), lives in the Caribbean Province.

---

## 93  PLACUNA SELLA
### Saddle Jingle Shell

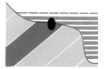

**Family**  Anomiidae

**Shell**  Large (3 inches or more), light, thin, rounded outline. It has a distinctive saddle shape, which gives it its specific name. The shell is so large, thin and transparent that a related species is used in China instead of glass in windows. It varies in color from a translucent white to a violet brown. The sculpture consists of thin circular lamellae that are very prominent at the margins of the valves. The entire shell is finely scored by very thin radial grooves. Though it belongs to the family *Anomiidae* the members of the genus *Placuna* do not have a hole on the right valve for the byssus. The hinge is edentulous and has two thickenings arranged as inverted V's, called *crura*. The ligament is internal. There is a single large muscle scar (monomyarian) and the pallial line is smoothly curved (integropalliate).

**Body**  It has a pair of gills, each consisting of two series of widely connected filaments, forming in all four series of lamellae (filibranch). The foot is fairly small, in keeping with the sedentary life of the species.

**Habitat**  Muddy bottoms in the infralittoral zone, on which the species rests but is not attached, unlike all other *Anomiidae*.

**Distribution**  From the Indo-Pacific Province, limited to the Western Pacific.

## 94 PLEUROTOMARIA AFRICANA
### African Pleurotomaria

**Family**  Pleurotomariidae
**Shell**  Large size (4 to 5 inches), conical, wider at its base than at its height, rounded whorls, and a moderately impressed suture. Viewed from below, the shell has a moderate umbilicus and aperture lips that are complete, except for a deep slit in the outer edge, about halfway up the body whorl. This slit leaves as the shell grows, a stripe (slit band), which runs through all the whorls in their lower third. The sculpture consists of thin concentric lines, covering the whole surface and partly broken by growth lines, which are often irregular. The latter are more prominent along the slit band. There is a horny, round operculum.

**Body**  It has primitive characteristics: two gills, a heart with two auricles, two nephridia. The anus is immediately underneath the base of the slit in the aperture lip, so the feces are rapidly expelled through this and don't foul the mantle cavity. The radula is rhipidoglossan.
**Habitat**  It is fished up, rather rarely, from soft bottoms in the bathyal level of the aphytal zone.
**Distribution**  Confined to the South African Province.

---

## 95 POLINICES DUPLICATUS
### Shark Eye

**Family**  Naticidae
**Shell**  Medium size (1 to 2½ inches), fairly thick and robust, swollen whorls, very low conical spire, with the body whorl covering a large part of the preceding one (involute), generally greater in breadth than in height, and a barely incised suture. The surface is smooth and lacks any trace of sculpture, except for the growth lines, a few of which are bigger and stand out. The base has a broad umbilicus. The aperture is semicircular, with a thin outer lip and a large columellar callus that covers part of the umbilicus. Grayish brown, with a slightly darker reddish-brown subsutural band, a black apex, and a light-hazel or cream base. The columellar callus, usually light chestnut, varies in color with changes in diet. The operculum is horny, chestnut, thin, paucispiral, with a roughly central nucleus.
**Body**  A very developed foot that, when expanded, can cover the head and part of the shell with the anterior portion (propodium). The distinct head has two tentacles, each with an eye behind its base. The eggs are deposited, bound with the sand, in a sort of very thin large collar. The radula is taenioglossan. All the naticids are predators.
**Habitat**  Sandy bottoms in the infralittoral zone.
**Distribution**  *P. duplicatus* is a fairly common species in the Carolinan and Caribbean provinces. Massachusetts to Florida and Gulf of Mexico.

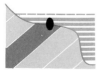

## 96 PTEROPURPURA MACROPTERA
### Frill-wing Murex

**Family** Muricidae

**Shell** Medium size (2 to 3 inches), fairly thin, light, not very fragile, high spire, rather long siphonal canal, giving an overall spindle shape. The whorls are moderately convex, and the suture is impressed. The aperture is roughly circular, the outer lip has slight denticulation/teething, and the columellar lip is lightly callused. The aperture projects slightly, in the shape of a thin swelling. The margins of the siphonal canal are fused ventrally. The axial sculpture consists of three broad-winged varices, with undulating edges, on each whorl; the spiral sculpture is made up of five broad ribs with thinner ribs irregularly interspersed. The color is a darkish chestnut with darker areas along the spiral ribs that cross the varices. The operculum is horny, chestnut, with a lateral nucleus.

**Body** As with all muricids, it has a fairly stout anteriorly truncated foot; the head is distinct, has a long retractile proboscis and two tentacles, each with an eye at its base. The hypobranchial gland is well developed. The radula is rachiglossan, and the rachidial teeth have five principal cusps and four pairs of accessory cusps.

**Habitat** An infralittoral species that appears to live on soft bottoms, but there is no precise information.

**Distribution** Californian Province.

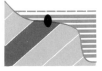

---

## 97 PURPURELLUS AND MARCHIA
### Wing Murex

**Family** Muricidae

**Shell** Usually medium small in size (1½ to 3½ inches), fairly thick, not fragile, despite the delicate appearance of the sculpture. The spire is very high, and the long siphonal canal gives the shell a markedly elongated-spindle shape. The aperture is pear-shaped, and the outer lip has thin folds on its inner surface; the columellar callus is raised above the body whorl. The axial sculpture is distinctive, consisting of three leaflike varices, sometimes with the posteria lateral apex pointed or spined on the body whorl, while on the preceding whorls it consists of only broad and flat spines. The two species illustrated, *Marchia elongata* (left) and *Purpurellus gambiensis* (right), belong to different genera. The siphonal canal is open along the ventral line in *M. elongata* and is closed in *P. gambiensis*. The operculum is horny, chestnut and has an apical nucleus.

**Body** No literature on the morphology and anatomy of the members of these uncommon genera. The radula is rachiglossan and the rachidial teeth have five cusps, two of which (the intermediate) are, in *P. elongatus,* much smaller.

**Habitat** Sandy or muddy bottoms in the infralittoral and circalittoral zones.

**Distribution** Of the two species illustrated *M. elongata* lives throughout the Indo-Pacific Province, and *P. gambiensis* in the West African Province.

## 98 RANELLA OLEARIA
### Little Frog Triton

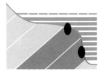

**Family** Cymatiidae

**Shell** Very large in size (2 to 6 inches), high spire, regularly rounded, whorls, very impressed almost caniculated suture. All the whorls have two large symmetrical varices, which edge their lateral margins. The round aperture has a thickened outer lip, with a varix and not very developed but prominent teeth; the inner lip has a slight columellar callus that is only very slightly extended on to the ventral surface of the body whorl and has thin ridges. The canal is rather long. The sculpture consists of fine spiral ridges that intersect fairly developed axial ribs, sometimes disappearing; such ribs can be nodular or smooth. There is rather thick hazel periostracum, which gives a velvety appearance to the shell. The shell is chestnut or hazel in color, sometimes with lighter spiral bands. The operculum is horny, thick, multispiral and has an apical nucleus.

**Body** As in all cymatiids the foot is well developed, anteriorly truncated, rounded posteriorly. The head has a long and thick retractile proboscis, two tentacles and an eye at the base of each, on the outer side. The radula is taenioglossan.

**Habitat** It lives on muddy or detrital-muddy bottoms in the circalittoral zone or at even greater depths in the aphytal zone.

**Distribution** Peculiar, as its range is made up of provinces that are not adjacent: the Lusitanian, South African and New Zealand provinces.

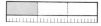

## 99 RINGICULA SEMISTRIATA
### Orbign's Helmet-Bubble

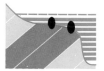

**Family** Ringiculidae

**Shell** Very small (⅛ inch), rather thick and solid. Moderately high conical spire, very rounded whorls, strongly impressed suture; spherical to roughly pear-shaped. The aperture has a deep anterior notch, through which the mantle siphon emerges. The outer lip is thick and is strengthened by a large swelling. The columellar lip has a thick callus, it covers a fairly large part of the ventral surface of the body whorl and has strong teeth; these teeth are among the diagnostic characteristics for the recognition of species of the genus *Ringicula*. Pure white in color. The sculpture consists of thin spiral grooves that, under high magnification, appear dotted. Lacks an operculum.

**Body** The foot is rather short. The head is expanded to form a shield (the cephalic shield) and is posteriorly extended, furling its margins to form a sort of siphon. As in all opisthobranchs it is hermaphroditic. The radula lacks rachidials and has only one series of laterals on each side.

**Habitat** Soft bottoms in the infralittoral and circalittoral zones.

**Distribution** Widely distributed in the Atlantic, including the Lusitanian, Celtic, Boreal (the edge) Carolinan and Caribbean provinces.

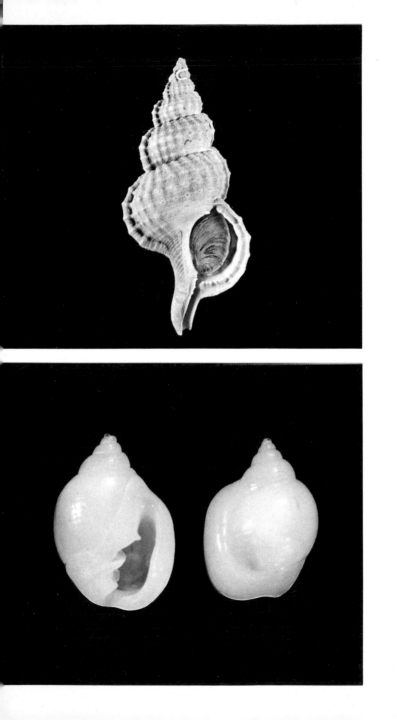

## 100 SCAPHANDER LIGNARIUS
### Canoe-Bubble

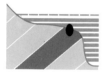

**Family** Cylichnidae

**Shell** Medium size (1 inch), rather thin and fairly fragile, sunken spire, with an umbilicus. A wide body whorl, expanded anteriorly, completely enfolding (convolute) and overhanging the preceding whorls. In overall appearance, an elongated oval. The aperture is rather narrow to the rear, but broad at the front. The outer lip is thin, fragile and sharp; the columellar lip has a light callus, usually of little extent. The sculpture consists of fine, very incised spiral grooves, almost equally spaced. The shell is yellowish brown, except for the spiral grooves, which are white. There is a thin reddish-brown, rather persistent periostracum. It lacks an operculum.

**Body** It has a wide, rather thick foot, which cannot be completely retracted into the shell. The wide head lacks tentacles, but has two short posterior holes. The eyes are sessile. The mantle cavity contains the gill, and the osphradium. It feeds on scaphopods.

**Habitat** *S. lignarius* lives on detrital muddy bottoms in the circalittoral zone.

**Distribution** It lives on the Boreal, Celtic and Lusitanian provinces, extending into the Mediterranean.

---

## 101 SCAPHARCA INAEQUIVALVIS
### Unequal arc

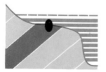

**Family** Arcidae

**Shell** Medium size (2½ inches), inequivalve, particularly in juvenile forms, the margin of the left valve usually overlaps the right valve's margin, inequilateral, roughly trapezoidal in shape. The brown periostracum is easily rubbed off in the sea, and so is usually restricted to the areas between the ribs of the sculpture; often the periostracum has regularly spaced bristles. The yellowish shell has fairly marked grayish veinings. The sculpture consists of broad ribs radiating from the umbones. The ribs, particularly on the left valve, are coarsely granular. The ligament is wide, dark chestnut and external. The straight hinge is taxodont. It is dimyarian, anisomyarian and has a smoothly curved pallial line (integropalliate).

**Body** It is a filibranch, having a pair of gills each with two series of connected filaments, forming four series of lamellae. The foot, not very developed, secretes by way of the byssal (pedal) gland a byssus with almost triangular filaments.

**Habitat** It usually lives buried in sandy or muddy bottoms in the infralittoral zone, but it also can be attached to rigid objects by the byssus.

**Distribution** Originally from the Indo-Pacific. The example photographed came from the Mediterranean, where it was introduced, presumably at the end of the sixties; it seems to have acclimatized well.

## 102 SCAPHELLA JUNONIA
### Junonia

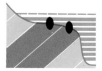

**Family** Volutidae

**Shell** Large size (5 to 6 inches), moderately thick, robust, fairly high conical spire, tapered in shape, the body whorl is moderately convex and covers a large part of the preceding one. The suture is very incised. The aperture is elongated, ellipsoidal, with a thin outer lip and a columellar lip that has four not very strong folds. The sculpture is almost invisible and consists of very thin spiral and axial grooves on the apical whorls and of spiral grooves alone on the body whorl. Yellowish or creamy yellow with irregular brown patches arranged in a spiral. There is a very thin chestnut periostracum; it lacks an operculum.

**Body** The same color as the shell, but it has larger and more irregular patches. The foot is well developed. The distinct head has two tentacles and a lateral lobe at the base of each, bearing the eyes; only the left lobe is at the base of the mantle siphon. The radula is a modified rachiglossan, as it has only a row of rachidial teeth, Y-shaped, single-cusped.

**Habitat** Soft bottoms in the deeper levels of the infralittoral and in the circalittoral zone.

**Distribution** Mainly Carolinan and in the northern part of the Caribbean Province. North Carolina to east and west coasts of Florida, to Texas and Mexico.

## 103 SCHILDERIA HIRASEI
### Hirase's Cowrie

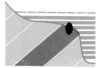

**Family** Cypraeidae

**Shell** Medium size (1½ to 2¼ inches), pear-shaped, the body whorl completely surrounds the preceding ones and the anterior extremity protrudes. The base is convex, the aperture is fairly broad and straight, with a slight posterior curvature. The labial teeth are rather small and well spaced, the columellar teeth little developed. Devoid of any sculpture, the surface is smooth and glossy. The base is white, the sides of the shell are dotted with chestnut or pinkish-brown spots about 2 millimeters in diameter. The back is cream, has a very variable pattern of lightish, irregular chestnut or reddish-brown patches. There is no operculum.

**Body** The foot is moderately developed, the distinct head has two tentacles, with an eye at the base of each. The mantle, as in all Cypraeids, has two lobes that, when completely expanded, can enfold the shell. The literature does not give any information on the coloration of the animal or on whether there are papillae on the mantle. The radula is taenioglossan.

**Habitat** The relatively few specimens found have usually come from soft bottoms in the circalittoral zone.

**Distribution** Confined to a restricted area of the Japonic Province.

## 104 SEPIA OFFICINALIS
### Common Cuttlefish

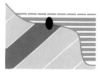

**Family**  Sepiidae

**Shell**  Large size (4 to 6 inches), fairly thick but very light, no trace of a spiral, placed inside the body of the animal in a pouch in the mantle. It can be subdivided into three portions: posterior, a strong spine called the rostrum; dorsal, a compact plate, called the pro-ostracum; and ventrally, a spongy mass composed of successive rows of tightly packed lamellae strongly angled to the pro-ostracum (these lamellae are thought to be homologous to the septa in the shell of *Spirula*)

**Body**  Much larger (15 to 20 inches) than the shell, which, as stated, is enclosed in a pouch. The head is very large, with large and complex eyes, similar to vertebrate eyes in structure. The mouth has two horny jaws like a parrot's beak. The foot has been transformed into a funnel, which, due to valved mantle lobes, is the only way the water contained in the mantle cavity can be expelled, eight oval arms and two longer, tentacular arms. The mantle has two fins, which run laterally along its whole length. There are two gills inside the mantle cavity.

**Habitat**  All sepiids are cephalopods adapted to benthonic life in relatively shallow water.

**Distribution**  An Atlantic species (western) it extends into the Mediterranean as far as the Black Sea.

## 105 SEPIOLA
### Deep-Water Cuttlefish

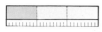

**Family** Sepioliidae
**Shell** Small, thin, fragile, limited to a small plate or feather contained in the shell pouch of the mantle.
**Body** A rather large head in relation to the visceral mass; pair of large eyes of complex structure, and a mouth that has strong mandibles. The foot has evolved, as in all cephalopods, into a ventral funnel through which the water that has entered the mantle cavity flows out, eight oval arms with suckers over all their inner surfaces, and two longer tentacular arms, which can be completely retracted into appropriate pockets and have suckers only on their distal portions. The mantle has two lateral fins, which are situated posteriorly and are almost circular in shape.
**Habitat** Like the Sepiidae, the sepioliids are cephalopods that have adapted to a benthonic life at relatively low depths, generally on sandy or detrital bottoms.
**Distribution** Temperate Eastern Atlantic and extending into the Western Mediterranean.

---

## 106 SINUM CONCAVUM
### Lamarck's Baby-Ear

**Family** Naticidae
**Shell** Medium size (1 to 2 inches), rather thin, light, fragile, flattish spire. The whorls enlarge rapidly, so that the body whorl is much larger than the preceding ones, in the shape of a depressed sphere, much greater in breadth than in height. The base has a narrow umbilicus; the ovoidal aperture has a thin sharp outer edge, sharply angled to the columellar axis; the inner lip is slightly turned back on to the columellar. The sculpture consists of thin ribs, much narrower than the spaces between them; there can be up to sixty on the body whorl, and they tend to disappear in the area around the umbilicus. There are also very weak growth lines that are more deeply incised at the base of the shell. The apical whorls are whitish, while the others are cream or light hazel, the base is whitish. The operculum is horny, as in other naticids.
**Body** There is no morphological or anatomical information concerning the genus *Sinum*. Probably, in general characteristics it resembles the description of other naticids.
**Habitat** No precise information, but it seems to live on soft bottoms in the circalittoral zone.
**Distribution** Confined to the West African Province.

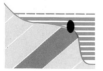

## 107 SIPHOCYPRAEA MUS
### Mouse Cowrie

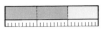

**Family** Cypraeidae
**Shell** Medium size (2 inches), spherical, rather thick and robust, the body whorl completely enfolds and hides the preceding ones. The back of the shell has a raised median zone, in the rear third. In some specimens, thought to be particularly old individuals, there are, in the posterior zone, one or, more often two midlateral tubercles. The base is flat, the aperture is very wide, slightly bulged at the rear, with roughly parallel margins in the posterior half, which tend to diverge anteriorly and then contract at the margins of the siphon. The teeth are rather large, narrower than the spaces between them, and they form a continuous row on the outer lip, while on the columellar lip the row is broken by a smooth zone about halfway along the shell. Hazel with patches of chestnut, varying in intensity on the back, beige flaming on the sides and dark-chestnut teeth. In the position corresponding to the apex (hidden by the body whorl) there is often a large patch of a chestnut color.
**Body** No exact information on the coloration of the animal or on the presence of papillae on the lobes of the mantle, which cover the shell. The radula is taenioglossan.
**Habitat** It is presumed—but the information is not definite—that it lives on sandy bottoms in the infralittoral zone.
**Distribution** Caribbean Province, restricted to the northern coasts of South America, Colombia and Venezuela.

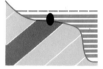

---

## 108 SIPHONALIA SIGNUM
### Lined Siphonalia

**Family** Buccinidae
**Shell** Medium size (1 ½ inches), not very thick, robust, shortish spire, short twisted shell canal, very convex, keeled whorls, suture markedly impressed. The aperture edge is faintly four cornered, and the outer lip has thin spiral folds on the inside; the inner lip has a thin callus, which is thickened and gives a characteristic tooth to the rear end. The sculpture consists of large nodules on the keel of the whorls and some spiral grooves on the anterior portion of the body whorl. Grayish in color, with chestnut spiral lines; there are also irregular patches of the same color; other examples can be completely white, yellow or chestnut. The operculum is horny, light chestnut and has an apical nucleus.
**Body** Like all buccinids, it has a long mantle siphon and the head has a long retractile proboscis. The mantle cavity contains the gill, the osphradium and, in males, a long, thick penis situated behind the right tentacle. The radula is rachiglossan.
**Habitat** Infralittoral, presumably soft bottoms, but there is no precise information in the literature concerning this.
**Distribution** Restricted to the Japonic Province.

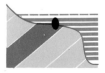

## 109 SOLEMYA TOGATA
### Common Awning Clam

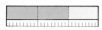

**Family** Solemyacidae

**Shell** In size 1 inch, equivalve, inequilateral, umbones no prominent, roughly rectangular in shape. It has a dark-chestnu periostracum that extends beyond the margins of the valve as fringe. The sculpture is almost nonexistent, the hinge is eden tulous, the ligament is internal, carried by a chondrophore. Th two adductor muscle scars differ in size. Unlike the scars o other bivalves, the anterior scar is larger than the posterior; th pallial line is smoothly curved (integropalliate). The shell is ver thin and is composed exclusively of homogenous arago nite crystals.

**Body** This species, along with all members of the subclas Cryptodonta, has many primitive characters. The foot is pis tonlike and by its lengthening and contraction causes the ex pulsion of water from the mantle cavity through an anterio aperture between the edges of the mantle that are fused ven trally. The gills are ctenidial (protobranch).

**Habitat** In the Mediterranean this species has been found o the sand, associated with *Posidonias*. It feeds on organic de tritus in the sand in which it actively burrows.

**Distribution** From the Mediterranean it follows the southern coasts of Spain and extends as far as the coast of Senegal.

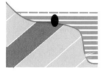

---

## 110 SOLEN VAGINA
### Jackknife clam

**Family** Solenidae

**Shell** Large (5 inches), fragile, equivalve and inequilatera the umbones are not prominent, an elongated rectangle wit the two ends truncated and gaping. The periostracum is ligh brown, while the shell is yellowish. The sculpture consists o weak concentric growth lines and a rather deep furrow paralle to the anterior margin of the valve. The dark-chestnut ligamer is not extensive. The hinge is heterodont, consisting of onl one cardinal tooth on each valve. The inner surface of the valv has two adductor-muscle scars that differ in size (dimyariar anisomyarian) and the pallial line has a deep posterior sinu (sinopalliate). The shell has a crossed-lamellae structure.

**Body** A beautiful yellowish white, the fingerlike foot is ver mobile and well developed, by means of which it burrows ac tively and deeply into the substrate. There are two long siphor (inhalant and exhalant). Each of a pair of gills consists of tw series of lamellae extensively fused by interlamellar junction (eulamellibranch).

**Habitat** Sandy or sandy-muddy bottoms in the infralittora zone.

**Distribution** The Boreal, Celtic, Lusitanian and West Africa provinces, extending into the Mediterranean and as far as th Black Sea.

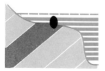

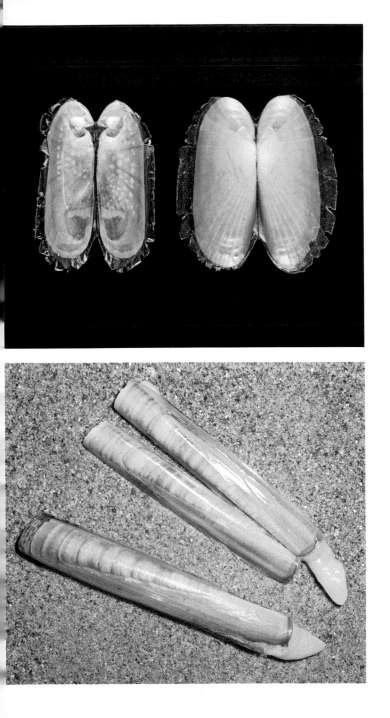

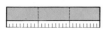

## 111  STELLARIA SOLARIS
### Sun Carrier Shell

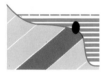

**Family**  Xenophoridae
**Shell**  Large size (3½ inches), rather thin and fragile, flattish spire, breadth greater than height, convex whorls, incised suture flattened or slightly convex base with a narrow but deep umbilicus. The aperture is strongly slanted. Characteristic of this species is the row of long tubular spines borne by a light but definite keel, above the suture at the periphery of the whorls. There is a thin, not very persistent, yellowish periostracum. The sculpture consists of thin granular spiral bands, which tend to become radial toward the lower margin of the whorls and run on to the spines. The base is granular, due to the intersection of the spiral elements with the growth lines, much more marked than on the upper surface of the whorls. Hazel colored. The operculum is yellowish, horny, ellipsoidal, paucispiral and with a lateral nucleus.
**Body**  Unlike the majority of xenophorids, it does not bind foreign material to its shell. It has the characteristics described for *Xenophora crispa*—i.e., the foot is divided into two portions, an anterior, locomotory, and a posterior one that produces the operculum. The very distinct head has two tentacles with a sessile eye at the base of each. The mantle cavity contains the gill, osphradium and, in males, the penis. The radula is taenioglossan.
**Habitat**  Muddy circalittoral bottoms.
**Distribution**  Fairly widespread, the Indo-Pacific and South African provinces.

## 112  STROMBUS GALLUS
### Rooster-Tail Conch

**Family**  Strombidae
**Shell**  Large size (4 to 6 inches), thick, solid, high spire, convex whorls, with a strong nodular keel in the upper part, very incised suture. The body whorl ends in an aperture with very broad margins, bluntly toothed and with two long siphons, one anterior, slightly twisted, and one posterior, straight. The surface has flattish spiral ribs, often irregular, sometimes as broad as the spaces between them; as already mentioned, all the whorls have a strong nodular keel in the upper part; the thin growth lines are almost invisible. The color varies; whitish, pink, pale violet, red, yellow, darkish chestnut often with whitish specks or very dark-chestnut patches. The periostracum is a fairly dark hazel. The operculum is horny, sickle-shaped, like all strombids' opercula.
**Body**  Narrow, curved foot, divided into a smaller anterior lobe and a larger posterior one, which bears the operculum and enables the mollusk to leap. The ocular peduncles are long and joined to the tentacles, which are slightly above the eyes. The mantle cavity contains one gill, one osphradium and, in males, a penis. The radula is taenioglossan.
**Habitat**  Sandy bottoms with a cover of seaweed in the infra- and circalittoral zones.
**Distribution**  *S. gallus* is mainly from the Caribbean Province.

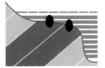

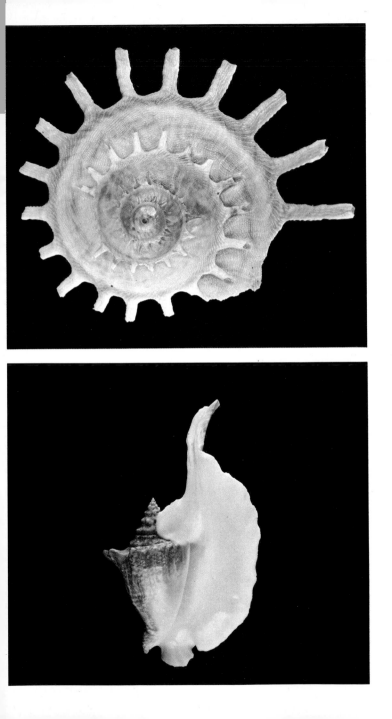

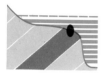

**STROMBUS LISTERI**
Lister's Conch

**Family**  Strombidae

**Shell**  Large (4½ to 6 inches), rather thin and fragile, very high conical spire. The apical whorls are regularly convex, the others have a median (upper in the body whorl) keel, above which the surface is slightly concave, while below it, it is almost flat. The aperture lips are very broad with a marked posterior spatula-shaped protuberance, a short anterior siphon and a wide anteriolateral sinus. The sculpture varies: on the apical whorl it consists of thin axial ribs and very fine spiral grooves; in the intermediate ones the spiral grooves tend to be more incised and the axial ribs fade. On the last whorls the surface is smooth and glossy. The base color is chestnut with wavy axial white lines, which become <-shaped specks arranged in spiral lines toward the end of the body whorl. The aperture is porcelaneous. The operculum is horny and sickle-shaped, as in all strombids and has an apical nucleus.

**Body**  It has the same characteristics as those described for other strombids.

**Habitat**  Up until a few years ago the species was thought to be very rare, because of the general ignorance of its true habitat. Today, very deep dredges (down as far as 800 meters, or 2,600 feet) on muddy bottoms, produce numerous specimens of this beautiful species.

**Distribution**  Indo-Pacific, it seems to be confined to the Gulf of Bengal.

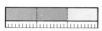

## 114 FAMILY STRUTHIOLARIIDAE
### Struthiolariid Conchs

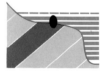

**Shell** Medium or medium-small (1 to 3½ inches), moderately thick and fairly robust, flattish conical spire, rounded whorls, sometimes with one or more nodular keels, an impressed or even slightly caniculated suture. The aperture is slightly broadened toward the bottom, the outer lip is thickened, having a light varix, and the inner lip is callused. There is a very short not very prominent siphon. The sculpture consists of thin spiral grooves, and there can be one or two nodular keels, varying within the same species, on the body whorl. Reddish brown or pink in color, with darker axial flaming. The operculum is very small, horny, long and narrow, with an apical nucleus. The illustration shows *Struthiolaria populosa* (Martyn 1784) on the left, and *Pelicaria vermis* (Martyn 1784) on the right.

**Body** It has a very extensive and mobile foot, fairly narrow and oval in shape. The distinct head has two short tentacles and a long proboscis, which ends in a circular-oval disc, rich in nerve receptors. There is a mantle tentacle situated toward the right margin of the mantle. It has, in the male, a long and narrow penis behind the right tentacle. The mantle cavity also contains the gill and osphradium.

**Habitat** The members of this family live on sandy or muddy bottoms in the infralittoral zone.

**Distribution** The Struthiolariidae are almost completely restricted to the New Zealand and eastern Australian provinces.

---

## 115 TAGELUS PLEBEIUS
### Stout Tagelus

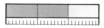

**Family** Solecurtidae

**Shell** Medium size (2 to 3½ inches), fairly swollen valves, almost cylindrical, gaping at the two ends, which are rounded, rather thin and fragile. The umbones are almost median, slightly displaced to the rear and with the apices pointed backward, unlike the great majority of bivalves. The sculpture consists of light, slightly incised growth lines. The periostracum, moderately thick and persistent, especially along the margin, is olive green or brownish yellow in color; the shell is white. The ligament is external and posterior to the umbones, the hinge heterodont, consisting solely of cardinal teeth, two on the right valve and one on the left. The muscle scars on the inside of the valves are almost identical (dimyarian, isomyarian), and they are linked by a pallial line with a deep sinus (sinopalliate).

**Body** The foot is rather long and thick. The siphons are highly developed. The mantle cavity contains a pair of gills, each of which is formed by two series of lamellae extensively fused by interlamellar junctions (eulamellibranch).

**Habitat** Sandy or muddy bottoms in the mesolittoral and infralittoral zones.

**Distribution** *T. plebeius* is fairly common in the Carolina and Caribbean provinces.

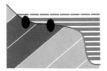

## 116 TAPES AUREUS
### Golden Venus

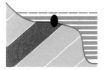

**Family** Veneridae
**Shell** Solid, medium size (1¾ inches), moderately convex valves, roughly rhomboidal, equivalve and inequilateral. The periostracum is thin and glossy. The color can be pale yellow white or chestnut with broken zigzag lines, or dark-chestnut patches. On the other hand, the inside of the valves is consistently golden yellow, hence its specific name. The sculpture is confined to moderately impressed concentric growth lines. The lunule is well defined and heart-shaped. The hinge is heterodont, with three cardinal and no lateral teeth on each valve. The two muscle scars are similar (dimyarian, isomyarian) and very prominent on the inside of the valve. The pallial line has a large sinus, which does not reach the middle of the shell.
**Body** It has a pair of gills each of which is made up of two series of lamellae, entirely fused by interlamellar junctions (eulamellibranch). The foot is normally dark, and the two siphons, of moderate length, have their apertures surrounded by cirri.
**Habitat** Sandy, sandy-muddy or muddy bottoms in the upper levels of the infralittoral zone. Actively fished for food.
**Distribution** Confined to the Celtic and Lusitanian provinces extends into the Mediterranean as far as the Black Sea.

---

## 117 TATCHERIA MIRABILIS
### Miraculous Thatcheria

**Family** Turridae
**Shell** Medium large (4 to 5 inches), thin, light, fragile, fairly high, conical spire, spindle-shaped; the outline resembles a pagoda. The whorls have a strong keel, above which they are flat or even slightly concave. The suture is deeply impressed. The aperture is wide, roughly triangular, extended at the front into a broad, short siphon; the outer lip is thin and sharp and has a wide and deep sinus above the shoulder. The sculpture consists of very thin growth lines. Yellowish or hazel except for the aperture and columellar, which are white. Lacks an operculum.
**Body** No information, even approximate, on this not very rare species. The radula is toxoglossan.
**Habitat** Deep water, presumably on muddy bottoms in the circalittoral zone.
**Distribution** Exclusive to and characteristic of the Japonic Province.

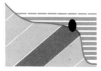

## 118 TELLINA PULCHELLA
### Beautiful Tellin

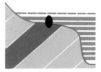

**Family** Tellinidae

**Shell** Medium size (2 to 3 inches), fragile and thin, faintly trapezoidal in shape, equivalve and inequilateral. The posterior extremity of the valve is slightly beaked and curved to the right. The valve is a fairly intense pink, and lighter radial stripes or bands extend over the whole surface. The only sculpture is the thin growth lines; at the posterior, both valves have a keel. The umbones are directed backward; the external ligament is situated behind them. The hinge is heterodont. The two muscle scars on the inside of the valves are alike (dimyarian, isomyarian), and the pallial line has a deep sinus (sinopalliate). The shell has a mainly crossed-lamellae structure.

**Body** It has a pair of gills each consisting of two series of lamellae extensively fused by interlamellar junctions (eulamellibranch); the foot is thin, mobile, and actively digs the substrate; like all tellinids, it has two very long siphons (inhalant, exhalant).

**Habitat** *T. pulchella* lives deeply buried in fine sands in the infralittoral zone.

**Distribution** Lusitanian, exclusively from the coasts of the Mediterranean.

## 119 TELLINA RADIATA
### Sunrise Tellin

**Family** Tellinidae

**Shell** Medium size (2 to 4 inches), elongated, very slightly swollen, equivalve and inequilateral. The coloration is variable, cream, pink, with fairly intense red rays or yellow; the umbones are usually a shade of red. Internally the valves are a beautiful strong yellow. Lacks sculpture, and the surface is smooth and glossy. The ligament is external, the hinge is heterodont, with two cardinal teeth, one being bifid, on both the valves and lateral teeth as in all members of the subfamily Tellininae. The two muscle scars are fairly similar (dimyarian, isomyarian). The posterior pallial sinus is so deep that it almost reaches the anterior adductor muscle scar.

**Body** It has a pair of gills each of which consists of two series of lamellae extensively fused by interlamellar junctions (eulamellibranch). The foot is elongated and mobile, and allows the animal to burrow deeply and rapidly into the sand. Two very long siphons ensure the circulation of water in the mantle cavity.

**Habitat** It lives at various depths on sandy bottoms in the infralittoral zone, but it seems that it can extend into the circalittoral zone.

**Distribution** As well as being found in the Carolinan Province, it is typical of the Caribbean Province—South Carolina to south of Florida, Bermuda to northern South America.

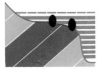

## 120 TYPHINELLUS SOWERBY
### Sowerby's Typhus

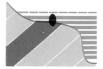

**Family** Muricidae

**Shell** Small size (¾ inch), rather thin, light, fairly fragile, moderately high spire, an elongated oval in shape. The whorls are convex, strongly keeled, as they are divided into an upper flat portion and a lower portion, almost at right angles to the preceding. The aperture is ovoidal, the outer and columellar lips have thin, slightly raised swellings. The sculpture is made up of four equally spaced lamellar varices on each whorl; the varices form a spine on the keel and between adjacent spines there is a fistular spine, which can be rather long in well-preserved examples. These open spines characterize the whole subfamily Tyrhinae. Whitish or a uniform brown, sometimes the upper part of the whorls is darker. The operculum is horny, with an apical nucleus.

**Body** White, with a foot that is truncated anteriorly and rounded at the back. The evaginable proboscis is not very long. The tentacles are long and thin, and the rachidial teeth have three principal cusps as well as two, sometimes more, accessory cusps.

**Habitat** Rather rare, it lives on sandy or fairly coarse-textured detrital bottoms in the infralittoral zone.

**Distribution** *T. sowerby* is found on both sides of the Atlantic, in the Lusitanian and Caribbean provinces.

## 121 TONNA GALEA
### Giant Tun

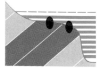

**Family** Tonnidae

**Shell** Very large (5 to 7 inches), thin, light and fragile, very swollen whorls, suture deeply impressed, even caniculated, its height greater than its breadth, with an almost ovoidal aperture, whose outer lip is thin, but not sharp, and whose inner lip has a slight callus, which partially covers the body whorl. The columellar is twisted, the base has a narrow umbilicus, the aperture has a short canal. The sculpture consists of large rather flat spiral ribs, which are much broader than the gaps between them, sometimes alternating with thinner ridges. The growth lines are prominent. It varies from a yellowish color (in young examples) to hazel or darkish chestnut. Like all tonnids it does not have an operculum.

**Body** It has a very large foot, short and broad, the distinct head has two short tentacles which contain the eyes. The proboscis is highly developed and tractile. As well as the gill and osphradium, the mantle cavity contains, in males, a large and flattened penis, placed behind the right tentacle. The radula is taenioglossan.

**Habitat** Found on sandy or fairly coarse detrital bottoms mainly in the circalittoral but also in the infralittoral zone.

**Distribution** A cosmopolitan species, except for particularly cold seas.

## 122    TRACHYCARDIUM EGMONTIANUM
### Prickly Cockle

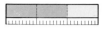

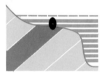

**Family**   Cardiidae

**Shell**   Medium size (2 inches), rather thick and robust, fair[ly] swollen, equivalve and slightly inequilateral; in shape an elon[-]gated oval. The sculpture consists of radial ribs, varying [in] number from 27 to 31; these ribs have blunt spines anterior[ly] and sharp ones at the rear. The margin of the shell is toothe[d] anteriorly and ventrally, but is spiny at the posterior. Outside, [it] is whitish with yellowish patches or with chestnut, often broke[n] concentric bands; inside, it is pink. The heterodont hinge ha[s] strong cardinal and lateral teeth on both valves. The extern[al] ligament is posterior to the umbones. The two thick muscl[e] scars are similar (dimyarian, isomyarian), and the pallial line [is] smoothly curved (integropalliate). The shell has a main[ly] crossed-lamellae structure.

**Body**   A well-developed, usually cylindrical, foot, used as i[n] all cardiids, in leaping movements. There are two gills, eac[h] consisting of two series of lamellae, extensively fused by inte[r]lamellar junctions (eulamellibranch).

**Habitat**   Sandy and also muddy infralittoral bottoms.

**Distribution**   *T. egmontianum* is restricted to the Caribbea[n] Province, where it is rather common. North Carolina to Florid[a] and West Indies.

---

## 123    FAMILY TRIPHORIDAE
### Sinistral Miniature Horn Shells

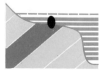

**Shell**   Small or very small in size (1/5 to 2/5 inch), sinistra[l] very high, regularly conical spire, almost flat or slightly conve[x] whorls. The base is convex or very flat. The aperture lips a[re] thin and sharp, with a short canal, dorsally curved, whic[h] sometimes is longish and closed, forming a tube. The sculptu[re] consists of a few very nodular spiral belts, sometimes with [a] smooth band in the middle. The base may either lack sculptu[re] or have one or two smooth concentric bands. The protoconc[h] always has different sculpture, and often this is made up [of] very fine slanted axial ribs. The coloration varies greatly. Th[e] operculum is horny, paucispiral, with an almost-central n[u]cleus. The illustration shows, from left to right *Triphora pe[r]versa* (L.1758), *Iniforis lifuana* (Hervier 1897) and *Viriola* sp.

**Body**   It has a narrow foot. The distinct head has long tent[a]cles. The mantle cavity contains a gill, an osphradium, b[ut] lacks, in males, a penis. The radula is of a very particular typ[e] halfway between the taenioglossan and the ptenoglossa[n] having one rachidial, one lateral (per side) and many elongate[d] and narrow marginals. Because of this and for other reason[s] the Triphoridae should, according to some Japanese autho[r]ities, be classified in a separate order, the Heterogastropod[a].

**Habitat**   Extremely varied, usually soft bottoms in the infral[it]toral zones, but some species are circalittoral or bathyal.

**Distribution**   Found in all the world's seas.

## 124 TRISIDOS TORTUOSA
### Twisted Arc

**Family** Arcidae
**Shell** Almost equivalve, inequilateral, medium size (3
inches). It has a characteristic shape, the valves being twisted
(hence its specific name). So, looking at the ventral side of the
shell, the valve margins do not meet in a straight line but in a
sinuous one. The periostracum, which is missing in the illustrated example, is rather thick and dark chestnut. The shell
color is very variable: whitish, yellow, orange or pink. The
sculpture consists basically of slightly raised radial ridges
which cross large furrows caused by growth stoppages. The
taxodont hinge is straight. The ligament is external. The muscle
scars on the inner surface of the valves are almost identical
(dimyarian, isomyarian), and they are joined by a smooth
curved pallial line (integropalliate). Like the shells of all arcids
the shell of *T. tortuosa* has a mainly crossed-lamellae structure.
**Body** It has a pair of gills, each made up of two series of filaments widely connected to form in all four series of lamellae
(filibranch); like all arcids it lacks siphons. There is no information on the morphology of the foot or the byssus.
**Habitat** It lives on muddy bottoms, mainly in the infralittoral
zone, but it seems that it can also be found in the mesolittoral
zone.
**Distribution** Indo-Pacific Province, confined to the Western
Pacific.

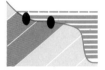

## 125 TROPHON VAGINATUS (PAGODULA)
### Sheath Trophon

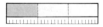

**Family** Muricidae
**Shell** Small size (⅞ inch), rather thin, fragile, light, very high
spire and long siphonal canal, giving it an elongated spindle
shape in overall appearance. The whorls are angular, almost
keeled. The suture is very impressed. The aperture is ovoidal
with a thin and sharp outer lip. The inner lip has a very thin
callus, which does not extend very far on to the ventral surface
of the body whorl. The axial sculpture consists of six platelike
varices, which elongate above the keel, forming longish spines.
Pink or light chestnut in color, and there is a thin yellowish
periostracum. The operculum is light chestnut, horny, and has
an apical nucleus.
**Body** There is no known literature, even approximate, on the
morphology and anatomy of this rather rare species. Even the
radula, which, as in all the other muricids, should be rachiglossan, has never been described.
**Habitat** A rather rare species, it is only infrequently found on
fairly coarse detrital bottoms in the circalittoral and aphytic
zones.
**Distribution** *P. vaginatus* is a species of the Lusitanian Province, found especially in the Mediterranean.

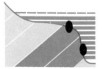

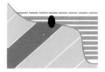

## 126 TURBINELLA
### Chank Shells

**Family** Turbinellidae
**Shell** Large or very large in size (7 to 14 inches), thick and robust, fairly high conical spire and a moderately long siphonal canal, overall it is spindle-shaped. The aperture is ovoidal and rather elongated, the outer lip has no teeth or internal folds, but the columellar lip has a callus that covers a large part of the ventral surface of the body whorl and has three or four large, well-spaced folds. The axial sculpture may be absent or may consist of large blunt ribs that form a stout nodule on the whorl's shoulder; the spiral consists of thinnish bands, restricted to the basal area and the canal. The coloration varies from species to species; it can be white or yellowish with chestnut patches. The operculum is horny, thick, chestnut and nail-shaped. The illustration shows *T. angulata* (on the left) and *T. pyrum* (on the right). The latter shell, when it is sinistral—a rarity—is revered by the Indians, who consider it a symbol of the God Vishnu.
**Body** The foot is very large, the head is distinct and has two tentacles. The mantle cavity contains the gill, the osphradium and, in males, the penis. The radula is rachiglossan.
**Habitat** The members of the genus *Turbinella* live on soft bottoms in the infralittoral zone.
**Distribution** Of the two species illustrated, *T. pyrum* is found in the Indo-Pacific Province, limited to the coasts of India, and *T. angulata* in the Caribbean Province.

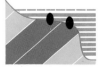

## 127 SUBFAMILY TURRINAE
### Turret Shells

**Family** Turridae
**Shell** Generally of medium size (among the many species within this subfamily there is much variation in size), moderately thick and robust, with a very high, conical spire, spindle-shaped, the whorls are very convex and the suture is impressed. The aperture is an elongated oval, a long anterior canal, a thin and sharp outer lip, which has a narrow deep slit in line with the shoulder of the body whorl. Obviously the color varies from species to species, but in general it consists of spiral stripes or rows of points or patches arranged in spiral bands. There may be no axial sculpture or it may consist of furrows or fairly fine and raised ribs. The operculum is horny, hazel or chestnut, triangular or almond-shaped, with an apical nucleus. The illustration shows *Turris similis* (left), *Turris babylonia* (center) and *Xenoturris cingulifera* (right).
**Body** The foot is moderately developed, elongated, the head has two tentacles, which carry the eyes, and a very long proboscis. The mantle cavity contains the gill, osphradium and, in males, the penis. The radula is toxoglossan.
**Habitat** Very varied, always on soft bottoms, muddy, sandy or coral sands. The infralittoral and circalittoral zones.
**Distribution** The subfamily Turrinae has species in all seas, but mainly intertropical.

## 128 SUBFAMILY TURRITELLINAE
### Turret Shells

**Family** Turritellidae

**Shell** Medium or large size (1 to 6 inches), usually light and fairly strong, very high conical spire (turreted). The whorls vary from flat to very convex, the suture from barely incised to impressed, a flat or slightly convex base, always lacking an umbilicus, with a thin and sharp aperture lip, often sinuous in outline, circular or roughly square in shape. The sculpture is mainly spiral from thin, not very prominent ridges to thick bands, often grooved longitudinally. The coloration is also variable, but is always based on whitish or brown hues, often with reddish-brown flamings. The operculum is horny, round with a central nucleus and fringed margins. The illustration shows from left to right *Turritella acutangula, T. crocea, T. nivea* and *T. mediterranea* (Monterosato 1872).

**Body** The foot is moderately developed, the distinct head has two tentacles, and the eyes are at their bases, set on two swellings. The mantle cavity contains one gill, with very long lamellae and one osphradium. Males do not have a penis.

**Habitat** The *Turritellinae* include species living on sandy, muddy and fairly coarse detrital bottoms, in the infralittoral and also in the circalittoral zone.

**Distribution** Found in all seas.

---

## 129 SUBFAMILY UMBONIINAE
### Button Shells

**Family** Trochidae

**Shell** Medium small (½ to 1 inch), rather thin and light, not fragile, flattish spire, so the shell is lens-shaped in general appearance. The whorls are swollen and the suture is barely incised. The base is convex, with a strong columellar callus, which occupies a third or more of the whole surface and conceals the umbilicus. The inside of the aperture is mother-of-pearl. The coloration is variable, both between and within species; it can be whitish, reddish, chestnut, grayish; with patches, tessellations or radial flamings of different colors. The columellar callus is usually whitish or pink. The surface can be smooth or scored, so forming blunt spiral bands. The horny operculum is round and has a central nucleus. The illustration shows *Umbonium giganteum* (left) and *U. moniliferum* (the two examples on the right).

**Body** Like all trochids, the *Umboniinae*, besides having primitive characters (such as two nephridia and the heart's ventricle being crossed over by the posterior part of the intestine) also have more evolved ones—i.e., a mantle cavity with only one gill and osphradium. The radula is rhipidoglossan.

**Habitat** The members of this subfamily usually live on fine infralittoral sands.

**Distribution** The *Umboniinae* are restricted to the Indo-Pacific Province.

## 130 VENUS VERRUCOSA
### Warty Venus

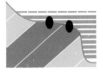

**Family** Veneridae
**Shell** Medium size (2½ inches), round outline, equivalve an
inequilateral. The periostracum is thick, not very persisten
and brown in color. The sculpture consists of concentric lamel
lar ribs, which are broken up posteriorly into blunt processe
(the "warts" of the specific name). Between the ribs there ar
thin radial grooves that give a reticulated appearance to youn
examples. The ligament is external and posterior to the
bones, the hinge is a typical heterodont, with three cardina
teeth on each valve. The two muscle scars are almost identica
(dimyarian, isomyarian). The shell has a violet patch. The pallia
line has a prominent sinus (sinopalliate).
**Body** It has a pair of gills, each of which consists of two se
ries of lamellae, extensively fused by interlamellar junction
(eulamellibranch). Normally, the foot is dark, the two siphon
are of moderate length, as the animal does not burrow deeply
**Habitat** V. verrucosa normally lives on sandy or fairly coars
detrital bottoms in the infralittoral zone, but it can extend int
the circalittoral zone.
**Distribution** An Atlantic species with a wide distribution fro
the Celtic to the Lusitanian and West African Provinces. Fro
the English Channel (uncommon) and west coast of Scotlan
south to Mediterranean sea and Angola; also from Cape o
Good Hope to Durban.

## 131 VOLUTA MUSICA
### Music Volute

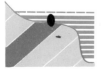

**Family** Volutidae
**Shell** Medium large size (2 to 2½ inches), fairly thick and ro
bust, moderately high conical spire, elongated spheric
shape, whorls that are slightly convex below the shoulder an
concave above it, incised suture. An elongated fairly wide a
erture. The thick outer lip is bent slightly outward, the columel
lar lip has a callus, which covers part of the ventral surface
the body whorl and has raised folds of variable thickness. Th
sculpture is confined to axial folds that form nodules, whic
sometimes fade, on the shoulder. Variable in color, usual
ivory or pink, with a patterning of spiral chestnut lines an
patches that resemble a musical score, from which it gets
specific name. The operculum is elongated, horny and has a
apical nucleus.
**Body** Large foot, anteriorly divided by a longitudinal furro
a light ivory in color, with dots or scattered reddish-brow
patches. The eyes are found at the base of the tentacles. T
mantle siphon is moderately long and has two lobes at its bas
The modified rachiglossan radula has only a single row of m
ticuspid rachidial teeth.
**Habitat** Sandy infralittoral bottoms.
**Distribution** Confined to the southern Caribbean Province

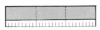

## 132 VOLUTOCONUS BEDNALLI
### Bednall's Volute

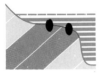

**Family** Volutidae
**Shell** Large size (4 inches), fairly thick, robust, relative
light, moderately high conical spire, elongated-oval in shape
the body whorl, which encloses a large part of the preceding
one, is gently convex, an impressed suture. Characteristic of
the entire genus *Volutoconus* is the calcarella, a very small
spiny process projecting upward from the apex of the first
whorl of the protoconch. The aperture is moderately wide, the
outer lip is thick, and the columellar lip has four thick fold
There is no sculpture. Cream in color with a coarsely textured
grid pattern of a chestnut color. It lacks both an operculum and
a periostracum.
**Body** In preserved animals it is pink, anteriorly the foot is b
partite. The head is distinct, has two not very long tentacle
and at their bases two highly developed lateral lobes on whic
the eyes are located. The mantle siphon has two short lobes
slightly different sizes. The modified rachiglossan radula ha
only the single row of rachidial teeth; these teeth have thre
curved cusps, triangular in section; the middle one is muc
longer than the other two.
**Habitat** Sandy infralittoral and perhaps circalittoral bottom
**Distribution** Indo-Pacific, confined to the northern coasts
Australia.

---

## 133 XENOPHORA CRISPA
### Curly Carrier Shell

**Family** Xenophoridae
**Shell** Medium size (2 to 3 inches), moderately thin but r
bust, a regular conical and fairly flat spire, at most the heig
equals the breadth. The whorls are almost flat, and the sutu
is incised. The base is flat or slightly convex, with a distin
deep umbilicus. The aperture is strongly slanted. All the whor
have a small but clearly visible keel, immediately above the s
ture. The animal binds fragments of rock or, more frequentl
gastropod or bivalve shells onto this keel. The first are a
ranged radially at regular intervals and attached by one en
the latter are always fitted so that the concave face is turne
upward. The sculpture consists of spiral ribs, often broke
sometimes granular, on the whorl's surface and a fairly regul
granulation, due to the intersection of the spiral ribs and th
growth lines, on the base. The operculum is horny, yellowis
ellipsoidal, paucispiral, with a lateral nucleus.
**Body** The foot is developed and divided transversally into
locomotory anterior portion and a posterior part that forms th
operculum. The head is distinct and carries two tentacles wi
the sessile eyes at their bases. The mantle cavity contains on
one gill, one osphradium and, in males, the penis. The radula
taenioglossan.
**Habitat** Coarse detrital bottoms in the circalittoral zone.
**Distribution** Lusitanian.

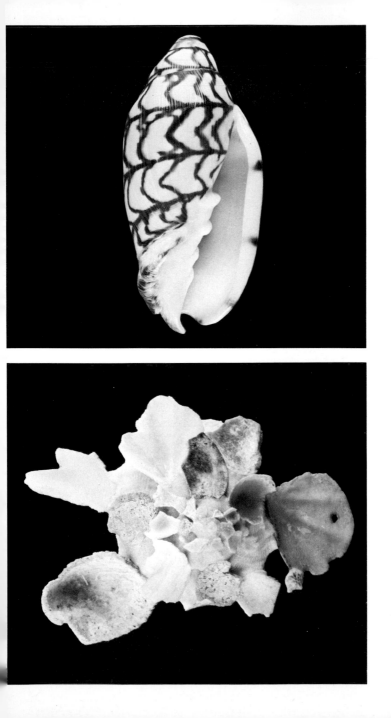

## 134 ACANTHOPLEURA
### Chitons

**Family**   Chitonidae
**Shell**   Medium large (2 to 3 inches), made up, as in all Poly-placophora of eight articulated plates which are very thick and robust. The tegmentum of the intermediate plates (II–VII) is divided into a central and two lateral areas, which are not always easily distinguishable. Plate VIII, which has an almost central mucro, is divided into a central and a posterior area. All the teeth inserting into the perinotum are pectinate—i.e., divided by thin distal furrows, into minute elongated teeth. The apophyses are roughly central. The surface is almost always eroded and encrusted, and therefore it is impossible to see any type of sculpture.
**Body**   The foot is very large and muscular. The head is distinct, with a central mouth. The gills are placed lateroposteriorly in the mantle cavity. The mantle extends beyond the edge of the valves forming the perinotum and bears fairly thick and short spicules.
**Habitat**   All the species of the genus *Acanthopleura* live on rocks in the supralittoral or the top of the mesolittoral zone.
**Distribution**   The genus *Acanthopleura* is confined to tropical waters.

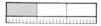

## 135 SUBFAMILY ALVANIINAE
### Alvanias

**Family**   Rissoidae
**Shell**   Small size (less than 1/5 inch), generally thick and robust, moderately high spire, sometimes globular, with convex whorls and an impressed suture. The base, except in rare cases, lacks an umbilicus. There are no canals; the outer lip often has a strong varix; sometimes the inner surface of the lip is toothed. Sculpture always present, and it almost always consists of axial ribs and spiral grooves or bands with one or the other predominating. If the two types of sculpture are equally prominent, the surface has a reticulated appearance. The coloration is very variable, generally whitish or shades of brown. There is always a thin horny operculum with an almost central nucleus. The illustration shows, from left to right, *Alvania montagni*, *A. cimex* and *Folina costata*.
**Body**   Members of this subfamily have a long, narrow foot, a distinct head, eyes at the base of two long tentacles. The rather long penis is behind the right tentacle. There is only one gill and one osphradium. The radula is taenioglossan.
**Habitat**   Rather varied, most of the species live on rigid substrates or rocks, but also seaweeds or marine Phanerogams, usually in the infralittoral zone, but there are also circalittoral and bathyal species.
**Distribution**   The illustrated species live in the Mediterranean, but members of the Alvaniinae may be found in all seas

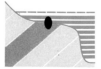

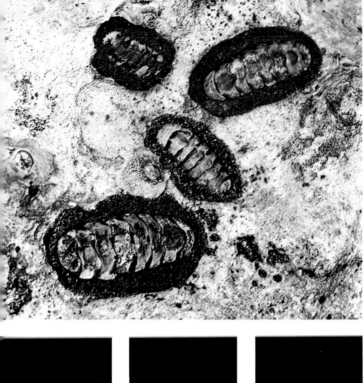

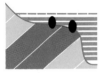

## 136  ANOMIA SIMPLEX
### Common Jingle Shell

**Family**  Anomiidae

**Shell**  Fragile, light, medium size (1 to 2 inches), varying in shape, depending upon the substrate on which it rests. Inequi valve and inequilateral. The right valve has a circular hole be neath the umbo and is smaller than the left valve, which is also much more convex. Color is yellow to orange, sometimes silve or black or red. The sculpture consists of irregularly shaped concentric lamellae; the hinge is edentulous, and the ligamen is internal. There is only one muscle scar inside the valve (monomyarian), the pallial line is smoothly curved (integropal liate). The shell has a leaved structure.

**Body**  It has a pair of gills, each consisting of two series of fil aments, widely connected, forming in all four series of lamellae (filibranch). The foot is reduced, as in many sessile bivalves The byssus is characteristic, as it is calcified and emerge. through the hole in the right valve. It is so firmly attached to the substratum that when collecting the shell the byssus must be detached from the foot.

**Habitat**  Rigid substrates, rocks, commonly other shells From shallows to more than 150 meters (500 feet)—i.e., infra littoral and circalittoral zones.

**Distribution**  Eastern Atlantic, Carolinan and Caribbean prov inces, Cape Cod, Massachusetts to Florida, Texas to Brazil Bermuda.

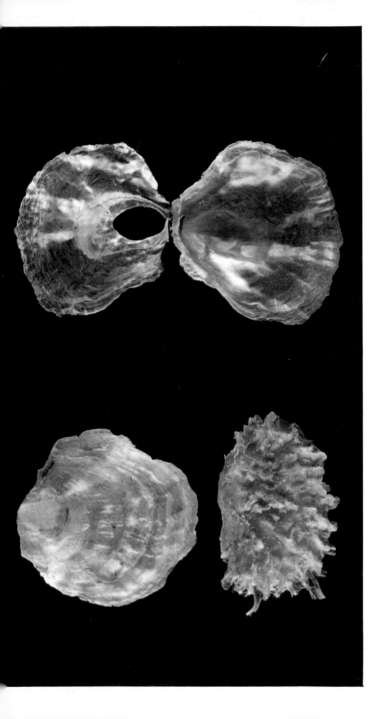

## 137 ARCA NOAE
### Noah's Arc

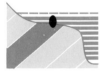

**Family** Arcidae

**Shell** Equivalve and inequilateral, rectangular, size 2½ to 3 inches, roughly trapezoidal in shape. The chestnut periostracum has fairly extensive and amply fringed lamellae. The periostracum tends to wear off with the development of the individual but is especially persistent along the large rib running from the umbo to the posterioventral extremity of the valve. The shell is basically whitish, with reddish-brown parallel, often W-shaped, bands. The external ligament is dark chestnut and occupies a large dorsal area between the umbones. The hinge is straight and taxodont. It is dimyarian, isomyarian and integropalliate. The shell has a mainly crossed-lamellae structure.

**Body** It has a pair of gills, each consisting of two series of filaments, widely connected forming in all four series of lamellae (filibranch). The foot is little developed, as an adaptation to sessile life; on the other hand, the byssus is well developed, essentially proteinaceous, secreted by the foot and it firmly anchors the animal to rigid substrates.

**Habitat** As has been said, this animal prefers rigid substrates, choosing cracks in the rocks in the infralittoral zone.

**Distribution** Mainly Mediterranean, it extends into the Atlantic northward along the Portuguese coast and south to Angola.

---

## 138 ASTRAEA BUSCHII
### Philippi's Star Shell

**Family** Turbinidae

**Shell** Medium size (1½ inches), thin and robust, high regular conical spire, height one and a half times breadth, flat or moderately convex whorls, incised suture, flat or even concave base, a broad umbilicus. The aperture points downward, forming a moderately acute angle to the axis of the shell. The outer lip is thin. The sculpture consists of large slanted axial ribs, narrower than the gaps between them; toward the base of the body whorl and above the suture on the others, these ribs project and expand, forming stout triangular spines. On the base there are growth lamellae and a spiral, roughly median rib. Underneath the thin fibrous periostracum the shell is brownish green, patterned with chestnut, green or white. The operculum (top right in the illustration) is calcareous, is paucispiral, and has a lateral nucleus and two smooth external ribs.

**Body** It has a broad foot, anteriorly truncated with a latero-dorsal fold (epipodium), which has long tentacles. There is only one gill and one osphradium. The head is very distinct. The radula is rhipidoglossan, the second marginal teeth are broader than the others.

**Habitat** Rocks in the lower levels of the mesolittoral zone or the upper levels of the infralittoral zone.

**Distribution** Confined to the southern Panamic and Peruvian provinces.

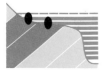

## 139 BARBATIA CANDIDA
### White Bearded Ark

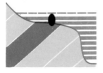

**Family** Arcidae

**Shell** Medium size (1½ to 2½ inches), robust, fairly thick, faintly trapezoidal in shape, with a narrow ventral aperture between the two valves through which the byssus emerges. The brown periostracum is quite thick, with short fringed lamellae which are highly developed at the posterior. The shell is a milk-white color. The sculpture is made up of fairly broad, slightly raised radial ribs, which carry blunt tubercles; these are more prominent on the posterior ribs. There are also fairly prominent, thin, growth lamellae. The ligament is external and very long, stretching in front of and behind the umbones. The hinge is taxodont. The two thick muscle scars are almost identical (dimyarian, isomyarian), joined by a smoothly curved pallial line (integropalliate). The shell has a crossed-lamellae structure.

**Body** A poorly developed foot, in keeping with the sessile life of the species; fixed to the substratum by a strong byssus. It has a pair of gills, each consisting of two series of filaments widely connected, forming four series of lamellae in all (filibranch).

**Habitat** Usually lives attached by its byssus to the lower surfaces of stones in the infralittoral zone.

**Distribution** An Atlantic species, the Carolinan and Caribbean Provinces, Southern Florida and off Texas and the West Indies to Brazil.

---

## 140 BERNAYA MARGINATA
### Marginated Cowrie

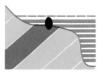

**Family** Cypraeidae

**Shell** Medium size (2 to 2½ inches), delicate and fragile appearance. The back is regularly spherical, the base is flat. At the margin between the base and the back there is a thin callus, which tends to broaden anteriorly and posteriorly into thin plates. As in the majority of cowries, there is no sculpture. The aperture is fairly narrow, straight for the anterior two thirds and smoothly curved in the posterior third. The teeth are quite large and well developed. Those on the outer lip extend right across it, almost to the margin of the base. The coloration is variable; besides albinos, there are quite extensively chestnut spotted examples, the spots varying in size and shade. The margins, on both dorsal and basal sides have patches; these are generally round and dark chestnut.

**Body** It has a translucent white foot, a distinct white head, two black tentacles and a colorless siphon. The mantle, which as in all cypraeids, is extended in two lobes to cover the shell, is transparent, pink or hazel and lacks papillae. The radula taenioglossan.

**Habitat** This rather rare species seems to live at varying depths in the infralittoral zone, often on sponges.

**Distribution** Characteristic of the Australian Province.

## 141 BRACHIDONTES VARIABILIS
### Variable Mussel

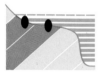

**Family** Mytilidae

**Shell** Medium small (2½ inches), equivalve, inequilateral, almost triangular in shape. It has a thin beige periostracum, and the shell varies from reddish brown to dark green in color, always paler toward the umbones. The sculpture consists of numerous bifid radial ribs, which produce further branched, radial ribs and extend over the whole surface of the valves. Beneath the umbones, almost terminal, there is a row of five teeth, not however, homologous to the five hinge teeth. The ligament is external and posterior to the umbones. The valve margins are crenulated. The two muscle scars differ greatly, as in all mytilids (dimyarian, anisomyarian). There is a smoothly curved pallial line (integropalliate).

**Body** It has all the typical characteristics of the Mytilidae—i.e., a pair of gills each consisting of two series of filaments widely connected to form one row of four lamellae (filibranch), small foot and strong byssus.

**Habitat** Usually rocky bottoms in the mesolittoral zone; it can also extend into the upper levels of the infralittoral zone, where it lives in very large colonies. Sometimes found on densely packed sand and shell detritus.

**Distribution** African coasts, both Atlantic and Indian Oceans, extending as far as the Red Sea and the Suez Canal; from there it has recently entered the Mediterranean, adapting so well to the southern Mediterranean that it has partly displaced the endemic populations of *M. galloprovincialis*.

## 142 BUCCINULUM CORNEUM
### Horn Whelk

**Family** Buccinidae

**Shell** Medium size (2 inches), rather thick and robust, high spire, moderately long and slightly twisted siphonal canal, spindle-shaped in overall appearance. The whorls, very convex, are concave in their posterior fifth. The suture is barely incised. The aperture is ovoidal, the outer lip has a thin edge; sometimes it has faint internal folds. The columellar lip has a thin callus, which tends to form a blunt tooth toward the posterior end. The spiral sculpture is imperceptible, consisting of very slightly raised bands, which are sometimes more marked near the canal. The only axial sculpture is the straight growth lines. The color is variable, the base color may be pink, orange, hazel or quite darkish chestnut; the patterning consists of reddish-brown patches or flames. The grayish-brown periostracum is very thin and quite persistent. The horny operculum is light chestnut and has an apical nucleus.

**Body** A very bright orange-yellow in color. The morphological characteristics of the foot and head are the same as other members of the Buccinidae. The radula is rachiglossan.

**Habitat** *B. corneum* lives hidden beneath stones in the infralittoral zone; sometimes it is found also on coarse detrital bottoms in the circalittoral zone.

**Distribution** Lusitanian Province, confined to the Mediterranean.

## 143 CALLIOSTOMA GLORIOSUM
### Glorious Top Shell

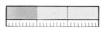

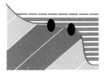

**Family**  Trochidae

**Shell**  Small size (1 inch), fairly high conical spire, the height is usually greater than the breadth. Almost flat whorls with a very impressed suture. The sculpture consists of ten spiral ridges; those on the higher part of the whorls, up to the fifth tend to be fairly prominently granular. The base, bordered by a rather blunt keel, has a series of very tightly packed smooth bands; no umbilicus. The aperture is roughly square, the outer lip is thin and sharp, the lower part of the columellar lip is broadened and bent back on to the columella. The shell, except for the white apical whorls, is yellowish, with irregular, indistinct and elongated reddish-brown patches grouped into two spirals following the whorls. The operculum is horny, multispiral, with a central nucleus, and is light hazel in color.

**Body**  It has a well developed elongated foot, with an epipodium that has cirri. The distinct head has two tentacles, the ocular peduncles are fused to their base, and these bear the pit eyes. The mantle cavity contains one gill and one osphradium. The heart has two auricles and one ventricle, which is crossed by the posterior part of the intestine. The radula is rhipidoglossan.

**Habitat**  Not very common, it lives on the seaweeds of the infralittoral and sometimes the circalittoral zone.

**Distribution**  Californian Province, San Francisco to San Diego

---

## 144 CALLIOSTOMA ZIZIPHINUS
### Painted Top Shell

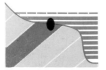

**Family**  Trochidae

**Shell**  Medium small size (1 ½ inches), solid, moderately high conical spire, height almost equaling breadth, flat base, never with an umbilicus, with a round continuous aperture (holostoma). The sculpture consists of broad spiral ribs; two of these ribs can fuse fairly completely. There are thin growth lines which, in the apical whorls, intersect the ribs and often form a series of small nodules. The nuclear whorls have a characteristic reticulated sculpture. The aperture forms an angle of about 120 degrees to the axis of the shell. The outer lip is thin and sharp. The coloration is variable; besides the most common reddish forms, sometimes patched or flamed, there are albino yellowish or bright-violet individuals. The operculum is horny and round, concave and yellowish.

**Body**  A very distinct head, two long tentacles with slight peduncles at their bases, which bear the eyes. The mantle margin is minutely lobed. The foot is large and has lateral papillae and an epipodium with four or five tentacles per side. The radula is rhipidoglossan.

**Habitat**  Essentially found on firm substrates in the infralittoral zone, in the northern part of its range. It also spreads into the mesolittoral or circalittoral zones and soft bottoms.

**Distribution**  The Boreal, Celtic (part of) and Lusitanian provinces.

**FAMILY CREPIDULIDAE**
**Cup-and-Saucer Shells**

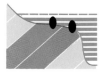

**Shell**   Medium or small size (¼ to 2 inches; average 1 inch), usually light and often very fragile; limpet, very low conical shape. A characteristic of the family is that the inner surface of the shell curls back to form a septum, which differs in shape in the various genera. The sculpture is variable. The color is also variable, usually whitish or chestnut, sometimes with flames or patches lighter or darker than the background. Always lacks an operculum. The illustration shows *Calyptraea chinensis* (top left), *Cheilea undulata* (bottom left), *Crepidula moulinsi* (top right) and *Crepidula fornicata* (bottom right). The first three of these are viewed from below, the last from above.

**Body**   The foot is short, reduced, usually discoidal. The distinct head has two tentacles with an eye at the base of each. Inside the mantle cavity there is the gill, the osphradium and, in males, the penis. The calyptraeids, like the epitoniids and the janthinids are protandrous hermaphrodites. A curious case occurs in *Crepidula fornicata*: a few individuals (up to ten) live on top of the others, the largest (and therefore oldest) below. In this way, there is an almost continuous progression of ages and of sexual conditions, from female (the larger) to male (the smaller) passing through hermaphrodites (in the middle). The radula is taenioglossan.

**Habitat**   All the species live on a rigid substratum, either rocky or coarse detrital bottoms. The species usually live in the infralittoral zone or, at the highest, the mesolittoral zone.

**Distribution**   All seas, preferring temperate or warm seas.

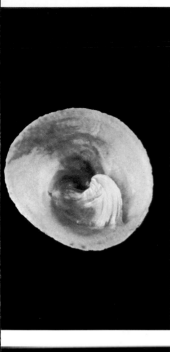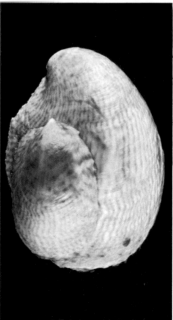

## 146 CAPULUS UNGARICUS
### Common Cap Shell

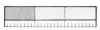

**Family**  Capulidae

**Shell**  Small size (¾ inch), very distinctive fool's-cap shape, fairly thin, but robust, the aperture is usually a regular circle. There is a rather thick light-chestnut periostracum, formed by bristled circular lamellae that overhang the margins of the aperture. The sculpture consists of thin radial ridges, varied in size and well spaced. There are always growth lines, some are particularly impressed. The external coloration is whitish, hazel or chestnut; the internal is white or pink. No operculum.

**Body**  A reduced circular foot. The head is distinct, has two tentacles and an eye at the base of each. The mantle cavity contains the gill and the osphradium and, when the individual is in the male phase, a penis; capulids are protandrous hermaphrodites—i.e., initially they are male, then they become female. The larva has a sort of supplementary shell called the echinospire, which enfolds the larval shell. The radula is taenioglossan.

**Habitat**  *C. ungaricus* attaches itself to rocks or sometimes to other mollusks in the infralittoral or circalittoral zone.

**Distribution**  Lusitanian, Celtic, and a very small part of the Boreal Province.

---

## 147 CAPULUS INCURVATUS
### Incurved Cap Shell

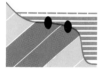

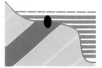

**Family**  Capulidae

**Shell**  Small size (½ inch), moderately thin, robust, very low spire; the whorls can even be separated (devolute) from one another, very rounded, swollen, enlarging rapidly, so the body whorl is much larger than the preceding ones. The aperture is continuous, circular or ovoidal, rather thin but never sharp. The periostracum is a light-yellowish chestnut, made up of successive rows of small tufts, which attach along the growth lines. The sculpture consists of blunt spiral ribs. Sometimes they are sharp, often as broad, or even broader, than the spaces between them. There are also faint concentric growth lines. Whitish or cream in color. Like all capulids it lacks an operculum.

**Body**  The foot is circular, the head distinct, with a pair of short tentacles with an eye at the base of each. There is a long proboscis. As with all mesogastropods the mantle cavity has only one gill, one osphradium and, when in the male phase, the penis. The radula is taenioglossan.

**Habitat**  Rocks in the upper levels of the infralittoral zone.

**Distribution**  Uncommon, found in the Carolinan and Caribbean provinces, North Carolina to Florida and to Brazil. Some authors erroneously consider it a Mediterranean species.

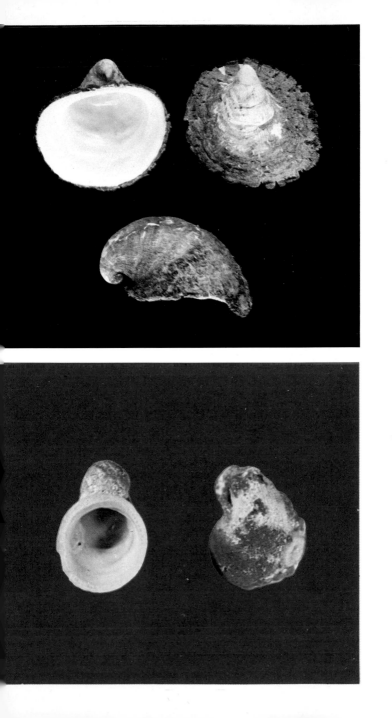

# CARDITA CRASSICOSTA
## Large-Ribbed Cardita

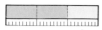

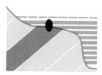

**Family**  Carditidae

**Shell**  Medium size (1½ inches), robust, roughly rectangular, equivalve and inequilateral. Extremely variable in color; the base color can be white, pink, yellow or red, on which there can be almost concentric, more intense stripes or rays of a different color. The sculpture consists of large radial ribs covered in lamellae, which in fresh examples are well developed, have the free end slightly broadened, and extend well beyond the margins of the valve. The ligament is external and posterior to the umbones. The hinge is heterodont, with two elongated cardinal teeth on the right valve, on the left valve the anterior cardinal is small, but the posterior one is elongated. The two muscle scars differ in size (dimyarian, anisomyarian). The pallial line is smoothly curved (integropalliate).

**Body**  In keeping with its sedentary life, the foot is rather reduced. There is a pair of gills, each consisting of two rows of lamellae, extensively fused by interlamellary junctions (eulamellibranch). The species is viviparous.

**Habitat**  It is found on both firm substrates and soft ones with a coarse texture, always being attached to solid objects by means of the very strong byssus.

**Distribution**  *C. crassicosta* lives in the Australian and Indo-Pacific provinces, in the area between the southern coasts of the Philippines and Australia.

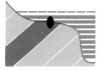

## 149 CERATOSTOMA BURNETTI
### Burnett's Purpura

**Family** Muricidae
**Shell** Large size (4 to 5½ inches), rather thick, robust, except for the thin lamellar varices which decorate it. The spire i
fairly high, and the siphonal canal is not very long, giving it a
overall ovate-spindle shape. The whorls are convex, incise
suture. The aperture is ovoidal, the outer lip is smooth internally and has a stout, strong spiny process in the lower third
The columellar lip has a thin marginal swelling, only slightl
raised relative to the ventral surface of the body whorl. The
axial sculpture consists of three leaflike varices, with fingere
edges, on each whorl. The spiral sculpture consists of large
ribs alternating with thinner ones; both types of rib are only
slightly raised, almost disappearing. A fairly reddish, chestnu
color. The operculum is horny with a marginal nucleus.
**Body** Anteriorly the foot is truncated, rounded posteriorly
The head has a long retractile proboscis and two rather long
and thin tentacles with an eye at the base of each. Inside the
mantle cavity there is the gill, the osphradium, in males the
penis, and also a well-developed hypobranchial gland. The ra
dula is rachiglossan.
**Habitat** Rocky bottoms in the infralittoral zone.
**Distribution** *C. burnetti* is found only in the Japonic
Province.

---

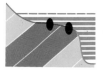

## 150 CERATOSTOMA FOLIATUM
### Foliated Thorn Purpura

**Family** Muricidae
**Shell** Large size (2 to 3 inches), fairly thick, robust an
heavy, moderately high conical spire, elongated ovoidal shape
convex whorls, very impressed suture. The aperture is ovoida
the outer lip has a wide, external leaflike varix, and it tapers t
an edge, with a tooth at the anteriolateral margin. The colume
lar lip has a slightly raised callus that does not extend ove
much of the ventral surface of the body whorl. The margins c
the siphonal canal are fused along the ventral line. The axia
sculpture consists of three winged varices on each whorl, wit
bluntly fingered margins and a few evanescent, intersperse
ribs. The spiral sculpture consists of bands of various thick
ness, which produce small, blunt nodules at the intersection
with the axial ribs. White in color with brown patches betwee
the varices. The operculum is horny, chestnut, and has a ma
ginal nucleus.
**Body** A fairly broad, well-developed foot. The distinct hea
has two tentacles with an eye at the base of each. The mantl
cavity contains the gill, osphradium and, in males, a penis be
hind the right tentacle. The radula is rachiglossan.
**Habitat** Rocky substrata in the infralittoral and, sometime
the circalittoral zone.
**Distribution** From the eastern North Pacific Boreal and Cal
fornian provinces. Alaska south to San Pedro, California.

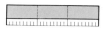

## 151 CHARONIA TRITONIS
### Triton's Trumpet

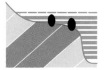

**Family** Cymatiidae
**Shell** Very large (up to 15 inches), it is one of the larges members of the phylum Mollusca, a very high spire, with an in cised suture and only moderately swollen whorls, with a fev slightly raised varices. The aperture is ovoidal, with an outer li that has white teeth arranged in twos on brown patches. Th inner lip has a not very thick or extensive chestnut callus, wit thin white folds running through it. The canal is short an broad. The sculpture consists of large rounded ribs, slightl raised, much broader than the gaps between them. The colora tion consists of chestnut, whitish or violet crescent-shape patches, roughly arranged along undulating axial lines. Th operculum is horny, with a central nucleus and concentri growth. *C. tritonis* is considered by some modern authors a conspecific with *C. variegata*, while others consider it as a sep arate species.
**Body** Creamy pink with reddish patches. A well-develope foot, truncated anteriorly and elongated posteriorly. The hea has a large proboscis, two moderately long tentacles with a eye at the base of each. The highly developed penis is situate behind the right tentacle. The radula is taenioglossan.
**Habitat** Normally rocky bottoms in the infralittoral and circa littoral zones.
**Distribution** Indo-Pacific Province.

---

## 152 CHICOREUS POMUM
### Apple Murex

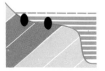

**Family** Muricidae
**Shell** Fairly large (2 to 4½ inches), thick, solid, not very hig spire, slightly elongated spherical shape, very convex whorls very incised suture. The aperture is round, the outer lip i toothed internally, and the columellar lip has a callus, whic has thin folds and covers a small part of the ventral surface c the body whorl. The canal is rather short, there is also a narro anal slit at the rear of the aperture. The spiral sculpture cor sists of alternating thick and thin ribs, which become nodular c even lamellar or spiny at the intersections with the axial sculp ture; this consists of three or four nodules or sometimes blunt spined varices on each whorl. In color a brownish gray wit lighter or darker, even blackish, spiral bands or stripes. Th aperture is yellow or chestnut yellow. The operculum is horny dark chestnut, multispiral, and has an apical nucleus.
**Body** Same characteristics as those of other *Chicoreu* members. The radula is rachiglossan, and the rachidial teet have five cusps, like all members of the subfamily Muricinae.
**Habitat** It lives on the various substrates, where there are th oysters on which it feeds, in the mesolittoral and infralittora zones.
**Distribution** Like *C. spectrum*, this species lives in th Caribbean Province from North Carolina to Florida and to Braz and Bermuda.

## 153 CHITON SQUAMOSUS
### Squamose Chiton

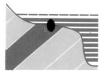

**Family** Chitonidae

**Shell** Medium size (2 to 3 inches), divided, as are all polypla cophoran shells, into eight plates, jointed with one another roughly trapezoidal apophyses. The intermediate plates (II–VI are divided into a central area and two lateral ones. The poste rior plate (VIII) has a rather narrow central area and a broa posterior region. There is only light sculpture, which is foun on the anterior plate, on the lateral areas of plates II–VII, an on the posterior of valve VIII; it consists of extremely fain granular, radial bands. All the valve insertion teeth are pectin ate, split by thin distal furrows into numerous teeth. The brigh blue color of the lower surface of the plates is characteristi (right-hand illustration).

**Body** The same general characteristics as *C. tuberculatu* (*q.v.*). The radula, as in all polyplacophorans, is formed of row of fifteen teeth; one rachidial and seven lateral on each side the outer ones are reduced to small plates.

**Habitat** Rigid substrates in the upper levels of the infralittore zone.

**Distribution** Confined to the Caribbean Province, Wes Indies.

---

## 154 CHITON TUBERCULATUS
### Common West Indian Chiton

**Family** Chitonidae

**Shell** Medium large (2 to 3 inches), divided, like all polypla cophorans, into eight plates or valves and with joints consistin of roughly trapezoidal apophyses between them. The interme diate plates (II–VII) have a tegmentum that is divided into central area and into two raised lateral areas; plate VIII (poste rior) with the mucro shifted forward is split into a rather sma central area and a large posterior area. The central areas valves II–VII and the posterior area of plate VIII have faint nodular radial ribs. The teeth inserted into the perinotum ar pectinate (i.e., divided by thin distal furrows into numerou teeth).

**Body** The foot is very large, muscular and ovoidal. Th mouth is at the center of a distinct head. The gills start immed ately behind the head and extend as far as the anal aperture The perinotum, which projects beyond the margin of the valve bears roughly rhomboidal calcareous scales.

**Habitat** Rocky substrates, in the mesolittoral and upp levels of the infralittoral zone.

**Distribution** Confined to the Caribbean Province. Southea Florida and West Indies, Bermuda.

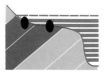

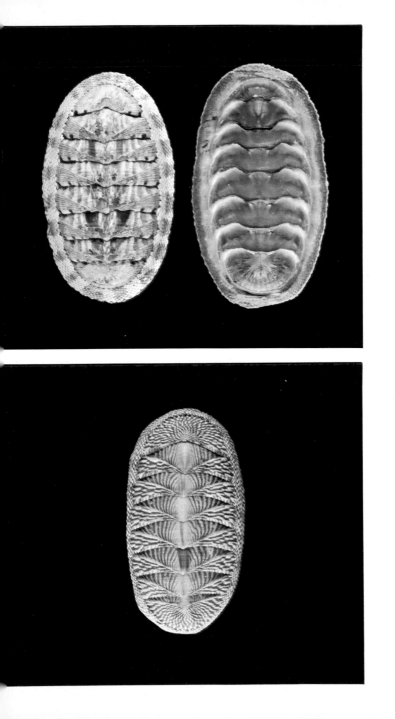

## 155 CHLAMYS NODOSUS (LYROSPECTEN)
### Lion's Paw

**Family** Pectinidae

**Shell** Large (3 to 6 inches), robust, inequivalve and inequilateral. To the side of the umbones the shell expands to form two "ears," the anterior being more developed than the posterior. There is no periostracum. The color varies greatly, from red to orange yellow, but most common is brownish red. The sculpture is made up of 7 to 9 larger coarsely nodular radial ribs, giving it its specific name. Furthermore, the whole surface is covered by thin radial ridges, which intersect light-growth lamellae. It is edentulous, with an internal ligament, triangular in section. There is only one muscle scar (monomyarian) and the pallial line is smoothly curved (integropalliate).

**Body** It has a circular flattened foot. Two gills, each consisting of two series of filaments, widely connected to form in all four series of lamellae (filibranch). The mantle edges have sensitive fingerlike processes with eyes in between.

**Habitat** A member of the epifauna—i.e., it rests on the surface of the bottom, almost always a rocky bottom. Normally found down to a depth of 30 meters (100 feet) in the infralittoral zone.

**Distribution** Carolinan and Caribbean provinces from North Carolina to Florida, Texas, the West Indies and Brazil.

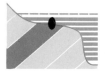

---

## 156 CITTARIUM PICA
### West Indian Top Shell

**Family** Trochidae

**Shell** Large (2 to 4 inches), thick and robust, fairly high conical spire, convex whorls, faintly angular in young examples but smoothly rounded in adults. The base is moderately convex, with a deep and wide umbilicus. The aperture is turned downward, at an angle to the axis of the columella. The outer lip is thin. No defined sculpture, a rough and often irregularly eroded surface. The coloration consists of pitch-black radial zigzags on a dirty-white base. The white areas of the shell are often more deeply eroded than the black ones. There is a horny, round, flattened operculum, dark chestnut in color, with a central nucleus and multispiral.

**Body** As in all trochids, the foot has a well-developed sole with a laterodorsal fold (epipodium). There are pit eyes at the bases of two long tentacles (laterodorsal) on the well-developed head. There is only one gill, but there are still two auricles in the heart. The rear section of the intestine crosses over the ventricle. The radula is rhipidoglossan.

**Habitat** It lives on rocks in the mesolittoral, or in the upper parts of the infralittoral zone. A species of the genus *Acmaea* is often found on the lower surface of the shell.

**Distribution** Confined to the north-central part of the Caribbean Province. No longer lives in Florida, but only in the West Indies.

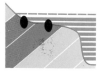

## 157 COLUMBELLA MERCATORIA
### Common Dove Shell

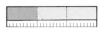

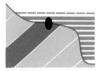

**Family** Columbellidae

**Shell** Small size (½ to ¾ inch), not very thick, but robust moderately high spire and an almost nonexistent siphonal canal, spherical in shape. The whorls are convex, with a light keel, the suture is incised. The aperture is narrow, the outer lip has a strong internal, toothed thickening. The columellar lip is weakly toothed and has a very slight callus. The sculpture consists of flat, equidistant bands that are broader than the gaps between them. The coloration is extremely variable, from yellow to red, chestnut and black with whitish- or reddish-brown patches or more often flamings. The operculum is horny and very small, about a quarter of the size of the aperture, normally oval and yellowish in color.

**Body** The foot is rather long and very narrow. The distinct head has two very long and thin tentacles with an eye at the base of each. The mantle siphon is not very long. The mantle cavity contains the gill, the osphradium and, in males, a not very long penis. The radula is rachiglossan.

**Habitat** It generally lives on seaweed, on which it scrapes its food, in the upper levels of the infralittoral zone.

**Distribution** The southern Carolinan Province and the whole of the Caribbean Province. Northeast Florida to the West Indies and Brazil. Bermuda.

## 158 CONUS subgenus CHELYOCONUS
### Cones (Purple Cone and California Cone illustrated)

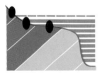

**Family** Conidae

**Shell** Medium or medium-small (1 to 2 inches), fairly solid somewhat high conical spire. The body whorl almost completely enfolds the preceding one. The shoulder is rounded above it the whorl's surface is flat or concave. The suture is incised. The sculpture is absent or, in some species, very weak consisting of small nodules on the shoulder and faint spiral grooves in the anterior part of the body whorl. The coloration is very variable; usually there are broken spiral stripes. Normally the periostracum is brown and rather thin. The operculum is horny, small, and has an apical nucleus. The illustration shows *Conus purpurascens* (left) and *C. californicus* (right).

**Body** It has an elongated, ovoidal foot, widened and truncated anteriorly. The head is distinct and has two quite long tentacles, with an eye about halfway along each. The mantle siphon is moderately developed. The radula is toxoglossan. *C. purpurascens* feeds on fish, while *C. californicus* feeds on mollusks and annelids.

**Habitat** *C. purpurascens* lives on rocky supralittoral or mesolittoral bottoms, while *C. californicus* lives on sandy bottoms in the infralittoral zone.

**Distribution** Both illustrated species live mainly in the Panamic Province. *C. californicus* north to California.

## 159 CONUS subgenus STEPHANOCONUS
### Cones (Crown Cone, Brown Cone & Prince Cone illustrated)

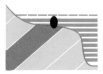

**Family**   Conidae

**Shell**   Medium or medium-small in size (1½ to 5 inches), solid, not very heavy. The body whorl covers the preceding one up to the angular shoulder, rather low spire, obconical in shape. The part of the whorls above the shoulder is flat or often concave. The aperture is narrow and elongated, the outer lip is thin and sharp. The sculpture consists of light tubercles, often fading, on the shoulders and on thin spiral bands; these can be missing on the anterior of the body whorl. The coloration is very variable; on a yellowish or darkish background, darker axial or spiral lines stand out or there are chestnut or whitish patches. The periostracum is generally thin. The small operculum is horny and has an apical nucleus. The illustration shows *Conus regius* (top left), *C. brunneus* (top right), and *C. princeps* (bottom).

**Body**   Similar to other members of this genus already described. The radula is toxoglossan. Of the three illustrated species, only the diet of *C. brunneus* is known, it being annelids.

**Habitat**   Unlike most conids, the three species described here generally live among rocks or corals, rather than sand, in the infralittoral zone.

**Distribution**   *C. regius,* Caribbean Province, while *C. brunneus* and *C. princeps* come mainly from the Panamic Province.

## 160 CRYPTOPLAX LARVAEFORMIS
### Burrow's Chiton

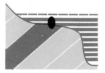

**Family**  Acanthochitonidae
**Shell**  Medium size (3 inches), divided like all polyplacophorans into eight plates; a characteristic of the genus *Cryptoplax* is that five of the plates are jointed with one another by means of elongated triangular apophyses, while the last three are free and separated by the perinotum. In the illustrated example, the surface of the tegmentum is worn, and so it is not possible to see any details of the sculpture; usually, however, *Cryptoplax* sp. have a jugal area, furrowed longitudinally and two lateropleural areas covered with small nodules or tightly packed tubercles. The mucro of plate VIII is displaced at the posterior end.
**Body**  The foot is very long and thin, but in other polyplacophorans it is usually ovoidal. The head is distinct, with a semicircular profile and the mouth at its center. The gills are confined to the lateroposterior part of the mantle cavity. The mantle, which projects well beyond the valve margins and, as seen, encircles the three posterior valves, has short quite thick spicules.
**Habitat**  Rigid infralittoral substrates.
**Distribution**  *Cryptoplax* sp. are found throughout the Indian Ocean and in the western Pacific.

## 161 CYMATIUM LOTORIUM
### Lotorium Triton

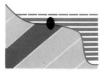

**Family**  Cymatiidae
**Shell**  Large size (5 inches), thick, robust, heavy, rather high spire, convex angular whorls, incised suture. On each whorl there is a large varix, which marks an old aperture. The aperture is ovoidal, the outer lip is slightly broadened at the anterior, strongly thickened with a few robust stout teeth that continue as folds into the aperture. The columellar lip has a not very thick or extensive callus, which has evanescent ridges. The sculpture consists of slightly raised irregular spiral bands and a strong median keel with, in general, four rows of three nodules (arranged vertically) between one varix and the next. The shell is yellowish in color, with the aperture, the varices and the edge of the canal chestnut with whitish patches. The periostracum is thin and light chestnut. The operculum is horny with a roughly central nucleus.
**Body**  The foot is well developed, truncated at the front and rounded at the rear. The very distinct head has a long retractile proboscis and two tentacles, each with an eye on the outer side of its base. Inside the mantle cavity there is the gill, the osphradium and, in males, a large penis. The radula is taenioglossan.
**Habitat**  Infralittoral, on corals or rocks.
**Distribution**  The entire Indo-Pacific Province.

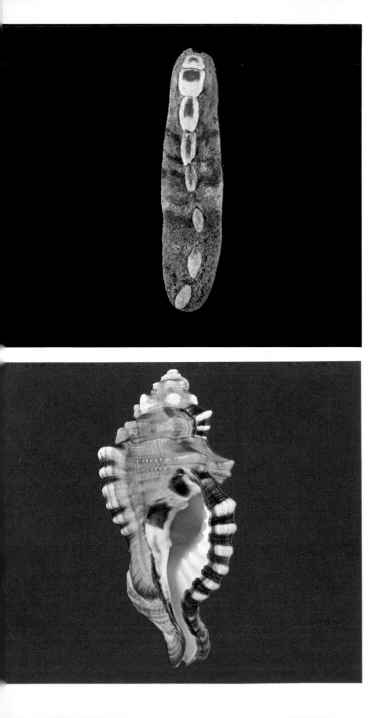

## 162 DIODORA GRAECA
### Common Keyhole Limpet

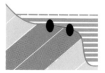

**Family** Fissurellidae
**Shell** Small size (1 inch), secondarily symmetrical, conical fairly high, with an almost central hole. The sculpture consists of twenty principal radial ribs, usually alternating with thinner secondary ones and a dozen rather raised concentric lamellar bands; the crossing of these two series of elements produces a regular grid. The apical hole is edged internally by an ovoidal swelling, usually one end is truncated. The margin of the shell is finely toothed. The coloration varies from grayish brown, uniform or speckled with brown or white, to whitish green or reddish. The inner surface is usually white.
**Body** It has all the primitive characteristics of the Fissurellidae—i.e., a pair of gills, two osphradia, two auricles, two nephridia. The foot is well developed, usually orange, and it covers part of the shell margin. The radula is rhipidoglossan, the fifth lateral tooth is dominant.
**Habitat** It is found mainly on rocky substrates in the infralittoral zone, but it can also be found in the circalittoral zone.
**Distribution** Lusitanian, also the southern portion of the Celtic Province.

## 163 ECHININUS NODULOSUS
### False Prickly Winkle

**Family** Littorinidae
**Shell** Small size (½ to 1 inch), moderately thick, robust, high conical spire, and height generally exceeds breadth; the whorls are angular and have a raised, median keel; the base is flat and lacks an umbilicus; the lip of the aperture is thin and sharp, and the columella does not have a callus. The sculpture consists of two nodular keels, giving it its specific name, one median and one basal, visible only on the body whorl; there are also two or three spiral ridges with small, stout nodules. The base is covered by concentric granular bands. The coloration is grayish with white patches. These are mainly on the sculpture. There is a horny operculum, which, as in all species of the subfamily Echininae, is multispiral with a central nucleus.
**Body** A moderately developed foot, very distinct head, with two long tentacles, an eye at the base of each. There is a rather large penis behind the right tentacle. The mantle cavity has only one gill and one osphradium. The radula is much longer than the animal's body and is taenioglossan.
**Habitat** Prefers supralittoral rocks but occasionally mesolittoral.
**Distribution** Confined to the north-central part of the Caribbean Province. Southeast Florida and the West Indies, Bermuda.

# SUBFAMILY EMARGINULINAE
## Limpets

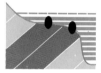

**Family** Fissurellidae

**Shell** Secondarily symmetrical, size ½ to 2 inches, shape varying from conical with backward pointing apex to flattened. Characteristic of this subfamily is a fairly deep slit in the anterior margin of the shell. The illustration shows three species belonging to three different genera: *Scutus unguis* (left), *Hemitoma octoradiata* (top right) and *Emarginula puncticulata* (bottom right). Generally, except for *Scutus,* the sculpture consists of fairly large principal radial ribs alternating with secondary or even tertiary ribs, which never reach the apex of the shell; concentric lamellae cross these ribs and so the surface has a gridlike appearance. There is almost always a yellow-brown periostracum, which obscures the shell's usually whitish color. All the species lack an operculum.

**Body** They have all the Fissurellid's primitive characteristics which have been described. In the genus *Scutus*, the foot is much larger than the shell and partly covers it, but in the other two genera it is usually covered by the shell.

**Habitat** All the Emarginulinae are restricted to rigid substrates, the three illustrated species are infralittoral but other species even from the same genera, can be circalittoral.

**Distribution** Members of this subfamily are found in all seas

## 165 EROSARIA SPURCA ACICULARIS
### Atlantic Yellow Cowrie

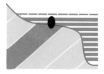

**Family** Cypraeidae

**Shell** Small size (½ to 1¼ inches), spherical, light and solid the ends protrude very slightly, the body whorl completely er folds and hides the preceding ones (convolute). The smoo back is very convex, as is the base, though to a lesser degre The latter has a thick callus, which extends to its edges, whe it tapers sharply, forming a sort of marginal "step"; above th the callus gradually thins out as it goes dorsally. It is one of th few cypraeids with any sculpture, which in this case consists very small pits arranged linearly on the marginal step. The bac is yellow with dense, chestnut specks surrounded by a rin which is lighter than the background color. The base is whit as is the marginal callus, which has chestnut dots. The pits to are chestnut.

**Body** Chestnut yellow. No information in the literature abo the presence of papillae on the lobes of the mantle and the s phon. Like all cypraeids the mantle cavity contains only on gill, one osphradium and, in males, a penis. The radula taenioglossan.

**Habitat** It lives hidden between stones or sometimes, amor corals in the infralittoral zone.

**Distribution** This subspecies is found from South Carolina Florida, Mexico, and the West Indies. The range of the speci also includes the Lusitanian and West African provinces.

## 166 FAVARTIA CELLULOSA
### Pitted Murex

**Family** Muricidae

**Shell** Small size (1 inch), rather thick, robust, fairly hi spire, spindle-shaped, very convex whorls, with a very incise suture. The aperture is ovoidal, the outer lip is thick, and inte nally it undulates, matching the sculpture of the whorl. Th inner lip has a thin callus, and at the rear this is attached to th ventral surface of the body whorl, while it is detached a teriorly. The siphonal canal is moderately long. The ax sculpture consists of five varices and of thin lamellae, varyi in size, which extend over the whole surface. The spiral scul ture consists of five thick bands on the body whorl, and oft there are additional thinner ones on the shoulder. Where the ribs and the varices intersect, a lamella is formed. Pale bro in color, becoming darker on the spiral ribs. The horny, che nut operculum has a roughly central nucleus.

**Body** See the descriptions of other muricids. The radula rachiglossan, the rachidial tooth has five cusps, roughly eq in size.

**Habitat** Rocky substrates in the mesolittoral or upper lev of the infralittoral zone, near the banks of mussels on whi they feed.

**Distribution** Typical of and confined to the Caribbean Pr ince. North Carolina to Gulf of Mexico to Brazil and Bermud

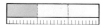

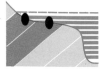

## 167 FISSURELLA NODOSA
### Knobby Keyhole Limpet

**Family** Fissurellidae
**Shell** Small size (1 to 1½ inches), symmetrical, flattened-cone shape, characterized, as all Fissurellidae, by an apical hole, the equivalent of the shell holes of the Haliotidae and the slit in the aperture edge in the Pleurotomariidae. The sculpture consists of large radial ribs, irregularly alternating with thinner secondary ones, which normally do not reach the apex. All the ribs bear strong nodules, giving it its specific name. The inner margin of the shell is crenulated, around the hole there is an internal callus of constant thickness. Whitish in color, however, it is almost always hidden by encrustations.
**Body** It retains many primitive characteristics—i.e., two gills, two osphradia, two auricles, two nephridia, the left being much smaller than the right. The large foot is attached to the shell by a series of muscles arranged in a horseshoe shape. The radula is rhipidoglossan, the fifth lateral tooth is dominant.
**Habitat** It lives firmly attached, by means of the strong foot, to rocks in the mesolittoral and splash zones exposed to waves.
**Distribution** Typical of the central region of the Caribbean Province.

---

## 168 GIBBULA FANULUM
### Gmelin's Top Shell

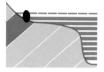

**Family** Trochidae
**Shell** Small size (½ inch), fairly thick, robust, rather high conical spire, the height almost equaling the breadth, swollen whorls and very incised suture. In the median portion of the body whorl and above the suture in the preceding ones, there is a sharp depression, characteristic of the species. The upper parts of the whorls are slightly convex and bear blunt radial ribs. The base is also convex, but it has three or four spiral ribs and a wide and deep umbilicus; furthermore the whole shell surface is covered by thin spiral grooves. Variable in coloration—white, grayish, chestnut, densely spotted, with large radial chestnut or red patches on the upper surfaces of the whorls and with regularly spaced brown spots in the lateral hollows. The operculum is horny, round, and has a central nucleus.
**Body** Though it has only one gill and one osphradium in the mantle cavity, *G. fanulum* retains some primitive characters—i.e., two nephridia (present at the same time), and the rear part of the intestine crosses the ventricle of the heart. The radula is rhipidoglossan.
**Habitat** It usually lives on top of stones or rocks in the infralittoral and sometimes the circalittoral zone.
**Distribution** Lusitanian, especially the Mediterranean.

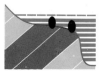

**GLOSSODORIS VALENCIENNESI**
**Cantraine's Blue Doris**

**Family    Dorididae**
**Shell**    Absent, as in all nudibranchs.
**Body**    Medium size, elongated, the foot has a sole. The fairly thick mantle border forms an undulating laterodorsal keel along the entire body. The surface is covered with slightly raised papillae and warts, arranged in irregular longitudinal lines. The head has two moderately long rhinophores, finger-like, retractile and well spaced. No mantle cavity, the gill is transformed into a tuft of branched dorsal papillae, arranged in a ring round the anal aperture. These gills can be retracted into an internal cavity. The radula has a very large number of teeth. The illustration shows the whole animal (top), a detail of the head (bottom left) and a detail of the branchial tuft (bottom right).
**Habitat**    It lives on calcareous seaweeds, detrital bottoms or even Posidonia leaves in the infralittoral zone. It is rarely found on sponges, on which, however, it appears to feed.
**Distribution**    Lusitanian Province, including the entire Mediterranean.

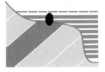

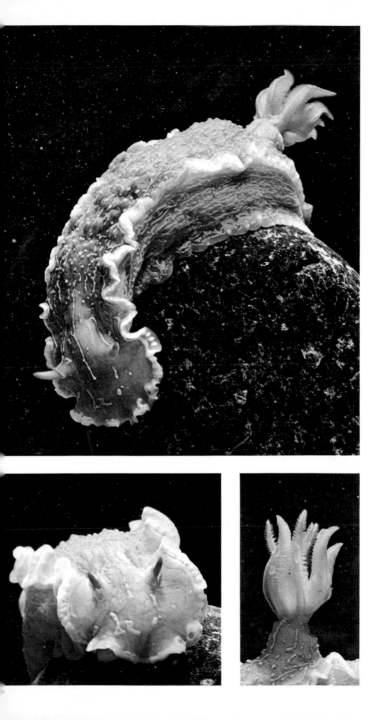

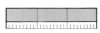

## 170 HALIOTIS FULGENS
### Green Abalone

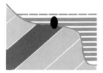

**Family** Haliotidae

**Shell** Very large (7 to 8 inches), thick and robust, rounded ear-shaped. The whorls enlarge rapidly, so that the body whorl is much larger than the others. The shoulder, the zone below the dorsal and lateral areas of the whorl, has a series of holes with slightly raised margins, only the last five or six of them being open. The periostracum is thin, chestnut and very persistent, hiding the reddish-chestnut color of the shell. The inner surface is iridescent, with bluish or green highlights. The sculpture consists of slightly raised, blunt, spiral bands, roughly similar in size, and there are faint radial ribs and thin growth lines. It lacks an operculum.

**Body** It has, like all members of the superfamily Pleurotomariacea, primitive characteristics—i.e., two gills and osphradia, the rear section of the intestine crosses the ventricle of the heart. The epipodium (a fold of the mantle bearing cirri), when extended, projects beyond the shell. The radula is rhipidoglossan.

**Habitat** Like many haliotids it lives on infralittoral rocks.

**Distribution** *H. fulgens* is a Pacific species. Californian Province. Point Conception, California, to Baja California.

## 171 HALIOTIS LAMELLOSA
### Mediterranean Abalone

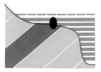

**Family** Haliotidae

**Shell** In size about 3 inches, these shells are ear-shaped (they are, in fact, called sea ears); they are made up of a few whorls, which rapidly enlarge; the body whorl is much larger than the others and has a row of holes, the equivalent of the slit in the lip of the Pleurotomariidae. The sculpture consists mainly of a series of fairly large spiral bands. The shell growth frequently, but not always, causes the formation of undulating lamellar crests, giving rise to the specific name. Variable coloration, greenish or reddish brown, sometimes bright red, often with tawny or whitish-gray patches. The operculum is present in the larval stage but not in the adult.

**Body** It has such primitive characters as two gills, two auricles and two nephridia, pit eyes and, on the foot, a lateral fold (epipodium), which has many sensory papillae. The radula is rhipidoglossan.

**Habitat** Firmly attached by its strong foot to rigid substrates, usually under stones, in the infralittoral zone.

**Distribution** Exclusively Mediterranean; some authorities consider it to be merely a Mediterranean subspecies of the Lusitanian, *H. tuberculata*.

## 172 HALIOTIS RUFESCENS
### Red Abalone

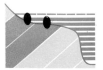

**Family** Haliotidae

**Shell** Very large size (10 to 12 inches), rather thick, robust, very low spire. The whorls enlarge rapidly, and so the body whorl is much larger than the preceding ones. The specific name comes from the brick-red coloration of the outer surface; the inner surface is mother-of-pearl with greenish highlights. The sculpture consists of blunt, dissimilar, spiral ribs, rough radial, extensively broken and thick folds, ending in line with the apertures of the dorsolateral margin of the shell. There are also fine, deeply incised growth lines. The periostracum is thin, rather persistent and chestnut. Larval forms have an operculum, but adults do not.

**Body** It has a large circular foot, which is often eaten barbequed, like a steak. The head and tentacles are black. Inside the mantle cavity there are two gills, two osphradia, but no penis in males; fertilization is external. The rear section of the intestine crosses over the ventricle. The radula is rhipidoglossan.

**Habitat** A common species, it lives on rocks in the mesolittoral, infralittoral and even circalittoral zones. Collection of this species is controlled by American authorities to prevent extinction of the species.

**Distribution** Eastern Pacific coasts, Oregon and California provinces.

---

## 173 HEXAPLEX PRINCEPS (MURICANTHUS)
### Prince Murex

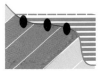

**Family** Muricidae

**Shell** Large size (5 inches), very thick, heavy, solid, moderately high spire and a rather short and broad siphonal canal, producing an ovate-spindle overall shape. Convex whorls, incised suture, the aperture is fairly broad, ovate, the outer lip lacks internal teeth or folds, the columellar lip has a slight callus, which is fully attached to the body whorl. The axial sculpture consists of five or six varices on each whorl, with large spines and slightly jagged edges. The spiral sculpture is made up of rather thin bands, roughly similar in thickness. White with dark-chestnut bands, alternating with spiral lines, but these never reach the distal ends of the spines. It is often impossible to see the characteristics described, as the shells are heavily and solidly encrusted with calcareous seaweed and bryozoans. The operculum is horny, dark chestnut, with an almost apical nucleus.

**Body** Like all muricids, it has a broad, not very elongated foot. The radula is rachiglossan, the rachidial tooth has five cusps, the outer two and middle being larger and roughly similar.

**Habitat** Mesolittoral rocks or in the upper levels of the infralittoral zone.

**Distribution** The Panamic and Peruvian provinces.

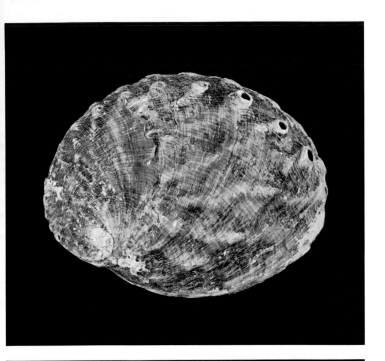

## 174 HIATELLA ARCTICA
### Arctic Saxicave

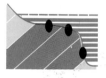

**Family** Hiatellidae

**Shell** Small (1 inch; rarely to 3 inches), robust, moderately swollen, mildly inequivalve and inequilateral. Varies in shape depending on the substrate, but tends to be rectangular. The white shell is covered by a thin grayish-brown periostracum. The sculpture consists of rather irregular concentric growth lines, with two ribs from the umbones to the posterior margins of the valves. In young examples these ribs have spines. The ligament is external, the heterodont hinge has, on the right valve, one cardinal tooth that fits between two cardinal teeth on the left valve. In larger shells these teeth are often eroded. The two muscle scars are almost equal (dimyarian, isomyarian), and the pallial line has a deep sinus (sinopalliate). The shell structure is mainly crossed-lamellae.

**Body** It has a pair of gills, each of which consists of two series of lamellae extensively fused by interlamellar junctions (eulamellibranch). The foot and the siphons are well developed.

**Habitat** This species bores into soft rocks or hides itself in their nooks and crannies, at depths varying from a few centimeters down to 3,000 meters (10,000 feet).

**Distribution** Very widespread, *H. arctica* can be found in all the seas of the Northern Hemisphere, and some authors say that it is found also in the Southern Hemisphere.

## 175 HINIA INCRASSATA
### Angulate Nassa

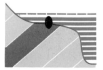

**Family** Nassariidae

**Shell** Small size (½ inch), fairly thick, robust, fairly high conical spire, short, twisted and rather open siphonal canal, an elongated-ovate overall appearance. The whorls are very convex and the suture is markedly impressed. The aperture is rounded, the outer lip has a thin edge, a distinct external thickening and thin internal folds. The columellar lip has a light, not very extensive, callus on the ventral surface of the body whorl. The axial sculpture consists of strong ribs, which are as broad as the gaps between them. The spiral is made up of thin bands extending over the whole surface. The color is extremely variable, there are a few uniformly yellow, reddish or chestnut examples, besides the more common yellowish individuals with spirally arranged chestnut spots. The operculum is horny, yellowish, roughly triangular, and the inner and outer margins are jagged.

**Body** It has an elongated triangular foot with two small pointed processes at the rear. The head has two tentacles and a fairly long proboscis. The mantle siphon is very long. The radula is rachiglossan.

**Habitat** *H. incrassata* lives hidden in small pockets of sand under stones or between rocks in the infralittoral zone.

**Distribution** Eastern Boreal, Celtic and Lusitanian provinces.

## 176 IRUS IRUS
### Irus Venus

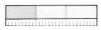

**Family** Veneridae
**Shell** Medium-small size (1 to 1 ¼ inches), moderately swollen shape varies according to the substrate; equivalve and inequilateral. The periostracum is thin and virtually colorless, the shell is white, sometimes, yellow or red; the umbones are often chestnut or reddish. The sculpture consists of thin, undulating concentric, well-developed lamellae; there are also thin radial grooves or furrows. The ligament is external, buried between the valves, posterior to the umbones. The heterodont hinge has three cardinal teeth and no lateral teeth on each valve. The two muscle scars are almost identical (dimyarian, isomyarian) and are linked by a pallial line that has a posterior sinus (sinopalliate).
**Body** It has a pair of gills, each consisting of two series of lamellae extensively fused by interlamellar junctions (eulamellibranch). The foot is poorly developed, and the siphons are not very long; these bivalves do not bury deeply.
**Habitat** *I. irus* lives in holes in rocks bored by other animals, in crevices or in very coarse detritus in the mesolittoral or, more commonly, the infralittoral zone.
**Distribution** Rather widespread. The Celtic, Lusitanian and West African provinces; extends into the Mediterranean as far as the Black Sea.

---

## 177 LEMINTINA ARENARIA
### Mediterranean Worm Shell

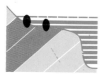

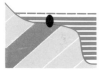

**Family** Vermetidae
**Shell** Fairly large (variable—up to 5 inches), moderately thick and robust, tubular irregularly wound and separated whorls. The terminal portion, with the aperture, points upward and usually is free of the substrate that adheres to the rest of the shell. The aperture lips are thin and sharp. The sculpture consists of longitudinal grooves or ribs that can vary in thickness among individuals and are usually granular. The growth lines are prominent, and some are strongly incised. Frequently there are curved plates along the shell, marking the apertures of previous stages of development. The coloration varies from light hazel to dark chestnut, sometimes the lighter forms have darker longitudinal lines or bands. The operculum is usually absent.
**Body** The foot is cylindrical. The distinct head has two tentacles. The males lack a penis. It has a distinctive method of capturing food; a gland in the foot secretes long mucus filaments, which the food particles stick to (similar to liming a twig). The radula is taenioglossan.
**Habitat** It lives fixed to rigid substrates, usually rock, but also large shells in the infralittoral zone.
**Distribution** Lusitanian, confined to the Mediterranean.

## 178 LEUCOZONIA NASSA
### Chestnut Latirus

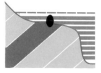

**Family** Fasciolariidae

**Shell** Medium-small (1½ inches), very thick and robust, moderately high conical spire, a not very long siphonal canal, spherical-spindle shaped in overall appearance. The whorls are very convex, sometimes bluntly keeled, and the suture is incised. The aperture is ovoidal; the outer lip tapers to an edge, with a very faint, blunt tooth near the anterior margin; on the inner surface there are thin bands. The columellar lip is anteriorly thickened and forms three or four strong folds. The sculpture consists of thin spiral grooves and coarse, indistinct, sometimes evanescent axial ribs. Darkish chestnut except for a thin, white, spiral stripe on the anterior third of the body whorl, which starts on the tooth of the outer lip. The operculum is horny, dark chestnut and nail-shaped.

**Body** Bright red, the foot is well developed and large. The head is distinct and has two tentacles with an eye at the base of each. The mantle siphon is rather short. The mantle cavity contains one gill, one osphradium and, in males, the penis. The radula is rachiglossan.

**Habitat** Rocky infralittoral bottoms.

**Distribution** Widespread throughout the Caribbean Province.

---

## 179 LIMA LIMA
### Spiny Lima

**Family** Limidae

**Shell** In size 1 to 1½ inches, variable shape, from the roughly rhomboidal to almost triangular, moderately convex, equivalve and inequilateral. To the sides of the umbones there are two ears, the posterior one is smaller and protrudes less than the anterior one. The periostracum is darkish brown, the shell is milk-white. The sculpture is made up of large radial ribs, which in fresh examples bear roughly concentric, thin lamellae. The byssus emerges posteriorly between the valves. The hinge is edentulous, the strong ligament is internal. There is only one muscle scar (monomyarian). The smoothly curved pallial line is faint (integropalliate). The shell has crossed aragonite lamellae internally and calcite prisms externally.

**Body** It has a pair of gills, each consisting of two series of lamellae extensively fused by interlamellar junctions (eulamellibranch). The foot secretes a strong byssus. The fingers at the periphery of the mantle lobes are distinctive.

**Habitat** Found in rocky infralittoral habitats, tending to hide in cracks in the rocks or under stones, anchored by the byssus. If disturbed and detached, it is capable of swimming (badly) by "beating" the valves; related species, which habitually use this movement, do so more elegantly.

**Distribution** Several subspecies are found in tropical seas in the Atlantic, northward into the Mediterranean.

## 180 LITHOPHAGA LITHOPHAGA
### Common Date Mussel

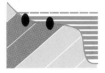

**Family** Mytilidae

**Shell** Medium size (3 inches), equivalve and inequilateral, very elongated, roughly rectangular shape, rounded umbones not prominent and often worn. The shape and the chestnut color of the periostracum are reminiscent of a date, and this species is known as the date mussel. The shell is whitish. The sculpture consists of light growth lines sometimes crossed by microscopic radial furrows. The ligament is long and external. The hinge lacks teeth (edentulous). The two muscle scars are very different (dimyarian, anisomyarian), the pallial line is smoothly curved (integropalliate). The shell has an outer prismatic layer and an inner mother-of-pearl one.

**Body** It has a pair of gills, each consisting of two series of widely connected filaments, which form in all four series of lamellae (filibranch). The foot is poorly developed. Unlike all other mytilids, it lacks a byssus.

**Habitat** This species, by means of an acid mantle secretion, bores into calcareous rocks in the mesolittoral and, especially infralittoral zones. Individuals are discovered only because of the holes which allow the posterior end of the valves to be seen. One has to break the rocks to get them out.

**Distribution** Typical of the Mediterranean. Some authors hold that it is found on the Atlantic coasts of Portugal and Morocco and also the Red Sea.

---

## 181 LITTORINA SAXATILIS
### Northern Rough Periwinkle

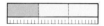

**Family** Littorinidae

**Shell** Small (¼ to ½ inch), thick and robust. In appearance spherical or high conical spire, marked suture and very swollen whorls. The base lacks an umbilicus. The lip is thin and sharp, the lower part of the aperture is slightly broadened. The sculpture varies; as well as completely smooth examples, there are others with spiral grooves or ridges, with varied spacing. The coloration is even more variable, it can be uniformly yellowish, orange, greenish or chestnut, or there may be white spots or spiral lines of the above colors, sometimes these white spots are arranged in a zigzag pattern. There is a horny semicircular operculum, slightly elongated at the top, paucispiral, with the nucleus displaced strongly toward the columellar side.

**Body** The foot is not highly developed. The distinct head has two long tentacles with an eye at the base of each. The single gill is moderately developed, while the osphradium is rather long. Behind the right tentacle there is a rather large penis. The taenioglossan radula is extremely long, two or three times the animal's length. It is a viviparous species.

**Habitat** Like all *Littorina* sp., this species lives on rocks in the mesolittoral zone, but it can extend up to the supralittoral zone.

**Distribution** Widespread, the Arctic, Boreal, Celtic and Lusitanian provinces.

## 182 LITTORINA ZICZAC
### Zebra Periwinkle

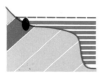

**Family** Littorinidae
**Shell** Small size (½ to ¾ inch), thinnish, robust, very hig
conical spire. The height is almost double the breadth. Th
whorls are slightly convex or flat, the suture is incised. The a
most flat base is marked off by a slight angle on the body whor
The outer lip is thin and sharp, the columella is callused. Th
sculpture consists of 20 to 26 thin spiral lines on the uppe
spire whorls; these lines tend to disappear on the body whor
The color varies in intensity from whitish to grayish. The pa
terning is made up of thin radial chestnut lines; these may be a
a slight angle to the shell axis or even zigzagged. The operce
lum is horny, faintly semicircular, with a pointed upper part, a
almost central nucleus; paucispiral, as is the entire Littorinina
subfamily.
**Body** The foot is small. The head is very distinct and has tw
long tentacles. The penis is behind the right tentacle. Each eg
is placed in a floating cylindroconical capsule.
**Habitat** As in all littorinids, it lives on rigid substrates in th
mesolittoral zone.
**Distribution** Caribbean Province, recently introduced to th
Pacific coasts of Panama.

## 183 LOTTIA GIGANTEA
### Giant Owl Limpet

**Family** Acmaeidae
**Shell** Large size (3 to 4 inches), thick and robust, limpe
shaped, oval, the apex is shifted forward close to the margin
Dark chestnut in color, with darker, irregular patches, often ra
dially arranged. The inner surface is chestnut, fading slight
near the horseshoe-shaped scar of the foot muscle. The scar
bluish, the area within it is grayish, sometimes with irregula
indistinctly edged chestnut patches. The sculpture consists o
flattened, radial ribs, often irregular and worn, due to the ere
sion of the shell. There are also growth lines some of which ar
deeply incised. The larval stages have an operculum, but it i
missing in adults.
**Body** The foot is large, discoidal, lacks an epipodium, b
has cirri. The head is very distinct and has two tentacles, wi
an eye at the base of each. In the mantle cavity the single g
and the osphradium are on the left, behind the head. The an
aperture and the nephridiophore are on the right. There are tw
nephridia, the right, the larger, is used as a gonoduct. Th
radula is docoglossan, without a rachidial tooth and only tw
lateral and two marginal teeth per side.
**Habitat** *L. gigantea* lives on rocks above the water; supral
toral or the upper level of the mesolittoral zones.
**Distribution** Californian Province, Crescent City, Californi
to Baja California.

## 184 LYNCINA REEVEI
### Reeve's Cowrie

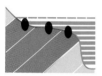

**Family** Cypraeidae
**Shell** Medium-small size (1 ¼ to 1 ½ inches), spherical, rather thin and light. The body whorl is highly developed but does not completely cover the preceding whorls, these are visible posteriorly. The back is regularly convex and swollen, while the base is only moderately convex and has a not very prominent callus. The aperture is gently and regularly curved, the two sides are almost parallel. The teeth are small, well defined, but not extensive. The base is white, the ends are red, and the back is a quite uniform grayish color.
**Body** The foot is a creamy white. The head is distinct with two black tentacles, the lobes of the mantle are yellow with short, branched gray papillae, as well as yellow ones. The radula is taenioglossan.
**Habitat** Rarely found alive, usually under stones or in cracks in the rocks in the mesolittoral zones or, more often, in the infra- or circalittoral zones.
**Distribution** Western Australian Province.

## 185 LYROMANGELIA TAENIATA
### Banded Turrid

**Family** Turridae
**Shell** Small size (about ¼ inch), not very thick but robust, high conical spire, spindle-shaped, the whorls are convex beneath the shoulder and concave above it, the suture is deeply impressed. The aperture is ovoidal, with a moderately developed canal at the anterior. The outer lip is strengthened by an external rib. The sculpture consists of strong well-spaced axial ribs, which form a rounded angle on the shoulder. The coloration is fairly distinctive; on a white or light-hazel base there are golden-yellow or chestnut spiral stripes (generally two on the body whorl). There are also thin chestnut lines. There is no operculum.
**Body** Although L. taeniata is not rare, there is no information on the morphology or anatomy of this species, not even the type of radula is known. Presumably it is toxoglossan, but in the Turridae it shows marked variation and is an important taxonomic character for determining the subfamily.
**Habitat** Hidden beneath stones or other rigid substrates in the infralittoral zone.
**Distribution** Lusitanian Province, confined to the Mediterranean Sea.

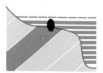

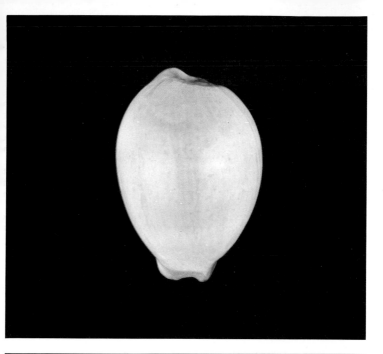

**MACROCYPRAEA**
**Large Cowrie**

**Family**   Cypraeidae

**Shell**   Medium or rather large size (2 to 7 inches), swollen, rather light for their size, body whorl generally completely covers the preceding whorls (convolute). The sides are almost parallel. The three species of this genus are all rather alike. The back is a dark hazel with lighter transverse bands and still lighter round spots, the base is a grayish hazel, and the teeth, quite extensive on both lips, are dark chestnut. *M. zebra* (bottom left) is distinguished from the others by the narrower aperture, the almost parallel sides, and the oculated spots (with a dark center and lighter outer ring), *M. cervus* (top) and *M. cervinetta* (bottom right). These all differ. The second has more extensive teeth. *M. cervinetta* is cylindrical in overall shape, but *M. cervus* is more swollen.

**Body**   Only *M. zebra* is mentioned in the literature. This has very thick mantle lobes, is dark chestnut in color with short conical papillae and longer branched ones. Inside the mantle cavity, like all cypraeids, there is only one gill, one osphradium and, in males, a penis. The radula is taenioglossan.

**Habitat**   The three species live under rocks or among corals, usually in the infralittoral, but also in the mesolittoral, zone.

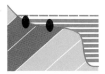

**Distribution**   It has already been mentioned that all three species are Central American—to be exact, *M. cervinetta* Panamic; *M. cervus* and *M. zebra* Caribbean.

## 187 MAURITIA HISTRIO
### History Cowrie

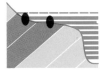

**Family** Cypraeidae

**Shell** Medium size (1 to 2¾ inches), fairly thick and robust, flattish conical spire; the body whorl only partly covers the preceding ones, leaving the apical whorls visible. The back is regularly spherical, the margins are never roughly parallel, the two ends are only moderately protruded, the base is slightly convex and has a callus that extends to the margin of the shell. The aperture is straight, the sides are parallel at the rear; they tend to diverge anteriorly and then draw in near the canal. The teeth are narrower than the interstices and extend very little. The background color is a grayish green, with two or three broad, transverse, chestnut-green bands; the entire back is covered by a network of polygonal, chestnut units. The marginal callus has dark-chestnut, round patches, the base is a chestnut or greenish gray, the teeth are chestnut.

**Body** The foot is dark gray, the distinct head has two black tentacles. The siphon is fringed and the chestnut-gray mantle lobes, when completely extended, enfold the shell and have numerous, short, conical papillae. The radula is taenioglossan.

**Habitat** Lives in shallow waters. Often found under stones in the infralittoral zone but also in tidal pools in the mesolittoral.

**Distribution** Indo-Pacific, confined to the Indian Ocean, not found in the Red Sea.

## 188 MAXWELLIA
### Maxwell Murexes (illustrated are St. Rosana Murex and Gem Murex)

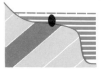

**Family** Muricidae

**Shell** Medium-small (1½ inches), quite thick, robust, flattish spire, rather long siphonal canal. The whorls are convex and the suture is deeply impressed. It is a characteristic of the genus to have five or six varices on each whorl, the free edge is bent backward, producing a stout spine on the shoulder, and this fuses to the varix of the preceding whorl. The aperture is oval, the outer lip is completely smooth internally, and the columellar lip has a light callus attached to body whorl. The color varies among the three known species of this genus; this is very apparent from the photographs. In the illustration are *M. santarosana* (Dall 1905), right, and *M. gemma* (Sowerby 1879), left. The operculum is horny with an apical nucleus.

**Body** Like all muricids, the foot is rather stout and truncated at the front. The head has a long retractile proboscis and two tentacles with an eye at the base of each. The rachidial tooth of the rachiglossan radula has five main cusps and some small accessory ones.

**Habitat** The species of this genus live on rocky or coarse detrital bodies in the infralittoral zone.

**Distribution** Of the three known species of *Maxwellia* the two illustrated ones live in the Californian Province, the other is from the Peruvian Province.

## 189 MEGATHURA CRENULATA
### Great Keyhole Limpet

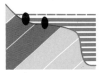

**Family** Fissurellidae

**Shell** Large size (2½ to 4 inches), secondarily symmetrical, moderately thick, ellipsoidal, flattened, a large apical hole equivalent to the series of holes in the shell of haliotids and the slit in the aperture lip of the pleurotomariids. The surface is scored by radial grooves that cross the highly impressed growth lines, producing a granular sculpture. Generally light hazel in color. The white porcellaneous inner surface is smooth except for a small swelling around the hole and the finely crenulated margin.

**Body** Like all fissurellids, it has many primitive characteristics—i.e., two gills, osphradia, auricles, and two nephridia of which the left one is reduced. The foot is enormously developed and is yellow. The mantle is black or dark chestnut and almost completely covers the shell. The radula is rhipidoglossan.

**Habitat** *M. crenulata* is a mesolittoral species, also found in the upper levels of the infralittoral zone, it lives on rocks and is attached to them by its large foot.

**Distribution** Confined to the Californian Province, Monterey, California, to Baja California.

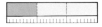

## 190 MONODONTA TURBINATA
### One-Toothed Turbin

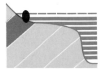

**Family** Trochidae

**Shell** Medium-small (1 inch), solid, moderately high conical spire, convex whorls, poorly marked incised suture, flattened base, no umbilicus, no canals. The sculpture consists of spiral belts, which become broader and lower from whorl to whorl. The base is covered by from seven to nine broad concentric bands. The growth lines are thin and often unnoticeable, on its median part the slightly oblique columella has a moderately extensive raised tooth, with a pearly sheen (characteristic of the genus *Monodonta*). The outer lip is sharp. The inside of the aperture is mother-of-pearl. The background color is pale—white, yellow, gray or greenish—with a series of red, brown, violet or blackish patches regularly arranged on each spiral band. It has a horny, yellowish operculum.

**Body** Grayish-green in color, with epipodial cirri. It has some primitive characters—i.e., two heart auricles (despite having one gill), two nephridia of different sizes. The radula is rhipidoglossan, with five roughly equal lateral teeth.

**Habitat** Rigid substrates, mesolittoral zone.

**Distribution** Lusitanian. Confined, in the Atlantic, to the southern waters of Portugal and the northern waters of Morocco, extending throughout the Mediterranean, except for the Black Sea.

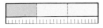

## 191 MURICOPSIS
### Hexagonal Murex and Aradas's Murex

**Family** Muricidae

**Shell** Medium or decidedly small (1 to 1 ½ inches), fairly thick and robust, high spire and moderately long siphonal canal, spindle-shaped. The whorls are not very convex, and the suture is barely incised. The aperture is ovoidal or pear-shaped, the outer lip is strongly toothed internally, and the columellar lip has a thin callus, which is not attached at all to the ventral surfaces of the body whorl but projects at right angles to it for a short distance. The axial sculpture consists of six to eight varices bearing blunt or sharp spines; the spiral one consists of quite large bands, the spines occurring where these cross the varices. The chestnut operculum is horny and has an apical nucleus. The illustration shows *M. aradasii* (left) and *m. oxytatus* (right).

**Body** As a whole, the foot is slimmer than in other muricids, generally whitish or cream in color. The rachidial tooth of the radula (rachiglossan) has seven cusps, the central one is larger than the others.

**Habitat** The species of this genus live on rocky or coarse detrital bottoms from the mesolittoral to the infralittoral zone.

**Distribution** *M. aradasii* is confined to the Mediterranean Sea (Lusitanian Province). *M. oxytatus* lives in the Caribbean Province.

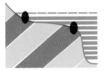

---

## 192 MYTILUS GALLOPROVINCIALIS
### Mediterranean Mussel

**Family** Mytilidae

**Shell** In size, 2 to 4 inches, equivalve and inequilateral, faintly triangular in shape, with pointed umbones. It has a very thin light-colored periostracum, which allows the blue-black shell color to show through. There are some very rare darkish brown forms with a few black lines fanning out from the apex. No sculpture. The ligament is external, posterior to the umbones, and rather long. The shell lacks a hinge (dysodont). The posterior muscle scar is very large, the anterior one is small and very close to the umbones. The pallial line is smoothly curved (integropalliate). The shell has an outer prismatic layer and an inner mother-of-pearl one. It is quite common to find little pearls, of paltry value, within the mantle.

**Body** It has a pair of gills, each of which is made up of two series of filaments, widely connected to form in all four series of lamellae (filibranch). The digitiform foot is very reduced. The byssus, which anchors the animal to rocks or other rigid substrates, is highly developed.

**Habitat** Gregarious, firmly attached to rigid substrates in the mesolittoral and infralittoral zones. It is eaten as food and it is intensively farmed in various Mediterranean regions.

**Distribution** A Mediterranean species that seems to extend into other Lusitanian areas, where it lives side by side with its more widely distributed relative *M. edulis*.

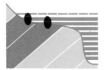

### 193 NERITA PELORONTA
### Bleeding Tooth

**Family** Neritidae

**Shell** Medium-small (¾ to 1½ inches), rather robust, very flattened spire, a spherical body whorl that covers a good part of the others. The sculpture is made up of blunt, very slightly raised, spiral ribs. The outer lip of the aperture is slightly thickened and has a small tooth at the top. The columellar lip has a callus, which covers part of the base of the shell and has one or two strong central teeth. Yellowish white with red or brownish tessellations, or lines. The aperture lips are yellowish except for an orangey-red patch at the center of the columellar callus; the tooth or teeth of the inner lip are white. The operculum is calcareous, orange inside, and externally partly reddish and smooth and partly bluish green and papillate.

**Body** Like all neritids, it has characteristics intermediate between the Archeogastropoda and the Mesogastropoda. It lacks an epipodium and has only one gill and one nephridium, but the heart has two auricles and the posterior section of the intestine crosses over the ventricle. The radula is rhipidoglossan. Males have a penis.

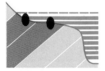

**Habitat** Exposed rocks in the mesolittoral and infralittoral zones.

**Distribution** Very common in the Caribbean Province: Southeast Florida, Bermuda and West Indies.

---

### 194 NERITA SCABRICOSTA
### Rough-Ribbed Nerite

**Family** Neritidae

**Shell** Medium size (1 to 1½ inches), very thick and robust, low spire, globular shape, regularly rounded, not very projecting whorls, suture slightly impressed. Lacks an umbilicus. The outer lip is thick, sharp and finely toothed on the inner surface. The inner lip is thickened, toward the aperture, has some large teeth, as well as being folded on to the columella forming a strong callus. The sculpture consists of very large spiral ribs, which are much broader than the gaps between them. Dark gray in color, except for inner surfaces of the aperture and the columellar callus, which are white. The operculum is calcareous, semicircular, grayish externally, with a granular surface; internally it has a small process, or apophysis, which is hinged under the columellar edge.

**Body** The foot is rather large, lacks an epipodium, a very distinct head that has two tentacles. A characteristic of neritids is that a single spherical chamber is formed within the shell through the restoration of the internal walls of the whorls. The radula is rhipidoglossan.

**Habitat** Like other neritids, this species lives in supralittoral rocks.

**Distribution** Confined to the Southern Californian and the Panamic provinces, Baja California to Ecuador.

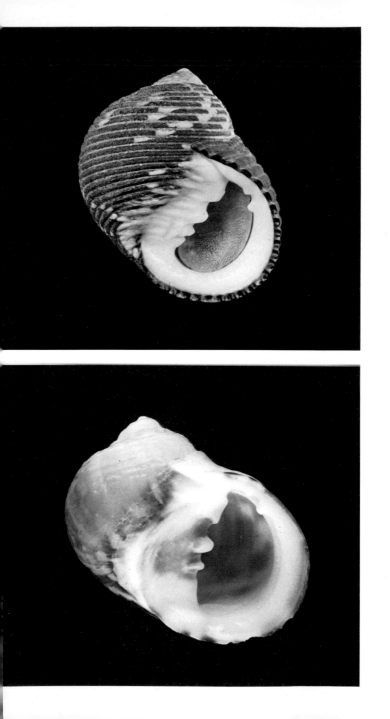

## 195 OCTOPUS VULGARIS
### Common Atlantic Octopus

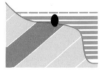

**Family** Octopodiidae

**Body** In size, up to 3 feet, with a radial spread of 7 feet. Shell absent throughout the order *Octopoda*. The head is rather large, with a pair of large eyes as complex as the eyes of vertebrates and a mouth that has a pair of strong jaws, like a parrot's beak. The foot is transformed into a large, very mobile funnel and eight equally long arms proximally linked by a membrane; these have two rows of suckers on their inner surface. The visceral spherical mass is enfolded by the mantle and lacks fins. Normally the animal moves by "walking" with its arms, but it can also "swim" by expelling a strong jet of water through its funnel. Very variable in color, depending on the conditions in which it finds itself; all skin divers are well aware of how easy it is to lose sight of an octopus through its ability to change color rapidly to match its background.

**Habitat** Benthonic; it lives on rigid substrates, generally infralittoral. Usually it hides itself in holes, which it then closes with some object that it finds on the bottom—i.e., a stone, a shell, et cetera.

**Distribution** Throughout the temperate Atlantic and extending into the Mediterranean.

## 196 OPEATOSTOMA PSEUDODON
### Thorn Latirus

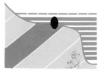

**Family** Fasciolariidae

**Shell** Medium size (1 to 1½ inches), fairly thick, solid, moderately high conical spire, very short and broad siphonal canal, spherical shape. The whorls are convex below the shoulder, but concave above it. The suture is barely incised. The aperture is ovoidal. The outer lip is tapered and has a distinctive, very long tooth near the anterior end. The columellar lip has a thin callus. The sculpture consists of very thin spiral ridges, some of which are fused, forming very slightly raised, almost equidistant bands. Except for the bands, which are dark brown, it is white in color. The periostracum is chestnut, thin and rather persistent. The operculum is horny, chestnut, and has an apical nucleus.

**Body** It has a well-developed foot, which is truncated anteriorly. The distinct head bears two tentacles with an eye at the base of each. The mantle siphon is moderately long. The mantle cavity contains the gill, the osphradium and, in males, the penis. The radula is rachiglossan.

**Habitat** It lives hidden between or under rocks usually in the upper levels of the infralittoral zone.

**Distribution** Panamic and Peruvian provinces, Gulf of California to Peru.

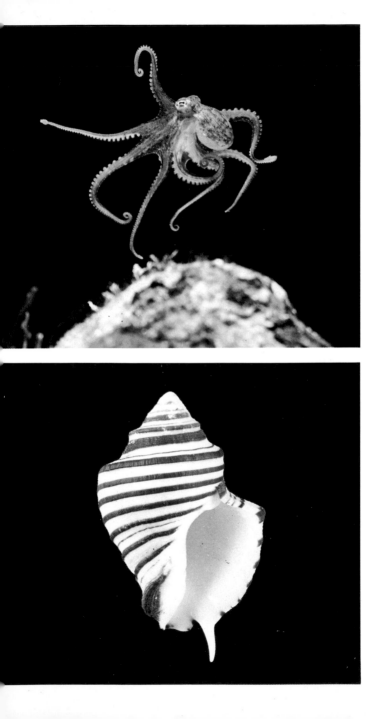

## 197 OSTREA EDULIS
### Edible Oyster

**Family** Ostreidae
**Shell** Medium-large (3 to 5 inches), rather thick and robust valves, shape varying according to the substrate that it rests on or adheres to, but tending to circular. Sometimes it has two not very prominent ears at the sides of the umbones; the posterior one is more developed than the anterior one. The right valve (the upper one) is flat or slightly convex, while the left one, which can be quite extensively stuck to the substrate, is markedly convex. The sculpture consists of concentric lamellae on both the right and left valves, but on the left they are less prominent and are crossed by radial ribs. The rather large ligament is external and is inserted on to two triangular "ligamentary" areas. There is no hinge. There is only one muscle scar inside the valve (monomyarian), and the pallial line is smoothly curved (integropalliate).
**Body** The foot is poorly developed, like all sessile species. There is a pair of gills, each consisting of two series of lamellae, extensively fused by interlamellar junctions (eulamellibranch). It incubates its eggs inside the mantle cavity.
**Habitat** Very varied. It can live on sandy, muddy, fairly coarse detrital and rocky bottoms in the mesolittoral and infralittoral zones.
**Distribution** Celtic and Lusitanian provinces, including the Black Sea.

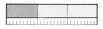

## 198 OVATELLA MYOSOTIS
### Mouse-Eared Marsh Snail

**Family** Melampidae
**Shell** Small (⅓ inch), rather thin, light but not fragile, fairly high conical spire, whorls weakly convex, suture faintly impressed, rather elongated ovoidal shape. The aperture is almond-shaped, not very wide; the outer lip is flared anteriorly, sometimes thickened on the inside and toothed. The columellar lip can have three folds, one basal, one parietal and one in its upper third. The surface almost always has an irregular axial grooving and is lightly ribbed, especially on the body whorl. The embryonic whorls have stippled spiral grooves. Reddish brown or violet in color.
**Body** Variable in color, generally gray but also white. The head may be uniformly blackish and has two cylindrical, slightly extensible tentacles and anteriorly two other tentacular protrusions. The penis is short and broad. Like all pulmonates it is hermaphroditic. The radula has a very large number of rows of teeth.
**Habitat** Hidden in cracks in rocks or under stones or buried in damp ground in the supralittoral zone.
**Distribution** An Atlantic species, found in the southern Boreal, Celtic, Lusitanian, Carolinan and Caribbean provinces.

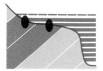

**PATELLA CAERULEA**
**Blue Patella**

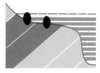

**Family** Patellidae

**Shell** Medium size (1 ¼ inches), moderately thick, fairly high, conical spire, roughly central apex, ovoidal to polygonal margins. The sculpture is made up of small radial furrows that disappear in some forms or give way to quite strong radial ribs in others. The concentric sculpture consists of growth lines and is usually faint. The margin is sharp, variable in color, from whitish forms with chestnut rays or spots to reddish or grayish forms with irregular white patches. However color and sculpture are almost always hidden by incrustations. The color of the inner surface also varies, from whitish to a shiny gray with blue highlights (the sky blue of the name) and indistinct darker-gray rays.

**Body** It has a large discoidal grayish or orange foot. The prominent head has two tentacles. The true gills are replaced by a row of secondary gills of mantle origin, arranged in a semicircle in the rear part of the mantle cavity. The radula is docoglossan.

**Habitat** Mesolittoral rocks or the upper levels of the infralittoral zones; some examples can be found at greater depths.

**Distribution** Lusitanian, mainly mediterranean. *P. c. pontica* is found in the Black Sea.

## 200 PATELLA COCHLEAR
### Snail Patella

**Family**  Patellidae
**Shell**  Medium size (1 1/5 inches), solid, low pear-shaped, the anterior end is compressed laterally and projects out. The sculpture, which is often hidden by incrustations or worn away, consists of strong radial ribs, these vary in breadth and length; these ribs produce a deeply corrugated margin. The irregular growth lines cross the radial sculpture giving a certain roughness to the shell. The color of the surface of the shell varies from white to yellow brown. Internally it is white with lead-gray highlights at the margins, reddish brown edged with violet in the center.
**Body**  Foot discoidal. Distinct head with two short tentacles. A row of secondary gills, as in *P. caerulea*. The radula is docoglossan.
**Habitat**  Mesolittoral rocks, or at the farthest the upper levels of the infralittoral zone. They are so numerous in some areas that they cover entire stretches of coast. Young individuals are often found attached to larger adult individuals.
**Distribution**  Confined to the South African Province.

## 201 PATELLA LATICOSTATA
### Wide-Ribbed Patella

**Family**  Patellidae
**Shell**  Large size (3 inches or more), very solid, roughly ovate, variable height, the apex blends into the anterior third. The sculpture consists of coarse radial ribs of variable width, those that reach the apex are called primary ribs, the others secondary or tertiary according to their length. The growth lines are almost invisible. The external coloration of radial chestnut stripes can be seen only in young individuals, as adults are frequently worn and encrusted. Very often shells have oval hollows, caused by the acmaeid *Patelloida nigrosulcata*. The inner surface is porcellaneous, the color varies according to the area; the central part is whitish or yellow brown, often surrounded by an orange band, round this the shell is milk-white and at the periphery there is a narrow band of dark chestnut spots.
**Body**  Like other *Patella* sp., it has a discoidal foot, a distinct head with two tentacles and a row of secondary mantle gills arranged in a semicircle in the rear of the mantle cavity. The radula is docoglossan.
**Habitat**  Rocky surfaces in the infralittoral zone.
**Distribution**  Confined to the western part of the Australian Province.

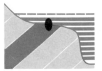

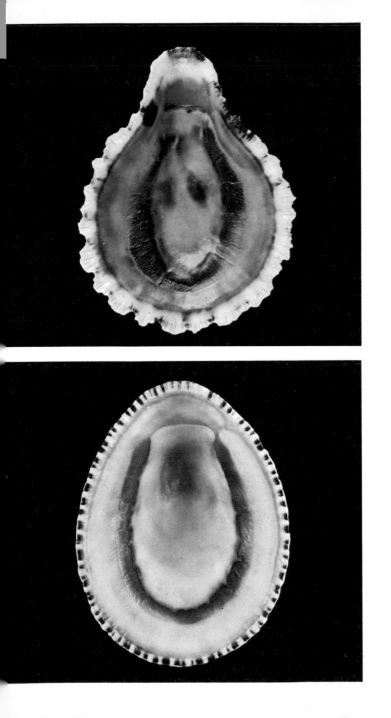

## PETRICOLA LITHOPHAGA
### Rock-eating Petricola

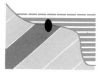

**Family** Petricolidae
**Shell** Medium small (1½ inches), fragile, varying in shape according to the substratum, rather swollen, equivalve and inequilateral. It has a grayish-brown periostracum, which hides the milk-white color of the shell; in some cases there are radial chestnut stripes, restricted to the rear part of the valves. The sculpture consists of radial ridges, and because of the large growth furrows, the ridges are not straight. The ligament is external. The heterodont hinge has three cardinal teeth on the left valve, but only two on the right one. The two muscle scars are roughly equal (dimyarian, isomyarian). The pallial line has a deep sinus (sinopalliate). Basically the shell has a crossed-lamellae structure.
**Body** It has a pair of gills, each gill consisting of two series of lamellae extensively fused by interlamellar junctions (eulamellibranch). The foot is well developed, and the siphons are rather long.
**Habitat** Infralittoral, it lives in cracks in the rocks or in holes that it bores. For this reason, the shell varies in shape and is often irregular.
**Distribution** Exclusively Lusitanian.

---

## PINCTADA IMBRICATA
### Pearl Oyster

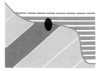

**Family** Pteriidae
**Shell** Medium-large (up to 3 inches), inequivalve and inequilateral, vaguely resembles a wing in shape. It has two ears. The posterior is more developed than the anterior. The coloration is very variable, from white through all the shades of yellow, green, red and chestnut, to almost pitch black, almost always there are dark-chestnut rays, frequently broken by wavy whitish lines. The valves bear concentric leaved lamellae and have many spiny processes, particularly prominent on the ventral and posterior margins. The ligament is external and posterior to the umbones. Young individuals have some rudimentary toothlike processes, but these are completely missing in adults. The species is monomyarian and integropalliate. The insides of the valves have a shiny layer of mother-of-pearl.
**Body** The gills, fused to the mantle, consist of two series of filaments each, widely connected, to form four series of lamellae (filibranch). The well developed foot secretes a strong byssus, which emerges through a deep byssal sinus in the right valve. It produces small but valuable pearls.
**Habitat** It lives attached to rigid substrates—rocks, zostera leaves or the valves of other members of the same species.
**Distribution** Widely distributed in warm tropical waters. Since the opening of the Suez Canal it has entered the Mediterranean and is well established in its southern water.

## 204  PISANIA MACULOSA
### Spotted Pisania

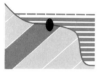

**Family**  Buccinidae
**Shell**  Small size (¾ inch), very thick, robust, fairly high coni
cal spire, elongated ovoidal shape, whorls only weakly convex
and suture barely incised. The aperture is an elongated oval
the outer lip is tapered, almost sharp, with folds on the inne
surface; the columellar lip has a very slight callus; anteriorly
this is thickened and has three or four teeth, posteriorly it has
one strong tooth. The sculpture consists of very thin, unequally
spaced spiral grooves and small bands confined to the anterio
part of the body whorl. It is variable in color, grayish or chest
nut, with a darkish axial flaming and patches arranged along
spiral bands. The inside of the aperture is violet with a thin
white band in the middle of the outer lip. The operculum is
horny, nail-shaped, light chestnut, with a central black zone
shaped like an elongated triangle and an apical nucleus.
**Body**  See the descriptions of the other buccinids. Black with
yellowish spots. Rachiglossan radula.
**Habitat**  It lives on rocks or, more often, hidden beneath
them, in the infralittoral zone.
**Distribution**  Rather common in the Lusitanian Province.

---

## 205  PROPUSTULARIA SURINAMENSIS
### Surinam Cowrie

**Family**  Cypraeidae
**Shell**  Medium size (1 to 1½ inches), fairly robust and solid
rather low conical spire, the body whorl is elongated-spherica
and completely covers and hides the preceding ones (convo
lute). The ends are markedly protruded, even beaked. The ap
erture is narrow, smoothly curved over its entire length. The
outer and columellar lips have calluses that cover the whole
base up to the margins of the shell, where they sharply tape
and disappear. The columellar teeth are not extensive, the la
bial ones extend across about half the outer lip. The base is
brownish-orange, tending to fade toward the aperture; the
teeth are orange. The back is orange, and it has irregularly ar
ranged darker-orange patches; these patches never occur on
the areas above the two ends. Like all cypraeids it does no
have an operculum.
**Body**  There is no information in the literature on the colora
tion of this rare cypraeid or on whether the mantle lobes have
papillae. The mantle cavity contains one gill, one osphradium
and, in males, the penis. The radula is taenioglossan.
**Habitat**  Not known. Possibly rigid substrates, probably
mainly circalittoral, but also infralittoral.
**Distribution**  The few known examples have come mostly
from the southern Caribbean Province, southeast Florida to
Brazil.

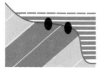

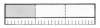

## 206 PSEUDOCHAMA GRYPHINA
### Left-Handed Jewel Box

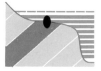

**Family** Chamidae

**Shell** Small size (¾ inch), very robust, inequivalve and in equilateral. The right (lower) valve is attached to the substrate and is strongly convex, while the left (upper) valve is free and almost flat. On the other hand, the related genus *Chama* fixed to the substrate by the left valve. Rather variable in colo ation, generally whitish. The sculpture of the upper valve con sists of highly developed, sinuous and often deeply incise concentric lamellae. The ligament is external, and the hinge pachyodont. The inner surface of the valves, whose edges ar finely crenulated, has two roughly similar muscle scars (d myarian, isomyarian) and the pallial line is smoothly curve (integropalliate).

**Body** Like all cemented forms the foot is greatly reduced. has a pair of gills, each of which consists of two series of la mellae extensively fused by interlamellar junctions (eulame libranch).

**Habitat** It belongs to the epifauna—i.e., the fauna that live on the surface of the substrate—in the infralittoral zone. O top of and beneath rocks, even in shallow water. The large forms, usually in fairly exposed positions, are often encruste and have worn concentric lamellae.

**Distribution** Mediterranean coasts and in the Atlantic, th southern coasts of Spain, Portugal and Madeira.

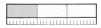

---

## 207 PUPERITA PUPA
### Zebra Nerite

**Family** Neritidae

**Shell** Small size (⅓ to ½ inch), thin, not fragile, flattish spire spherical, the body whorl covers much of the preceding ones the apex is often eroded. The aperture is semicircular. Th outer lip has a thin sharp edge, but it is slightly thickened from its margin. The columellar lip has a callus that covers large part of the base of the shell. The surface is smooth b not glossy. Lacks sculpture and is covered by a very thi glassy, yellow periostracum. Whitish with black axial streaks o bands arranged as zigzags. The columellar callus is yellow e even orange. The operculum is calcareous and yellow.

**Body** Like all neritids, it resorbs the internal walls of th whorls, forming an undivided, spherical cavity. The foot lack an epipodium. The head has two long tentacles with one of th ocular peduncles joined to the base of each. Inside the mant cavity, there is a single gill, one osphradium and, in males, penis. The heart has two auricles, and the posterior portion the intestine crosses over its ventricle. The radula rhipidoglossan.

**Habitat** It lives in brackish waters on rigid substrates in th supralittoral zone.

**Distribution** Fairly common in the islands of the Caribbea Province, southeast Florida, Bermuda and the West Indies.

## 208 RAPANA BEZOAR
**Bezoar Rapana**

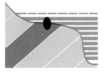

**Family** Thaididae
**Shell** Medium size (2 inches), fairly thick and robust, low conical spire, short canal and a wide aperture, spherical overall shape. The whorls are very convex and the suture deeply incised. The umbilicus is surrounded by a highly developed swelling. The outer lip of the aperture is solid and has internal folds, the columellar lip has a thin callus that is attached to a small part of the ventral surface of the body whorl. The sculpture consists of spiral ridges of irregular thickness, two of these, one on the shoulder and one just under it, are more prominent. There are also axial lamellae, and these bear small plates where they cross the spiral ribs. Hazel in color except for the aperture, which is white. The operculum is horny, chestnut, and has a marginal nucleus.
**Body** The foot is very large, truncated at the front and elongated at the rear. The head has two long tentacles with an eye at the base of each, and a retractile proboscis. The mantle cavity contains a gill, an osphradium and, in males, a long and fairly thick penis. The radula is rachiglossan.
**Habitat** Various substrates in the infralittoral zone.
**Distribution** Confined to the Japonic Province.

## 209 RISSOINA BRUGUIEREI
**Bruguiere's Risso**

**Family** Rissoidae
**Shell** Small size (⅛ inch), thick and robust, very high conical spire (turreted), moderately convex whorls, impressed suture. The base lacks an umbilicus. The aperture lips are continuous and edged externally by a slightly upward-angled varix. The sculpture is made up of slightly angled and winding axial ribs that are narrower than the gaps between them; there are also thin spiral ridges, which are more prominent in the gaps between the ribs, but they also cross over them. Milk-white in color. There is a horny operculum with a roughly central nucleus.
**Body** It has all the characteristics already listed for other rissoid species—i.e., a long and narrow foot, tapered at the rear, a distinct head with two tentacles and an eye at the base of each. The mantle cavity contains a gill, which has only a small number of branchial lamellae, an osphradium and, behind the right tentacle, in males, a penis. The radula is taenioglossan, its rachidial tooth has two basal, accessory cusps and its lateral teeth have two long lateral appendices.
**Habitat** Rigid substrates in the infralittoral zone.
**Distribution** *R. bruguierei* is mainly Mediterranean, but the genus *Rissoina* is widely distributed in tropical seas.

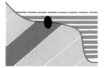

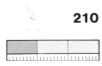

## 210 SIPHONARIA SIRIUS
### Sirius False Limpet

**Family** Siphonariidae
**Shell** Small size (1 inch), moderately thick, rather light, not fragile, limpetlike, flattened, oval outline and toothed margin. The sculpture consists of a variable number of strong radial ribs (usually six), the secondary ridges between the ribs are much smaller and are always narrower than the gaps between them. Both kinds of rib project beyond the margins of the shell, thus giving it a star shape. Dark brown, even black, except for the ribs, which are white. Internally the external shell color shows through at the periphery, while it is whitish at the center.
**Body** The foot is large, ovoidal and muscular. The distinct head lacks tentacles. The mantle cavity is very wide and contains an osphradium, as well as a developed gill, even though it is a pulmonate. It has a hermaphrodite gonad and a single genital aperture. The radula has small rachidil teeth and a lot of lateral teeth.
**Habitat** Like all siphonariids, it lives attached to rigid substrates in the mesolittoral zone.
**Distribution** Confined to the Japonic Province.

## 211 SPONDYLUS PRINCEPS
### Prince Thorny Oyster

**Family** Spondylidae
**Shell** Large (up to 5 inches), and thick, inequivalve and in equilateral. As with all spondylids, their right valve is convex the region of the outer surface close to the umbones is ce mented to the substrate. The left valve is free and is almost fla or moderately convex. There are two triangular ears at the sides of the umbones. The coloration varies from white to red in white forms the umbones are often intense pink. Large radia ribs, bearing flat, at times spatula-shaped, spines, extend over the surface and alternate with thinner ribs. Between the rib there are fine grooves formed by overlapping scales. The liga ment is internal, roughly trapezoidal in section, born by a ro bust chondrophore. The hinge is isodont. There is only on muscle scar (monomyarian). The pallial line is smoothly curve (integropalliate). The shell has layers of calcite externally an aragonite lamellae internally.
**Body** As in many sessile forms the foot is reduced; here it i circular and flattened. Each of the two gills consists of two se ries of filaments widely connected to form, in all, four series o lamellae.
**Habitat** Rocks or other rigid substrates, in the infralittora zone.
**Distribution** Panamic Province, Gulf of California to Panam

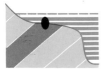

## 212 TALPARIA CINEREA
### Atlantic Gray Cowrie

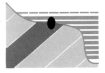

**Family** Cypraeidae

**Shell** Small size (¾ to 1½ inches), solid, spherical, the end protrude a little, the body whorl almost completely enfolds th preceding ones, allowing them to project slightly (involute). Th back is regularly convex, as is the base, which has a larg callus that extends to the margins of the shell, which are there fore heavily thickened. The aperture is rather narrow, is regu larly curved, and has strong teeth; these are as wide as th gaps between them, but they extend only very slightly on bot the columellar and outer sides. The back is a grayish hazel wit pinkish shading and two lighter transverse bands. The bas and marginal calluses are pinky cream. The sides are densel covered by fine blackish dots.

**Body** The whole body is a dark chestnut, the head's two ten tacles, with an eye at the base of each, are black. The mantl lobes enfold the shell when completely extended and hav densely packed conical papillae. The radula is taenioglossan

**Habitat** Found on both soft bottoms and rocky bottoms under stones or among corals. Always infralittoral.

**Distribution** The Caribbean Province, North Carolina to Flor ida and the West Indies, Bermuda, and Brazil.

## 213 TECTARIUS MURICATUS
### Beaded Periwinkle

**Family** Littorinidae

**Shell** Small size (½ to 1 inch), thick and robust, high conica spire; its height is about one and a half times its width. Th whorls are slightly convex, the suture is incised, the base lack an umbilicus. The outer lip is thin and sharp, the columella side is slightly broadened, and the columella has a small callu The sculpture consists of ten ridges (on the body whorl); thes are narrower than the gaps between them and are made up rather widely spaced nodules. Externally the shell is ash gra and dark chestnut internally. Like all the subfamily *Tectariina* the horny operculum is paucispiral, the nucleus is slight shifted toward the columellar edge.

**Body** It has all the typical littorinid characteristics: the foot not very developed, is truncated at the front; the very distin head has two tentacles with an eye at the base of each. Unlik the other littorinids, *T. muricatus* has a penis that is thin and si uated behind the right tentacle. The eggs are laid singly floating egg capsules; these are rather flattened cylinder rounded at both ends.

**Habitat** Confined to supralittoral rocks.

**Distribution** North-central Caribbean Province, South Flo ida, West Indies, Bermuda.

## 214   TEGULA FASCIATA
### Smooth Atlantic Tegula

**Family**   Trochidae

**Shell**   Small (½ to ¾ inch); solid, moderately high spire, the whorls are rounded, slightly hollowed at the top, incised suture, convex base with a deep umbilicus. The columella has two teeth at the base, the outer lip is rather large, and the aperture lacks any canal (holostoma). Internally there is a beautiful layer of mother-of-pearl. The surface is smooth. The background color is extremely variable, from yellowish to reddish, grayish and olive green, with countless white, red, chestnut or black spots, often arranged in spiral lines. Examples with a lighter-colored spiral band at the periphery of the body whorl are common. The umbilicus and the basal zone around it are white. The operculum is horny, round and yellowish.

**Body**   Like the other trochids, it retains many primitive characters. The heart has two auricles despite there being only one gill; there are two nephridia, the left is reduced. There are long tentacles on the laterodorsal fold (epipodium) of the large foot. The head is very distinct and has a pair of tentacles with an eye at the base of each. The radula is rhipidoglossan.

**Habitat**   Rigid substrates. It lives under stones in the lower part of the mesolittoral zone or in the upper parts of the infralittoral.

**Distribution**   Caribbean, extending from the southern tip of Florida to Brazil.

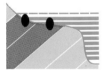

---

## 215   THAIS
### Rock Shells (illustrated are Girdled Rock Shell and Florida Rock Shell)

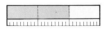

**Family**   Thaididae

**Shell**   Usually medium or medium-large (1½ to 3 inches), thick, solid spire, almost flat or low, very short siphonal canal, spherical or elongated-spherical overall shape. The aperture is ovoidal or pear-shaped. The outer lip is quite thick with longitu-dinal internal folds, and the columellar lip is smooth. The sculpture is mainly spiral, usually very strong ribs or thin ridges, sometimes with fairly marked nodules, especially on the shoulder of the whorls. The axial sculpture is usually confined to thin growth lines. The color is variable. The aperture is usually a different color, sometimes rather bright. The opercu-lum is horny and has a lateral nucleus.

**Body**   The well-developed foot is truncated anteriorly and rounded at the rear. The distinct head has two tentacles, an eye at the base of each. The mantle siphon is very short. As well as the gill and the osphradium, the mantle cavity has a hy-pobranchial gland, which produces a purple secretion and, in males, a long penis. The radula is rachiglossan.

**Habitat**   All the species are normally found on rocky coasts in the mesolittoral or upper levels of the supralittoral zone.

**Distribution**   Illustrated are: *T. cingulifera* (L.1758), left, found in the South African Province, and *T. haemostoma flor-idana* (Conrad 1837), right, in the Caribbean Province.

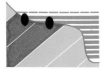

## 216 TRUNCATELLA SUBCYLINDRICA
### Subcylindrical Truncatella

**Family** Truncatellidae

**Shell** Very small (about 1/5 inch), high spire, cylindrical-conical, the whorls are only moderately swollen, and the suture is very incised; the base lacks an umbilicus, the outer lip is uninterrupted and externally strengthened by a small varix. There may or may not be sculpture in different individuals in the same population; where present it consists of numerous axial ribs. A characteristic of this species is that it loses the apical whorls during growth (giving it its generic name), therefore adult shells are roughly cylindrical, and hence the specific name. In the illustration, from left to right are, the juvenile form, the adult form without sculpture and with sculpture. Whitish or sometimes yellowish in color. It has a horny yellowish, paucispiral operculum with a roughly central nucleus.

**Body** Developed foot, very distinct head with two tentacles and an eye at the base of each. The mantle cavity has one gill and one osphradium; these are retained in terrestrial truncatellids. The lateral tooth of the taenioglossan radula has a short lateral appendix.

**Habitat** It lives on stones, pebbles and decomposing vegetation in the supralittoral zone. Occasionally found in the mesolittoral.

**Distribution** Lusitanian; confined to the Mediterranean.

## 217 UMBRACULUM MEDITERRANEUM
### Mediterranean Umbrella Shell

**Family** Umbraculidae

**Shell** Medium size (3 inches), limpetlike, very thin, fragile, light, roughly central apex; thin and sharp margins, which are smaller than the mollusk that secretes them. No sculpture except the almost imperceptible growth lines. The shell is yellowish, with the apex and surrounding area chestnut-colored.

**Body** The mantle has a fringed margin and covers part of the shell. The foot lacks parapodia and is larger than the shell, very thick, fleshy, and the dorsal surface has large warts. The head is always hidden beneath the shell and has two filiform tentacles with sessile eyes at their base. The gill is very large, on the right-hand side, under the shell, pointing backward as in all opisthobranchs. The mantle cavity is rather reduced. The radula has a rachidial tooth and many lateral teeth.

**Habitat** It creeps over rigid substrates in the infralittoral or, more rarely, in the circalittoral zone.

**Distribution** As the specific name suggests, this Lusitanian species is confined to the Mediterranean.

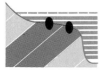

## 218  VITULARIA SALEBROSA
### Panamaic Vitularia

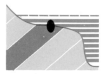

**Family**  Muricidae
**Shell**  Medium size (2½ inches), moderately thick, robust, fairly light, short spire, long and broad siphonal canal, overall appearance is spindle-shaped. The whorls are angular, almost keeled, the suture is deeply impressed. The aperture is pear-shaped, the outer lip is strongly thickened, and inside it has twelve to sixteen robust and closely packed teeth. The columellar lip has a thin callus, which is fixed to part of the ventral surface of the body whorl. The axial sculpture consists of six or seven sharp lamellar varices, the spiral is a blunt keel on the shoulder of the whorls. The whole surface is covered by microscopic nodules of irregular size and arrangement. It is dark chestnut with four or five even darker bands. The internal surface of the aperture is white. The operculum is horny.
**Body**  There is no information on the morphology of this species. Presumably it differs from other muricids only in details. The rachiglossan radula has a rachidial tooth with seven roughly equal cusps.
**Habitat**  It lives under rocks in the infralittoral zone.
**Distribution**  Mainly Panamic Province, as far as the Galapagos Islands.

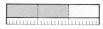

---

## 219  ZONARIA ANNETTAE
### Annette's Cowrie

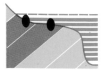

**Family**  Cypraeidae
**Shell**  Medium size (1 to 1½ inches), fairly thin and light, elongated roughly cylindrical; anterior end slightly protrudes but the posterior end does not. The body whorl completely enfolds and conceals the preceding ones (convolute). The back is regularly convex, the base only very slightly so. There is a conspicuous basal callus, which extends on to the margins, forming a light thickening, then tapering on the sides. The aperture is fairly wide and straight, except for the slightly curved posterior portion. It has thin well-spaced teeth on both sides of the aperture; these are not extensive. The back has a grayish background color, with four transverse, chestnut bands; this color is almost completely concealed by a dense array of dark-chestnut spots. The base is pink chestnut, as is the marginal callus, which has well-spaced chestnut patches. The teeth are whitish.
**Body**  The mantle is light hazel with fairly extensive chestnut patches. The tentacles are dark chestnut. The mantle is thin and has many rather long cylindrical papillae. The siphon is weakly fringed at its free end. The radula is taenioglossan.
**Habitat**  It lives under stones in the mesolittoral zone or in the upper levels of the infralittoral zone.
**Distribution**  The Californian, Panamic and Peruvian provinces; there are large gaps in its range.

## 220 ZONARIA PYRUM
### Pear Cowrie

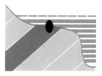

**Family** Cypraeidae

**Shell** Medium-small (1 inch), pear-shaped, rather light but not fragile, the body whorl completely covers and conceals the preceding ones (convolute). The back is regularly convex, the base is poorly so. The ends project a little. The aperture is fairly broad, curved at the rear, and has moderately extensive teeth on both lips. The background color of the shell is a reddish chestnut, with two yellowish transverse bands and an array of spots varying from yellowish to chestnut all over the back. The margins and base are also reddish chestnut, but the teeth are creamy-white.

**Body** The foot is whitish with a gray reticulation. The distinct head has two white tentacles with a short ocular peduncle at the base of each. The siphon is fringed; the mantle lobes, thin transparent and whitish, and they bear short cylindroconical papillae. The radula is taenioglossan.

**Habitat** It lives on Posidonias and on top of and beneath stones in the infralittoral zone.

**Distribution** Lusitanian and West African provinces.

---

## 221 ZONARIA SPADICEA
### Chestnut Cowrie

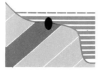

**Family** Cypraeidae

**Shell** Medium size (1 to 2 inches), fairly light, elongated ovate, the two ends protrude. The body whorl completely enfolds and hides the preceding ones (convolute). The back and base are regularly convex. The base has a thickening that extends to the margins of the shell, forms a lateral callus and tapers off on the back. The aperture is moderately broad, the margins are almost parallel at the rear, diverging a little at the front. The labial and columellar teeth are quite strong, little narrower than the gaps between them, extending very little on the columellar side and not at all on the labial side. The coloration consists of a brilliant chestnut patch that covers almost all the dorsal surface; this patch is edged with an irregular band that darkens to a very dark brown and then becomes yellow. The base is whitish and the marginal callus is grayish.

**Body** Brilliant orange. The two lobes of the mantle, which when completely expanded can enfold the shell, have rather short and stout, cream papillae. The radula is taenioglossan.

**Habitat** Unlike other cypraeids, it lives in the open among seaweeds or on stones at various depths in the infralittoral zone.

**Distribution** Confined to the Californian Province—Monterey, California to Cerros Island, Baja California.

# CORAL DWELLERS

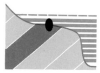

# GENUS AMORIA
## Amoria Volutes (illustrated are Waved Volute, Damon's Volute and Channeled Volute)

**Family**  Volutidae

**Shell**  Medium or large size (2 to 5½ inches for illustrated species), fairly thin and light but solid, conical spire, usually high, varying in shape from an elongated sphere to markedly elongated. The whorls are moderately convex; the body whorl is large and enfolds much of the preceding one, the suture is barely incised or, sometimes, is canaliculated. The aperture is long, the outer lip can have a tapered edge, be bordered by a light external swelling or be thickened internally by a callus. The columellar lip has numerous strong folds, sometimes there is a callus. No sculpture. Color and patterning vary greatly. No periostracum or operculum. The illustration shows *A. undulata* (bottom), *A. damonii* (top right), *A. canaliculata* (top left).

**Body**  Distinguished by very beautiful and striking colors and patterns. The foot is large, anteriorly divided by a longitudinal furrow; the head is distinct, has two lobes lateral to the tentacles with an eye at the base of each. The mantle siphon has two roughly similar basal appendices. The modified rachiglossan radula has a single series of monocuspid and Y-shaped rachidial teeth.

**Habitat**  The members of the genus *Amoria* generally live on coral or sandy infralittoral bottoms.

**Distribution**  All the species of this genus live mainly in Australian waters.

## 223 ANGARIA MELANACANTHA
### Black-Tankard Angaria

**Family**  Trochidae

**Shell**  Medium size (2 inches), fairly thick, moderately high spire, deep and wide umbilicus. The aperture lips are continuous, with a striking internal layer of mother-of-pearl. This species (synonym *A. imperialis*) is especially elegant with its long, thin file of spines set on the laterosuperior margins of the whorls. The sculpture is made up of spiral lamellar bands, which extend over the whole surface. Some of these bands—one laterosuperior, two lateral and three interior—have lamellae that have been transformed into spoutlike spiny processes. The growth lines are very fine. The base color of the shell is a violet pink while the lamellae and spiny processes are a dark chestnut, tending to greenish at the ends. There is a dark chestnut, fairly persistent periostracum. The operculum is round, flattened, multispiral (i.e., the spiral has many turns), and there is a central nucleus (the start of the spiral).

**Body**  No detailed information about this species, but presumably, like other *Angaria* sp., it has a large foot with a laterodorsal fold (epipodium) carrying long tentacles. The radula is rhipidoglossan with large rachidial teeth, five almost identical laterals and not very many marginals.

**Habitat**  It lives on rigid substrates, both rocks and coral formations in the infralittoral zone.

**Distribution**  Indo-Pacific Province; appears to be restricted to the Philippines.

## 224 ASTRAEA CAELATA
### Carved Star Shell

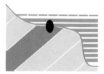

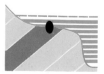

**Family**  Turbinidae

**Shell**  Medium size (2 to 3 inches), rather thick and robust, high conical spire, height almost equals width. The whorls are convex, the suture very incised and the base flat. The sculpture consists of numerous spiral bands, up to ten on the body whorl, and radial ribs of different sizes, usually two or three thinner ones between two double-thick ones. Where these two sculptures cross there are short, stout, spiny scales. Also prominent, especially on the base, between the spiral ribs, are some thin-growth lamellae. The coloration varies, usually yellowish white or yellow pink, with indistinct greenish, brown or reddish irregular patches of tessellations. The operculum is calcareous, very often white with a very convex outer surface.

**Body**  Cream with brownish flaming. The foot has a marginal fold with long cirri. The distinct head has two tentacles with a pit eye at the base of each. The mantle cavity has a single gill and an osphradium, but the heart has two auricles.

**Habitat**  Infralittoral rocks.

**Distribution**  Moderately common, lives in the Caribbean Province, Southeast Florida and the West Indies.

## 225 ASTRAEA CALCAR
### Spurred Star Shell

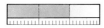

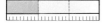

**Family** Turbinidae
**Shell** Medium size (3 inches), moderately thick and robust, with a rather variable regular conical spire, the height may be only half the breadth or equal it, the whorls are convex, suture impressed, base flattened, lacking an umbilicus. The aperture is pointed downward and forms a not very acute angle with the axis of the shell. The outer lip is thin and sharp, the lower parts of the lips are toothed. The sculpture is variable, consisting mainly of nodular slanting ribs that end at the base of the whorls in spiny spoutlike processes, often very pronounced. The base has lamellar, or leaved, spiral bands. The color can be white, yellow or pink, the spines are usually greenish. The columella is an intense bluish green, as is the calcareous operculum, which is ovoidal, paucispiral, with a lateral nucleus and strongly convex on the outer surface.
**Body** Well-developed foot, truncated anteriorly, has a tentacled epipodium. The very distinct head has two tentacles. There is only one gill and one osphradium. The radula is rhipidoglossan, with the second marginal tooth more developed than the others.
**Habitat** Coral formations, in the mid-reef section.
**Distribution** Indo-Pacific Province, restricted to Pacific coasts.

---

## 226 BISTOLIDA STOLIDA
### Stolid Cowrie

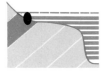

**Family** Cypraeidae
**Shell** Small size (1 inch), roughly cylindrical to pear-shaped, rather light. The body whorl completely enfolds the preceding ones, hiding them (convolute). The area corresponding to the apex is slightly sunken. The ends protrude, even beaked in some forms, especially in those from New Caledonia. The base is greatly convex, the aperture is slightly and smoothly curved, not very narrow, with fairly large teeth that extend in some forms over almost all the columellar and outer lips. The back is greenish with at least one central reddish-chestnut patch and small spots of the same color, especially toward the margins. The margins are a light reddish chestnut darkening toward the ends. The base is whitish. The illustration shows the typical form on the left and the beaked form, thought to be melanistic, from New Caledonia.
**Body** Foot, head and mantle lobes are extremely thin and lack papillae. The radula is taenioglossan.
**Habitat** It lives among corals in the midreef section of the infralittoral zone.
**Distribution** An Indo-Pacific species; it has never been found along the coasts of Continental Asia.

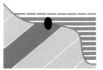

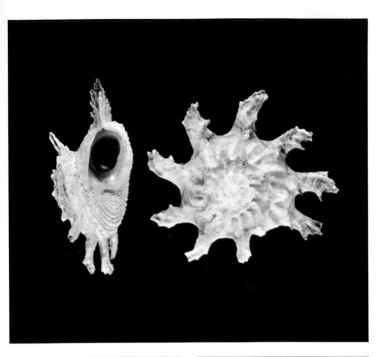

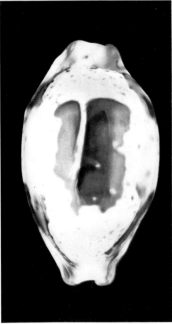
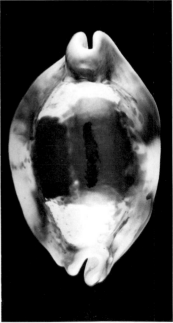

## 227 CANTHARUS SANGUINOLENTUS
### Bloody-Lined Cantharus

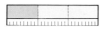

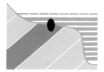

**Family** Buccinidae

**Shell** Small (1 inch), very thick, robust, moderately high conical spire, very short siphonal canal, spherical shape, convex whorls and incised suture. The aperture is ovoidal, the outer lip tapers to an edge after a strong thickening and, internally, has strong teeth, which continue as folds. The columellar lip has a thickish callus, covered with large pimples, which is fused to the ventral portion of the body whorl. The spiral sculpture is made up of thin ridges of variable thickness, the axial consists of stout angular nodules, particularly prominent on the weak keel of the whorls. Variable in color, yellowish on the tubercles and part of the surface, large greenish patches covering the remainder. The carmine color of the columellar callus is distinctive, the pimples are white. The operculum is horny and has an apical nucleus.

**Body** Though it is not rare, there is no literature, even an outline, on the morphology and anatomy of this species. Presumably similar to the other buccinids that have been described.

**Habitat** Lives close to large bodies of corals in the infralittoral zone.

**Distribution** Widespread in the Panamic Province, extending as far as the Galapagos Islands.

---

## 228 CLANCULUS PHARAONIUM
### Strawberry Top

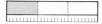

**Family** Trochidae

**Shell** Small (1 inch), thick and robust, moderately high conical spire, almost as high as it is broad. The whorls are slightly convex, and the suture is impressed. The convex base has a deep umbilicus whose aperture is bordered by a granular swelling. The aperture is pointed downward at an angle of 45 degrees to the shell axis. The lip is thickish and internally has a row of long, thin teeth. The sculpture consists of a dense array of granular spiral bands, a little broader than the gaps between them; on the base these bands tend to become thinner and continuous. Bright red in color; along two bands, one above the suture and one halfway up the whorl, there is one black-colored granule every two or three red ones. The operculum is small, horny, round and flattened.

**Body** Like other trochids it has some primitive characters: the heart has two auricles; the rear portion of the intestine crosses over the ventricle of the heart; two nephridia. It has a single gill and one osphradium. The radula is rhipidoglossan.

**Habitat** Coral formations in the mid-reef section.

**Distribution** *C. pharaonium* lives in the Indo-Pacific Province, confined to the Indian Ocean.

## 229 CODAKIA TIGERINA
### Pacific Tiger Lucine

**Family** Lucinidae
**Shell** Largish (5 inches), circular, thick and moderately convex valves, equivalve and inequilateral. Yellowish or white in color, tending to pink at the margins of the valves as the violet red color of the internal margin shows through. The sculpture consists of radial ribs, as broad as the gaps between them, intersecting concentric lamellae forming a network of squarish units. At the intersection of ribs and lamellae there are often fairly coarse nodules. The ligament is external, but deeply embedded in the region posterior to the umbones, the hinge is heterodont, with cardinal and lateral teeth. The two muscle scars visible on the inner surface of the valves differ (dimyarian, anisomyarian), the pallial line is smoothly curved (integropalliate).
**Body** It has a pair of gills, each consisting of two series of lamellae extensively fused by interlamellar junctions (eulamellibranch). The fairly well-developed foot enables it to partly bury itself in the substrate.

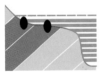

**Habitat** Outer reef coralline sands. It lives in the lower part of the Mesolittoral or the upper parts of the infralittoral zone.
**Distribution** As it lives in coral habitats it is confined to tropical waters, where it is found throughout the Indo-Pacific Province.

---

## 230 CONUS ARENATUS
### Sand-dusted Cone

**Family** Conidae
**Shell** Medium-small (1 ½ inches), very thick, heavy, angular whorls, lowish spire, with the body whorl almost completely enfolding the preceding (involute), obconical in shape, suture barely impressed. The aperture is narrow and elongated with roughly parallel margins and a thin edge to the outer lip. The sculpture consists of very stout nodules, broad based, placed far apart and just above the shoulder. Creamy white with a pattern of chestnut dots irregularly scattered over the whole surface, more densely packed in two or three irregular spiral bands. The periostracum is thin and transparent. The operculum is horny, very small, with an apical nucleus.
**Body** The same general characteristics already described for other species of this genus: an elongated ovoidal foot; a distinct head with two fairly long tentacles, the eyes are about halfway along the tentacles; the mantle cavity contains the gill, the osphradium and, in males, the penis behind the right tentacle. The radula is toxoglossan.

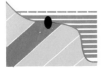

**Habitat** *C. arenatus* lives on coral sands in the upper level of the infralittoral zone.
**Distribution** Fairly common throughout the Indo-Pacific Province.

## 231 CONUS BULLATUS
### Bubble Cone

**Family** Conidae

**Shell** Medium-large size (2 to 3 inches), fairly thick, solid and heavy, flattish spire, sometimes almost sunken, the body whorl is rather swollen, so the shape tends to the elongated-spherical rather than the obconical. Incised suture. The aperture rather wide, the outer lip tapers to an edge. No sculpture, the shell of this species is smooth and glossy, porcellaneous in appearance. It varies from orange to bright-red in color, with triangular whitish or cream spots irregularly scattered over the entire surface and indistinct dark-chestnut spiral lines. No information on the periostracum. The operculum is horny, chestnut, small, and has an apical nucleus.

**Body** Fairly well-developed foot, posterior end rounded and anterior broadened and truncated. The head has two tentacles, the eyes are halfway along these. The mantle cavity contains the gill, the osphradium and, in males, the penis behind the right tentacle. The radula is toxoglossan.

**Habitat** Buried beneath coral sand in the infralittoral zone.

**Distribution** Though there are gaps in its range, *C. bullatus* is found in the Pacific Province and in the Japonic Province.

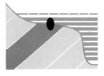

---

## 232 CONUS CHALDAEUS
### Vermiculated Cone

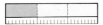

**Family** Conidae

**Shell** Small (½ inch), thick and robust, the whorls are angular and the spire flattish, the body whorl is slightly convex below the shoulder and extensively enfolds the preceding one. Suture very incised. Narrow aperture, roughly parallel margins, thin outer lip. The surface can be smooth, or it can have nodular bands on the anterior part of the body whorl. The shoulder has well-spaced and fading nodules. The coloration consists of axial black stripes, which are fairly undulating and are broken just below the shoulder and are about halfway up the body whorl; the remainder of the shell is white. The periostracum is thin and yellowish. The operculum is horny and small.

**Body** The foot is roughly rectangular, the distinct head has two tentacles and halfway along these, the eyes. Both the proboscis and the mantle siphon are fairly long. The mantle cavity contains the gill, the osphradium and, in males, the penis, behind the right tentacle. The radula is toxoglossan.

**Habitat** Hidden among rocks or corals in the infralittoral zone.

**Distribution** The entire Indo-Pacific Province, though there are gaps in its range.

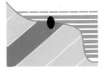

## 233 CONUS COCCINEUS
### Berry Cone

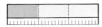

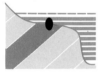

**Family**   Conidae
**Shell**   Small (1 ½ inches), moderately thick, robust, flattish conical spire, the body whorl encircles the preceding one up to the shoulder; above this the whorls are convex. The suture is impressed; overall it is biconical in appearance. The aperture is narrow and elongated, roughly parallel margins with a thin and sharp outer lip. The coloration is fairly unusual, as well as being variable; the shell is a darkish chestnut except for a spiral band halfway up the body whorl; this is whitish with black dots or spots arranged in spiral stripes or lines. The sculpture consists of, besides the very small nodules on the shoulder of the body whorl, thin spiral, finely nodular grooves. The periostracum is thin and transparent. The operculum is horny, small, with an apical nucleus.
**Body**   No literature referring to the morphology and anatomy of this species in particular. It is unlikely to differ substantially from other *Conus* sp. that have been described. The radula is toxoglossan.
**Habitat**   Buried in the sand in the inner-reef section of the infralittoral zone.
**Distribution**   *C. coccineus* lives in the Indo-Pacific Province, confined to the Southwestern Area.

---

## 234 GENUS CONUS SUBGENUS CYLINDER
### Tent or Textile Cones (illustrated are Glory-of-the-Sea Cone and Textile Cone)

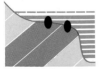

**Family**   Conidae
**Shell**   Medium or large size (up to 5 inches), rather light never very thick, moderately high spire, biconical. The body whorl has a rounded shoulder, slightly concave above it and convex beneath it. The narrow aperture is roughly rectangular. No trace of sculpture; the surface is usually smooth and glossy. The coloration of this subgenus is characteristic; on a yellowish-chestnut background there are triangular white spots of various sizes, generally rather small; in the areas free of these spots, there are tightly packed zigzag axial lines. The periostracum is thin, yellowish and glossy. The operculum is horny, small, elongated, and it has an apical nucleus. The illustration shows *C. gloriamaris* (Chemnitz 1777), left (thought, until a few years ago, to be very rare), and *C. textile* (L.1758), right.
**Body**   The foot is elongated, posteriorly rounded and truncated at the front. The end of the mantle siphon has three colored, transverse bands; black proximally, creamy-white in the middle and red distally. The radula is toxoglossan. The sting of *C. textile* can cause serious illness or death to a man.
**Habitat**   Live on coral sandy bottoms in the infralittoral or muddy bottoms in the infralittoral and circalittoral zones.
**Distribution**   The subgenus *Cylinder* is widely distributed in the Indo-Pacific Province, but it is not confined to it.

## 235 GENUS CONUS SUBGENUS DAUCICONUS
### Cone Shells (illustrated are Carrot Cone and Lithograph Cone)

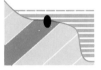

**Family** Conidae

**Shell** Usually medium or medium-small size (2 inches), spire very low, the body whorl encircles the preceding ones up to the shoulder, obconical, sometimes slightly concave above the shoulder. The suture is barely incised. The aperture is a very elongated rectangle, the outer lip is thin and sharp. Sculpture completely absent. The coloration is rather variable, the base color is usually chestnut or hazel, with a broken white band on the shoulder and, halfway up, the whorls; patterning spiral lines are often added. The periostracum is very thin. The operculum is chestnut, horny, small, with an apical nucleus. The illustration shows *C. daucus* (left) and *C. lithoglyphus* (right).

**Body** The foot is elongated, roughly rectangular, broadened and truncated anteriorly. The head is distinct and the eyes are halfway along the tentacles. The proboscis, when evaginated, is rather long. The radula is toxoglossan.

**Habitat** Like many *Conus* sp. these two live on coral sand bottoms in the infralittoral zone.

**Distribution** *C. lithoglyphus* is fairly common throughout the Indo-Pacific Province; *C. daucus* lives in the Caribbean Province.

---

## 236 CONUS GEOGRAPHUS
### Geography Cone

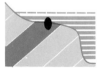

**Family** Conidae

**Shell** Large size (5 inches), rather thin, light, fairly fragile, differs in shape from other *Conus* sp., as the body whorl is slightly swollen and so the shell tends to be an elongate sphere rather than conical. Above the shoulder the whorls are concave. The aperture is rather wide, widening slightly at the anterior, the outer lip is thin and sharp. The sculpture is confined to a row of well-spaced, small nodules on the keel. The coloration is chestnut with hazel patches and largish dots. The periostracum is thin and has well-spaced spiral rows of bristles. The operculum is horny, small, with an apical nucleus.

**Body** The foot is well developed, roughly rectangular, widened and truncated anteriorly. The distinct head has a thick proboscis and two long and thin tentacles, the eyes are halfway along their length. The radula is toxoglossan. This species, which normally feeds on fish, can kill a man with the poison that its teeth inject.

**Habitat** It usually lives in pockets of sand, near the edges of coral bodies in the infralittoral zone.

**Distribution** Relatively common throughout the Indo-Pacific Province.

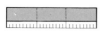

## 237 CONUS IMPERIALIS
### Imperial Cone

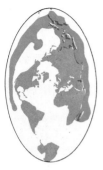

**Family** Conidae
**Shell** Medium-large size (3 to 4 inches), solid, very flat spire. The whorls are strongly angular; the body whorl enfolds the preceding one up to the shoulder. Obconical shape. The narrow aperture has a canal, roughly parallel margins, and the outer lip has a thin edge. The sculpture consists of squat, well-spaced nodules on the shoulder of the whorls. The coloration is very variable and complex. The base color is lightish chestnut or greenish, with white patches; the patterning consists of spiral chestnut lines, often broken, differing in thickness and unequally spaced. The operculum is, as it is in all *Conus* sp. horny, very small and elongated.
**Body** The foot is roughly rectangular, slightly truncated at the front. The distinct head has two tentacles with an eye at the base of each. The end of the mantle siphon is pink. The mantle cavity contains the gill, the osphradium and, in males, the penis behind the right tentacle. The radula is toxoglossan. This species feeds mainly on annelids. A sting by the ''harpoon'' of its radula can cause a mild sickness in a human victim.
**Habitat** It lives on the sand among the corals in the outer-reef section of the mesolittoral and the infralittoral zones.
**Distribution** Throughout the Indo-Pacific Province.

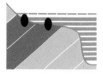

## 238 GENUS CONUS SUBGENUS LEPTOCONUS
### Cone Shells (illustrated are General Cone and Jasper Cone)

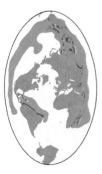

**Family** Conidae
**Shell** Small or medium in size (½ to 3 inches), moderately thick and heavy, high spire. The species of this subgenus have a characteristic, fairly marked concave outline to the spire. The aperture is narrow, the outer lip has a thin, sharp edge. The sculpture may be completely missing or may consist of fairly broad and raised spiral bands. The coloration is very variable. The periostracum is brown, opaque, thick in some species, thinner in others. The operculum is horny, small, elongated, with an apical nucleus. The illustration shows *C. generalis* (left) and *C. jaspideus* (right).
**Body** Elongated foot. The distinct head has two long, thin tentacles, the eyes are halfway along these. The proboscis and mantle siphon are also long. The mantle cavity contains the gill, the osphradium and, in males, the penis behind the right tentacle. The females lay the eggs in flattened ovoidal capsules, on rigid substrates, as do all *Conus* sp. The radula is toxoglossan.
**Habitat** Both species illustrated here live on coral sands in the infralittoral zone.
**Distribution** *C. generalis* is widely distributed throughout the Indo-Pacific Province; *C. jaspideus* lives in the Caribbean Province.

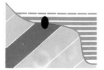

## 239 GENUS CONUS SUBGENUS LITHOCONUS
### Stone Cones (illustrated are Letter Cone and Graded Cone)

**Family**   Conidae
**Shell**   Medium size (2 to 5 inches), but some species are very large, generally solid, heavy, angular whorls, flattish spire; the body whorl enfolds the preceding one up to the shoulder. The upper part of the whorls are, in some species, slightly concave. The suture is incised. The narrow aperture is long, with roughly parallel margins, a thin and sometimes sharp outer lip. No sculpture apart from quite marked growth lines. The coloration consists mainly of chestnut, black, reddish or even yellowish spots arranged in spiral rows. The periostracum is, in some species, chestnut and very thick. The operculum is horny and small, as in all *Conus* sp. In the illustration are *C. litteratus* (left) and *C. gradatus* (right).

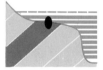

**Body**   Roughly rectangular foot. The head is distinct, has two tentacles, and the eyes are halfway along these. The radula is toxoglossan, and the teeth are used like a harpoon to capture the annelids, which are the usual diet of the species of this genus. The sting of *C. litteratus* causes in man an injury similar to that caused by the sting of a wasp.
**Habitat**   The members of this subgenus live on coral sands or mud in the infralittoral zone.
**Distribution**   The subgenus *Lithoconus* lives in all the tropical provinces.

## 240 CONUS MARMOREUS
### Marble Cone

**Family**   Conidae
**Shell**   Large size (4 inches), thick and robust, very flat spire, the body whorl almost completely enfolds the preceding one, obconical shape, barely incised suture. The aperture is narrow, the outer lip has a thin, sharp edge. The shoulder has squat well-spaced nodules (crowned shoulder). There is no other sculpture. The base color is a very dark brown or even black with roughly triangular white patches over the whole surface. This species is very similar to *C. bandanus* (Brugière 1792), which differs in having two spiral stripes, slightly smaller white patches, and therefore the base color is more apparent. The operculum is horny, chestnut, small and elongated. The periostracum is thin and transparent.
**Body**   As in all *Conus* sp., the foot is relatively narrow and long, and the mantle siphon is moderately developed. The eyes are halfway along the tentacles. The radula is toxoglossan. This species feeds on other mollusks.
**Habitat**   Coral sands in the infralittoral zone.
**Distribution**   Moderately common in the Indo-Pacific Province.

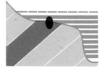

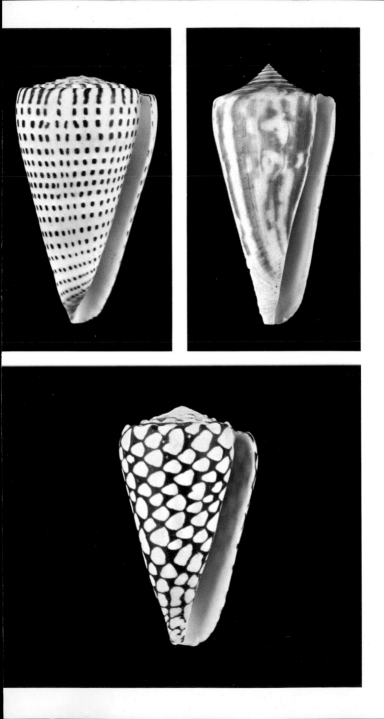

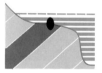

## 241 CONUS NUSSATELLA
### Nussatella Cone

**Family** Conidae

**Shell** Medium or medium-small in size (3 inches), fairly thick and solid. Moderately high conical spire, the first whorls rise above the others to form a short, stout stiletto. The body whorl has a very rounded receding shoulder, the margins are gently curved, it covers the preceding one, though the shoulder is left free and the suture is impressed and not incised as in many other *Conus* sp. The overall shape is vaguely cylindrical. At the posterior the aperture is narrow, but it is wider at the front; the outer lip is thin and sharp. The sculpture consists of thin, minutely granular spiral ridges (lyre-shaped). Creamy white with axially directed orangy-chestnut flamings, patches or bands and spiral stripes made up of densely packed blackish dots. The periostracum is thin and transparent. The operculum is small, horny and has an apical nucleus.

**Body** The same general characteristics as other *Conus* sp. elongated foot, two tentacles on the head with the eyes halfway along them, moderately long mantle siphon. The radula is toxoglossan.

**Habitat** It lives hidden among the corals in the mid-reef section of the infralittoral zone.

**Distribution** Widespread and fairly common throughout the Indo-Pacific and Japonic provinces.

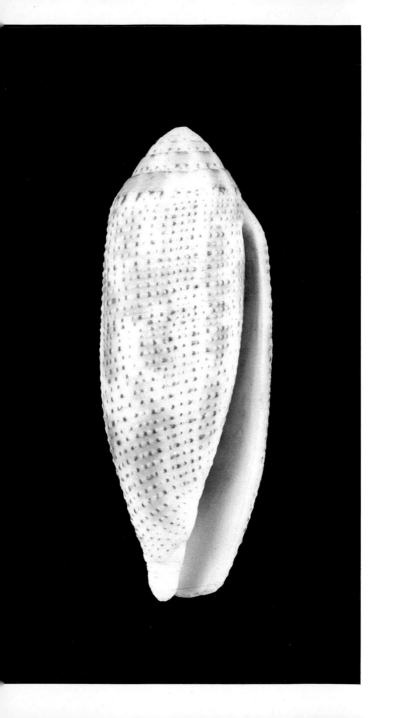

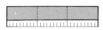

## 242 CONUS STRIATUS
### Striated Cone

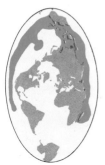

**Family** Conidae
**Shell** Large size (3 to 6 inches), fairly thick, robust, heavy, flattish spire, slightly biconical. The body whorl is slightly convex below the lightly keeled shoulder. All the whorls are markedly concave above the suture, which is barely incised. The aperture is narrow, with a wide anterior notch for the emergence of the mantle siphon, and a thin, sharp outer lip. The sculpture consists of a dense array of thin spiral grooves, which cover the entire surface. The coloration is extremely variable both as to the base color, which can be pinkish chestnut or white, and the patterning, which is made up of patches of various shapes and sizes. The periostracum is thin and transparent. The operculum is horny, small and has an apical nucleus.
**Body** As in all *Conus sp.*, the foot is roughly rectangular, rounded posteriorly and slightly broadened and truncated at the front. The eyes are halfway along the head's long, thin tentacles. The toxoglossan radula has two rows of lateral teeth, which are used one at a time, like a harpoon, to capture the fish that it feeds on.
**Habitat** *C. striatus* lives hidden in pockets of sand among the corals in the infralittoral zone.
**Distribution** Fairly common throughout the Indo-Pacific Province.

---

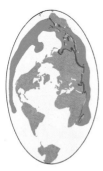

## 243 CONUS VEXILLUM
### Vexillum Cone

**Family** Conidae
**Shell** Large size (3 inches), moderately thick, robust, relatively light, flattish spire, suture barely incised; the body whorl is flat or slightly concave above the shoulder; biconical in shape. As in all *Conus* sp., the aperture is elongated and narrow, and has a thin outer lip. Lacks any trace of sculpture. Chestnut in color, with two whitish, extensively broken bands, one on the shoulder, the other halfway up. The periostracum is thinnish and somewhat transparent. The operculum is horny, chestnut, much smaller than the aperture, and has an apical nucleus.
**Body** The animal is black and has the same characteristics as other Conids: roughly rectangular foot slightly broadened and truncated at the front; long, eye-bearing tentacles; fairly long mantle siphon. The toxoglossan radula has harpoon-shaped teeth, which it uses to catch the annelids that it feeds on.
**Habitat** It lives hidden among the corals in the mid-reef section of the infralittoral zone. It appears to prefer moving waters.
**Distribution** Indo-Pacific, more common in the southern part of the province.

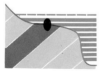

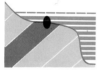

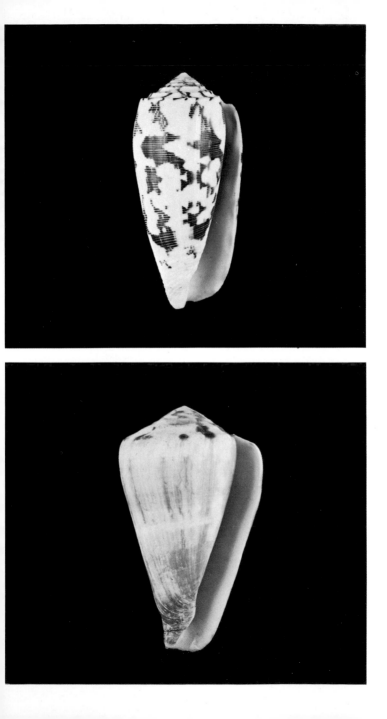

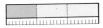

## 244 CORCULUM CARDISSA
### Heart Cockle

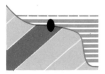

**Family** Cardiidae
**Shell** In size 3 inches, heart-shaped, very distinctive as the valves are longitudinally compressed but laterally strongly broadened and keeled; the shell is therefore very flattened. According to some malacologists *C. cardissa* should be split into at least three different species. The color is extremely variable, from almost pure white to pinkish yellow and intense red with radial lines of darker color than the rest of the shell, often spotted brown. The sculpture consists of equally spaced, flattened radial ribs, those on the lateral margins carry spiny processes. The ligament is small, external and posterior to the umbones. The two adductor-muscle scars are almost equal (dimyarian, isomyarian). The pallial line is smoothly curved. As with all Cardiidae the shell has a crossed-lamellae structure.
**Body** No literature on the morphology of this species, but presumably it does not differ substantially from other Cardiidae.
**Habitat** *C. cardissa* lives on soft bottoms in the outer-reef section of the coral bodies, in the infralittoral zone.
**Distribution** Throughout the tropical strip of the Indo-Pacific Province.

## 245 CYMATIUM RUBECULUM
### Ruby Triton

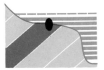

**Family** Cymatiidae
**Shell** Small (1 inch), rather thick, robust, high spire, spindle-shaped, swollen whorls and very incised suture; the aperture is ovoidal; the outer lip is thickened by a strong varix and has well-defined and widely spaced teeth inside. The columellar lip has a moderately thick callus with raised folds, which give way to thin teeth. The sculpture consists of spiral ribs that are as broad as the gaps between them and intersect thinner axial bands; well-developed nodules are formed at the intersections of these two sculptures. There are one or two large varices on all the whorls. As the specific name suggests, it is red, very often rather intense in color, with a median whitish stripe on the body whorl and white patches on the varices. The periostracum is chestnut yellow with tufts of bristles arranged in longitudinal rows along the axial grooves. The operculum is rounded and horny.
**Body** It has a rather developed, anteriorly truncated foot. The distinct head has a long proboscis and two tentacles with an eye at the base of each. In males the mantle cavity contains, behind the right tentacle, a large penis. The radula is taenioglossan.
**Habitat** It lives hidden beneath or among the corals of the mid- and inner-reef sections of the infralittoral zone.
**Distribution** Throughout the Indo-Pacific Province.

**GENUS CYMBIOLA**
**Volutes (illustrated are Imperial Volute and Aulica Volute)**

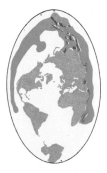

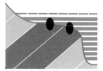

**Family**   Volutidae

**Shell**   Medium or large size (4 to 10 inches), moderately thick, robust; the spire is never very high, the body whorl enfolds a large part of the preceding one, elongated-spherical shape. The whorls are moderately convex below the shoulder and flat or fairly concave above it. The aperture is rather wide, the outer lip tapers to an edge, the columellar lip has three or four folds, and a callus that extends over a good part of the ventral portion of the body whorl. The protoconch is very large and spherical. The sculpture consists of fairly prominent axial ribs, which form nodules, flattish or even fairly long, backward-pointing spines on the shoulder. The color is very variable. There is never an operculum, the periostracum is present in some species. In the illustration are *C. imperialis* (top) and *C. aulica* (bottom).

**Body**   The few species whose morphology and anatomy are known have the same characteristics as other volutids. They have a modified rachiglossan radula—i.e., they have a single row of tricuspidate rachidial teeth.

**Habitat**   The known species of this genus live on coral sandy or muddy bottoms in the infralittoral and circalittoral zones.

**Distribution**   The members of the genus *Cymbiola* live in the Indo-Pacific Province, confined to the eastern Indian and western Pacific Oceans.

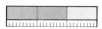

## 247 CYPRAEA PANTHERINA
### Panther Cowrie

**Family** Cypraeidae

**Shells** Medium large (2½ inches), quite thick and robust, oblong-spherical, the ends, especially the anterior one, protrude. The back is smooth and very rounded, while the base is only slightly convex. The aperture, quite wide, has roughly parallel margins posteriorly, but at the front they diverge and then draw in at the end of the canal. The teeth are quite fine and very distinct, not extending far on the columellar lip and not at all on the outer lip. The coloration is made up of round chestnut spots with quite indistinct edges, the background changes from pure white to dark chestnut. The base is always white.

**Body** Though it is a very common species, there is no information in the literature on the color of the foot, head, siphon or the lobes of the mantle; these latter can cover the shell. Like all *Cypraea* sp., the mantle cavity contains a gill, an osphradium and, in males, a penis. The radula is taenioglossan.

**Habitat** Infralittoral; it normally lives on top of corals, and so it is easy prey even for inexpert collectors.

**Distribution** Indo-Pacific Province, confined to the Red Sea and neighboring African coasts.

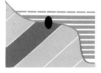

---

## 248 CYPRAEA TIGRIS
### Tiger Cowrie

**Family** Cypraeidae

**Shell** Medium large to notably large (2½ to 4½ inches), spherical, the body whorl completely covers and hides the preceding ones (convolute). The dorsal surface is regularly convex, the ends are less protruding than in the similar *C. pantherina*, but on the whole the outer and columellar lips are farther apart and the teeth are coarser. The back has round patches, usually chestnut with indistinct edges on a whitish, beige or, sometimes, chestnut background. The base is white, and at its edges there are patches like those on the dorsal surface.

**Body** The foot has a gray-yellow pattern and a white margin; the distinct head has a pair of dark-gray tentacles, the gray-yellow siphon is fringed at its free end. The two mantle lobes, which can completely encircle the shell, bear branched papillae up to a centimeter (⅓ inch) long, they are white except for the middle part which is gray-yellow. The radula is taenioglossan.

**Habitat** *C. tigris* lives over a range of depths in the infralittoral zone, usually on corals in the mid- and inner-reef sections.

**Distribution** Widespread throughout the Indo-Pacific Province, except for the Red Sea, where it is replaced by the related *C. pantherina*.

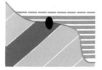

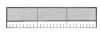

## 249 CYPRAECASSIS RUFA
### Bull Mouth Helmet

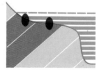

**Family**   Cassidae
**Shell**   Large size (6 inches), thick, solid, rather heavy, flattish spire, the body whorl covers a large part of the preceding one. Spherical, rather squat, very impressed suture. The aperture is narrow, almost straight; the anterior canal is directed posterio-laterally, and there is a posterior canal notch. The outer lip is strongly thickened with irregular-sized teeth internally, and it has a strong external rib. The inner lip has a thick callus that extends over the base and up the lateral margins of the body whorl; there are also thin extensive teeth. The sculpture consists of spiral ribs of variable width and flattish, apart from four, which are thicker and nodular; there are also prominent, very incised, axial grooves. There is a very narrow umbilicus. Brownish red in color, which gives it its specific name, with irregular lighter patches that shade into white. This species is used in jewelry workshops for making cameos. The operculum is horny, circular, very small and has a roughly central nucleus.
**Body**   A developed foot, distinct head with two narrow and long tentacles. The eyes are near the bases of the tentacles. The radula is taenioglossan, with very thin marginal teeth.
**Habitat**   Fairly coarse coral sands in the infralittoral and mesolittoral zones.
**Distribution**   Quite common in almost all the Indo-Pacific Province.

## 250 CYPRAECASSIS TESTICULUS
### Reticulated Cowrie-Helmet

**Family**   Cassidae
**Shell**   Medium large (1 to 3 inches), not very thick, solid, squatly pear-shaped, flattish spire, the body whorl extensively encircles the preceding one. The aperture is rather narrow with roughly parallel, almost straight, margins and a short, dorsally pointed canal. The outer lip is thickened by a robust callus, has internal teeth and an external varix. The columellar lip also has teeth and a not very thick callus, which almost completely covers the ventral surface of the body whorl. The sculpture consists of a network of closely packed axial furrows and about a dozen spiral furrows; this gives the surface a reticulated appearance. It is a light chestnut or cream in color, with reddish-brown patches of variable size, shape and position. The posterior two thirds of the columellar callus is orange while the front third is whitish. Juveniles have an operculum, but adults do not.
**Body**   The whole body is brownish orange in color. The head has two tentacles, with an eye at the base of each. The penis in males, is behind the right tentacle in the mantle cavity. The taenioglossan radula has two rather long, thin marginal teeth.
**Habitat**   It lives on coral formations in the infralittoral zone.
**Distribution**   There are two recognized subspecies; one lives in the Caribbean Province, and the other lives in the West African Province.

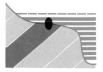

## 251 DISTORSIO ANUS
### Common Distorsio

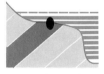

**Family** Cymatiidae

**Shell** Medium-large (3 inches), the variation of coiling of the axis between the whorls is characteristic, hence the generic name. The whorls are very convex with an incised suture. Overall, the shell is fairly thick and solid, apart from a wide parietal callus, which entirely covers the ventral surface of the body whorl and the penultimate whorl and projects as a thin and fragile plate beyond their margins. The aperture is very narrow, the outer lip has a varix and strong teeth; halfway along the inner lip there is a broad, deep sinus, it also has teeth. The entire surface is covered by nodules formed at the intersection of spiral and axial ribs. The whorls have varices. A darkish chestnut in color with some lighter, even white, spiral bands. The operculum is horny, dark chestnut, and very small.

**Body** No precise information about the morphology of this mollusk, presumably it is similar to other members of the *Cymatiidae*. The radula is taenioglossan.

**Habitat** This species lives hidden under and among corals in the infralittoral zone.

**Distribution** *D. anus* is found throughout the Indo-Pacific Province.

## 252 DRUPA MORUM
### Purple Drupe

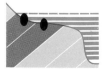

**Family** Thaididae

**Shell** Small size (1 inch), very thick and robust, flattish spire spherical. The aperture has a very short, rather open, siphonal canal; the outer lip is strongly thickened internally and carries three or four double teeth (sometimes triple or quadruple). The inner lip has a large callus, which covers part of the ventral surface of the body whorl; the anterior third of the callus is thickened and has three robust teeth. There is only spiral sculpture, consisting of fairly prominent and developed bands that bear large, squat nodules, whitish except for the nodules, which are black. The aperture is violet or purple. The operculum is horny, very dark chestnut, elongated, and has an apical nucleus.

**Body** The foot is fairly well developed; the head has two long, thin tentacles, with an eye at the base of each. The proboscis is retractile. The mantle cavity contains the gill, the osphradium, in males the long penis, and the hypobranchial gland, which is well developed and secretes a colored substance. The radula is rachiglossan.

**Habitat** *D. morum* lives on corals in the mesolittoral or in the upper levels of the infralittoral zone.

**Distribution** Widespread throughout the Indo-Pacific Province.

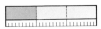

## 253  EROSARIA NEBRITES
### Nebrite Cowrie

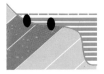

**Family**  Cypraeidae
**Shell**  Small size (1 to 1¼ inches), robust. The spire is very low, and only a very small part of it remains uncovered as the body whorl enfolds and hides it (involute). The base is moderately convex, with a strong callus extending to the shell margins and forming a conspicuous marginal thickening. The aperture is almost straight. The dorsal surface of the shell is smooth except for some thin radial ridges that extend, at the anterior and posterior, over the upper part of the marginal callus. The teeth are as thick as the gaps between them and, while the columellar teeth do not extend far, those on the outer lip extend across its whole breadth as far as the margin. The back is chestnut, with small, round, greenish patches, of variable diameter. The marginal callus has chestnut spots, with two larger dark-chestnut spots in the middle (one per side). The radial ridges are also chestnut. The base is whitish, with thin chestnut lines.
**Body**  The mantle lobes, which can cover the shell when completely extended, are gray, like the rest of the body and have papillae of the same color. The radula is taenioglossan.
**Habitat**  Infralittoral, occasionally mesolittoral, it lives on coral or stones.
**Distribution**  Indo-Pacific Province, confined to the Red Sea the Gulfs of Aden and Oman and the central East African coasts.

## 254  GLYCYMERIS PECTINIFORMIS
### Scalloplike Bittersweet

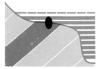

**Family**  Glycymeridae
**Shell**  Medium size (1½ inches), thick and robust, moderately swollen, circular outline, rather large and slightly protruding umbones. The thickish periostracum is made up of very short lamellae of a darkish-hazel color. The shell is whitish or cream with irregularly arranged reddish patches. The sculpture consists of broad, low, radial ribs, smoothly rounded in section. There are also thin, concentric growth lines. The external ligament is very wide and extends both in front of and behind the umbones. The hinge is taxodont and has fairly large teeth. Inside the valves there are two almost-equal muscle scars (dimyarian, isomyarian), the pallial line is smoothly curved (integropalliate). The shell has a crossed-lamellae structure.
**Body**  The foot is moderately developed and is used to dig quite deeply into the substratum. There is a pair of gills each consisting of two series of filaments widely connected and forming, in all, four series of lamellae (filibranch).
**Habitat**  It lives moderately buried in sandy bottoms in the outer-reef section of coral formations in the infralittoral zone.
**Distribution**  Widespread throughout the Indo-Pacific Province. Some authors would divide it into subspecies or even species living in different areas.

## 255 HARPA DAVIDIS
## Madras Harp

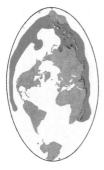

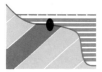

**Family**  Harpidae

**Shell**  Medium-large (2¼ to 3½ inches), not very thick, solid, low spire. The body whorl is swollen and almost completely enfolds the preceding one; lacks a siphonal canal; spherical, impressed suture. The aperture is wide, the outer lip is smooth internally and has a sharp rib externally. The columellar has a very light callus, which covers much of the ventral surface of the body whorl. The axial sculpture is made up of sharp, equally spaced ribs, which have a blunt spine near the posterior end; the spiral sculpture consists of very thin, almost invisible grooves in the gaps between the ribs. Like all *Harpa* sp., it lacks a periostracum and an operculum.

**Body**  It has a very large foot, which cannot be completely withdrawn into the shell; anteriorly there is a broadened semicircular region, and it is pointed at the rear. There are known cases of autonomy of the posterior part of the foot—that is, when the animal is disturbed it can amputate this part. The radula is rachiglossan.

**Habitat**  *H. davidis* lives, like many others of its genus, buried beneath the sand in the infralittoral zone.

**Distribution**  It is not very common, lives in the Indo-Pacific Province. Maldives, Ceylon and Eastern India to Burma, Thailand and Sumatra.

## 256 HARPA MAJOR
## Large Harp

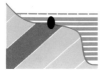

**Family** Harpidae

**Shell** Medium-large size (2½ to 4 inches), rather thin, ne fragile, light, moderately high conical spire, broad, swolle body whorl, which almost completely enfolds the precedin one; very impressed suture. The aperture is very large, th outer lip is thickened by a strong rib; in section it is triangula like the others on the surface of the shell. The inner lip has light callus, which partly covers the ventral surface of the bod whorl. The sculpture consists of thin spiral grooves confined t the gaps between the ribs as well as the ribs themselves, whic are characteristic of all species of the genus *Harpa*. The colo ation is quite variable, and the pattern is rather complex. N operculum or periostracum.

**Body** It has a large cream-colored foot with fine chestnu spots; the posterior end is elongated and the front is broad ened and semicircular. The head has two long, thin tentacle each with an eye on its proximal third. The mantle siphon i rather long. The female encloses the eggs in discoidal eg capsules, which are laid in strings. The radula is rachiglossar

**Habitat** *H. major*, like the other species of the genus, live buried under the sand in the infralittoral zone.

**Distribution** Indo-Pacific Province. East Africa to Hawaii an Marquesas Islands.

---

## 257 HIPPOPUS HIPPOPUS
## Horses Hoof

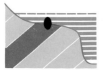

**Family** Tridacnidae

**Shell** Very large (up to 15½ inches), thick and robust valves rather swollen, equivalve inequilateral, elongated-triangular i shape. The umbones point backward. The sculpture consist of thirteen or fourteen moderately convex radial ribs, with secondary radial sculpture, both on and between the ribs, c small ridges that can bear rows of spoutlike spines, which stic out in all directions, giving the valves a prickly appearance White or cream with concentrically arranged strawberry-col ored patches. The ligament is secondarily anterior to the um bones. The hinge has one cardinal tooth on each valve, tw lateral teeth on the right valve and one on the left. Only the pos terior adductor muscle is present, therefore the species i monomyarian, the pallial line is smoothly curve (integropalliate).

**Body** The edges of the mantle lobes are fused. As in all othe tridacnids, the mantle has symbiotic microscopic algae, zoo xanthellae living in it; these are partly responsible for the strik ing mantle coloration. The byssus is present only in juveniles

**Habitat** Lives on sandy bottoms in association with coral for mations, down to a depth of 6 meters (20 feet).

**Distribution** Indo-Pacific Province, Malay Peninsula to Eas ern Melanesia.

## 258 HOMALOCANTHA SCORPIO
### Scorpion Murex

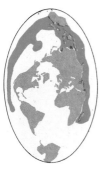

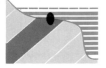

**Family** Muricidae

**Shell** Medium small (2 inches), rather thin and light, but fairly robust; spire not very high; long canal, spindle-shaped shell. The whorls are swollen, keeled; the zone posterior to the keel is almost flat, the suture is almost canaliculated. The aperture is roughly ovoidal, the outer lip is internally smooth or sometimes has a light ridge. The columellar lip has a callus that is not fused to the ventral part of the body whorl but sticks up, forming a thin swelling. The axial sculpture consists of six varices on each whorl; the spiral sculpture consists of alternating thick and thin ribs; where they intersect with the varices they form stout, spatulalike spines with slightly broadened ends. The color varies from darkish chestnut to black; there are rare whitish examples. The operculum is horny, reddish chestnut, ovoidal and, unlike that of other species from the subfamily Muricinae, the nucleus is lateral, near the outer margin.

**Body** Like all muricids, the foot is truncated at the front and rounded posteriorly. The head has a long retractile proboscis and an eye at the base of each tentacle. The radula is rachiglossan.

**Habitat** It appears that it lives on coral sands in the infralittoral zone. However, the information is not definite.

**Distribution** Fairly common throughout the Indo-Pacific Province, Philippines, Indonesia and the Red Sea.

---

## 259 HYDATINA ALBOCINCTA
### White-Banded Bubble

**Family** Hydatinidae

**Shell** Small (1 inch), very thin, fragile and light, sunken spire, the large and spherical body whorl enfolds the preceding ones and exceeds them in height. The suture is impressed. The aperture is rather wide, the outer lip is thin, and the columellar lip lacks a callus. No sculpture except for thin growth lines. Chestnut with five white bands (hence the specific name), one subsutural, one basal and three intermediate, equally spaced ones. Lacks an operculum. The periostracum is thin and yellowish.

**Body** The robust foot has two broad parapodia and lateral lobes that can cover the shell. The head has been transformed into a cephalic disc with two posterior lobes and four lateral tentacles, the two anterior ones are coiled. The mantle cavity contains the gill and the osphradium. The penis, as in almost all opisthobranchs, all of which are hermaphrodites, can be retracted into a muscular sheath.

**Habitat** It lives on coral sandy bottoms in the infralittoral zone.

**Distribution** It lives in the Japonic Province and the Indo-Pacific Province, restricted to the western coasts of the Pacific Ocean.

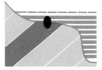

## SUBFAMILY IMBRICARIINAE
### Miters (illustrated are Papilio Miter and Almost Cancellated Miters)

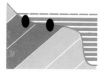

**Family** Mitridae

**Shell** Small to medium-large (2 to 3 inches), thick, sometimes thin, high conical spire, tapered or elongated-ovate overall shape, convex or angular whorls, sometimes concave above the shoulder and convex beneath it; sometimes almost canaliculated suture. The aperture is elongated with a wide anterior notch; the outer lip has a thin edge; in some species it is sharp. The inner lip has a slight callus and from three to ten strong columellar folds. The sculpture generally consists of fairly strong, sometimes sharp, well-spaced spiral ribs; frequently there are very incised axial growth lines, prominent in the gaps between the spiral sculpture. The coloration is very variable, and it is hidden by an opaque periostracum. There is never an operculum. The illustration shows, from left to right *Neocancilla papilio* (Link 1807) and *Subcancilla* sp.

**Body** The foot is rather narrow and long, the head is distinct, has a pair of tentacles, with the eyes on their proximal third; the proboscis is very long. The mantle cavity contains the gill, the osphradium and, in males, the penis. The radula is rachiglossan.

**Habitat** Almost exclusively coralline sands or, rarely, muddy bottoms in the mesolittoral and infralittoral zones.

**Distribution** The species of this subfamily are limited to warm tropical seas.

---

## JENNERIA PUSTULATA
### Pustulate Cowrie

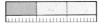

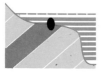

**Family** Ovulidae

**Shell** Small size (½ to ¾ inch), rather solid, pear-shaped; the ends slightly protrude; the body whorl completely enfolds the preceding whorls, hiding them (convolute). The back is regularly convex, the margins are slightly keeled; the base is almost flat. The sculpture is distinctive; it consists of pointed tubercles on the back and margins and radial ribs on the base; these are extensions on both the columellar and outer sides of the aperture teeth. The aperture is rather narrow, straight at the anterior and curved near the posterior end. The background color is grayish chestnut on the back and chestnut on the base; the back also has two median chestnut patches on the canals. The tubercles are red or orange red ringed with chestnut, the teeth are white.

**Body** The foot and head are grayish, the siphon, with smooth margins and the tentacles, which have the eyes at their base, are black with dense red dotting. The mantle lobes when completely expanded can cover the shell and have branched papillae with red, yellowish and black rings. The radula is taenioglossan.

**Habitat** It lives on the corals in the infralittoral zone.

**Distribution** It lives in the Panamic Province and in the southern part of the Californian Province; West Coast of Mexico to Ecuador.

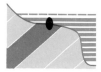

# GENUS LAMBIS
## Spider Conchs (illustrated are Orange Spider Conch, Violet Spider Conch and Arthritic Spider Conch)

**Family**  Strombidae

**Shell**  Large or very large size (3 to 12 inches), moderately high conical spire; all the species have aperture lips that are greatly expanded and almost cover the preceding whorls and have a variable number of long fingers. The suture is barely incised, the whorls always have a median or suprasutural keel; this is strongly and stoutly nodular; above it the surface is concave or, at most, flat. The body whorl usually has other rows of tubercles or nodules arranged in spiral lines. The entire surface of the shell is covered in the majority of cases by thin spiral ribs. The outer lip has fingerlike spiny processes, sometimes spoutlike, very often fused along the ventral line, with a curved end pointing apically. The columellar lip is usually thickened to form a callus. As in all strombids, there is a short anterior canal and an anteriolateral notch (the stromboid notch). The aperture may be smooth or finely toothed. The background color is usually whitish or beige with darkish-chestnut lines, patches or irregular flamings. The aperture varies in color, in some cases it is responsible for the specific name *Lambis crocata, L. violacea*. There is always a horny operculum, sickle-shaped, a characteristic of the Strombidae. The illustration shows  *L. crocata* (top left); *L violacea* (top right); and *L chiragra arthritica* (bottom).

**Body**  Not substantially different from other strombids—i.e., a curved foot with a reduced anterior part and a large posterior one that carries the operculum and enables the animal to leap. The eyes are at the end of two long and thick peduncles, which are fused to the tentacles, which barely protrude above the eyes. The mantle cavity contains the gill, the osphradium and, in males, the penis.

**Habitat**  Except for a rather rare species (L. violacea) they all live in the infralittoral zone, particularly the mid-reef section of coral formations.

**Distribution**  The members of the genus *Lambis* are confined to the Indo-Pacific Province.

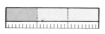

## 263 LATIAXIS PAGODUS
### Pagoda Latiaxis

**Family** Coralliophilidae
**Shell** Medium-small size (1 ¼ inches), rather thin, light, fragile, generally high conical spire and a not very long siphonal canal, spindle-shaped. The aperture is pear-shaped, the outer lip is not thickened and has slight internal folds; the columellar lip has a thin callus, which sticks out slightly from the ventral surface of the body whorl. The spiral sculpture is characteristic and consists of lamellar bands; of these the largest one is on the keel, and this bears highly developed triangular spines, which curve toward the apex of the shell. There is another quite large band but with less prominent spines, immediately beneath the keel band. White or light hazel. The operculum is light chestnut, and its laterally displaced nucleus is halfway along the outer margin.
**Body** It has a rather thick, short foot, the head is distinct and has two tentacles, with an eye at the base of each. The mantle cavity contains a gill, an osphradium and, in males, a penis. The eggs are enclosed in lens-shaped oviger capsules, which are laid singly. No radula.
**Habitat** Like all members of the Coralliophilidae family, *L. pagodus* lives on corals in the infralittoral and circalittoral zones.
**Distribution** Confined to the Japonic Province.

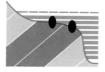

## 264 LATIAXIS PILSBRYI
### Pilsbry's Latiaxis

**Family** Coralliophilidae
**Shell** Medium-small size (1 ½ inches), very thin, fragile and light, flattened spire, overall shape faintly conical. The whorls have a strong keel; above this they are flat, while below it they are lightly convex. The suture is incised, and the whorls (especially the body whorl) are sometimes detached (devolute). The base has a wide umbilicus. The aperture is pear-shaped. The sculpture consists of thin spiral ridges and a crown of long triangular lamellar spines on the keel of the whorls. The umbilicus is bordered by lamellar spines. Pure white, sometimes very light hazel in color. The operculum is reddish chestnut, with a lateral nucleus halfway along the outer margin.
**Body** No literature on the morphology or anatomy, not even an outline of this rather rare species. Presumably in general features it is similar to *L. pagodus*. Like all coralliophilids, it lacks a radula.
**Habitat** It lives on corals in the circalittoral or even the aphytal zones.
**Distribution** Like *L. pagodus* it lives in the Japonic Province.

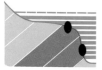

## 265 LIOCONCHA CASTRENSIS
### Zigzag Venus

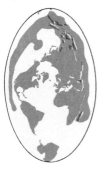

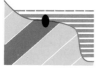

**Family** Veneridae
**Shell** Medium size (1¼ inches), robust, moderately swollen valves, thick, inequilateral and equivalve, rounded shape. It has a thin grayish-chestnut periostracum, the valves are white, cream or grayish, with quite dark chestnut zigzag lines. The only sculpture consists of the thin growth lines. The lunule is well defined and heart-shaped. The external ligament is deeply set along the posteriodorsal margin of the valves. The hinge is heterodont; the left valve has three cardinal teeth and one anterior lateral tooth, the right valve has three cardinal teeth and two anterior lateral teeth. The posterior muscle scar is a little larger than the anterior one. The pallial line has a small sinus. As with all venerids, the shell has a mainly crossed-lamellae structure.
**Body** As do all the Veneridae, *L. castrensis* has a pair of gills, each consisting of two series of lamellae, extensively fused by interlamellar junctions (eulamellibranch). The foot is highly developed, and the siphons are very long.
**Habitat** Typically it is found on coral sands in the outer-reef section.
**Distribution** Essentially Indo-Pacific, extending from the Red Sea to the islands of the Central Pacific.

## 266 LYNCINA ARGUS
### Eyed Cowrie

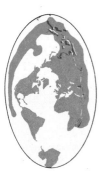

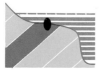

**Family** Cypraeidae
**Shell** Medium-large (3 inches), robust, the body whorl leaves a small part of the preceding whorls uncovered (involute). The anterior end protrudes a little; while the posterior end does not. The margins of the body whorl are roughly parallel, so the overall appearance of the shell is almost cylindrical. The base has a light callus; though this covers the two ends, it usually does not hide the apex of the shell. The aperture is slightly but smoothly curved and has well-defined teeth that do not extend far. The background color of the back is a light hazel with some darker transverse bands; the whole surface is covered with chestnut rings of various sizes and thicknesses. The base is hazel with two chestnut patches on the columellar side and sometimes two on the outer side. Aperture teeth, the same color as the base, are delimited by two chestnut lines (one on each side).
**Body** The color of the foot and head is not known. The mantle lobes are light chestnut with brown spots; they have both short and conical papillae and in smaller numbers long and branched ones. The siphon is fringed at its free end. The radula is taenioglossan.
**Habitat** Like many cypraeids, it lives under rocks or corals in shallow waters in the infralittoral zone.
**Distribution** Indo-Pacific Province. Not found in the Red Sea or over a large part of the coasts of continental Asia.

## 267 LYNCINA AURANTIUM
### Golden Cowrie

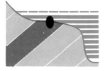

**Family** Cypraeidae
**Shell** Large (4 inches), spherical, sometimes roughly parallel sides; the ends project faintly; the body whorl leaves only a small part of the preceding ones uncovered (involute). The base is moderately convex and it has a callus that covers part of the apex of the shell. As the specific name suggests, the back is darkish orange. The base and the basal callus, which covers both ends, are creamy white. The aperture has well-developed, robust teeth, which are slightly narrower than the gaps between them. Like the back, it is orange.
**Body** As it is rather rare, the exact details of its soft parts are not known. Probably grayish or chestnut with a reddish tint. The mantle lobes, in preserved examples, are gray with white spots. These have both short smooth and long branched papillae. The very distinct head has two tentacles. The siphon is fringed at its free end. Like all cypraeids, the mantle cavity contains the gill, the osphradium and, in males, the penis. The radula is taenioglossan.
**Habitat** Normally it lives among the corals in the infralittoral zone.
**Distribution** Indo-Pacific Province, between the Philippines and Melanesia.

## 268 LYNCINA CAMELOPARDALIS
### Camel Cowrie

**Family** Cypraeidae
**Shell** Medium size (2 inches), pear-shaped. The body whorl completely enfolds and hides the preceding ones (convolute). The back is smoothly convex; so is the base, but much less so. The base has a callus that extends to the periphery of the shell, where it tapers and disappears. The aperture is rather wide; it is smoothly curved in the posterior half with numerous very small teeth that do not extend on to the columellar or the outer sides. The base, the two ends and the marginal callus are milk-white. The back is a darkish hazel with two slightly lighter transverse bands and roundish milk-white spots.
**Body** Though it is not very rare, there is no information in the literature on the color of the soft parts or whether the mantle lobes have papillae or not. As in all cypraeids, the mantle cavity contains the gill, the osphradium and, in males, the penis. The radula is taenioglossan.
**Habitat** It lives among corals in the infralittoral zone.
**Distribution** Indo-Pacific, confined to the southern Red Sea and the Gulf of Aden.

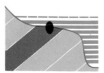

## 269 GENUS LYRIA
### Lyre Volutes (illustrated are Lyre-shape Volute and Kuroda's Volute)

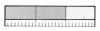

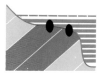

**Family** Volutidae

**Shell** Medium or sometimes large size (½ to 5½ inch), fairl thick, solid, high or very high conical spire, whorls weakly cor vex, suture impressed or, in some species, canaliculate varying from almost spherical to an elongated-spindle shap The aperture is elongated-ovoidal, rather wide; the outer li has a sharp edge. The inner lip has a callus; anteriorly thi covers part of the ventral surface of the body whorl; there ar also columellar folds, the anterior ones being more marke than the others. The sculpture consists of axial ribs; ofte these are very prominent, but sometimes they fade or are missing altogether. Some species have a faint spiral sculptur consisting of furrows or ridges, these are more prominent in the anterior part of the body whorl. There may or may not be periostracum. The operculum is horny, chestnut, and has nearly apical nucleus. The illustration shows, from left to righ L. lyraeformis and L. kurodai.

**Body** Its large foot in front is bipartite. The head has tw thick tentacles, each with an eye at its base. The rather lon penis is behind the right tentacle. The modified rachiglossa radula consists of a row of tricuspidate rachidial teeth.

**Habitat** Lives on coralline sandy bottoms in the infralittoral o on soft bottoms in the circalittoral zone.

**Distribution** L. lyraeformis is found on the coasts of Eas Africa; L. kurodai lives in the Japonic Province.

---

## 270 MAGILUS ANTIQUUS
### Magilus Coral Snail

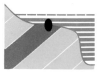

**Family** Coralliophilidae

**Shell** Medium size (1 to 3 inches), rather thin and fragile, ir regular shape as it grows between or in the bodies of the corals. The apical whorls are regularly convex with an incise suture and coiled in a spiral, then the shell grows as a tube wit an irregular course and a constant or very slightly increasing cross-sectional area. There is almost no sculpture in the spira part, but there are growth lamellae in the tubular part. White i color. Some authorities maintain that there is no operculum while others claim that there is one. Probably, as happens i other gastropods, it can be lost, even physiologically, and the reformed.

**Body** The body is not as large as the shell; in fact, it is muc smaller and occupies only the terminal part of its shell. As i grows it shifts its body and secretes a calcareous septum be hind it, closing off the part previously occupied. Other than thi there is no information in the literature on the morphology of it body. There is no radula.

**Habitat** It lives, as has already been said, between or in the bodies of corals in the infralittoral zone.

**Distribution** Spread throughout the Indo-Pacific Province.

## 271 MAURITIA EGLANTINA
### Eglantine Cowrie

**Family** Cypraeidae

**Shell** Medium size (1 ½ to 2 inches), thick and robust, moderately high spire; the body whorl does not completely cover the preceding ones and leaves the apical whorls exposed (involute). The back is regularly convex; the margins are moderately so; sometimes they are almost parallel. It is this characteristic that allows this species to be distinguished easily from the rest of the genus. The base is flat or moderately convex; its callus extends to the edges of the shell, but it is inconspicuous. The back has axial lines that have extensive breaks becoming rounded patches. The background color is greenish gray with three broad transverse chestnut bands. The shell margins have chestnut patches that extend partly on to the base. The faintly curved and rather narrow aperture has thin, not very extensive chestnut teeth. The base is a grayish beige. In the illustration the typical form is on the left, and the melanistic form, characteristic of New Caledonia, is on the right.

**Body** The foot is a very dark gray; the distinct head has two tentacles; the dark-gray siphon has its distal end extensively fringed. The mantle lobes, which can enfold the shell when completely extended, are almost black and have slightly darker short, conical papillae.

**Habitat** Commonly found under stones and corals in shallowish infralittoral waters.

**Distribution** Confined to the eastern zone of the Indo-Pacific Province.

## 272 MAURITIA MAPPA
### Map Cowrie

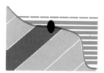

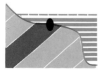

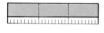

**Family** Cypraeidae

**Shell** Medium-large (4 inches), fairly thick and robust, the body whorl partly covers the preceding ones, leaving the shell apex visible (involute). It is spherical in overall shape; there are only rare cases with roughly parallel margins. The base is slightly convex, the ends are moderately protruded. The aperture is narrow, straight with only a slight curve at the rear and robust teeth, which are not extensive but are as broad as the gaps between them. The coloration is very variable; the background may be whitish, beige or pink, and on this there is an irregular pattern of extensively broken axial lines. The margins have chestnut spots. The base can be whitish or pink; sometimes it has a large dark patch on the columellar side. The teeth are either the same color or slightly orange.

**Body** There is no literature on the color of the foot, head or siphon. The two mantle lobes, which can enfold the shell, are a darkish chestnut and have numerous conical papillae. The radula is taenioglossan.

**Habitat** Like other cypraeids, M. mappa normally lives in the mid-reef zone, hidden among the corals in the infralittoral zone.

**Distribution** Indo-Pacific Province.

**GENUS MITRA**
**Miters (illustrated are Barbado Miter, Episcopal Miter, Fusiform Miter and Papal Miter)**

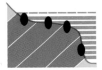

**Family**  Mitridae

**Shell**  From small to large size (¾ to 5 inches), typically very elongated-ovoidal, thick and solid, high spire, the whorls are very convex, sometimes flattened, the suture is markedly impressed. The aperture is elongated, with a wide notch for the mantle siphon; generally the outer lip tapers to an edge; the columellar lip usually has some sort of callus and from three to seven strong folds. Axial sculpture is uncommon; the spiral is made up of fairly stippled furrows or bands. The coloration is fairly uniform within a species but rather variable between different species. The patterning is usually patches, flamings or bands; these are darker than the background color. The darkish-chestnut periostracum is thin, though in some cases it is quite thick. There is never an operculum. The illustration shows *M. barbadensis* (top left), *M. mitra* (top center), *M. papalis* (top right) and *M. fusiformis zonata* (bottom).

**Body**  Though it is variable, the body coloration of *Mitra* sp. is usually whitish, and any patches are darker. The head has two tentacles, the eyes are in the proximal thirds of these. The proboscis is very long, and the end is bulbous. The mantle siphon is also long, and the radula is rachiglossan.

**Habitat**  Most species of this genus are limited to rocky or coral habitats, but some live on coralline sands or muds. They are found in all the zones of the phytal region and even (rarely) from the aphytal.

**Distribution**  Members of the genus *Mitra* are found in warm and temperate seas.

## 274 MODIOLUS AMERICANUS
### Tulip Mussel

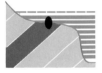

**Family** Mytilidae

**Shell** Medium size (2 to 4 inches), rather thin and fairly fragile, very swollen, equivalve and inequilateral, vaguely triangular; the umbones are rather stout, coarse and protruding. The periostracum is quite thick, chestnut, and has rather long and smooth bristles. The shell is dark chestnut at the anterior with a triangular yellowish band separating it from the lighter-chestnut posterior portion. The inside of the shell is mother-of-pearl with pink highlights. The ligament is external and posterior to the umbones. The hinge is completely lacking in teeth. As in all mytilids, the two muscle scars differ greatly (dimyarian, anisomyarian), and they are joined by a smoothly curving pallial line.

**Body** As in all related species, the foot is greatly reduced. The byssal gland is highly developed and produces a byssus with quite thick and strong filaments. Each of the two gills consists of two series of filaments, widely connected to form, in all, four series of lamellae (filibranch).

**Habitat** It lives among the corals, attached to them by its byssus, in the infralittoral zone.

**Distribution** It lives on both the Atlantic and Pacific coasts. In the Carolinan, Caribbean, Californian, Panamic and Peruvian provinces.

## 275 GENUS MONETARIA
### Money Cowries (illustrated are Gold-Ringed Cowrie and Money Cowrie)

**Family** Cypraeidae

**Shell** Small size (1 inch), moderately spherical, sometimes compressed (i.e., flattened dorso-ventrally), the body whorl completely enfolds and masks the preceding ones (convolute). The profile is variable (i.e., from quite rounded to polygonal, pear-shaped or, rarely, almost cylindrical). The base is moderately convex and has a thick callus that extends to the periphery, forming a conspicuous marginal callus. In *M. moneta* this callus sometimes, at the rear, has two tubercles or, more rarely, four. Sometimes, there are several coarse tubercles on the base. Yellowish or whitish, with an orange-yellow ring, hence the specific name of *M. annulus*. *M. moneta* gets its name from the fact that it is used as money in some places.

**Body** *M. moneta* has a black foot with yellow spots; the distinct head has two gray tentacles, the fringed siphon is grayish yellow. In *M. annulus* the two mantle lobes are dark gray with several sorts of papillae, usually yellowish gray and smooth. The radula is taenioglossan.

**Habitat** Shallow water in tidal pools in the mesolittoral zone and under stones or on seaweeds in the infralittoral zone.

**Distribution** The members of the genus *Monetaria* are widely spread in the Indo-Pacific Province.

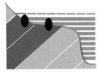

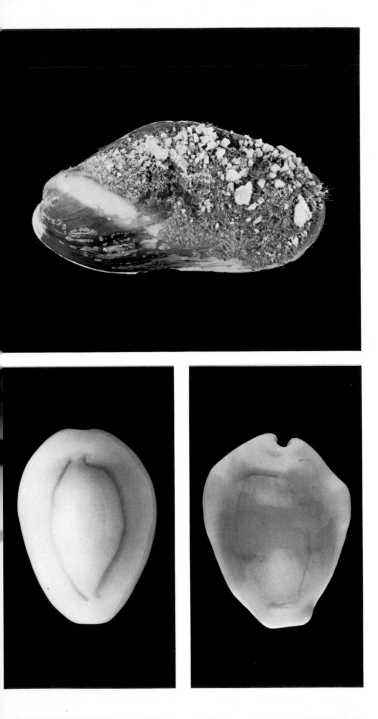

**GENERA MUREX, BOLINUS, AND HAUSTELLUM**
**Murex (illustrated are Scallop Murex, Snipe's Bill and Mediterranean Murex)**

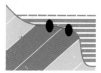

**Family** Muricidae

**Shell** Large size (3 to 6 inches), quite thin but not fragile, fairly high spire, incised or impressed suture, sometimes canaliculate; spherical shape with a siphonal canal that is much longer than the rest of the shell. The two margins of the canal are never fused. The sculpture consists of fairly fine and raised spiral ribs; in many cases, but not all, they form spines, sometimes very long, on the varices of the whorls. In some species there are also rounded axial ribs. The roughly circular aperture has an outer lip, which may be smooth and may have teeth or internal folds. The inner lip has a thin callus that can cover part of the body whorl. The coloration varies from species to species, it is hazel or chestnut with lighter or darker spiral lines or bands. The operculum is horny and ovoidal, and the nucleus is almost apical. The illustration shows *M. pecten* (top left); *M. haustellum* (top right); and *M. brandaris* (bottom).

**Body** The foot has a truncated front and an elongated posterior. The head has a long and retractile proboscis, two long, thin tentacles, each with an eye at its base. The mantle cavity contains a single ctenidial gill, in males a penis situated behind the right tentacle, and the hypobranchial gland, which, although present in other gastropods, is more developed in many muricids, secreting a purple substance, used in antiquity to dye cloth.

**Habitat** Rather varied. As a rule, *Murex* sp. live in the infralittoral and circalittoral zones on fairly coarse coralline detrital bottoms, on sands, muds or sometimes rocks.

**Distribution** Representatives in all warm seas, some species also live in temperate seas.

### 277 OLIVA BULBOSA
#### Swollen Olive

**Family**   Olividae
**Shell**   Medium size (1¾ inches), thick, robust, flattish spire. The body whorl is fairly spherical, and the suture is hardly incised. As in all olivids the aperture is narrow, the outer lip has no internal folds, and the columellar lip has a strongly toothed callus that extends posteriorly to cover part of the whorls and projects outward, forming a swelling. Like all members of the genus *Oliva* it lacks sculpture. The coloration is very variable, and the two examples illustrated here, give an indication of this. As well as albino and melanistic forms there are some with whitish or hazel backgrounds, with a dark-chestnut pattern of minute spots, zigzag axial lines, spiral stripes or bands, triangular patches. No operculum.
**Body**   It has a highly developed foot, which when completely extended covers a large part of the shell. The head has two long and thin tentacles, with eyes in their lower thirds. The mantle cavity contains the gill, the osphradium and, in males, the long, thin penis. The radula is rachiglossan.
**Habitat**   *O. bulbosa* lives buried in coralline sands in the infralittoral zone.
**Distribution**   Indo-Pacific Province; confined to the Indian Ocean, where it is very common.

### 278 OLIVA MINIACEA
#### Pacific Common Olive

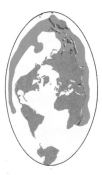

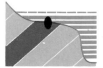

**Family**   Olividae
**Shell**   Medium size or sometimes medium-large (2½ to 3 inches), thick, solid, robust, flattish conical spire, the body whorl almost completely enfolds the preceding ones (involute). Almost cylindrical shape. The suture is incised between the apical whorls, becoming canaliculated between the later ones. The outer lip of the aperture lacks any internal teeth, and the columellar lip has a densely toothed callus that is expanded at the anterior. The surface is smooth and glossy. The coloration varies from white to orange or very dark chestnut, the most common base color is hazel, and the patterning consists of three broken chestnut stripes, one subsutural, one halfway along and one on the canal, as well as axial zigzag lines. Like all *Oliva* sp. it has no operculum.
**Body**   The foot is highly developed, as in all olivids, and when it is completely extended it covers the shell. The eyes are in the proximal third of the long, thin tentacles. The mantle siphon is very long, and it is the only part of the mollusk that projects above the sand when the animal is buried. The radula is rachiglossan.
**Habitat**   Coralline sands in the infralittoral zone.
**Distribution**   *O. miniacea* is one of the most beautiful and common olivids in the Indo-Pacific Province.

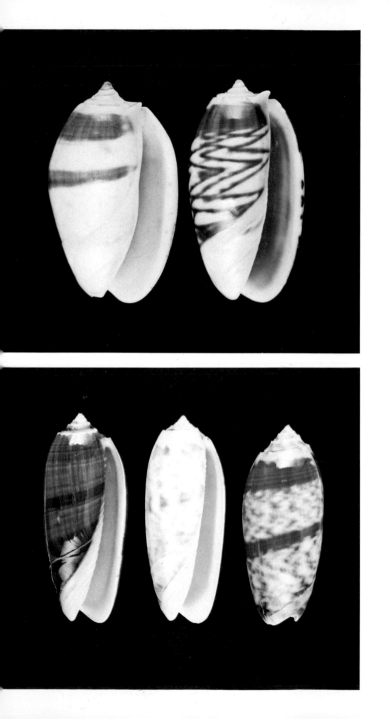

## 279 PISANIA PUSIO
## Miniature Triton Trumpet

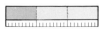

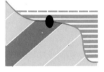

**Family** Buccinidae

**Shell** Small size (1 to 1½ inches), quite thick, robust, high conical spire, no siphonal canal, elongated shape, moderately convex whorls, suture barely incised. The aperture is elongated-ovoidal, the outer lip tapers and has thin internal folds. The inner lip has a slight, transparent callus and, toward the posterior end of the aperture, a strong tooth. The sculpture consists of thin spiral grooves; these may be absent, and on the apical whorls there are very small tubercles. The color is variable, usually a reddish chestnut with a lighter band halfway up the body whorl and spiral bands of darkish patches extending over the whole surface of the shell. The horny operculum has an apical nucleus.

**Body** The foot is quite thick and long. The distinct head, like all buccinids, has a long retractile proboscis; it also has two tentacles with an eye at the base of each. The mantle siphon is extremely long. The radula is rachiglossan.

**Habitat** Fairly common on or among corals in the infralittoral zone.

**Distribution** *P. pusio* is confined to the Caribbean.

---

## 280 POLINICES AURANTIUS
## Golden Moon Shell

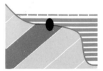

**Family** Naticidae

**Shell** Medium size (1⅛ inches), elongated-spherical, fairly thick and solid, with rounded whorls; the body whorl extensively covers the preceding one; its height is markedly greater than its breadth; barely incised suture. The aperture is semicircular, the outer lip is thin, the inner lip has a strong callus that partly covers the base, extending over the umbilicus and almost completely hiding it, leaving only a narrow, curved fissure free. Apart from very thin growth lines there is no sculpture. The yellowish or vivid orange color gives it its specific name, though the inner lip's callus and the apical whorls are white. The periostracum is opaque and chestnut orange. The horny operculum is the same color and is paucispiral, with a lateral nucleus.

**Body** The foot is highly developed, it can be completely retracted inside the shell or, when completely expanded, it can cover the shell quite extensively. The head has two rather short tentacles. The mantle cavity contains the gill, the osphradium and, in males, the penis. The radula is taenioglossan.

**Habitat** Sandy bottoms in the infralittoral zone.

**Distribution** Indo-Pacific Province, confined to the Pacific Ocean.

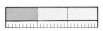

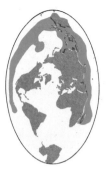

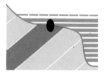

# PUSTULARIA CHILDRENI
## Children's Cowrie

**Family** Cypraeidae
**Shell** Small size (½ to ⅞ inch), roughly cylindrical, quite thin. The body whorl enfolds and masks the preceding whorls completely (convolute). The margins are roughly parallel. The back is regularly convex; so is the base, but gently so. The base has a callus that ends abruptly, forming a sort of step, at the margins of the shell. The ends are very protruded or even beaked. Unlike almost all other cypraeids, this species has a sculpture of thin transverse ridges, which are broken along a dorsal line and are extensions of the aperture teeth. These, obviously, extend across the whole base. The aperture is straight, very narrow and has parallel margins. It is a dark hazel, with yellowish shades.
**Body** Though it is not very rare and it has been collected alive many times, there is no information in the literature on the coloring of the soft parts or on whether the mantle lobes have any papillae. As in all cypraeids, the mantle cavity contains a single gill, one osphradium and, in males, a penis. The radula is taenioglossan.
**Habitat** It lives in the inner-reef section under corals, in the infralittoral zone.
**Distribution** Indo-Pacific Province; it has never been found on the coasts of Continental Asia, Africa or northern Australia.

---

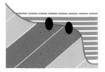

# FAMILY PYRAMIDELLIDAE
## Pyrams (illustrated are Needle Pyram and Miter Pyram)

**Shell** Small or very small (up to 1 inch), rather thin but robust, very high conical spire, turreted, the suture is incised or impressed. The embryonic whorls (protoconch) are heterostrophic (i.e., their axis of coiling is at an angle to the columella of the adult shell). The aperture has a complete ovoidal margin. The outer lip has a thin edge in some species; the inner lip generally has at least one strong, sharp columellar fold. The background color is white, hazel or chestnut, the patterning consists of rows of spots or irregularly arranged patches and thin spiral lines. Either there is no sculpture or it consists of closely packed axial ribs; sometimes the interstices are finely scored. The operculum is horny. The illustration shows *Pyramidella acus* (left) and *Otopleura mitralis* (right).
**Body** The foot is moderately developed. The head has two tentacles with an eye at the base of each, and a long evaginable proboscis. No radula, but the members of this species have a stiletto that pierces the integument of their prey. It lacks a gill. They are all hermaphroditic.
**Habitat** Many species are ectoparasitic on sponges, annelids, mollusks and tunicates; others are predatory, living on sandy, muddy or coralline sandy bottoms, as do the two illustrated species, in the infralittoral or circalittoral zone.
**Distribution** The Pyramidellidae are cosmopolitan.

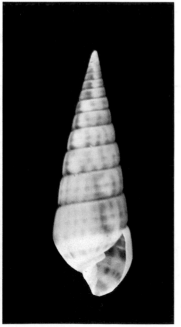

## 283 GENUS RHINOCLAVIS
### Horn Shells (illustrated are Striped Horn and Rough Horn)

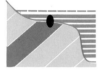

**Family** Cerithiidae

**Shell** Medium-large size (2 to 3½ inches), quite thick and robust, regular conical spire, very high (turreted), the whorls are almost flat, and the suture is weakly incised. The aperture is almond-shaped; the lip is slightly tapered, but never sharp; the columellar has a rather developed callus, and anteriorly it has a short, well-defined and dorsally pointed canal. The columella has a prominent central fold. The sculpture consists of thin spiral lines, which are faintly incised and often irregularly spaced on thin ridges. The axial sculpture consists of furrows, which extend from suture to suture on the embryonic whorls, but only over the upper third in the later ones. Other species have proper, weakly marked axial ribs; there are also sometimes blunt varices. The coloration is variable; there are white forms or forms with darkish-chestnut tessellations, spiral lines or stripes on a white background. The operculum is horny, yellowish, paucispiral, and it has an almost central nucleus. The illustration shows *R. fasciatus* (left); and *R. asper* (right).

**Body** The foot is rather thick, but not elongated. The head is very distinct and has two tentacles with ocular peduncles fused to their bases. The mantle cavity contains the gill and the osphradium, there is no penis in males. The radula is taenioglossan.

**Habitat** Fine sands in outer-reef sections of infralittoral zone.

**Distribution** Indo-Pacific Province.

## 284 STAPHYLEA CASSIAUI
### Cassiau's Cowrie

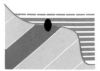

**Family** Cypraeidae

**Shell** Small size (½ inch), spherical, very thick and robust. The body whorl completely enfolds and hides the preceding ones (convolute). Both back and base are convex, the base has a large callus that extends to the borders of the shell, forming a marginal swelling. The two ends do not protrude. Like *Pustularia childreni*, this species is not smooth but sculptured. The aperture is narrow, almost straight, and has teeth. These teeth extend as thin ridges, over the base on to the marginal callus and the back of the shell, where there are spherical swellings, ending at a roughly median longitudinal furrow. The back is purple and the base is orange brown.

**Body** It is a very rare species. Only a score of examples have been collected, all without their soft parts.

**Habitat** Obviously, as no living specimens have been found, there is no information on its habitat. According to its discoverer, *S. cassiaui* lives in shallow waters, probably in the infralittoral zone.

**Distribution** The few known examples have all come from eastern Polynesia.

# STOMATELLA CALLOSA
## Callused Stomatella

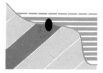

**Family**   Stomatellidae

**Shell**   Small size (¼ inch), thin, fragile and light; low spire; the whorls grow rapidly, so the body whorl is much larger than the preceding ones, ear-shaped, faintly similar to haliotid shells, but lacking the perforations on the margin between the dorsal and lateral surfaces of the whorls. The aperture is wide, with a very thin mother-of-pearl layer that allows the color of the back to show through; this varies greatly—white, yellow, reddish or chestnut, with quite large patches or flamings of various colors. The surface is smooth and glossy with no sculpture at all. It also lacks an operculum.

**Body**   The animal is larger than the shell. There is no literature on the anatomical characteristics of this family. The radula is rhipidoglossan, similar to the one in the subfamily *Gibbulinae*, with five lateral teeth per side.

**Habitat**   Like all Stomatellidae this species usually lives on corals in the mid-reef and outer-reef sections or, sometimes, attached to rocks or seaweeds in the infralittoral zone.

**Distribution**   Due to considerable systematic confusion over the entire genus, it is difficult to define the range of the species.

---

# STROMBUS PIPUS
## Seed Conch

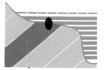

**Family**   Strombidae

**Shell**   Medium size (3 inches), quite thick and solid, moderately high conical spire, angular whorls, convex, incised suture. The sculpture consists of axial ridges on the first whorls and nodular bands all over the surface of the body whorl. The outer lip is slightly broadened and thickened. The aperture has an anterior, short, broad siphon and an anterolateral notch, characteristic of the strombids (the stromboid notch). White or cream with darkish-chestnut patches or undulating axial lines. The aperture is a pale violet on the inner side, darkening to purple or chestnut on the outer side. The operculum is horny, sickle-shaped with an apical nucleus.

**Body**   As of all strombids, the foot is arched and divided into a small anterior portion and a more developed posterior position, which bears the operculum and enables the animal to leap. The distinct head has two tentacles which are so extensively fused to the large ocular peduncles that their ends only just protrude beside the eyes. The mantle cavity contains one gill, one elongated osphradium and, in males, a penis.

**Habitat**   Sandy infralittoral bottoms in coral formations.

**Distribution**   Indo-Pacific Province, confined to the Pacific Ocean.

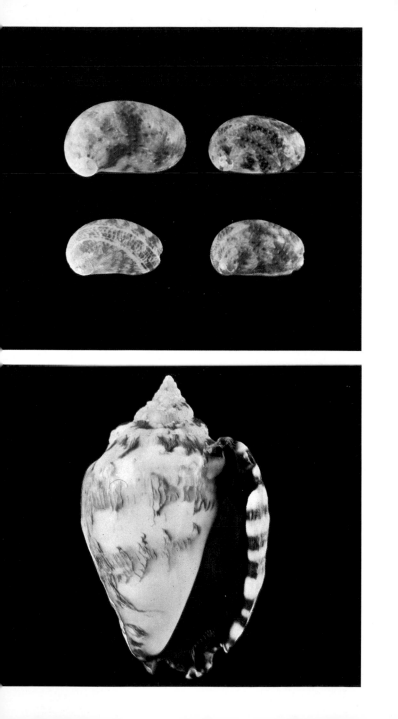

## 287 STROMBUS SINUATUS
### Laciniated Conch

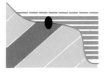

**Family** Strombidae
**Shell** Large size (4 inches), rather thick and robust, moderately high conical spire, the body whorl tends to broaden toward the aperture and partly covers some of the preceding whorls. The whorls are angular, with a nodular keel; the surface is concave both above and below it. The expanded aperture has three or four posterior fingers (pointed toward the apex), a short, broad anterior canal and an anteriolateral notch found in all strombids (the stromboid notch). The sculpture consists of axial ridges in the first turns and nodules on the keels of the others. Basically darkish chestnut with quite broad axial zigzag white lines. The aperture is, internally, violet, shading into white at its margins. The horny operculum is sickle-shaped, as in other strombids and assists in the leaping movements of these mollusks.
**Body** A narrow arched foot, only the anterior end rests on the bottom. Each of the long, thick ocular peduncles has a small tentacle at its end protruding through the anteriolateral notch in the aperture. There is only one gill, and the osphradium is very elongated. The radula is taenioglossan with very thick rachidial and lateral teeth, while the marginal teeth are thin.
**Habitat** Coralline sands in the outer-reef infralittoral zone.
**Distribution** Indo-Pacific Province, restricted to the western Pacific.

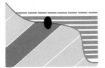

## 288 STROMBUS TRICORNIS
### Three-Cornered Conch

**Family** Strombidae
**Shell** Large size (4½ inches), very thick and robust, low conical spire; the body whorl expands near the aperture and partly enfolds some of the preceding whorls. There is a row of highly developed, squat, suprasutural nodules; the rest of the surface is concave. The suture is barely incised. The aperture edge is broadened, as in all strombids; it has a thickened outer lip that has a strong, broad posterior finger, a short anterior canal and an anteriolateral notch that is characteristic of all strombids (the stromboid notch). Apart from the suprasutural nodules, the only sculpture consists of the growth lines, some of these very incised. There is a thin, yellowish periostracum. The shell is whitish and has irregular chestnut patches, often with angular margins, some examples are almost completely chestnut. The aperture is white, tending to a brightish pink at the margins. The operculum is horny, sickle-shaped, with an apical nucleus (i.e., toward the anterior end).
**Body** The foot is arched and has a small anterior portion and a more developed posterior one that bears the operculum. The distinct head has two tentacles which are fused to the long, thick ocular peduncles. The mantle cavity contains a gill, an osphradium and, in males, a penis.
**Habitat** Sandy bottoms in coral formations; infralittoral zone.
**Distribution** Indo-Pacific Province in the Indian Ocean.

## 289 TECTUS CONUS
### Cone Top Shell

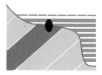

**Family** Trochidae
**Shell** Medium size (2 to 3 inches), moderately thick and robust, rather high, regular conical spire, flat whorls, incised suture, flat or slightly concave base, quite broad but shallow umbilicus. The aperture is strongly turned downward, so the angle it forms with the shell axis is not very acute. The outer lip is thin, the inner lip has a strong twisted columellar tooth characteristic of all *Tectus* sp. The sculpture consists of spiral ribs, broader than the interstices, with quite regular granules. At the bottom of each whorl, above the suture, one or sometimes two partly fused ribs protrude farther and are more coarsely nodular. The base of the shell has dense moderately corrugated concentric bands; these intersect with the thin growth lines. Whitish with darkish-pink flaming. The inner surface and the umbilical cavity are mother-of-pearl. The yellow operculum is horny, round, flat, with a central nucleus.
**Body** See *T. niloticus*. The radula is rhipidoglossan.
**Habitat** Rocky substrates in the upper level of the infralittoral zone, also mid-reef section of coral formations.
**Distribution** The entire Indo-Pacific Province, including the Red Sea.

## 290 TECTUS DENTATUS
### Toothed Top Shell

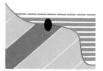

**Family** Trochidae
**Shell** Large size (3 inches), quite light and thin, very high conical spire, its height one and a half times greater than its breadth. Flat whorls, incised suture, base almost flat, no umbilicus. The aperture points downward; the angle that it forms with the shell axis is moderately acute. The outer lip is thin; the inner lip has a small columellar tooth. The surface has an irregular warty appearance caused by the very slanted growth lines intersecting with fading spiral ribs. The sculpture consists of a row of rather raised nodules or tubercles at the base of each whorl. The shell base is virtually smooth. White with fairly intense, oblique, reddish lines. There is a greenish stripe between the suprasutural nodules. The base is white with a broad green stripe around the columella. The inner surface is mother-of-pearl. The horny yellowish operculum is round and flat.
**Body** It has a large, soled foot, with a tentacled epipodium. The well-developed head has the pit eyes at the base of the tentacles. There is a single gill and one osphradium. The radula is rhipidoglossan.
**Habitat** Coral formations, inner- and mid-reef.
**Distribution** Indo-Pacific Province. It seems to be confined to the Red Sea or, at most, the western Indian Ocean.

## 291 TECTUS NILOTICUS
### Commercial Top Shell

**Family** Trochidae
**Shell** Large (3 to 5 inches), moderately thick and robust, high, regular conical spire; except for the body whorl, which is larger and flared, the whorls are flat; incised suture; the base is virtually flat with a broad, but not very deep, funnellike umbilicus. The aperture faces downward and is at an angle to the axis of the shell. The outer lip is thin. The sculpture, found only on the embryonic whorls (protoconch), consists of irregular, nodular, spiral ridges, the suprasutural one being larger than the others. The remainder of the shell, including the base, is smooth, apart from some vestigial spiral lines, which intersect the very thin growth lines. The operculum is horny, circular, and has a central nucleus.
**Body** It has a large foot, this is extracted by boiling, it is then smoked and can be eaten. Like the foot of other trochids, this foot has a laterodorsal fold (epipodium), which has long tentacles; pit eyes. A single gill and one osphradium. The heart has two auricles, and the rear portion of the intestine crosses over the ventricle. The radula is rhipidoglossan.
**Habitat** Coral formations, both inner-reef and mid-reef. Mainly infralittoral; also found in the lower levels of the mesolittoral zone.
**Distribution** Indo-Pacific Province, confined to the Pacific Ocean.

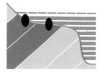

---

## 292 TELLINA FOLIACEA
### Leafed Telline

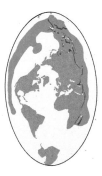

**Family** Tellinidae
**Shell** Medium size (3 inches), flattened valves, thin and fragile, slightly inequivalve and inequilateral. A thin brownish periostracum that often persists along the margins of the valves. Bright orange. The sculpture is restricted, over four fifths of the shell, to very thin growth lines; but in the posterior fifth, delimited by a radial keel, there are very small, irregularly distributed spiny processes. This area is edged by a dorsal keel bearing curved triangular backward-pointing spines. The umbones are very small; the external ligament is enclosed between the spiny dorsal keels of the valves. The hinge is heterodont. Inside the valves there are two roughly equal muscle scars (dimyarian, isomyarian). The pallial line has a moderately deep sinus (sinopalliate). As in all tellinids, there are two small muscle scars (left by the retractor muscles of the long siphons) below the pallial line and near the ventral margin of the valves.
**Body** No specific information concerning *T. foliacea*, but presumably it has the same morphological characteristics as other tellinids.
**Habitat** Fine sandy bottoms in the infralittoral zone.
**Distribution** Throughout the Indo-Pacific Province.

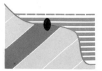

# FAMILY TEREBRIDAE I
## Auger Shells (illustrated are Triseriate Auger, Marlinspike, Eyed Auger, Crenulate Auger and Lance Auger)

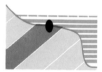

**Shell** Usually medium or large size (1 ½ to 10 inches), moderately thick, robust, very high spire, small almost flat whorls; in some species there is a slight shoulder immediately beneath the suture, which gives the whorls a weakly convex appearance; the suture is hardly incised, turreted shape. Small aperture, wide anterior notch prolonged in some cases into a very short canal. The outer lip is thin and sharp, the inner never has a callus but may have a small columellar tooth. The base always has a prominent band. As the illustration shows, the coloration is extremely variable. The sculpture may be completely missing or may consist of axial furrows; in some species there are rather flat and broad spiral bands. The operculum is horny, dark chestnut and has an apical nucleus. The illustration shows *Terebra triseriata* (left), *T. maculata* (top center), *T. guttata* (top right), *T. crenulata* (bottom center) and *T. lanceata* (bottom right).

**Body** The triangular foot is moderately developed. The head is distinct, the eyes may be about halfway along its two tentacles, or both eyes and tentacles may be absent. The penis is very long. The radula is toxoglossan, though in some species it is missing.

**Habitat** The members of this family usually live in coralline sands in the infralittoral zone.

**Distribution** All the illustrated species live in the Indo-Pacific Province; some extend into the Japonic and Panamic provinces.

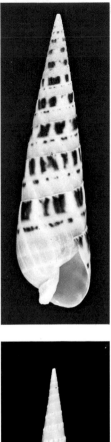

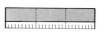

# FAMILY TEREBRIDAE II
## Auger Shells (illustrated are Flame Auger, Groved Auger, Senegal Auger, Atlantic Auger and Gray Auger)

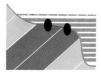

**Shell** Large size, medium or occasionally small (¾ to inches), usually thick, solid, very high turreted spire, the whorl are small and almost flat, they are slightly convex in only a fev species. The aperture is small; there may or may not be a shor siphon; the columellar lip does not have a callus, but it ma have a small tooth; the outer lip is always thin and sharp. Vari able coloration, often it consists of patches arranged quite reg ularly into spiral rows or axial lines or flamings. There is usuall no sculpture, but a few species have thin axial folds and one c two spiral furrows. The chestnut operculum is horny and has a apical nucleus. The illustration shows *Terebra taurinus* (left); *i strigata* (top center); *T. senegalensis* (top right); *T. disloca* (bottom center); and *T. cinera* (bottom right).

**Body** Little is known about the morphology and anatomy c the Terebridae. The triangular foot is moderately developec The distinct head may or may not have two tentacles, with th eyes halfway along these. The mantle cavity contains the gil the osphradium and, in males, a very long penis. The toxoglos san radula is missing in a few species.

**Habitat** A few species live on muddy substrates in the circa littoral zone. The others live in infralittoral coralline sands.

**Distribution** Apart from *T. strigata* which lives in the Panami Province, all the illustrated species live in the Caribbean an West African provinces.

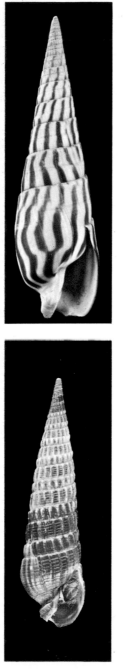

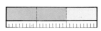

## 295 TEREBELLUM TEREBELLUM
### Terebellum Conch

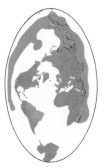

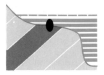

**Family** Strombidae

**Shell** Medium size (2 to 3 inches), rather thin but quite robust, flattish conical spire, characteristic ogive shape, anterior margin truncated, thin and sharp. The whorls are almost flat, suture barely incised. The outer lip is either thin or slightly thickened, the inner has a light callus. There is a slight notch where the outer lip attaches to the body whorl. No sculpture, the surface is smooth and glossy. Very variable coloration, generally whitish, with quite large, irregular, beige or chestnut spots, often arranged as spiral stripes. The horny sicklelike operculum has an apical nucleus.

**Body** As in other strombids the foot is elongated and arched, the anterior part is the smaller and the posterior part bears the operculum. The distinct head has two long, thick ocular peduncles; the tentacles are fused to these and project from the ends of them. The mantle cavity contains a gill and an osphradium and, in males, a penis. The radula is taenioglossan.

**Habitat** Like many strombids, it is quite characteristic of outer-reef sands in the infralittoral zone.

**Distribution** Throughout the Indo-Pacific Province.

---

## 296 SUBFAMILY THAIDINAE
### Rock Shells (illustrated are Vexillum Rock Shell and Sertum Rock Shell)

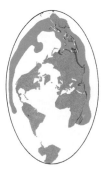

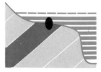

**Family** Thaididae

**Shell** Medium (1 to 2 inches), robust; generally high, sometimes flattened spire, siphonal canal virtually absent, spherical or elongated-spherical shape. The two illustrated species, *Nassa serta* (left) and *Vexilla vexillum* (right), differ in shape from all other thaidids. They have no sculpture or only thin, flat and inconspicuous bands. The aperture's outer lip is moderately thickened, and it lacks folds internally. The canal is rather broad. Even the coloration, especially of *V. vexillum*, is different, consisting of alternate dark and light bands. The chestnut operculum is horny and has a marginal nucleus halfway along the outer side.

**Body** Similar to the genus *Thais*. The radula of *N. serta* males differs slightly from the female radula.

**Habitat** The two illustrated species are restricted to corals in the infralittoral zone.

**Distribution** Both illustrated species live in the Indo-Pacific Province.

# GENUS TIBIA
## Tibia Conchs (illustrated are Spindle Tibia, Arabian Tibia and Martini's Tibia)

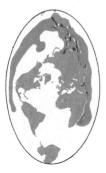

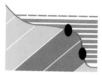

**Family**   Strombidae

**Shell**   Medium or large size (1 to 12 inches), very high conical spire (turreted), the whorls are markedly convex, impressed suture. Slightly expanded aperture lips, bordered by an external swelling, always smooth; there are usually fingers, sometimes rather long, on the outer lip. The columellar lip has a callus, which is sometimes very thick. There is always a sharp anterior canal; in *T. fusus* it is as long as the rest of the shell. At the point of attachment of the aperture to the body whorl there is always a notch or even a posterior canal. The sculpture is generally more marked on the first whorls, where it consists of axial ribs that cross fairly prominent spiral furrows. The other whorls are always finely scored by very thin spiral grooves, which are generally more obvious on the base of the body whorl. The color varies from yellowish to quite dark chestnut; some species also have darker or lighter spiral stripes or bands. The operculum is horny, ovoidal, slightly arched, with an apical nucleus. In the illustration are *T. fusus* (left); *T. insulae-chorab* (top right); and *T. martini* (bottom right).

**Body**   An elongated, curved foot, the posterior more developed and producing the operculum. The mantle margin is digitate. The head is distinct and has two long, thick ocular peduncles, the tentacles are fused to these and project from the top of them. The mantle cavity contains a gill, an osphradium and, in males, a penis. The radula is taenioglossan.

**Habitat**   The members of the genus *Tibia* are almost all deepwater or very-deep-water species, circalittoral or bathyal. Soft bottoms.

**Distribution**   Confined to the Indo-Pacific Province.

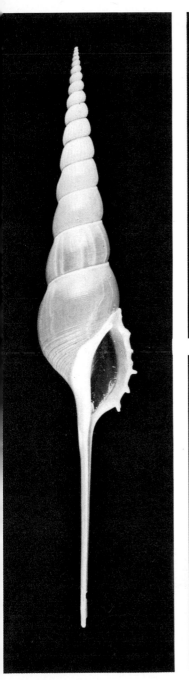

**TRIDACNA SQUAMOSA**
**Fluted Giant Clam**

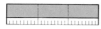

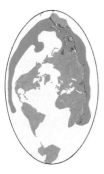

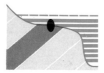

**Family** Tridacnidae

**Shell** Very large (up to 16 inches), semicircular, thick valves, robust, moderately swollen, equivalve and almost equilateral. The umbones are turned backward. Unlike most bivalves, tridacnids live with the ventral margin of the valve facing upward and the umbones downward, hence dorsal and ventral are reversed. Ventrally there is a roughly ellipsoidal hole through which the byssus emerges. The sculpture consists of four to twelve strong radial ribs, which bear a variable number of well-developed scales. These scales are almost always yellow, but the base color of the shell varies from white to yellow to pink. The ligament is secondarily posterior to the umbones. The hinge consists of one cardinal tooth on each valve, two lateral teeth on the right valve, and one on the left.

**Body** The anatomy of all tridacnids has been greatly altered because they rest on their umbones and the margins of the valves consequently face upward. One of the most obvious alterations is the rotation of the very reduced foot, except for the part that forms the byssus. The byssus remains physiologically ventral, but it emerges from the zone anterior to the umbones, which in normally orientated bivalves is dorsal.

**Habitat** *T. squamosa* lives firmly attached by its byssus to corals in the mid-reef section.

**Distribution** Indo-Pacific Province.

## 299 TROCHUS MACULATUS
**Maculated Top Shell**

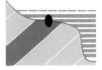

**Family** Trochidae

**Shell** Medium size (2 inches), robust, moderately thick, regular conical high spire, flat whorls, incised suture, flat base; wide, not very deep, funnel-shaped umbilicus. The aperture is turned downward and forms an acute angle with the shell axis. The outer lip is moderately thin, never sharp. The internal surface of the aperture and the umbilicus are mother-of-pearl, as are the teeth on the inner (columellar) lip. The lower parts of the aperture lips have blunt teeth. The sculpture consists of irregularly granular spiral ribs; there are sometimes axial ridges in the subsutural regions of the whorls. The base is covered by granular bands, which are finer than those on the surface of the whorls. Apart from some completely chestnut individuals, the coloration consists of irregular reddish or brown flamings on a dirty-white background. There is a not very persistent chestnut periostracum. The operculum is horny, round and yellowish.

**Body** Similar to *Tectus conus*. The radula is rhipidoglossan.

**Habitat** A typical species in the mid- and inner-reef sections of coral formations in the infralittoral zone.

**Distribution** Common throughout the Indo-Pacific Province, including the Red Sea.

---

## 300 TURBO CANALICULATUS
**Channeled Turban**

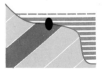

**Family** Turbinidae

**Shell** Medium size (2 to 3 inches), thick and robust, regular conical low spire. Its height is equal to, or slightly greater than, its breadth. The whorls are convex, and beneath the suture there is a deep smooth canal, which gives it its specific name. The convex base has a narrow umbilical fissure, which is shallow. The aperture is only moderately turned downward, the outer lip is rather thick. The sculpture consists of strong, smooth spiral ribs, there are sixteen or eighteen on the body whorl. The base color is a light hazel, with fairly extensive chestnut marbling or patches. The aperture is white. The calcareous operculum is paucispiral, flat on the inside and convex on the outer surface; there may be a lateral swelling.

**Body** Similar to other turbinids (i.e., a large anteriorly truncated foot, a very distinct head, with two tentacles and an eye at the base of each, one gill and one osphradium). The radula is rhipidoglossan, the second marginal tooth is more developed than the others.

**Habitat** The mid-reef and more often the inner-reef sections of coral formations.

**Distribution** Limited to the Caribbean Province, Southeast Florida and the West Indies, Brazil.

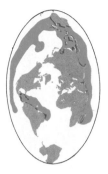

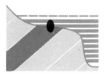

# GENUS VASUM
## Vase Shells (illustrated are Tube Vase, Caribbean Vase and Ceramic Vase)

**Family** Turbinellidae

**Shell** Usually medium, sometimes large size (2½ to 5 inches), very thick solid, heavy, spire may be low or, in some species, fairly high; short, very open, moderately broad siphonal canal. Overall shape, biconical. Elongated aperture, slightly wider at the rear. The outer lip has a spiny varix, but lacks internal folds and teeth. The columellar lip has a callus that extends moderately on to the ventral surface of the body whorl and has two or three robust, equidistant folds. The sculpture consists of fairly prominent spiral bands or ridges and large axial ribs on which there are stout spines. Almost always whitish with quite extensive dark-chestnut patches. The operculum is horny and thick, and it has an apical nucleus. The illustration shows *V. tubiferum* (top left), *V. muricatum* (bottom), and *V. ceramicum* (top right).

**Body** With a few exceptions, the several species of this genus are not rare, yet there is almost no literature, even brief, on their morphology or anatomy. The radula is rachiglossan.

**Habitat** Moderate depths in the infralittoral zone, on sandy bottoms, and they feed on bivalves or worms.

**Distribution** *V. tubiferum* lives in the Indo-Pacific Province, confined to the waters round the Philippines. *V. ceramicum* lives throughout the Indo-Pacific Province. *V. muricatum* lives in the Caribbean Province.

# SUBFAMILY VEXILLINAE
## Miters (illustrated are Little Fox Miter, Queen Miter, Food Miter and Eben Miter)

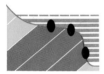

**Family**　Mitridae

**Shell**　Small or medium size (½ to 2 inches), quite high conical spire; general shape varies from ovate-spherical to elongated-spindle shape or even turreted. Convex whorls, impressed suture. Elongated aperture, short canal. In some species the outer lip has a thin, sharp edge. It can have internal teeth. The columellar lip has a thick callus with three to six strong folds. The sculpture is made up mainly of axial folds, which may be present or absent within the same species. The spiral sculpture consists of thin grooves. The coloration is very variable, generally spiral stripes or bands. The periostracum is thin and translucent. Like all mitrids it lacks an operculum. In the illustration are *Vexillum vulpecula* (above left); *V. regina* (top right); *V. trophonia* (bottom left); and *V. ebenus* (bottom right).

**Body**　Rather thin, elongated and multicolored foot. The distinct head has two long, thin tentacles, each with an eye near its base. The mantle siphon is short. The mantle cavity contains the gill, the osphradium and, in males, a long and curved penis. The radula is rachiglossan.

**Habitat**　Varied, generally the species of the subfamily live in the sand in the infralittoral zone, some live under rocks or between corals in the circalittoral zone.

**Distribution**　The subfamily is cosmopolitan.

**GENUS APLYSIA**
**Sea Hares**

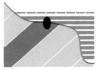

**Family**   Aplysiidae

**Shell**   Small or medium size, very thin, fragile, poorly calcified. Not visible from the outside; it is covered by the mantle which is much smaller than the animal that produces it; rounded disc shape anteriorly, angular at the rear. Hazel or light-chestnut color, growth lines are the only sculpture. The lower illustration has two views of the shell—from the ventral surface (left) and from the dorsal surface (right).

**Body**   Much larger (5 to 30 inches), than the shell, a well-developed foot with two broad parapodia, used for swimming. The head is very distinct, two tentacles lateral to the mouth, another two dorsal and posterior to the sessile eyes. When disturbed *Aplysia* releases a harmless red substance. The colored eggs are laid in gelatinous bands among the rocks and the seaweeds on which they feed. The radula has a lot of lateral teeth as well as rachidials.

**Habitat**   The members of the genus *Aplysia* live mostly on seaweeds, which they feed on, irrespective of the type of substrate; infralittoral zone.

**Distribution**   The genus is widely distributed in all warm and temperate seas.

# GENUS ARGONAUTA
## Paper Nautilus (illustrated are Common Paper Nautilus and Brown Paper Nautilus)

**Family**  Argonautidae

**Shell**  Like all Octopoda, genus Argonauta lacks a true shell. In size it is 4 to 8 inches. In females there is a structure with a parchmentlike appearance, secreted by two broadened arms; it encloses the eggs laid by the animal and part of the animal itself; it is called the pseudo shell, or nidamental shell. The illustration shows the nidamental shell of *A. argo* (top) and *A. hians* (bottom).

**Body**  The very distinct head has two large eyes, rivaling vertebrate eyes in complexity. The mouth has two strong jaws. The foot is transformed into a funnel and four pairs of tentacles. In the female, two of these are particularly broadened and form the nidamental shell. In males, during the reproductive season, a tentacle lengthens, loses its suckers and is detached once it has penetrated the mantle cavity of the female, fertilizing her with the spermatophores that it carries. The visceral sack lacks fins and is, in females, usually enclosed in the nidamental shell.

**Habitat**  Pelagic.

**Distribution**  Worldwide in warm waters.

## 305 ATLANTA PERONI
### Peron's Atlanta

**Family** Atlantidae
**Shell** Very small (½ inch) and fragile; thin, glassy, flatly coiled spire. Rounded whorls; the body whorl is angular at the periphery and has a well-developed keel, which gradually thins and disappears close to the aperture; this keel is made up of two very thin calcareous plates. The whole surface, including the embryonic whorls, is smooth and translucent apart from these very thin spiral grooves near the suture. The aperture is ovoidal; the longer axis is at right angles to the shell height. There is a deep notch halfway up the outer lip. Shell is glassy-white in color; the base of the keel may be brownish. Horny, thin, transparent, roughly triangular, paucispiral operculum with a nucleus close to the anterior margin.
**Body** Transparent, gelatinous appearance, a distinct head that has a large proboscis and two not very long tentacles with an eye at the base of each. The foot is subdivided into three lobes, an anterior flattened (propodium), transformed into a fin, a median (mesopodium), which has suckers and a posterior, operculum bearing one (metapodium). Taenioglossan radula.
**Habitat** Planktonic. It swims by means of its propodium in the upper levels of the sea, though it can extend down to 3,000 meters (10,000 feet). Predatory, it uses the mesopodial suckers to capture its prey and tears it with its radula.
**Distribution** Cosmopolitan.

## 306 BARLEEIA RUBRA
### Red Barley Shell

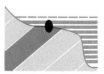

**Family** Rissoidae
**Shell** Very small (1/5 inch), moderately thick and robust, regularly conical, high spire, almost flat or slightly convex whorls, incised suture. The aperture lips lack a varix; no umbilicus. No real sculpture; apart from some more prominent growth furrows present in some individuals; the surface is smooth and glossy. Variable coloration, there are some light-hazel examples, others of a fairly intense reddish chestnut, and still others that are hazel with a chestnut stripe along the lower middle part of the whorls. There is a horny, yellowish operculum with an almost central nucleus.
**Body** Well-developed, long, narrow foot, pointed at the rear. The head is very distinct and has two tentacles with an eye at the base of each. The mantle cavity contains a single gill with relatively few branchial lamellae, one osphradium and, in males, a penis behind the right tentacle. The radula is taenioglossan.
**Habitat** Mainly infralittoral, usually living on seaweeds or marine phanerogams.
**Distribution** Lusitanian Province.

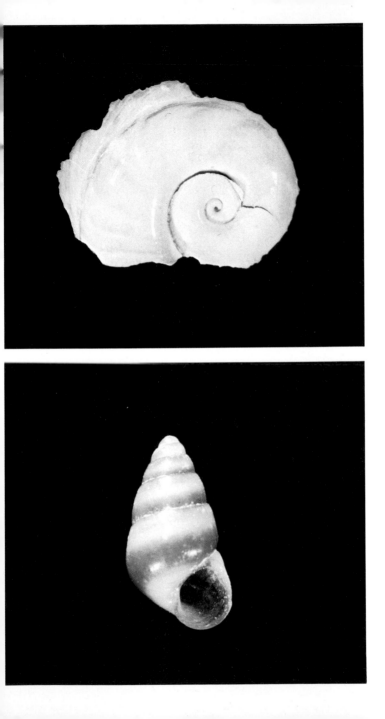

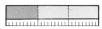

## 307 BERTHELINIA CHLORIS
### Bivalved Snail

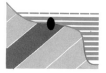

**Family**  Juliidae

**Shell**  Small (⅜ inch), light, fragile, thin; made up of two valves; this is very rare in gastropods. The left valve retains a trace of a spiraled apex, but there is none on the right valve. The right valve has developed from a lobe on the left side of the aperture, and by means of very small teeth, it articulates with the other valve; the two valves are linked by a ligament derived from the periostracum. Roughly trapezoidal shape. The sculpture consists of faint growth lines and thin radial grooves. As the specific name suggests it is a greenish-yellow color. The periostracum is thin and transparent.

**Body**  The foot is poorly developed, without parapodia, and is used in crawling; it can be completely retracted inside the shell, which is closed by an adductor muscle attached to the centers of the valves. The head has two auriculate tentacles and two smaller, oral tentacles. The mantle cavity contains a gill, and an osphradium. The radula consists of a single row of rachidial teeth.

**Habitat**  All *Berthelinia* sp. live on seaweeds in the infralittoral zone.

**Distribution**  Panamic Province, extending as far as the Galapagos Islands.

## 308 BULLA STRIATA
### Common Atlantic Bubble

**Family**  Bullidae

**Shell**  Small size (½ to 1 inch), moderately thick, fairly fragile and light, sunken spire, umbilicate. The body whorl completely conceals the preceding whorls; body whorl convex, ovoidal shape. Elongated aperture, narrow at rear, broadened anteriorly. The outer lip is thin, and the columellar lip has a light, not very extensive callus. The surface may be smooth, or there may be spiral grooves near the base and inside the apical umbilicus. Chestnut with indistinct lighter and darker patches, distributed irregularly over the whole surface. The aperture is whitish. No operculum.

**Body**  The foot is well developed, no parapodia. The head lacks tentacles, is broadened, and has a pair of sessile eyes. The mantle cavity contains the gill and the osphradium. Hermaphrodite. The radula has three rows of lateral teeth on each side, as well as the central rachidial teeth.

**Habitat**  Varied substrates, provided they are covered by seaweed, in the infralittoral zone.

**Distribution**  Both sides of the Atlantic, and Lusitanian and Caribbean provinces.

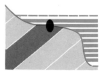

## CALPURNUS VERRUCOSUS
### Common Calpurnus

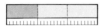

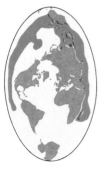

**Family** Ovulidae
**Shell** Small size (1 inch), rather thin and light, pear-shaped
The body whorl completely enfolds and hides the preceding ones (convolute). The back is very convex with a prominent blunt, median posterior, transverse rib. At the two ends, dorsal to the canals, are two rounded tubercles with deeply incised margins. Only the anterior end protrudes (slightly). The slightly convex base has a callus that continues on to the sides and even quite extensively on to the back of the shell, where it progressively fades away. The aperture is fairly narrow at the posterior but wider at the front and is gently but smoothly curved. Only the outer lip has teeth, these extend to its margin. The sculpture consists of very fine, almost invisible transverse grooves on the back. No operculum.
**Body** The entire body is yellowish white, the foot has well spaced blackish spots; on the mantle lobes this spotting is much denser; these lobes, when fully extended, can cover the shell. The siphon is not fringed. The radula is taenioglossan.
**Habitat** Like all ovulids, *C. verrucosus* lives on coelenterates, which it feeds on, in the infralittoral zone.
**Distribution** Fairly common throughout the Indo-Pacific Province except for the Red Sea.

---

**310**

## CAVOLINIA TRIDENTATA
### Three-Toothed Cavoline

**Family** Cuvieridae
**Shell** Small (up to ¾ inch), light, thin, fragile, spherical, apex posteriorly pointed, two long lateral furrows, which divide it into a dorsal, slightly convex portion that with three slightly raised folds, overhangs the ventral portion; the latter is spherical with a marked anterior swelling and numerous, thin, transverse ribs. The narrow arched aperture continues laterally as the furrows mentioned above. The specific name derives from its three posterior spines; one of these is on the apex, and the other two are at the points of union of the dorsal and ventral parts of the shell. A light hazel or honey color with darker bands along the lateral fissures and on the posterior part of the shell. The illustration shows three views of the shell: as seen in profile (left), ventrally (top right) and dorsally (bottom right).
**Body** Small foot, expanded laterally and anteriorly as two lobes (parapodia), which form the two fins that the mollusk swims with. The very reduced head has two unequal tentacles. The visceral sack is rotated through 180 degrees with respect to the anterioposterior axis, so the mantle cavity is ventral. The gill is reduced.
**Habitat** Planktonic, from the surface to a depth of 100 meters (300 feet).
**Distribution** A discontinuous range—Pacific and eastern Atlantic Ocean.

# FAMILY EPITONIIDAE
## Wentle Traps (illustrated are Precious Wentletrap, Magnificent Wentletrap, Lamellose Wentletrap and Noble Wentletrap)

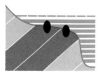

**Shell** Small to medium size (½ to 4 inches), generally light. High spire. Whorls convex, suture impressed; convex base with rare exceptions, no umbilicus. The aperture is round. The sculpture is variable; in a large number of species there is a distinct predominance of axial sculpture consisting of generally thin, often lamellar, ribs which may have a spiny process near the upper margin. There may be no spiral sculpture or it may consist of smooth, stippled or honeycombed microscopic grooves. The larval shell (protoconch) always differs in sculpture from the rest of the shell; the coloration also varies. White species are most common. The operculum is horny, pauci-spiral, and has a central nucleus. In Figure I the illustration contains *Epitonium scalare* (top left); *Amaea magnifica* (top right); *Epitonium lamellosum* (bottom left) and *Sthenorythis pernobilis* (bottom right).

**Body** A short foot. The eyes are at the bases of the two long tentacles. The mantle cavity contains a single gill and one rather long osphradium. There is no penis in male-phase individuals. The Epitoniidae are protandrous hermaphrodites. The pharynx has a sort of evaginable proboscis through which the food is taken in. The radula is ptenoglossan.

**Habitat** Varied. The Epitoniidae may be found on soft bottoms from the infralittoral to the lowest part of the aphytal zone. Many species are found associated with coelenterates (corals, sea anemones, etc.), and this is probably a general characteristic of the family.

**Distribution** This family is found in all seas, but warm and temperate seas have a much greater number of species than cold ones.

## 312 FLABELLINA AFFINIS
### Mediterranean Flabellina

**Family** Flabellinidae
**Shell** As for all Nudibranchs, absent.
**Body** Rather small size (about ¾ inch), elongated, narrow foot, pointed at rear and broadened to form two long lateral appendices at the front. The head has a pair of long tentacles lateral to the mouth and a posterior dorsal pair; these latter function as chemoreceptors and are called rhinophores. The eyes are sessile. No mantle cavity, the respiratory function of the gill is taken over by dorsal, branched projections, called cerata; to enable gaseous exchange their epithelium is richly vascularized. Internally the cerata contain diverticula of the liver; these store the stinging capsules (nematocysts) of the coelenterates on which it feeds. The radula consists of one row of rachidial teeth and one row of laterals on each side.
**Habitat** Infralittoral. It can live directly on rigid substrates, on seaweeds or on various animals, such as bryozoans or hydrozoans of the genus *Endendrium,* on which it feeds.
**Distribution** Lusitanian Province. Restricted to the Mediterranean Sea.

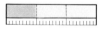

---

## 313 HIPPONIX CONICUS
### Cone-Shaped Hoof Shell

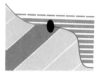

**Family** Hipponicidae
**Shell** Medium-small size (¾ inch), thick and robust, conical- or limpet-shaped; the spiral coiling is so loose and the growth so rapid that the shell is cap-shaped. The circular aperture has a complete and crenulated margin. The sculpture consists of coarse radial ribs, varying in size within the same individual. The growth lines are circular and visible. Usually lightish chestnut, tending to beige or white toward the apex. No operculum.
**Body** Reduced, discoidal foot, which secretes a thin calcareous plate on to the substrate to which the animal is attached. The large, cylindrical tentacles have sessile eyes at their bases. The mantle cavity contains a single gill, osphradium and, in males, a penis. The females lay the eggs in capsules that are attached to the calcareous plate secreted by the foot. The taenioglossan radula has strong rachidial and lateral teeth.
**Habitat** All *Hipponix* sp. live on rigid substrates, consisting exclusively of the shells of other mollusks.
**Distribution** Like all hipponicids, it is confined to warm seas. Indo-Pacific Province.

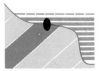

## 314 ISOGNOMON ALATUS
### Flat Tree Oyster

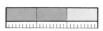

**Family** Isognomonidae

**Shell** Medium size (2 to 3 inches), inequivalve and inequilateral, vaguely rounded shape, strongly compressed. No periostracum. Color varies from grayish chestnut to reddish. The sculpture consists of very irregular growth lamellae. The anterior margin of the shell has a narrow fissure through which the byssus emerges. Edentulous, a very long, thick ligament. As in all other members of its family, the resilium is broken into small zones; these are parallel to each other and at right angles to the shell margin. A single muscle scar (monomyarian). The pallial line is smoothly curved (integropalliate). The inner surface of the shell is mother-of-pearl.

**Body** Moderately developed foot, two gills each consisting of two series of filaments, widely connected—in all, four series of filaments (filibranch). The foot secretes a strong byssus and this fixes it to the substrate.

**Habitat** Like many members of its genus it is attached to mangrove roots in the mesolittoral zone. It can also be found on submerged bodies and in sheltered places, but always in shallow water.

**Distribution** Mainly Caribbean—extending from Florida to Texas, the West Indies and Brazil.

---

## 315 JANTHINA JANTHINA
### Common Purple Sea Snail

**Family** Janthinidae

**Shell** Medium size (1 to 1½ inches), rather thin and compared to other species in the genus, quite robust, short spire, very swollen whorls, very impressed suture. The base lacks an umbilicus. The aperture lips are thin and sharp; in profile the outer lip has a deep notch, the bottom of which is in the lower third of the body whorl, in line with its blunt keel. The inner lip is bent back on to the columella. The axis of coil of the embryonic whorls (protoconch) is at an angle to the columella. The only sculpture consists of growth lines whose paths parallel the outer lip. There are also less prominent, irregularly spaced, frequently broken, spiral grooves. The base and keel of the body whorl are an intense violet, shading to white toward the apex and the basal zone around the columella. Larval forms have an operculum, adults do not.

**Body** Similar to *J. nitens*, apart from a few differences—e.g. it does not attach its eggs to "rafts" of gas bubbles; as it is ovoviviparous, it gives birth to larvae that have developed in the eggs that are incubated inside the mother. The males lack a penis. The radula is ptenoglossan.

**Habitat** Pelagic. It lives attached to pelagic coelenterates (*Physalia* or *Velella*) or floating by its own means.

**Distribution** Except for very cold seas it is almost cosmopolitan.

## 316 JANTHINA NITENS
### Mediterranean Purple Sea Snail

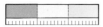

**Family** Janthinidae

**Shell** Small (1 inch), very thin and extremely fragile, spherical, moderately high spire, convex whorls and impressed suture. The base does not have an umbilicus. The aperture lips are thin and sharp. The axis of coil of the apex is at an angle to the rest of the whorls. The sculpture consists of growth lines; these are waved in the middle of the whorls; in the lower part of the body whorl there are numerous thin, discontinuous, spiral grooves. Violet coloration, more intense at the base of the whorls; in their upper portion there is a fairly prominent whitish subsutural band. No operculum.

**Body** Rather broad, short foot that secretes, at the anterior end a "float," made up of a large number of bubbles full of air, with thin but tough walls. This structure helps the animal to float and supports the egg capsules. The head has two bifid and unequal tentacles. The mantle cavity contains the gill, the osphradium. Individuals that are functionally male do not have a penis; like the Epitoniidae, the Janthinidae are protandrous hermaphrodites. The radula is ptenoglossan and lacks rachidial teeth.

**Habitat** Pelagic, like all Janthinids; it can float because of the "raft" secreted by its foot.

**Distribution** Lusitanian Province; mainly confined to the Mediterranean Sea.

## 317 LOLIGO VULGARIS
### Common Atlantic Squid

**Family** Loliginidae

**Shell** Relatively large size, thin, light, horny, not calcified, feather-shaped, transparent, corresponding to the proostracum of the sepia shell.

**Body** In size up to 24 inches, very elongated, well-developed head, a pair of complex lateral eyes. The mouth has a pair of strong jaws. The foot is transformed, as in all cephalopods, into a ventral funnel and ten arms; of these, eight are retractile and shorter than the remaining two, which can be completely retracted into pouches in the mantle. The mantle cavity contains a pair of well developed gills. The water circulates around the mantle cavity, entering through the gap between the anterior margin of the mantle and the foot, and leaving, expelled violently, through the funnel. There are two triangular, lateral fins in the posterior third of the body. The eggs are laid in gelatinous bands attached to submerged bodies.

**Habitat** Pelagic, over a range of depths.

**Distribution** *L. vulgaris* lives in the eastern Atlantic, confined to the North Temperate Zone and extending into the Mediterranean.

## 318 LOPHA CRISTAGALLI
### Cockscomb Oyster

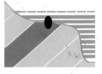

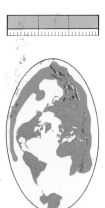

**Family**  Ostreidae

**Shell**  Fairly large (3½ inches), and thick, inequivalve and in equilateral, like all ostreids, as its attachment to rigid substrates affects the overall shape. The lower (left) valve has spoutlike projections, which adhere to the substrate. The thin periostracum is light hazel, but the valves are a quite purple violet. Internally the shell is golden yellow. The specific name derives from the strongly toothed (zigzagged) borders of the valves, which resemble a cock's comb. The sculpture consists of a dense, fine granulation over the whole surface of the valves. Edentulous, monomyarian and integropalliate, though the pallial line is often difficult to see. The ligament is internal, the shell has a leaved shell structure.

**Body**  It has a pair of gills, each of which consists of two series of lamellae, extensively fused by interlamellar junctions (eulamellibranch). This species and the rest of the genus incubate the eggs for some time.

**Habitat**  Rigid substrates in the infralittoral zone. Many species of the genus *Lopha* can live on either mangroves or gorgonids, and they have different shell characteristics (ecomorphs), depending on which of these two types of substrates they live on.

**Distribution**  Throughout the Indo-Pacific Province.

---

## 319 MODULUS MODULUS
### Atlantic Modulus

**Family**  Modulidae

**Shell**  Small (½ inch), quite thick and robust, moderately high conical spire, height almost equals breadth, flat whorls, slightly stepped impressed suture. The periphery of the body whorl is angular. The base is flat or moderately convex, with a narrow deep umbilicus. The aperture lips are thin, sharp and finely toothed internally. The columella has a sharp and finely internally toothed lip. The columella has a sharp tooth at its base. The sculpture consists of tightly packed, strong spiral ribs both on the surface of the whorls and on the basal region. Grayish with irregular darker patches; the columella and its tooth are whitish. There is a round, horny, multispiral operculum with a central nucleus.

**Body**  Thick, not very elongated foot. The very distinct head has a pair of long tentacles with the eyes about halfway along them. The mantle margin is fringed. The mantle cavity contains only one gill and one osphradium. The radula is taenioglossan, rather short, and one lateral tooth has a long basal appendix.

**Habitat**  Like almost all modulids, this species lives on sea weeds found on sandy or muddy bottoms in the infralittoral zone.

**Distribution**  Confined to the Caribbean Province, North Carolina to Texas and to Brazil, and Bermuda.

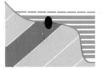

## 320 NAUTILUS POMPILIUS
### Chambered Nautilus

**Family** Nautilidae

**Shell** Very large size (4 to 8 inches), moderately thick, robust, coiled into a flat spiral, convolute (i.e., the body whorl completely covers the preceding ones). The aperture is very wide, and its margin is rather thin. The internal subdivision of the shell into successive chambers by calcareous septa is characteristic. These septa are laid down by the animal during its growth and have at their center a hole through which the mollusk, which occupies the last chamber, remains in contact with the previous ones. The shell surface is smooth and bears no trace of sculpture. The terminal third of the body whorl is white, the intermediate is white with orange-brown stripes, and the remaining third is black.

**Body** Like all cephalopods, the foot is transformed into a funnel and arms or tentacles; these are very numerous and are arranged in two concentric rows around the mouth. The eyes are of the primitive pit type. The extensive mantle cavity contains four large gills, hence the name "Tetrabranchia" given to the Nautiloidea.

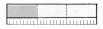

**Habitat** Pelagic, at depths of 50 to 100 meters (165 to 325 feet).

**Distribution** Like the rest of its genus it lives in the Indo-Pacific Province, restricted to the western Pacific.

---

## 321 NERITINA COMMUNIS
### Common Pacific Nerite

**Family** Neritidae

**Shell** Small size (¾ inch), rather thick and robust, moderately high spire, globular shape, regularly rounded whorls, each of which extensively covers the preceding one, slightly impressed suture, no umbilicus. The outer lip of the aperture is thin and sharp, the inner lip is finely toothed and thickened to form a marked whitish columellar callus. No sculpture; the surface is smooth and glossy. The background color is red, tending to crimson, though there are yellowish examples. The patterning is extremely variable, usually consisting of a quite broad white band in the middle of the body whorl and black perpendicular, undulating or even zigzag lines or stripes. The operculum is semicircular, calcareous, and as in all neritids, has a small apophysis pointing toward the columellar margin.

**Body** Rather large; the internal walls of whorls are reabsorbed, and so it occupies a large globular cavity. The foot is large and lacks an epipodium, the head is very distinct and has two long tentacles. There is one gill, one ospradium and one nephridium. The radula is rhipidoglossan.

**Habitat** Typical of muddy bottoms in areas of mangroves.

**Distribution** Indo-Pacific Province, confined to the west central Pacific.

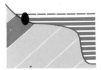

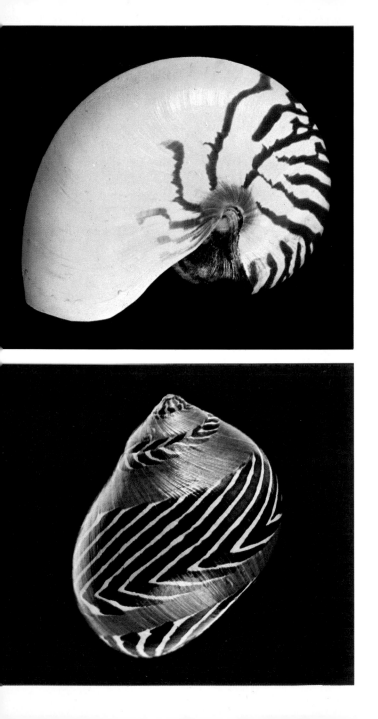

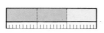

## 322 OVULA OVUM
### Common Egg Shell

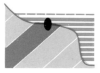

**Family** Ovulidae

**Shell** Large size (3 to 4 inches), quite thick and robust, por cellaneous appearance, elongated-spherical, the two ends ar very protruded, the posterior one is beaked. The body whor completely enfolds and hides the preceding ones (convolute The aperture is smoothly curved over its entire length, quit narrow at the rear, tending to widen at the anterior. The colu mellar side lacks both teeth and a callus, but the outer side i folded inward, lightly thickened, so as to form a sort of labi swelling; has a weakly lined surface bearing blunt, coarse, in regularly spaced and not very prominent teeth. The shell is mil white, the inner surface, visible through the aperture, is dar red.

**Body** The foot, the head with its two tentacles, the sipho and the mantle lobes are black with irregular scattered yellow white spots. The free end of the siphon is not fringed, and th mantle lobes have some very short papillae; these too are ye low-white. The radula is taenioglossan.

**Habitat** Like other ovulids, it lives in association with th coelenterates on which it feeds in the infralittoral zone.

**Distribution** Widespread in the Indo-Pacific Province.

## 323 PHASIANELLA AUSTRALIS
### Australian Pheasant Shell

**Family** Phasianellidae

**Shell** Medium-large size (3 inches), not thick, fragile, ver high conical spire, moderately convex whorls, impressed su ture, no umbilicus. The outer lip is thin and sharp. Neithe sculpture nor a periostracum, the shell is smooth and glossy Like all phasianellids the color and patterning is very variable simplifying matters a little, the background color may rang from white to orange, pink or chestnut, and the patterning ma be either vaguely perpendicular (axial) zigzag speckling or sp ral dashes, usually rather dense but sometimes widel spaced—these are dark chestnut, greenish or grayish, regu larly spotted by often oblique whitish patches. The white oper culum is calcareous, faintly almond-shaped, pointed at the top slightly convex, paucispiral with a basal nucleus.

**Body** The foot is long, narrow, longitudinally bipartite, th epipodium has long cirri (three per side). The head is very dis tinct and has two very long tentacles. The radula is rhipido glossan; the thin rachidial tooth does not have cusps; there ar five lateral teeth and many marginal; these have more cusp (up to six) toward the outer border.

**Habitat** It generally lives on marine plants (dicotyledons o the genus Cymodocea, in the infralittoral zone.

**Distribution** Confined to the Australian Province.

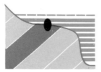

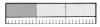

## 324 PSEUDOSIMNIA CARNEA
### Dwarf Red Ovula

**Family**  Ovulidae
**Shell**  Small size (⅓ to ½ inch), quite thin but solid, pear-shaped, ends markedly protruding, the body whorl completely enfolds and masks the preceding ones (convolute). The back is smoothly convex and completely covered by very thin transverse grooves. The base is smooth, convex, and has a callus that extends to the margins of the shell; this callus forms a swelling around the outer lip and above the two canals (anterior and posterior). The aperture is rather narrow, curved for its whole length, but more so at the rear. The columellar side lacks teeth, but the outer one is finely toothed. The coloration varies from pinkish white to brick red, frequently there is a dorsal patch, sometimes a stripe of a slightly paler color; the ends are also paler. There is no operculum.
**Body**  The narrow foot is pale red with scattered brownish dots. The distinct head has two whitish tentacles with an eye and a brownish patch at the base of each. The siphon has a smooth free end and is a glassy white, but the semitransparent mantle lobes have reddish-brown dots. The radula is taenioglossan and the marginal teeth are extensively fringed.

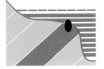

**Habitat**  Generally associated with red corals in the circalittoral zone.
**Distribution**  Found on both sides of the Atlantic, the Lusitanian and Caribbean provinces.

---

## 325 PTERIA HIRUNDO
### Wing Oyster

**Family**  Pteriidae
**Shell**  Medium size (3 inches), fragile, inequivalve and inequilateral, resembles a wing in shape. The ears, the extensions of the shell at the sides of the umbones, differ greatly, the posterior is sword-shaped and longer than the triangular anterior one. The periostracum is thin and yellowish. The shell is light brown, translucent; frequently having numerous irregular and quite broken, violet rays spreading from the umbones. The sculpture consists of growth lines that bear irregularly fringed concentric lamellae, which overlap one another. The ligament is posterior to the umbones and is carried in an oblique groove on the dorsal margin of the valves. Though it is edentulous, the hinge has one or two tooth-shaped processes. Monomyarian and integropalliate. The shell has a prismatic structure with crossed lamellae externally and mother-of-pearl internally.
**Body**  Though it is fixed to the substrate it has a well-developed foot and a strong byssus that emerges through a byssal notch deeply incised in the right valve.

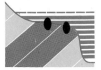

**Habitat**  It can be found in two different situations. Either solidly attached to gorgonias, in masses of individuals on muddy circalittoral bottoms.
**Distribution**  Lusitanian—from Southern England to the Mediterranean.

## 326 RAPA RAPA
### Papery Rapa

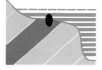

**Family** Coralliophilidae
**Shell** Large size (3 inches), thin, very light and fragile, very flat spire, moderately long canal, pear-shaped, resembling a turnip, as the generic and specific names suggest. The whorls are very swollen, and the suture is canaliculated. The aperture is almond-shaped and very wide; the outer lip is thin and toothed in the anterior third; the inner lip has a light callus; this is attached to a small part of the ventral surface of the body whorl and is more extensive in the anterior third. The sculpture consists of roughly equal spiral ridges, which are narrower than the gaps between them. Pure white or very light hazel. The horny operculum is yellowish and much smaller than the aperture.
**Body** The foot is well developed but short and stout. The distinct head has a long proboscis and two tentacles with an eye at the base of each. There is a large mantle cavity containing a gill, an osphradium and, in males, a penis. Like all coralliophilids, it does not have a radula.
**Habitat** It lives completely hidden with Alcyonacean coelenterates (soft corals) in the infralittoral zone.
**Distribution** Indo-Pacific Province, confined to the Western Pacific.

## 327 SUBFAMILY RISSOINAE
### Risso (illustrated are Variable Risso, Violet Risso and Golden-capped Risso)

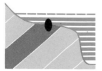

**Family** Rissoidae
**Shell** Small (¼ to ½ inch), thin and fragile, turreted or high conical spire, the whorls almost flat or markedly convex, the suture incised or very impressed. The base usually lacks an umbilicus, the aperture lacks canals and is externally thickened by a quite prominent varix. The sculpture varies from completely smooth forms to forms with well-developed axial ribs, usually fading at the base of the body whorl. Almost all the species have translucent or whitish shells; there may also be reddish-chestnut or violet pattern of flamings, tessellations or bands. Aperture lips may be chestnut or violet. The operculum is horny and has an almost central nucleus. In the illustration, from left to right are *Rissoa variabilis*, *R. violacea* and *R. auriscalpium*.
**Body** A long, narrow foot, pointed at the rear. Distinct head with two rather long tentacles, the penis is behind the right-hand tentacle. The mantle cavity contains a rather small gill and one osphradium. The radula is taenioglossan, one lateral tooth has a long lateral appendix.
**Habitat** All members live on seaweeds or marine phanerogams in the infralittoral zone.
**Distribution** The illustrated species all come from the Mediterranean. The subfamily itself is found in all seas.

## SUBFAMILY SIMNIINAE
### Simnias (illustrated are Common Volva, Flamingo Tongue, Single-Toothed Simnia, and Wheat Simnia)

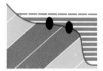

**Family** Ovulidae

**Shell** Generally small or rather large (½ to 4 inches), light, quite fragile, spindle-shaped; often very elongated; the body whorl completely enfolds and hides the preceding ones (convolute). The ends may project slightly or, much more frequently, they are beaked. The dorsal surface is smoothly arched, sometimes it has a blunt, median-posterior, transverse keel. The regularly convex base has a callus that is thicker and more robust on the outer side than on the columellar side and, so, frequently has a marginal swelling. This callus can extend on to the margins, and it can even cover the back almost completely (*Cyphoma gibbosum*). The aperture is generally rather wide, at least anteriorly, and never has teeth. The coloration is very variable both within and between species. It appears that shell-color pigments may come from the coelenterate species that the ovulids feed on. No operculum. In the illustration are *Volva volva* (top left); *Cyphoma gibbosum* (center top); *Simnia uniplicata* (top right); and *Simnia spelta* (bottom).

**Body** Generally highly colored, often the same color as the coelenterate on which the species live. The siphon may be smooth or fringed at its free end. The mantle lobes entirely cover the shell, may be smooth or have fairly developed papillae. The mantle cavity contains one gill, one osphradium and in males, a penis. The radula is taenioglossan.

**Habitat** The members of this subfamily live on coelenterates generally gorgonids. Therefore they usually live in the infralittoral and circalittoral zones, but they can also extend down to greater depths.

**Distribution** All seas, especially warm seas, but also temperate.

**329**

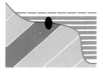

## SMARAGDIA VIRIDIS
### Emerald Nerite

**Family**  Neritidae

**Shell**  Very small size (¼ to ⅓ inch), thick and robust, very high spire, vaguely globular shape; the whorls are rounded, and each one almost completely covers the preceding one, the suture is barely incised, like all neritids, and it lacks an umbilicus. The aperture has a thin, sharp outer lip, and the inner (columellar) lip is finely toothed and thickened, forming a columellar callus. No sculpture; the surface is smooth and glossy. The coloration, as the specific name suggests, is a brilliant green; the body whorl has a pattern of small, white zigzag lines or stripes, often edged by a black line. The calcareous operculum is semicircular and green like the rest of the shell; its nucleus is laterobasal, and it is paucispiral with the internal apophysis characteristic of the Neritidae.

**Body**  A beautiful green, like the shell. A large foot, lacking an epipodium; a very distinct head with two long tentacles. The mantle cavity has one gill and one osphradium. The radula is rhipidoglossan.

**Habitat**  It usually lives on green seaweeds or eelgrass in the infralittoral zone.

**Distribution**  Found on both western and eastern coasts of the Atlantic Ocean.

---

**330**

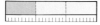

## SPIRULA SPIRULA
### Common Spirula

**Family**  Spirulidae

**Shell**  Small size (up to 1 inch), rather thin and light, but because of its structure, quite robust; coiled into a flat spiral with separated whorls; unlike *Nautilus* shells, which coil above the body, it is coiled ventrally. This species also has concave septa, which subdivide the cavity into quite a few chambers, which are linked by a siphon (siphuncle) that passes through off-center apertures (displaced toward the ventral margin). The surface undulates slightly as the shell is faintly constricted in the regions corresponding to the septa. White in color.

**Body**  It is much larger than the shell, which it almost completely covers. The distinct head has ten arms, eight of these having suckers over their entire inner surface, the remaining two being longer and having suckers only on the distal third. The funnel derived from the foot is formed by the fusion of two lobes along the ventral line. The mantle cavity contains only two gills, a characteristic of the subclass Coleoidea (dibranchia).

**Habitat**  A pelagic species found at depths of between 50 and 500 meters (165 to 1,650 feet).

**Distribution**  Cosmopolitan.

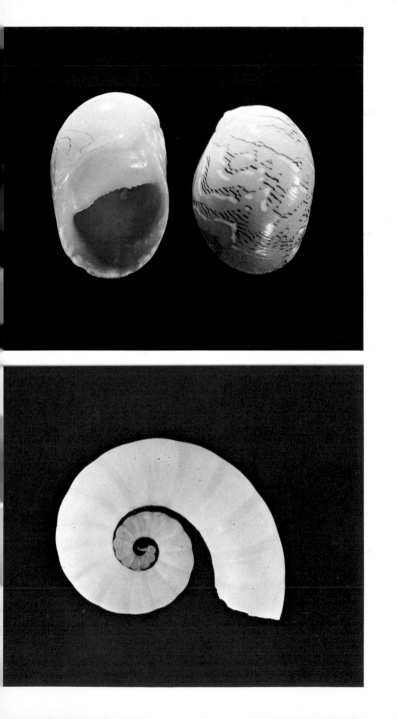

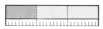

## 331 TRICOLIA SPECIOSA
### Showy Pheasant

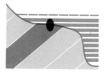

**Family** Phasianellidae
**Shell** Small size (about ½ inch), light, fragile; the conical spire is very high, and the height may be double the breadth; the whorls are regularly rounded, the suture is impressed, and the base lacks an umbilicus. The aperture slants moderately in relation to the shell axis. The lip is thin and sharp. There is neither a periostracum nor any sculpture; the shell is smooth and glossy. The coloration and pattern vary greatly. There are uniformly white, orange, red and chestnut forms or, much more frequently, examples with patterns made up of zigzag, generally perpendicular, white or chestnut stripes or lines. The operculum is ovoidal; the upper part is pointed, white, slightly convex; the nucleus is off center, and it is paucispiral.
**Body** A beautiful pea-green color. The foot is long and thin with a laterodorsal fold (epipodium) which has long cirri. The distinct head has two long tentacles, one gill and one osphradium. Rhipidoglossan radula; broad but cuspless rachidian tooth.
**Habitat** It lives almost exclusively on the leaves of posidonias (a marine plant) in the infralittoral zone.
**Distribution** Lusitanian Province, confined to the Mediterranean area.

## 332 TRIVIA ADRIATICA
### Adriatic Trivia

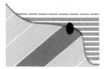

**Family** Eratoidal
**Shell** Small size (⅓ inch), light, quite fragile, spherical, very low spire; the body whorl completely covers the preceding ones (convolute); the ends are slightly beaked. The sides and back are rounded, but the base is almost flat. The aperture is cracklike, curved slightly at the rear and broadening a little anteriorly. The edge of the outer lip is bent inward and has from twenty-five to thirty-eight teeth, these are extensions of the ribs that cover the whole surface of the shell. The inner lip also has teeth, which have the same origin as those on the outer lip. A very light pink in color, the ribs and base are slightly lighter or whitish. No operculum.
**Body** The foot is rather long and narrow. The distinct head has two long tentacles with an eye at the base of each. The mantle has two lobes, which can emerge through the aperture and cover the shell completely. The mantle cavity contains one gill, one osphradium and, in males, behind the right tentacle, a fairly large penis. The radula is taenioglossan.
**Habitat** It appears to live on the Bryozoans of coarse detrital bottoms in the circalittoral zone.
**Distribution** Lusitanian Province, confined to the Adriatic Sea.

## 333 TRIVIA PEDICULUS
### Coffee Bean Trivia

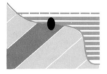

**Family** Eratoidal
**Shell** Small size (½ inch), fairly thick, robust, spherical, low spire; the body whorl completely covers and masks the preceding ones (convolute). The moderately wide aperture has almost parallel and straight margins, except for the posterior fifth, which is gently curved. The outer and columellar lips are lightly callused and possess teeth (from thirteen to seventeen on the outer lip) that continue as ridges on to the base, flanks and back up to a deep median furrow. Near this furrow the ridges swell, and their ends are pustular. Pinky brown in color, with three pairs of chestnut patches on the back; the margins and base of the shell are darker and more grayish than the back. There are some pink examples.
**Body** A quite narrow foot; the distinct head has two tentacles with an eye at the base of each. The two mantle lobes can extend to enfold the entire shell. The mantle cavity contains one gill, one osphradium and, behind the right tentacle in males, the penis. The radula is taenioglossan.
**Habitat** It lives on rigid substrates covered by colonial tunicates, and it deposits its eggs inside them. Infralittoral zone.
**Distribution** Carolinan and Caribbean, North Carolina to Florida and to Brazil, and Bermuda.

## 334 TYMPANOTONUS FUSCATUS
### Brown Cerith

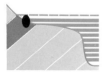

**Family** Potamididae
**Shell** Medium size (2 inches), moderately thick and robust, very high regular conical spire (turreted). The aperture is ovoidal; the outer lip is thin; toward the bottom there is a notch leading into a short canal. This species varies so much in shape and sculpture that many authors consider the two extreme forms to be distinct species: *T. fuscatus* (on the left in the illustration) and *T. radula* (on the right). In the first form the apical whorls are finely nodular, but toward the aperture they have a strong keel with highly developed spiny nodules. The second form has the same kind of sculpture, fine nodules, over its whole surface. The first whorls are often heavily eroded. Dark chestnut in color with greenish-yellow highlights. The horny operculum is round, multispiral and has a central nucleus.
**Body** A poorly developed foot. The distinct head has two tentacles, the eyes are set well away from the bases of the tentacles. The mantle cavity contains a single gill and one osphradium, the males do not have a penis. The radula is taenioglossan, the rachidial tooth has an extension.
**Habitat** Mesolittoral zone, muddy sands that are covered with organic material in areas of mangroves.
**Distribution** West African Province.

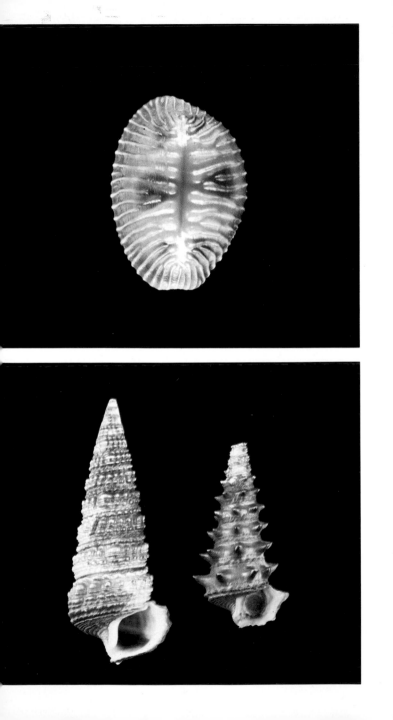

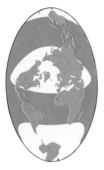

# SUBFAMILY VERMICULARIINAE, FAMILY TURRITELLIDAE AND FAMILY SILIQUARIDAE
## Worm Shells (illustrated are West Indian Worm-Shell and Slit Worm Shell)

**Shell** Medium or large size (up to 6 inches), moderately thick and robust, the first (apical) whorls are quite high and regularly conical, the later ones have an irregular path, furthermore though the first whorls are regularly fused along an incised suture, the others are separated. The aperture is circular and thin. In most cases the sculpture consists of rather irregular spiral bands, which are always thinner than the gaps between them. The genus *Siliquaria* has a spiral furrow, sometimes made up of successive ellipsoidal holes and deeply incised growth lines. Variable coloration, generally whitish or fairly dark chestnut, exceptionally, orange. There is always a horny circular operculum that is multispiral and has a central nucleus and fringed margins. The illustration shows *Vermicularia spirata* (top); and *Siliquaria ponderosa* (bottom).

**Body** A moderately developed foot. The distinct head has two not very long tentacles. Like all turritellids, the males do not have a penis. A single osphradium and one gill with filamentous lamellae.

**Habitat** Apart from a few exceptions these snails and close relatives live inside sponges in the infralittoral zone.

**Distribution** All warm and temperate seas.

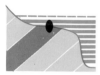

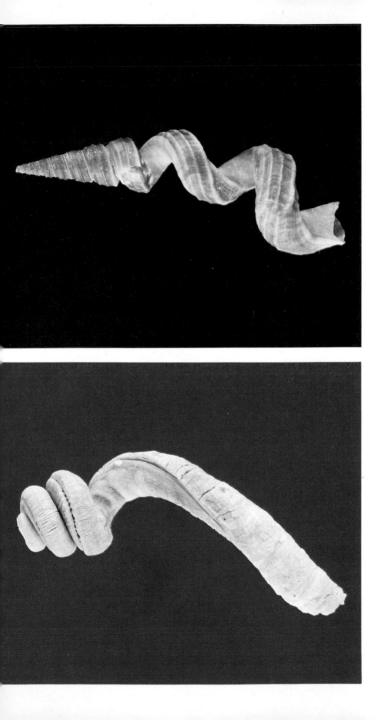

# LAND AND FRESH WATER MOLLUSKS

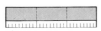

## 336 ACHATINA ACHATINA
### Common African Snail

**Family** Achatinidae
**Shell** Very large (8 inches), rather thick, robust, fairly high conical spire, slightly convex whorls, barely impressed suture, elongated-ovate in shape. It has a wide oval aperture, no canal, and in mature examples an outer lip that is bent slightly outward. The sculpture is restricted to fine axial growth lines. Chestnut in color with lighter flamings or irregular axial bands. The periostracum is thin, yellowish and rather persistent.
**Body** Chestnut color; large, elongated foot, pointed at rear. The upper pair of tentacles on the head are retractile and bear the eyes at their ends, the lower pair are also retractile, but are much shorter. Like all pulmonates, it is hermaphrodite. The eggs are rather large (up to 5 or 6 millimeters—0.20 to 0.24 inches) and have a calcareous shell. The radula consists of several rows with large numbers of teeth.
**Habitat** The genus is confined to Africa, except for one species that has been accidentally introduced to Florida, and many islands in the Pacific—Ceylon, Guam, Hawaii, etc. The infamous Giant African Snail (*A. fulica*) is a serious agricultural pest.

## 337 BITHYNIA TENTACULATA
### Faucet Snail

**Family** Hydrobiidae
**Shell** Small size (⅓ to ½ inch), rather thin but robust, fairly high conical spire; convex whorls; swollen, moderately impressed suture. The aperture is ovoidal, pointed at the top; the outer lip is thin. There is no trace of sculpture, and the surface is smooth, yellowish in color, horny. There is a rather thin calcareous operculum that is semitransparent, has a central nucleus, and has very marked concentric growth lines. The operculum is never, even when the animal is completely retracted, withdrawn inside the shell but juts out at the edge of the aperture.
**Body** The foot is expanded at the front into two lobes, and it is thin and pointed at the rear. The head is distinct and has two long threadlike tentacles, with eyes to the rear of their bases. The mantle cavity contains a single gill and, behind the right tentacle in males, a penis. The taenioglossan radula has one rachidial tooth and two lateral teeth and one marginal tooth per side.
**Habitat** Fresh water, on vegetation and on mud.
**Distribution** Continental Europe, Asia as far as the Himalayas and Africa north of the Sahara. Introduced into northeastern United States.

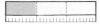

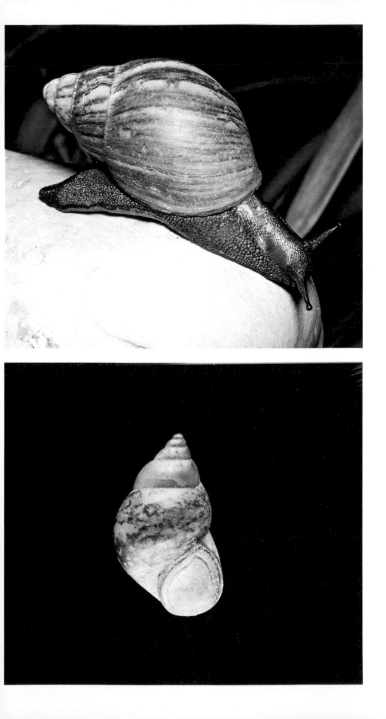

## FAMILY BULIMULIDAE
### Bulimulus Shells (Illustrated are Wagners Zaplagius and Tooth-Mouthed Bulimulus)

**Shell**   In general well developed, variable in size, small, medium, or even rather large (¾ to 2 inches); conical spire, generally quite high, moderately thick, rather solid, the whorls are quite convex, the suture impressed, the base has an umbilicus, which in adults is often closed off by a columellar callus. Generally the aperture is wide, round, sometimes almost triangular. The outer lip may be thin and sharp or bent outward or frequently, internally thickened. The columellar lip has a thick callus, and sometimes it is quite strongly toothed. Sculpture is almost always absent; some species have a very faint honeycomb pattern over the entire surface. The illustration shows from left to right *Zaplagius navicula* and *Odontostomus pantagruelinus.*

**Body**   The foot is large and well developed. The head has two pairs of tentacles, the upper pair, with an eye at the end of each, is longer than the lower pair. Like all pulmonates the members of this family are hermaphrodite. The radula consists of quite a number of rows, each of which has a large number of rather similar teeth.

**Habitat**   All bulimulids are terrestrial; generally they live on plants, some are arboreal.

**Distribution**   Central and South America, Australia, Pacific Islands. Southeastern United States, west to Texas.

---

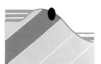

## CEPAEA NEMORALIS
### English Garden Snail

**Family**   Helicidae

**Shell**   Medium-small size (¾ to 4/5 inch), not very thick, moderately robust and solid, low conical spire; the body whorl enfolds a large part of the preceding one. The whorls are very convex, and the suture is impressed. The aperture lips are thin; the outer one is bent outward. No sculpture. Very variable coloration, usually a reddish-chestnut or yellow background color with spiral, sometimes broken, chestnut stripes; there are up to five on the body whorl. The stripes can merge, or in some examples a few may disappear. The aperture is white or chestnut. There is a thin, light hazel, transparent periostracum.

**Body**   The foot is well developed, often pale in color. The head has two pairs of tentacles, the eyes are at the ends of the upper; the lower pair is shorter. The radula consists of several rows, each with a large number of teeth. The hermaphrodite genital apparatus has a calcareous dart, kept in a pouch, which is used to stimulate the two partners during copulation.

**Habitat**   Meadows and woods.

**Distribution**   Widespread throughout Europe, part of Asia and North America.

## 340 CERION MARIELINUM
### Hand's Peanut Shell

**Family** Ceriidae
**Shell** Medium-small size (1½ inch), rather thick, solid and robust, very high conical spire, similar in shape to the pupae of some insects (e.g., flies). The whorls are moderately convex and the suture is very incised. Rounded aperture, the aperture lips are continuous, quite thick and bent outward. The columellar lip has two well-spaced and fairly prominent teeth. The sculpture consists of rather strong axial ribs, which are much thinner than the gaps between them. The apical whorls are smooth. The periostracum is quite thick and rather persistent particularly in the interstices between the ribs, its hazel color masks the cream color of the shell.
**Body** No information on the morphology of this species. Cerion radulae have large numbers of teeth per row. The genital atrium is rather broad, the penis is retractile, as in all pulmonates, and rather short. Hermaphrodite.
**Habitat** All members of this family live near the sea.
**Distribution** The example in the photograph came from Cuba; the genus *Cerion* is confined to the islands of the Caribbean, Bahamas, Cuba, Netherland Antilles and southeastern Florida.

## 341 CLAUSILIA CRUCIATA
### Crucified Clausilia

**Family** Clausiliidae
**Shell** Small size (½ inch), sinistral, like almost all clausiliids, moderately thick and robust; very high, conical spire, turreted, slightly convex whorls and rather impressed suture. The aperture is ovoidal, constricted at the rear, and the aperture lips are bent outward. The inner lip is always smooth, but the columellar one has a strong fold halfway along and two teeth in the rear part. The sculpture consists of quite tightly packed axial ridges, which are narrower than the gaps between them, and they are sometimes slightly oblique. The apical whorls are smooth and rather large. There is a thin, yellowish, transparent periostracum. The shell is dark chestnut. Like all pulmonates, it has no operculum, but it does have a narrow pedunculated lamella (clausilia), which fulfills the same function.
**Body** A narrow, elongated, rather developed foot. The head has two pairs of tentacles; the upper are rather long, the lower are reduced to conical papillae. Each row of the radula is made up of numerous teeth.
**Habitat** Tree trunks, moss covered rocks, above the tree line at rather high altitudes.
**Distribution** Boreal alpine.

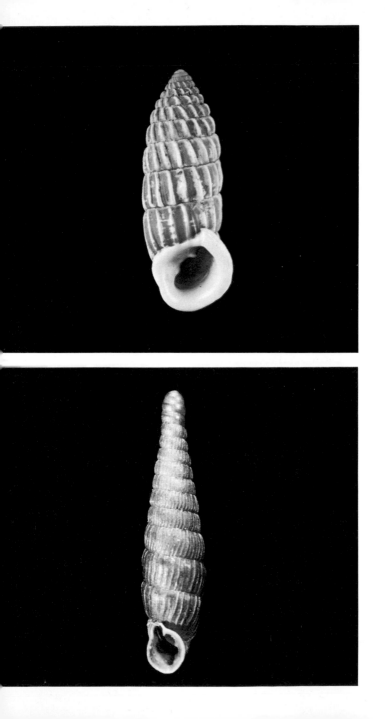

## 342 DREISSENA POLYMORPHA
### Many-Shaped Dreissena

**Family** Dreissenidae
**Shell** Medium-small size (1½ inches), roughly triangular, equivalve and inequilateral, valves swollen with a strong dorsal keel, umbones pointed. The periostracum varies in color from yellow to chestnut, the valves are yellow with a pattern of greenish-chestnut, wavy or angular, roughly concentric lines. The concentric growth lines are the sole sculpture. The external ligament is posterior to the umbones. Internally, beneath the umbones, the valves have a triangular septum. The two adductor-muscle scars differ in size (dimyarian, anisomyarian), the pallial line is smoothly curved (integropalliate).
**Body** It has a pair of gills, each of which consists of two series of lamellae, extensively fused by interlamellar junctions (eulamellibranch). It is sessile, so the foot is reduced and the byssus is well developed. The posterior margins of the mantle lobes are fused, forming two siphonlike apertures (inhalant and exhalant), ensuring water circulation in the mantle cavity.
**Habitat** An invasive species, attached to rigid substrates by its byssus, shallow waters. In Italy, in Lake Garda, it has been found down to a depth of 50 meters (164 feet). One of the few fresh-water bivalves to have a veliger.

**Distribution** In the past it was widely spread through Europe, but it was pushed back by the Ice Ages into Eastern Europe. Today it is recolonizing its old range.

---

## 343 LANCEOLARIA GRAYANA
### Gray's Naiad

**Family** Unionidae
**Shell** Medium size (3 to 4 inches), very elongated, moderately swollen valves, equivalve and strongly inequilateral. Covered by a robust and persistent periostracum, which is dark chestnut with greenish highlights. The sculpture consists of fairly regular fine, growth lines. One large radial rib runs from the umbones to the posterioventral edge of the valves. Anteriorly there is a similar rib, formed by the alignment of irregular, fairly raised warts. The external ligament extends both in front of and behind the umbones, these are often eroded. The actinodont hinge has two anterior teeth and one posterior tooth on the right valve, and one anterior and two posterior on the left valve. The muscle scars differ in size (dimyarian, anisomyarian), and they are linked by a smoothly curved pallial line (integropalliate).
**Body** It has a pair of gills each consisting of two series of lamellae extensively fused by interlamellar junctions (eulamellibranch). As in all Unionidae the larvae (glochidia) are incubated within the gills.
**Habitat** Muddy or sandy bottoms in inland waters.

**Distribution** China. A closely related species comes from Japan.

## 344 MUSCULIUM LACUSTRE
### Lake Fingernail Clam

**Family**  Pisidiidae

**Shell**  Small size (⅓ to ½ inch), thin and light, fragile, ovoidal, sometimes almost square, moderately convex, equivalve and almost equilateral. The thin, transparent periostracum is the same hazel color as the shell. Apart from the concentric growth lines, which are sometimes deeply incised and cover the whole shell surface, there is no sculpture. The umbones are rather large. The posterior ligament is embedded between the valves and is visible—with difficulty—from the outside. Heterodont hinge, two cardinal teeth on each valve, and anterior and posterior lateral teeth. It is hard to see the two adductor-muscle scars on the inside of the shell; they differ slightly (dimyarian, anisomyarian). The pallial line is smoothly curved (integropalliate).

**Body**  Unlike the related genus *Pisidium,* but like the genus *Sphaerium* (Musculium is sometimes considered as a subgenus of the latter), this species has mantle lobes that are fused at the rear, except for two short siphons. The foot is well developed and very mobile. It has a pair of gills, each consisting of two series of lamellae, extensively fused by interlamellar junctions. The eggs are incubated within the inner row of branchial lamellae.

**Habitat**  Rather stagnant fresh water, rich in algae, which the species lives on.

**Distribution**  Widespread in Europe and northern Asia.

---

## 345 MYTILOPSIS LEUCOPHAEATA
### Conrad's False Mussel

**Family**  Dreissenidae

**Shell**  Medium-small (½ to ¾ inch), moderately thick and robust, roughly triangular, vaguely mussellike (hence the generic name, which refers to *Mytilus*—mussel). It has a thin, smooth, glassy periostracum. The shell is a violet or a very dark chestnut. The irregular growth lines are the only sculpture. Inside the shell, immediately beneath the umbones there is a triangular calcareous septum; the anterior adductor muscle is attached to this; sometimes the septum has a small tooth to which the byssal muscle is attached. Though external, the ligament is deeply embedded in the valves. The hinge consists of a long plate beneath the ligament. The muscle scars differ (dimyarian, anisomyarian), and the pallial line is smoothly curved (integropalliate).

**Body**  A moderately developed foot; this emerges through an aperture between the two lobes of the mantle, which are extensively fused. To the rear there are two short siphons. There is a pair of gills, each consisting of two series of lamellae, extensively fused by interlamellar junctions (eulamellibranch).

**Habitat**  Fresh or brackish water, found in large numbers, attached by its byssus to underwater objects, especially near estuaries.

**Distribution**  Eastern and southern North America. New York to Florida, Texas and Mexico.

## 346 OBOVARIA RETUSA
### Dull Obovaria

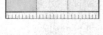

**Family** Unionidae
**Shell** Medium size (3 inches), very thick, quite swollen, equivalve and inequilateral. The chestnut periostracum is persistent, has greenish highlights and often has yellow-green rays. Sculpture virtually absent, confined to the concentric growth lines. The umbones are worn in young examples and are completely missing in adults—so much so that the apical part of the shell is flattened. The external ligament is posterior to the umbones. The hinge is actinodont with two anterior-lateral and two posterior teeth on the left valve, and three anterior and two posterior teeth on the right valve. Like all unionid shells the inside of the valve is mother-of-pearl and is colored a pale violet. The two muscle scars are roughly similar (dimyarian, isomyarian) and are linked by a smoothly curved pallial line (integropalliate).
**Body** In the subfamily Lampsilinae, to which *Obovaria retusa* belongs, the embryos are incubated in the rear part of the outer lamellae of each gill.
**Habitat** Muddy or sandy bottoms in inland waters.
**Distribution** Like the rest of the subfamily, *O. retusa* is confined to North America.

## 347 PHYSA FONTINALIS
### Common European Tadpole Snail

**Family** Physidae
**Shell** Small size (½ inch), sinistral, rather thin, light and fragile, moderately high spire, rounded whorls, very impressed suture, ovoidal shape; the body whorl makes up four fifths of the total length. The aperture is wide, broadened slightly at the front; the aperture lips are continuous; the fragile outer one is thin and sharp; the columellar one has a thin whitish callus, which extends a little way on to the ventral surface of the body whorl. The surface is covered by very thin longitudinal lines. It is a rather light-yellowish color.
**Body** The foot is very long, rounded at the front, thin and pointed at the rear. The broad head has two fairly long, thin tentacles, with an eye at the base of each. The mantle is large, the two lobes are fringed and can enfold part of the shell. The male genital aperture is behind the left tentacle, and the female one is below the *pneumostome*. Each row of the radula has a large number of teeth. The jaw is shaped like a plowshare.
**Habitat** Usually prefers still, muddy-bottomed fresh waters.
**Distribution** Old World.

## 348 PLANORBARIUS CORNEUS
### Horn-colored Ram's Horn

**Family** Planorbidae
**Shell** Medium-small size (¾ inch), moderately solid, thick, sunken spire, flattened, hence the generic name (i.e. flat wheel), convex swollen whorls, very impressed suture. Ovoidal, slightly expanded aperture; the outer lip has a thin, sharp edge, the columellar one has a slight callus, which does not extend far on to the ventral surface of the body whorl. The growth lines, which can be rather incised, are the only sculpture. As the specific name suggests, it is horn-colored, darker in the upper part of the whorls than the lower.
**Body** The foot is quite developed, truncated anteriorly and elongated at the rear. The distinct head has two long, thin tentacles, with an eye at the base of each. Like all pulmonates it is hermaphrodite. The radula is made up of quite a few rows each with a lot of rather similar teeth.
**Habitat** Calm, stagnant waters; found on the leaves of aquatic plants.
**Distribution** Throughout south-central Europe and Asia Minor. Pleistocene fossil shells belonging to this species have been found in many places in Europe.

---

## 349 POLYMITA PICTA
### Painted Polymita

**Family** Helminthoglyptidae
**Shell** Medium-small size (1 inch), rather thin, light, fairly fragile, low conical spire, vaguely spherical in shape, convex whorls, impressed suture. The body whorl almost completely enfolds the preceding one. Wide, ovoidal aperture; the outer lip is thin and sharp. No sculpture. Very variable coloration. The illustrated examples show some of the color and pattern variants of this beautiful species.
**Body** Large, well-developed foot, elongated posteriorly, truncated at the front. There are two pairs of tentacles, the upper pair is longer and has an eye at the end of each tentacle. Hermaphrodite, like all pulmonates. The genital system has a calcareous dart, which is used to stimulate and grip the partners during copulation.
**Habitat** Terrestrial, arboreal, rather common.
**Distribution** Characteristic of and exclusive to Oriente Province, Cuba.

## 350 QUADRULA QUADRULA
### Maple Leaf

**Family** Unionidae
**Shell** Medium size (up to 3½ inches), solid, rather thick valves, roughly quadrangular, projecting umbones. The moderately developed periostracum is brownish green. The sculpture consists of fairly coarse, irregular nodules or papillae, arranged in two radial lines, one perpendicular to and one oblique to the ventral margin; the latter splits the area of the valve posterior to the first row of papillae roughly in half. The concentric growth lines may be incised. The external ligament is rather developed. Actinodont hinge, one large and squat anterior tooth and an elongated posterior one on the right valve, two anterior and two posterior teeth on the left valve. The muscle scars on the inside of the valves are prominent and roughly equal (dimyarian, isomyarian). The pallial line is smoothly curved (integropalliate).
**Body** As in all unionids, the eggs are incubated in the gills. In this species all the lamellae are used. The foot is well developed.
**Habitat** No precise information.
**Distribution** Fresh water in Northern America—Mississippi River Drainage; part of St. Lawrence basin; Red River in Texas.

## 351 SUCCINEA PUTRIS
### Rotten Amber Snail

**Family** Succineidae
**Shell** Small size (½ inch), thin, fragile, light, moderately high conical spire; the whorls enlarge rapidly, so the body whorl is much larger than the preceding ones. The whorls are very convex, and the suture is deeply impressed. The aperture is ovoidal and very wide. The outer lip is thin, sharp and very fragile. The sculpture is restricted to weakly incised growth lines. Yellowish, hornlike in color.
**Body** Well-developed foot, its sole is tripartite. The distinct head has two pairs of tentacles, the upper, longer pair bears the eyes at its ends. Like all pulmonates, the gonad is hermaphrodite. The common genital atrium opens behind the upper right tentacle. The radula has several rows, each of which has many teeth.
**Habitat** Terrestrial, it needs high humidity. Commonly found on the stems or leaves of plants or on the mud near lakes, ponds or rivers.
**Distribution** Mediterranean, extending into Central Europe.

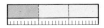

## 352 THEODOXUS LONGISPINA
### Long-Spined Nerite

**Family** Neritidae

**Shell** Small size (1 inch), rather thin, light, but not fragile; low spire; the spherical body whorl almost completely covers the preceding ones (involute). The columella base is covered by an extensive callus from the inner lip. The outer lip is thin and sharp. The only sculpture is a crown of long spines (which gives it its specific name) on the upper third of the body whorl. Blackish or sometimes, gray brown in color with slightly darker spots that merge into the base color. As in all neritids the operculum is calcareous, semicircular, with a lateroventral nucleus, paucispiral and an internal appendix.

**Body** It retains some primitive archaeogastropod characteristics, such as having two auricles in the heart and the posterior portion of the intestine crossing the ventricle of the heart, but unlike the Archaeogastropoda, the foot lacks an epipodium and males have a penis. The eggs are deposited on rigid substrates in hemispherical capsules. The radula is rhipidoglossan.

**Habitat** Still, fresh waters.

**Distribution** The Philippines.

## 353 THIARA AMARULA
### Spiny Theora Snail

**Family** Thiaridae

**Shell** Medium-small size (1½ inches), rather light and quite fragile, very high conical spire, more than twice as high as it is broad. The whorls are slightly convex and on their upper thirds they have a crown of fairly long spines pointing toward the apex. The aperture is ovoidal, the outer lip thin and sharp, the inner lip has a light columellar callus. The sculpture consists of widely spaced axial ribs that tend to fade out toward the base of the body whorl and form sharp, spiny processes in the upper thirds of the whorls. The growth lines are generally very prominent and incised. The apical whorls are often very eroded. The shell is a light chestnut-yellow and always has a dark-chestnut, almost black, very persistent periostracum. The operculum is horny with concentric whorls.

**Body** The foot is moderately developed. The head is distinct and has a pair of tentacles with the ocular peduncles at their bases. The mantle cavity contains a single gill. No penis in males. The radula is taenioglossan.

**Habitat** Like the rest of the family, it lives in fresh water in warm regions.

**Distribution** An African species.

## 354 TROPIDOPHORA CARINATA
### Carinated Tropidophora

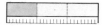

**Family** Pomatiasidae
**Shell** Medium-small size (1 inch), fairly thin, light, but rather robust, moderately high conical spire, breadth greater than height, very convex whorls, deeply incised, canaliculate suture. The sculpture consists of thin spiral ribs, some of which are keels, the mediodorsal and medioventral ones on the body whorl being more prominent. The base has an umbilicus. The aperture is ovoidal, with an almost central nucleus, paucispiral, internally horny, externally quite calcified.
**Body** The sole of the foot is divided by a median longitudinal furrow. The head is distinct and has two tentacles, with an eye at the base of each. The mantle cavity contains the osphradium and, in males, the penis, but no gill. Respiration takes place through the vascularized mantle. The radula is taenioglossan.
**Habitat** All members of this family are terrestrial, living hidden under stones, in the grass or on shrubs.
**Distribution** Pomatiasid species are found in Southern Europe, Africa and India.

## 355 TRUNCILLA TRUNCATA
### Deer Toe

**Family** Unionidae
**Shell** Medium size (up to 2½ inches), moderately swollen, very thick and robust valves, with a conspicuous layer of mother-of-pearl. The whitish coloration of the shell is masked by the very persistent periostracum, which is yellowish with darkish-green rays of different widths. The periostracum gives the shell a glossy appearance. The sculpture consists of very thin growth lines and a distinct and sharp radial rib extending dorsally and posteriorly from the umbones, thinning progressively, to about halfway along the shell. The external ligament is posterior to the umbones. The hinge is actinodont, with a strong anterior lateral tooth and a longer, narrow, posterior one. Inside the valves the two muscle scars are very prominent and almost equal (dimyarian, isomyarian). The pallial line that links them is smoothly curved (integropalliate).
**Body** There is a pair of gills, each consisting of two series of lamellae, extensively fused by interlamellar junctions (eulamellibranch). The posterior parts of the two outer rows of lamellae are modified into incubation chambers for the eggs.
**Habitat** Partly buried in sandy or muddy fresh-water bottoms.
**Distribution** North America. Mississippi Drainage-Western Pennsylvania west to Kansas, north to Minnesota and Michigan and south to northern Alabama and Texas.

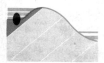

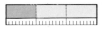

## 356 VIANA REGINA
### Queen Viana

**Family**  Helicinidae
**Shell**  Small size (⅜ inch), not thick, light, regularly conical
flattish spire, always greater in breadth than in height, whorls
regularly rounded, incised suture, convex base, umbilicus hidden by a thin columellar callus. The margin of the aperture is
angled at 45 degrees to the shell axis and has a notch in its
upper third. The sculpture consists of thin spiral bands, which
are slightly raised, are narrower than the gaps between them,
and almost disappear in the second half of the body whorl. Yellowish in color, faintly pink in the upper parts of the whorls with
a thin subsutural band. The calcareous operculum is almond-
shaped; its nucleus is off center, and there is a light callus toward the columellar side.
**Body**  A distinct head with long tentacles. Though *V. regina* is
a protobranch, the mantle cavity is transformed into a respiratory organ, with the consequent disappearance of the gill and
the osphradium. The posterior portion of the intestine does not
cross over the heart, which has only one auricle.
**Habitat**  Terrestrial, often living in trees.
**Distribution**  Confined to Cuba.

## 357 VIVIPARUS CONTECTUS
### Lister's River Snail

**Family**  Viviparidae
**Shell**  Medium size (1½ inches), thin, fragile, spherical overall
shape; six or seven regularly rounded and swollen whorls; very
deep suture; the base may or may not have a rather narrow umbilicus; the aperture lips are thin. The growth lines are occasionally more marked; otherwise virtually no sculpture. A
persistent greenish-yellow periostracum. The shell is yellowish
with three or four dark-red bands; these may merge or be
missing altogether. There is a horny, almond-shaped, concave
operculum; it has concentric growth and a nucleus that is almost central, usually displaced slightly upward. Due to its flexi-
bility the operculum can be withdrawn up to a fifth of the way
along the body whorl.
**Body**  Dark in color with greenish-yellow patches, a large foot
and a very distinct head with two long tentacles; the right one is
stouter, digitiform, and it functions as a penis. One gill and one
ctenidium. The heart has one auricle. The taenioglossan radula
has one rachidial tooth, two lateral teeth and one marginal
tooth, all very similar.
**Habitat**  Fresh water, especially ponds, lakes and marshes.
**Distribution**  European.

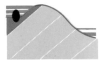

# CLASSIFICATION TABLE OF THE SPECIES MENTIONED IN THE TEXT

<small>POLYPLACOPHORA:</small> *Chiton magnificus* Deshayes.

## CLASS—POLYPLACOPHORA

**ORDER—Neoloricata**
SUBORDER—Ischnochitonina
    *FAMILY—ISCHNOCHITONIDAE*
        Ischnochiton rissoi Payraudeau, 1826
    *FAMILY—CHITONIDAE*
        Chiton squamosus L. 1764
        Chiton tuberculatus L. 1758
        Acanthopleura
SUBORDER—Acanthochitonina
    *FAMILY—ACANTHOCHITONIDAE*
        Cryptoplax larvaeformis Burrow, 1815

### CLASS—GASTROPODA

**Subclass Prosobranchia**
**ORDER—Archaeogastropoda**
SUBORDER—Pleurotomariinae
    **Superfamily**—Pleurotomariacea
    *FAMILY—PLEUROTOMARIIDAE*
        Pleurotomaria africana Tomlin, 1849
    *FAMILY—HALIOTIDAE*
        Haliotis lamellosa Lamarck, 1822
        Haliotis rufescens Swainson, 1822
        Haliotis fulgens Philippi, 1845
    **Superfamily**—Fissurellacea
    *FAMILY—FISSURELLIDAE*
    *Subfamily*—Fissurellinae
        Fissurella nodosa (Born, 1778)

*Subfamily*—Diodorinae
    Diodora graeca (L. 1767)
    Megathura crenulata (Sowerby, 1825)
*Subfamily*—Emarginulinae
    Scutis unguis (L. 1767)
    Hemitoma octoradiata (Gmelin, 1791)
    Emarginula puncticulata A. Adams, 1851
SUBORDER—Patellina
**Superfamily**—Patellacea
*FAMILY—PATELLIDAE*
*Subfamily*—Patellinae
    Patella caerulea L. 1758
    Patella cochlear Born, 1778
    Patella laticostata Blainville, 1825
*FAMILY—ACMAEIDAE*
*Subfamily*—Acmaeinae
    Lottia gigantea (Sowerby, 1834)
SUBORDER—Trochina
**Superfamily**—Trochacea
*FAMILY—TROCHIDAE*
*Subfamily*—Angariinae
    Angaria melanacantha (Reeve, 1842)
*Subfamily*—Monodontinae
    Monodonta turbinata (Born, 1780)
    Bathybembix argenteonitens (Lischke, 1871)
    Tegula fasciata (Born, 1778)
*Subfamily*—Gibbulinae
    Gibbula fanulum (Gmelin, 1790)
    Cittarium pica (L. 1758)
*Subfamily*—Calliostomatinae
    Calliostoma gloriosum Dall, 1871
    Calliostoma zizyphinus (L., 1758)
*Subfamily*—Trochinae
    Tectus niloticus (L. 1767)
    Tectus dentatus (Forskål, 1775)
    Tectus conus (Gmelin, 1791)
    Trochus maculatus L. 1758
    Clanculus pharaonium (L. 1758)
*Subfamily*—Umboniinae
    Umbonium giganteum (Lesson, 1831)
    Umbonium moniliferum (Lamarck, 1822)
*FAMILY—STOMATELLIDAE*
    Stomatella callosa Fischer, 1871
*FAMILY—TURBINIDAE*

*Subfamily*—Astraeinae
    Astraea caelata (Gmelin, 1791)
    Astraea calcar (L. 1758)
    Astraea buschii (Philippi, 1844)
    Guildfordia triumphans (Philippi, 1841)
*Subfamily*—Turbininae
    Turbo canaliculatus Hermann, 1781
*FAMILY—PHASIANELLIDAE*
    Phasianella australis (Gmelin, 1788)
    Tricolia speciosa (von Mühlfeld, 1824)
**Superfamily**—Neritacea
*FAMILY—NERITIDAE*
*Subfamily*—Neritinae
    Nerita peloronta (L. 1758)
    Nerita scabricosta Lamarck, 1822
    Puperita pupa (L. 1758)
    Neritina communis (Quoy and Gaimard, 1832)
    Neritina virginea (L. 1758)
    Theodoxus longispina (Recluz, 1841)
*Subfamily*—Smaragdiinae
    Smaragdia viridis (L. 1758)
*FAMILY—HELICINIDAE*
*Subfamily*—Stoastomatinae
    Viana regina (Morelet, 1849)

**ORDER—Mesogastropoda**
  **Superfamily**—Viviparacea
  *FAMILY—VIVIPARIDAE*
  *Subfamily*—Viviparinae
    Viviparus contectus (Millet, 1813)
  **Superfamily**—Littorinacea
  *FAMILY—LITTORINIDAE*
  *Subfamily*—Littorininae
    Littorina saxatilis (Olivi, 1792)
    Littorina ziczac (Gmelin, 1791)
  *Subfamily*—Tectariinae
    Echininus nodulosus (Pfeiffer, 1839)
    Tectarius muricatus (L. 1758)
  *FAMILY—POMATIASIDAE*
  *Subfamily*—Pomatiasinae
    Tropidophora carinata (Sowerby, 1842)
  **Superfamily**—Rissoacea
  *FAMILY—TRUNCATELLIDAE*
  *Subfamily*—Truncatellinae

Truncatella subcylindrica (L. 1767)
FAMILY—HYDROBIIDAE
   Bithynia tentaculata (L. 1758)
FAMILY—RISSOIDAE
Subfamily—Rissoinae
   Rissoa variabilis (Muehfeldt, 1824)
   Rissoa violacea Desmarest, 1814
   Rissoa auriscalpium (L. 1758)
Subfamily—Alvaniinae
   Alvania montagui (Payraudeau, 1826)
   Alvania cimex (L. 1758)
   Folinia costata (Adams, 1797)
FAMILY—RISSOINIDAE
Subfamily—Rissoininae
   Rissoina bruguierei (Payraudeau, 1826)
Subfamily—Barleeiinae
   Barleeia rubra (J. Adams, 1795)
**Superfamily**—Architectonicacea
FAMILY—ARCHITECTONICIDAE
   Architectonica perspectiva (L. 1758)
**Superfamily**—Cerithiacea
FAMILY—TURRITELLIDAE
Subfamily—Turritellinae
   Turritella acutangula Linne, 1758
   Turritella crocea Kiener, 1844
   Turritella nivea Anton, 1839
   Turritella mediterranea (Monterosato, 1872)
Subfamily—Vermiculariinae
   Vermicularia spirata (Philippi, 1836)
FAMILY—SILIQUARIIDAE
   Siliquaria ponderosa (Morch, 1860)
FAMILY—VERMETIDAE
   Lemintina arenaria (L. 1758)
FAMILY—MODULIDAE
   Modulus modulus (L. 1758)
FAMILY—CERITHIIDAE
Subfamily—Cerithiinae
   Cerithium adustum Kiener, 1841
   Cerithium nodulosum Bruguière, 1792
   Rhinoclavis fasciatus (Bruguière, 1792)
   Rhinoclavis asper (L. 1758)
FAMILY—POTAMIDIDAE
Subfamily—Potamidinae

Tympanotonus fuscatus (L. 1758)
FAMILY—THIARIDAE
Subfamily—Thiarinae
Thiara amarula (L. 1758)
FAMILY—TRIPHORIDAE
Triphora perversa (L. 1758)
Iniforis lifuana (Hervier, 1897)
Viriola sp.
**Superfamily**—Epitoniacea
FAMILY—EPITONIIDAE
Epitonium scalare (L. 1758)
Epitonium lamellosum (Lamarck, 1822)
Amaea magnifica (Sowerby, 1844)
Sthenorythis pernobilis (Fischer and Bernardi, 1857)
FAMILY—JANTHINIDAE
Janthina nitens Menke, 1828
Janthina janthina (L. 1758)
**Superfamily**—Eulimacea
FAMILY—EULIMIDAE
Leiostraca subulata (Donovan, 1804)
Eulima polita (L. 1758)
**Superfamily**—Hipponicacea
FAMILY—HIPPONICIDAE
Hipponix conicus (Schumacher, 1817)
**Superfamily**—Crepidulacea
FAMILY—CREPIDULIDAE
Calyptraea chinensis (L. 1758)
Crepidula moulinsi (Michaud, 1829)
Crepidula fornicata (L. 1758)
Cheilea undulata (Röding, 1798)
FAMILY—CAPULIDAE
Subfamily—Capulinae
Capulus ungaricus (L. 1767)
Capulus incurvatus (Gmelin, 1791)
FAMILY—XENOPHORIDAE
Xenophora crispa (König, 1831)
Stellaria solaris (1767)
**Superfamily**—Strombacea
FAMILY—STROMBIDAE
Strombus gallus L. 1758
Strombus listeri Gray, 1852
Strombus sinuatus (Humphrey, 1786)
Strombus tricornis (Humphrey, 1786)

Strombus pipus (Röding, 1798)
Lambis chiragra arthritica (Röding, 1791)
Lambis crocata (Link, 1803)
Lambis violacea (Swainson, 1821)
Tibia fusus L. 1758
Tibia insulae-chorab Röding, 1798
Tibia martini Marrat, 1877
Terebellum terebellum (L. 1758)
FAMILY—APORRHAIDAE
    Aporrhais pespelecanis (L. 1758)
    Aporrhais occidentalis Beck, 1836
FAMILY—STRUTHIOLARIIDAE
    Struthiolaria papulosa (Martyn, 1784)
    Pelicaria vermis (Martyn, 1784)
**Superfamily**—Triviacea
FAMILY—ERATOIIDAE
    Trivia adriatica Coen, 1933
    Trivia pediculus (L. 1758)
**Superfamily**—Cypraeacea
FAMILY—CYPRAEIDAE
Subfamily—Cypraeorbinae
    Bernaya marginata (Gaskoin, 1849)
    Siphocypraea mus (L. 1758)
Subfamily—Cypraeinae
    Cypraea tigris L. 1758
    Cypraea pantherina Lightfoot, 1786
    Talparia cinerea (Gmelin, 1791)
    Lyncina aurantium (Gmelin, 1791)
    Lyncina argus (L. 1758)
    Lyncina reevei (Sowerby, 1832)
    Lyncina camelopardalis (Perry, 1811)
    Macrocypraea cervus (L. 1771)
    Macrocypraea cervinetta (Kiener, 1843)
    Macrocypraea zebra (L. 1758)
    Mauritia eglantina (Duclos, 1833)
    Mauritia mappa (L. 1758)
    Mauritia histrio (Gmelin, 1791)
Subfamily—Nariinae
    Erosaria lamarcki (Gray, 1825)
    Erosaria nebrites (Melvil, 1888)
    Erosaria spura acicularis (Gmelin, 1791)
    Monetaria moneta (L. 1758)
    Monetaria annulus (L. 1758)
    Propustularia surinamensis (Perry, 1811)

Pustularia childreni (Gray, 1825)
Staphylea cassiaui (Burgess, 1965)
*Subfamily*—Cypraeovulinae
Bistolida stolida (L. 1758)
Schilderia hirasei (Roberts, 1913)
Zonaria annettae (Dall, 1909)
Zonaria pyrum (Gmelin, 1791)
Zonaria spadicea (Swainson, 1823)
*FAMILY—OVULIDAE*
*Subfamily*—Ovulinae
Ovula ovum (L. 1758)
Calpurnus verrucosus (L. 1758)
Pseudosimnia carnea (Poiret, 1789)
*Subfamily*—Simniinae
Simnia spelta (L. 1758)
Simnia uniplicata (Sowerby, 1848)
Cyphoma gibbosum (L. 1758)
Volva volva (L. 1758)
*Subfamily*—Eocypraeinae
Jenneria pustulata (Lightfoot, 1786)
**Superfamily**—Carinariacea
*FAMILY—ATLANTIDAE*
Atlanta peronii Lesueur, 1817
**Superfamily**—Naticacea
*FAMILY—NATICIDAE*
*Subfamily*—Naticinae
Naticarius millepunctatus (Lamarck, 1822)
Naticarius hebraeus (Martyn, 1786)
Natica canrena (L. 1758)
*Subfamily*—Polinicinae
Polinices aurantium (Röding, 1798)
Polinices duplicatus (Say, 1822)
*Subfamily*—Sininae
Sinum concavum (Lamarck, 1822)
**Superfamily**—Tonnacea
*FAMILY—TONNIDAE*
Tonna galea (L. 1758)
Malea ringens (Swainson, 1822)
*FAMILY—CASSIDAE*
Cassis fimbriata Quoy e Gaimard, 1833
Cassis madagascariensis Lamarck, 1822
Cypraecassis rufa (L. 1758)
Cypraecassis testiculus (L. 1758)

Phalium granulatum undulatum (Gmelin, 1790)
Phalium labiatum (Perry, 1811)
Cassidaria echinophora (L. 1758)
FAMILY—FICIDAE
    Ficus communis Röding, 1798
    Ficus filosa Sowerby, 1892
**Superfamily**—Cymatiacea
FAMILY—CYMATIIDAE
Subfamily—Cymatiinae
    Cymatium parthenopaeum (Salis, 1797)
    Cymatium femorale (L. 1758)
    Cymatium lotorium (L. 1767)
    Cymatium rubeculum (L. 1758)
    Charonia tritonis (L. 1758)
    Charonia nodifera (Lamarck, 1822)
    Distorsio anus (L. 1767)
    Distorsio clathrata (Lamarck, 1816)
Subfamily—Argobuccininae
    Ranella olearia (L. 1758)
FAMILY—BURSIDAE
    Bursa dunkeri Kira, 1962


**ORDER**—**Neogastropoda**
**Superfamily**—Muricacea
FAMILY—MURICIDAE
Subfamily—Muricinae
    Bolinus brandaris (L. 1758)
    Haustellum haustellum (L. 1758)
    Murex pecten Lightfoot, 1786
    Murex cervicornis (Lamarck, 1822)
    Phyllonotus pomum (Gmelin, 1791)
    Chicoreus spectrum (Reeve, 1846)
    Phyllonotus trunculus (L. 1758)
    Muricanthus princeps (Broderip, 1833)
    Marchia elongata (Lightfoot, 1786)
    Purpurellus gambiensis (Reeve, 1845)
    Homalocantha oxyacantha (Broderip, 1833)
    Homalocantha scorpio (L. 1758)
Subfamily—Muricopsinae
    Maxwellia gemma (Sowerby, 1879)
    Maxwellia santarosana (Dall, 1905)

Favartia cellulosa (Conrad, 1846)
Muricopsis aradasii (Poirier, 1883)
Muricopsis oxytata (M. Smith, 1938)
Vitularia salebrosa (King & Broderip, 1832)
*Subfamily*—Ocenebrinae
Ocenebra erinacea (L. 1758)
Pteropurpura macroptera (Deshayes, 1839)
Ceratostoma burnetti (Adams & Reeve, 1849)
Ceratostoma foliatum (Gmelin, 1791)
*Subfamily*—Trophoninae
Pagodula vaginatus (Cristofori and Jan, 1832)
*Subfamily*—Typhinae
Typhinellus Sowerby Broderip, 1833
*FAMILY—THAIDIDAE*
*Subfamily*—Thaidinae
Thais cingulifera (L. 1758)
Thais haemastoma floridana (Conrad, 1837)
Nassa serta (Bruguière, 1789)
Vexilla vexillum (Gmelin, 1791)
*Subfamily*—Drupinae
Drupa morum Röding, 1798
*Subfamily*—Rapaninae
Rapana bezoar (L. 1758)
*FAMILY—CORALLIOPHILIDAE*
Latiaxis pagodus (A. Adams, 1853)
Latiaxis pilsbry Hirase, 1908
Magilus antiquus Montfort, 1810
Rapa rapa (L. 1758)
*FAMILY—COLUMBARIIDAE*
Columbarium pagoda (Lesson, 1831)
**Superfamily**—Buccinacea
*FAMILY—BUCCINIDAE*
Buccinum undatum L. 1758
Neptunea lyrata decemcostata (Say, 1826)
Neptunea contraria (L. 1771)
Colus gracilis (Da Costa, 1778)
Colus islandicus (Gmelin, 1791)
Babylonia formosae (Sowerby, 1866)

Siphonalia signum (Reeve, 1843)
Pisania pusio (L. 1758)
Pisania maculosa (Lamarck, 1822)
Buccinulum corneum (L. 1758)
Cantharus sanguinolentus (Duclos, 1833)
FAMILY—COLUMBELLIDAE
Columbella mercatoria (L. 1758)
FAMILY—FASCIOLARIIDAE
Subfamily—Fasciolariinae
Fasciolaria tulipa (L. 1758)
Latirus infundibulum (Gmelin, 1791)
Leucozonia nassa (Gmelin, 1791)
Opeatostoma pseudodon (Burrow, 1815)
Subfamily—Fusininae
Fusinus longicaudatus (Lamarck, 1801)
FAMILY—NASSARIIDAE
Hinia incrassata (Müller, 1776)
Cyclope neritaeus (L. 1766)
Arcularia gibbosula (L. 1758)
FAMILY—MELONGENIDAE
Melongena corona (Gmelin, 1791)
Busycon contrarium (Conrad, 1840)
Syrinx aruanus (L. 1758)
**Superfamily**—Volutacea
FAMILY—OLIVIDAE
Ancilla urasima Taki, 1955
Ancilla albocallosa (Lischke, 1868)
Olivancillaria urceus (Röding, 1798)
Olivella biplicata (Sowerby, 1825)
Olivella volutella (Lamarck, 1811)
Oliva bulbosa Röding, 1798
Oliva incrassata Lightfoot, 1786
Oliva miniacea Röding, 1798
Oliva porphyria L. 1758
Oliva sayana Ravenel, 1834
FAMILY—TURBINELLIDAE
Turbinella angulata (Lightfoot, 1786)
Turbinella pyrum (L. 1758)
Vasum ceramicum (L. 1758)
Vasum muricatum (Born, 1778)
Vasum tubiferum (Anton, 1839)
FAMILY—HARPIDAE
Harpa costata L. 1758
Harpa davidis Röding, 1798

Harpa major Röding, 1798
FAMILY—*VOLUTIDAE*
*Subfamily*—Volutinae
Voluta musica L. 1758
*Subfamily*—Lyriinae
Lyria lyraeformis (Swainson, 1821)
Lyria kurodai (Kawamura, 1964)
*Subfamily*—Fulgorarinae
Fulgoraria clara (Sowerby III, 1914)
*Subfamily*—Cymbiinae
Cymbium glans (Gmelin, 1791)
Melo amphora (Lightfoot, 1786)
Cymbiola imperialis (Lightfoot, 1786)
Cymbiola aulica (Sowerby I, 1825)
Cymbiolacca peristicta McMichael, 1963
*Subfamily*—Zidoninae
Harpulina arausiaca (Lightfoot, 1786)
*Subfamily*—Odontocymbiolinae
Volutoconus bednalli (Brazier, 1878)
*Subfamily*—Scaphellinae
Scaphella junonia (Lamarck, 1804)
Amoria undulata (Lamarck, 1804)
Amoria damonii Gray, 1864
Amoria canaliculata (McCoy, 1869)
*Subfamily*—Calliotectinae
Neptuneopsis gilchristi Sowerby III, 1898
FAMILY—*MARGINELLIDAE*
Marginella haematita Kiener, 1834
Marginella goodalli Sowerby, 1825
Marginella pseudofaba Sowerby, 1846
Bullata elegans (Gmelin, 1791)
**Superfamily**—Mitracea
FAMILY—*MITRIDAE*
*Subfamily*—Mitrinae
Mitra mitra (L. 1758)
Mitra barbadensis (Gmelin, 1791)
Mitra fusiformis zonata (Marryat, 1817)
Mitra papalis (L. 1758)
*Subfamily*—Imbricariinae
Neocancilla papilio (Link, 1807)
Subcancilla sp.
*Subfamily*—Vexillinae
Vexillum ebenus (Lamarck, 1811)
Vexillum regina (Sowerby, 1828)

Vexillum trophonia (Dall, 1889)
Vexillum vulpecula (L. 1758)
*FAMILY—CANCELLARIIDAE*
Cancellaria cancellata (L. 1767)
**Superfamily—**Conacea
*FAMILY—CONIDAE*
Conus marmoreus L. 1758
Conus imperialis L. 1758
Conus litteratus L. 1758
Conus gradatus Wood, 1828
Conus chaldaeus Röding, 1798
Conus arenatus Bruguière, 1792
Conus purpurascens Sowerby, 1833
Conus californicus Reeve, 1844
Conus regius Gmelin, 1791
Conus brunneus Wood, 1828
Conus princeps L. 1758
Conus generalis L. 1767
Conus lithoglyphus Bruguière, 1792
Conus jaspideus Gmelin, 1791
Conus daucus Bruguière, 1792
Conus mercator L. 1758
Conus vexillum Gmelin, 1792
Conus geographus L. 1758
Conus bengalensis (Okutani, 1968)
Conus gloriamaris Chemnitz, 1777
Conus textile L. 1758
Conus figulinus L. 1758
Conus genuanus L. 1758
Conus striatus L. 1758
Conus bullatus L. 1758
Conus nussatella L. 1758
Conus coccineus Gmelin, 1791
Asprella arcuata (Gray, 1838)
Asprella australis Holten, 1802
*FAMILY—TEREBRIDAE*
Terebra lanceata L. 1767
Terebra maculata (L. 1758)
Terebra guttata (Röding, 1798)
Terebra triseriata Gray, 1834
Terebra crenulata (L. 1758)
Terebra strigata Sowerby, 1825
Terebra taurinus Lightfoot, 1786
Terebra senegalensis Lamarck

Terebra dislocata (Say, 1822)
Terebra cinerea (Born, 1778)
*FAMILY—TURRIDAE*
*Subfamily*—Turrinae
Turris similis (Bivoña, 1838)
Turris babylonia (L. 1758)
Xenoturris cingulifera (Lamarck, 1822)
*Subfamily*—Mangeliinae
Lyromangelia taeniata (Deshayes, 1834)
*Subfamily*—Tatcheriinae
Tatcheria mirabilis Angas, 1877
**Subclass Opisthobranchia**


**ORDER—Entomotaeniata**
*FAMILY—PYRAMIDELLIDAE*
Pyramidella acus (Gmelin, 1791)
Otopleura mitralis (A. Adams, 1855)


**ORDER—Cephalaspidea**
**Superfamily**—Acteonacea
*FAMILY—ACTEONIDAE*
Acteon tornatilis (L. 1767)
*FAMILY—RINGICULIDAE*
Ringicula semistriata Orbigny, 1842
*FAMILY—HYDATINIDAE*
Hydatina albocincta (van der Hoeven, 1839)
**Superfamily**—Bullacea
*FAMILY—BULLIDAE*
Bulla striata Bruguière, 1792
**Superfamily**—Cylichnacea
*FAMILY—CYLICHNIDAE*
Scaphander lignarius (L. 1758)


**ORDER—Sacoglossa**
SUBORDER—Juliacea
*FAMILY—JULIIDAE*
Berthelinia chloris (Dall, 1918)

**ORDER—Aplysiacea**
  *FAMILY—APLYSIIDAE*
    Aplysia sp.
  *FAMILY—UMBRACULIDAE*
    Umbraculum mediterraneum (Lamarck, 1819)

**ORDER—Thecosomata**
SUBORDER—Euthecosomata
  *FAMILY—CUVIERIDAE*
    Cavolinia tridentata (Niebuhr, 1775)

**ORDER—Nudibranchia**
  *FAMILY—DORIDIDAE*
  *Subfamily*—Glossodoridinae
    Glossodoris valenciennesi (Cantraine, 1835)
SUBORDER—Aeolidoidea
  *FAMILY—FLABELLINIDAE*
    Flabellina affinis (Gmelin, 1791)
    **Subclass Pulmonata**
SUPERORDER—Pulmonata

**ORDER—Basommatophora**
  **Superfamily**—Siphonariacea
  *FAMILY—SIPHONARIIDAE*
    Siphonaria sirius Pilsbry
  **Superfamily**—Melampidacea
  *FAMILY—MELAMPIDAE*
    Ovatella myosotis (Draparnaud, 1801)
  **Superfamily**—Lymnaeacea
  *FAMILY—LYMNAEIDAE*
    Lymnaea sp.
  **Superfamily**—Physacea
  *FAMILY—PHYSIDAE*
    Physa fontinalis (L. 1758)
  **Superfamily**—Planorbiacea
  *FAMILY—PLANORBIDAE*
    Planorbarius corneus (L. 1758)

**ORDER—Stylommatophora**
SUBORDER—Mesurethra
    **Superfamily**—Clausiliacea
    *FAMILY—CLAUSILIIDAE*
    *Subfamily*—Clausiliinae
        Clausilia cruciata Studer, 1820
    *FAMILY—CERIONIDAE*
        Cerion Marielinum Hand, 1926
SUBORDER—Heterurethra
    **Superfamily**—Succinacea
    *FAMILY—SUCCINEIDAE*
    *Subfamily*—Succineinae
        Succinea putris (L. 1758)
SUBORDER—Sigmurethra
    **Superfamily**—Achatinacea
    *FAMILY—ACHATINIDAE*
    *Subfamily*—Achatininae
        Achatina achatina (L. 1758)
    **Superfamily**—Bulimacea
    *FAMILY—BULIMULIDAE*
    *Subfamily*—Bulimulinae
        Zaplagius navicula (Wagner, 1827)
    *Subfamily*—Odontostominae
        Odontostomus pantagruelinus (Moricand,
           1837)
    **Superfamily**—Helicacea
    *FAMILY—HELMINTHOGLYPTIDAE*
    *Subfamily*—Cepoliinae
        Polymita picta (Born, 1780)
    *FAMILY—HELICIDAE*
    *Subfamily*—Helicinae
        Helix pomatia L. 1758
        Helix aspersa Müller, 1774
        Cepaea nemoralis (L. 1758)

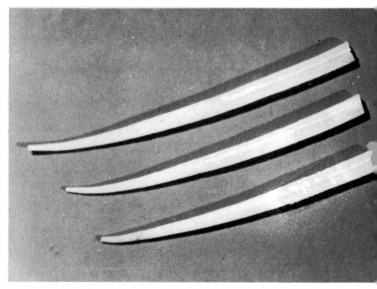

SCAPHOPODA: *Dentalium ceratum* Dall.

## CLASS—SCAPHOPODA

*FAMILY—DENTALIIDAE*
 Dentalium inaequicostatum Dautzenberg,
  1881
*FAMILY—SIPHONODENTALIIDAE*
 Cadulus jeffreysi (Monterosato, 1875)

BIVALVIA: *Spondylus americanus* Hermann.

### CLASS—BIVALVIA

### Subclass Paleotaxodonta

**ORDER—Nuculoida**
    **Superfamily**—Nuculacea
    *FAMILY—NUCULIDAE*
        Nucula nucleus (L. 1758)
        **Subclass Cryptodonta**

**ORDER—Solemyoida**
    **Superfamily**—Solemyacea

*FAMILY—SOLEMYACIDAE*
Solemya togata (Poli, 1795)
**Subclass Pteriomorphia**


**ORDER—Arcoida**
**Superfamily—Arcacea**
*FAMILY—ARCIDAE*
*Subfamily—Arcinae*
Arca noae L. 1758
Barbatia candida (Helbling, 1779)
Trisidos tortuosa (L. 1758)
*Subfamily—Anadarinae*
Scapharca inaequivalvis (Bruguière, 1789)
**Superfamily—Limopsacea**
*FAMILY—GLYCYMERIDAE*
*Subfamily—Glycymeridinae*
Glycymeris pectiniformis (Lamarck, 1819)


**ORDER—Mytiloida**
**Superfamily—Mytilacea**
*FAMILY—MYTILIDAE*
*Subfamily—Mytilinae*
Mytilus galloprovincialis Lamarck, 1819
Brachidontes variabilis Krauss, 1848
*Subfamily—Lithophaginae*
Lithophaga lithophaga (L. 1780)
*Subfamily—Modiolinae*
Modiolus americanus (Leach, 1815)
Modiolula phaseolina (Philippi, 1844)
**Superfamily—Pinnacea**
*FAMILY—PINNIDAE*
Pinna rudis L. 1758


**ORDER—PTERIOIDA**
SUBORDER—Pteriina
**Superfamily—Pteriacea**
*FAMILY—PTERIIDAE*
Pteria hirundo (L. 1758)
Pinctada imbricata Röding, 1798
*FAMILY—ISOGNOMONIDAE*

Isognomon alatus (Gmelin, 1791)
*FAMILY—MALLEIDAE*
Malleus albus Lamarck, 1817
**Superfamily—Pectinacea**
*FAMILY—PECTINIDAE*
Amussium japonicum (Gmelin, 1791)
Pallium incomparabilis (Risso, 1826)
Lyropecten nodosus (L. 1758)
Chlamys senatoria (Gmelin, 1791)
Chlamys flabellum (Gmelin, 1791)
Placopecten magellanicus (Gmelin, 1791)
Pecten jacobaeus (L. 1758)
*FAMILY—SPONDYLIDAE*
Spondylus princeps Broderip, 1833
**Superfamily—Anomiacea**
*FAMILY—ANOMIIDAE*
Anomia simplex Orbigny, 1842
Placuna sella (Gmelin, 1791)
**Superfamily—Limacea**
*FAMILY—LIMIDAE*
Lima lima (L. 1758)


**ORDER—Ostreina**
**Superfamily—Ostreacea**
*FAMILY—OSTREIDAE*
*Subfamily—Ostreinae*
Ostrea edulis L. 1758
*Subfamily—Lophinae*
Lopha cristagalli (L. 1758)
**Subclass—Palaeoheterodonta**


**ORDER—Unionoida**
**Superfamily—Unionacea**
*FAMILY—UNIONIDAE*
*Subfamily—Unioninae*
Lanceolaria grayana (Lea, 1834)
*Subfamily—Quadrulinae*
Quadrula quadrula (Rafinesque, 1820)
*Subfamily—Lampsilinae*
Obovaria retusa (Lamarck, 1819)
Truncilla truncata Rafinesque, 1820

**ORDER—Trigonioida**
    **Superfamily—**Trigoniacea
    *FAMILY—TRIGONIIDAE*
        Neotrigonia margariacea (Lamarck, 1804)
    **Subclass Heterodonta**


**ORDER—Veneroida**
    **Superfamily—**Lucinacea
    *FAMILY—LUCINIDAE*
    *Subfamily—*Lucininae
        Codakia tigerina (L. 1758)
    *Subfamily—*Myrteinae
        Myrtea spinifera (Montagu, 1803)
    **Superfamily—**Chamacea
    *FAMILY—CHAMIDAE*
        Pseudochama gryphina (Lamarck, 1819)
        Arcinella arcinella (L. 1767)
    **Superfamily—**Carditacea
    *FAMILY—CARDITIDAE*
    *Subfamily—*Carditinae
        Cardita crassicosta Lamarck, 1819
    *Subfamily—*Carditesinae
        Cardites antiquata (L. 1758)
    *Subfamily—*Carditamerinae
        Carditamera floridana Conrad, 1838
    **Superfamily—**Crassatellacea
    *FAMILY—ASTARTIDAE*
    *Subfamily—*Astartinae
        Astarte borealis (Schumacher, 1817)
        Gonilia calliglypta (Dall, 1903)
    **Superfamily—**Cardiacea
    *FAMILY—CARDIIDAE*
    *Subfamily—*Cardiinae
        Cardium costatum L. 1758
        Acanthocardia aculeata (L. 1758)
    *Subfamily—*Trachicardiinae
        Trachycardium egmontianum (Shuttle-
            worth, 1856)
    *Subfamily—*Fraginae
        Corculum cardissa (L. 1758)
    *Subfamily—*Protocardiinae
        Nemocardium lyratum (Sowerby, 1841)
    *Subfamily—*Laevicardiinae

Laevicardium crassum (Gmelin, 1791)
Cerastoderma glaucum (Bruguière, 1789)
**Superfamily**—Tridacnacea
*FAMILY—TRIDACNIDAE*
   Tridacna squamosa Lamarck, 1819
   Hippopus hippopus (L. 1758)
**Superfamily**—Mactracea
*FAMILY—MACTRIDAE*
*Subfamily*—Mactrinae
   Mactra glauca Born, 1778
**Superfamily**—Solenacea
*FAMILY—SOLENIDAE*
   Solen vagina L. 1758
**Superfamily**—Tellinacea
*FAMILY—TELLINIDAE*
*Subfamily*—Tellininae
   Tellina radiata L. 1758
   Tellina pulchella Lamarck, 1818
   Tellina foliacea L. 1758
*Subfamily*—Macominae
   Macoma balthica (L. 1758)
   Macoma melo (Sowerby, 1870)
*FAMILY—DONACIDAE*
   Donax variabilis Say, 1822
   Donax variegatus (Gmelin, 1791)
*FAMILY—PSAMMOBIIDAE*
*Subfamily*—Psammobiinae
   Gari costulata (Turton, 1822)
*FAMILY—SOLECURTIDAE*
*Subfamily*—Solecurtinae
   Pharus legumen (L. 1758)
   Tagelus plebeius (Lightfoot, 1786)
**Superfamily**—Dreissenacea
*FAMILY—DREISSENIDAE*
   Dreissena polymorpha (Pallas, 1771)
   Mytilopsis leucophaeata (Conrad, 1831)
**Superfamily**—Arcticacea
*FAMILY—ARCTICIDAE*
   Arctica islandica (L. 1767)
**Superfamily**—Glossacea
*FAMILY—GLOSSIDAE*
   Glossus humanus (L. 1758)
**Superfamily**—Corbiculacea
*FAMILY—PISIDIIDAE*
   Musculium lacustre (Müller, 1774)

**Superfamily**—Veneracea
*FAMILY—VENERIDAE*
*Subfamily*—Venerinae
   Venus verrucosa L. 1758
*Subfamily*—Pitariinae
   Pitar lupanarius (Lesson, 1830)
   Callista chione (L. 1758)
   Lioconcha castrensis (L. 1758)
*Subfamily*—Tapetinae
   Tapes aureus (Gmelin, 1791)
   Irus irus (L. 1758)
*Subfamily*—Chioninae
   Bassina disjecta (Perry, 1811)
*FAMILY—PETRICOLIDAE*
   Petricola lithophaga (Retzius, 1786)
   Petricola pholadiformis (Lamarck, 1818)


**ORDER—Myoida**
  **Superfamily**—Myacea
  *FAMILY—MYIDAE*
    Mya arenaria L. 1758
  *FAMILY—CORBULIDAE*
  *Subfamily*—Corbulinae
    Corbula gibba (Olivi, 1792)
  **Superfamily**—Hiatellacea
  *FAMILY—HIATELLIDAE*
    Hiatella arctica (L. 1767)
SUBORDER—Pholadina
  **Superfamily**—Pholadacea
  *FAMILY—PHOLADIDAE*
  *Subfamily*—Pholadinae
    Cyrtopleura costata (L. 1758)
  *FAMILY—TEREDINIDAE*
  *Subfamily*—Teredininae
    Teredo sp.
    **Subclass Anomalodesmata**


**ORDER—Pholadomyoida**
  **Superfamily**—Poromyacea
  *FAMILY—CUSPIDARIIDAE*
    Cuspidaria cuspidata (Olivi, 1792)
    Cuspidaria rostrata (Spengler, 1793)

**Superfamily**—Clavagellacea
*FAMILY—CLAVAGELLIDAE*
Penicillus australis (Chenu, 1843)

Cephalopoda: *Nautilus pompilius* Linné.

## CLASS—CEPHALOPODA

**Subclass Nautiloidea**
*FAMILY—NAUTILIDAE*
    Nautilus pompilius L. 1758
**Subclass Coleoidea**

**ORDER—DECAPODA**
SUBORDER—Sepioidea
    **Superfamily**—Spirulacea
    *FAMILY—SPIRULIDAE*
        Spirula spirula (L. 1758)
    *FAMILY—SEPIIDAE*
        Sepia officinalis L. 1758
    *FAMILY—SEPIOLIDAE*
    *Subfamily*—Sepiolinae
        Sepiola rondeleti Leach, 1817
SUBORDER—Teuthoidea
    **Superfamily**—Loliginacea
    *FAMILY—LOLIGINIDAE*
        Loligo vulgaris Lamarck, 1799


**ORDER—Octopoda**
SUBORDER—Incirrata
    **Superfamily**—Octopodacea
    *FAMILY—OCTOPODIDAE*
    *Subfamily*—Octopodinae
        Octopus vulgaris Cuvier, 1797
    *Subfamily*—Eledoninae
        Eledone sp.
    **Superfamily**—Argonautacea
    *FAMILY—ARGONAUTIDAE*
        Argonauta argo L. 1758
        Argonauta hians Lightfoot, 1786
        Argonauta nodosa Lightfoot, 1786

GASTROPODA: *Polymita picta* Beck.

# GLOSSARY

*The scientific terms in the introduction and species descriptions are all explained in the text. Following are a few of the terms most frequently employed in describing the shells.*

**actinodont**   Descriptive of bivalve shell having a hinge with teeth that radiate outward from the umbones.

**anisomyarian**   Descriptive of bivalve shell with the scars of the two adductor muscles on the interior being of different sizes. The posterior scar is usually larger than the anterior

**aperture**   Principal opening from which the body parts of a gastropod shell emerge.

**apex**   The point at the end of the spire of a gastropod shell.

**apophysis**   The articulating plate on valves II to VII of a chiton shell.

**articulamentum**   Internal layer of a chiton shell.

**auricle**   Anterior or posterior projection along the hinge line of a bivalve shell.

**auricular crus**   Blunt internal ridge that defines the bottom boundary of the auricles of certain bivalve shells.

**basal fasciole**   A special band on the base of a shell formed by a series of more or less curved growth lines that define the siphonal sinus (canal).

**base**   Part of the shell surface opposite the apex.

**biconical**   Descriptive of shell with the apex and the base both cone-shaped (see illustration p. 58 bottom——2).

**body whorl**   Last whorl of a gastropod shell next to the aperture, containing all the major body parts except the visceral mass.

**byssal sinus**   Recess in the anterior of the valve of some bivalve shells to provide an outlet for the byssus notch.

**callus**   Thicker section of the aperture of a gastropod; it may partly or completely cover the umbilicus.

**cardinal teeth**   Projections on the hinge line, located directly below the umbones on bivalve shells.

**carina**   (Literally, a keel.) A fold or spiral thickening of the shoulder.

**chondrophore**   Spoon-shaped pit on the interior surface of a bivalve shell, containing the internal ligament (resilium).

**columella**   Solid or hollow axis of a gastropod shell.

**conical**   Cone-shaped—especially, describing a shell with a flattened base and whorls that are so shaped.

**costa**   Large, cordlike ridge that runs longitudinally, spirally, or concentrically on a shell rib.

**dextral**   Right-handed, as in gastropod shells having the aperture on the right side of the shell facing the observer when the apex is held upward.

**dimyarian**   Denoting, in the bivalve mollusks, the characteristic of having two (anterior and posterior) adductor muscles.

**ententate**   Without teeth—descriptive of a type of bivalve shell with a hinge that lacks teeth.

**escutcheon**   Area on the surface of the valve of a bivalve shell, parallel to the hinge, where the ligament is attached.

**fusiform**   Spindle-shaped; thicker in the middle and with pointed ends.

**girdle**   Edge of the chiton mantle, bordering the shell and covered with hard structures.

**growth line**   Line parallel to the edge of a shell, representing the position of the edge at a previous stage of the animal's life.

**heterodont**   Descriptive of bivalve shell that has a hinge with small teeth of different sizes, having both cardinals and laterals.

**hinge line**   Dorsal boundary of the valve on a bivalve shell where it contacts the opposite valve.

**holostomate**   Characterizing an aperture lip of a gastropod shell that is uninterrupted by any anterior sinus or notch.

**insertion teeth**   Articulating processes that unite the valves of a chiton to the girdle or insertion plates.

**isodont**   Descriptive of bivalve shell that has a hinge with one pair of teeth and one pair of pits on one valve that articulate with two pits and two teeth on the other.

**isomyarian**   Descriptive of bivalve shell having the two adductor-muscle scars on the inner surface approximately equal in size.

**lateral section**   More or less raised area on the tegmentum of valves II to VII of a chiton shell, bounded by the posterior edge of the valve and by a line from the midpoint to the anteriolateral edge.

**lateral teeth**   Projections of the hinge line that are almost parallel to it and located anterior or posterior or both to the cardinal teeth.

**ligament**   More or less calcified, horny structure that holds the two valves of a bivalve shell together when the shell is open.

**lunule**   Curved or flat heart-shaped area on the outside of a bivalve shell along the hinge line and anterior to the umbones.

**median section**   Triangular area of the tegmentum of valves II to VII of a chiton shell, bounded by the anterior edge of the shell and by the lateral sections.

**monomyarian** Descriptive of bivalve shell with only one adductor-muscle scar on the inner surface of each valve.

**mucro** High point on Valve VIII, of a chiton shell.

**muscle scar** Slight depression on the inner surface of the valve of a bivalve shell where a muscle is attached.

**obconic** In the form of an inverted cone——with a conical base and a flattened spire.

**outer lip** Edge of the shell aperture opposite the columellar axis.

**ovate** Egg-shaped, with rounded base and apex.

**pachyodont** Descriptive of bivalve shell with one heavy, blunt, and shapeless hinge tooth.

**pallial line** Impression or scar on the inner surface of a bivalve shell, parallel to the ventral edge, by the insertion of the muscles that attach the mantle to the shell.

**pallial sinus** Indentation in the posterior part of the pallial line. It defines the site of the siphons when retracted.

**patelliform** Shaped like a limpet shell——cap-shaped and without whorls.

**periphery** Part of the shell containing the whorls farthest from the axis.

**peristome** Edge of the aperture on a gastropod shell.

**plait** Spiral plication produced on the columella by local thickening of the shell.

**posterior section** Area of the tegmentum of valve VII of a chiton shell bounded by the posterior edge of the valve and anteriorly by two lines from the mucro to the anteriolateral edge of the valve.

**pseudoumbilicus** Depression or cavity in the base of the shell, involving only the body whorl, so that it is not a true umbilicus.

**resilifer** On a bivalve shell, a socketlike structure that supports the internal part of the hinge ligament (resilium).

**resilium** Part of the hinge ligament of a bivalve shell inside the edges of the valves.

**schizodont** Descriptive of actinodont hinge of which the individual teeth have denticulated edges.

**shoulder** Prominent angulation of the gastropod whorls, forming a shelf or ridge.

**sinistral** Left-handed (as opposed to right-handed) in the gastropod shell having the aperture on the left side of the shell facing the observer when the apex is held upward. The whorls run counterclockwise.

**siphonostome** Descriptive of shell with a discontinuous peristome, interrupted anteriorly by a sinus that may be prolonged into a shell siphon——called the siphonal notch.

**spire** All the whorls of a gastropod shell with the exception of the body whorl.

**spire angle** Angle formed by two tangents to the opposite sides of a gastropod shell with two or more whorls.

**suture** Line joining two successive whorls on a gastropod shell.

**taxodont**    Descriptive of bivalve shell that has a hinge with numerous almost identical teeth on each valve.

**tegmentum**    Outermost layer, with sculpture and coloration, of a chiton shell.

**turbinate**    Shaped like a toy top, usually with a rounded base.

**turreted**    Having a very high spire, the base usually flattened or slightly convex.

**umbilicus**    Central cavity in a gastropod shell, formed by the internal walls of the whorls.

**umbo (pl. umbones)**    The beak, or apex on a bivalve shell; the point from which the shell begins to grow.

**varix**    Ridge, crest, or series of spines, parallel to the growth lines on a gastropod shell, that mark the positions of the aperture at previous stages of growth.

**whorl**    Complete single turn in a spirally twisted gastropod shell.

# INDEX OF ENTRIES

*Acanthocardia aculeata* 1
*Acanthopleura* 134
*Achatina achatina* 336
*Acteon tornatilis* 2
Adriatic trivia 332
African pleurotomaria 94
*Alvania cimex* 135
*Alvania montagni* 135
Alvanias 135
*Alvaniinae* 135
*Amaea magnifica* 311
American pelican's foot 5
*Amoria* 222
*Amoria canaliculata* 222
*Amoria damonii* 222
*Amoria undulata* 222
Amoria volutes 222
Almost cancelled miter 260
*Amussium japonicum* 3
*Ancilla* 4
*Ancilla urasima* 4
Ancillas 4
*Angaria melanacantha* 223
Angel wing 45
Angular triton 42
Angulata nassa 175
Annette's cowrie 219
*Anomia simplex* 136
*Aplysia* 303
*Aporrhais occidentalis* 5
*Aporrhais pespelecani* 6
Apple murex 152
Arabian tibia 297
Arada's murex 191
*Arca noae* 137
*Architectonica perspectiva* 7
*Arcinella arcinella* 8
Arctic saxicave 174
*Arctica islandica* 9
*Arcularia gibbosula* 10
*Argonauta* 304
*Argonauta argo* 304
*Argonauta hians* 304
Arthritic spider conch 262
*Asprella* 11
*Asprella arcuata* 11
*Asprella australis* 11
*Astarte borealis* 12
*Astraea buschii* 138
*Astraea caelata* 224
*Astraea calcar* 225
*Atlanta peroni* 305
Atlantic auger 294
Atlantic deepsea scallop 31

Atlantic distorsio 47
Atlantic gray cowrie 212
Atlantic modulus 319
Atlantic yellow cowrie 165
Auger shells 293, 294
Aulica volute 246
Australian pheasant shell 323

*Babylonia Formosae* 13
Balthica macoma 64
Banded turrid 185
Barbado miter 273
*Barbatia candida* 139
*Bassina disjecta* 14
*Bathybembix    argenteonitens* 15
Beaded periwinkle 213
Bean horse-mussel 71
Beautiful tellin 118
Bednall's volute 132
Bengal cone 36
*Barleeia rubra* 306
*Bernaya marginata* 140
Berry cone 233
*Berthelinia chloris* 307
Bezoar rapana 208
*Bistolida stolida* 226
*Bithynia tentaculata* 337
Bivalved snail 307
Black-tankard angaria 223
Bleeding tooth 193
Bloody-lined cantharus 227
Blue patella 199
*Bolinus* 276
Boreal astarte 12
*Brachidontes variabilis* 141
Broad-ribbed cardita 20
Broderip's homalocantha 62
Brown cone 159
Brown paper nautilus 304
Bruguiere's risso 209
Bubble cone 231
*Buccinulum corneum* 142
*Buccinum undatum* 16
*Bulimulidae* 338
Bulimulus shells 338
Bull mouth helmet 249
*Bulla striata* 308
*Bullata elegans* 69
Burnett's purpura 149
Burrow's chiton 160
*Bursa dunkeri* 17
*Busycon contrarium* 70
Button shells 129

Cadulus jeffreysi 18
California cone 158
Calliostoma glorosium 143
Calliostoma ziziphinus 144
Callused stomatella 285
Calpurnus verrucosus 309
Calyptraea chinensis 145
Camel cowrie 268
Cancellaria cancellata 19
Cancellated nutmeg 19
Canoe-bubble 100
Cantharus sanguinolentus 227
Cantraine's blue Doris 169
Capulus incurvatus 147
Capulus ungaricus 146
Cardita crassicota 148
Carditamera floridana 20
Cardites antiquata 21
Cardium costatum 22
Caribbean vase 301
Carinated tropidophora 354
Carrot cone 235
Carved star shell 224
Cassiau's cowrie 284
Cassidaria echinophora 23
Cassis fimbriata 24
Cassis madagascariensis 25
Cavolinia tridentata 310
Capaea nemoralis 339
Ceramic vase 301
Cerastoderma edule 26
Ceratosderma glaucum 26
Ceratostoma burnetti 149
Ceratostoma foliatum 150
Cerion marielinum 340
Cerithium 27
Cerithium adustum 27
Cerithium nodulosum 27
Cervicornis murex 28
Chambered nautilus 320
Chank shells 126
Channeled turban 300
Channeled volute 222
Charonia tritonis 151
Cheilea undulata 145
Chestnut cowrie 221
Chestnut latirus 178
Chicoreus pomum 152
Chicoreus spectrum 29
Children's cowrie 281
Chiton squamosus 153
Chiton tuberculatus 154
Chitons 134
Chlamys flabellum 30

Chlamys magellanicus (placopecten) 31
Chlamys nodosus (lyrospectin) 155
Chlamys senatoria 32
Cittarium pica 156
Clanculus pharaonium 228
Clausilia cruciata 341
Clear volute 54
Cockscomb oyster 318
Codakia tigerina 229
Coffee bean trivia 333
Colorful Atlantic natica 74
Columbarium pagoda 33
Columbella mercatoria 157
Colus 34
Colus 34
Colus gracilis 34
Colus islandicus 34
Comb Venus 92
Commercial top shell 291
Common African snail 336
Common Atlantic bubble 308
Common Atlantic octopus 195
Common Atlantic squid 317
Common awning clam 109
Common basket-shell 38
Common calpurnus 309
Common cap shell 146
Common coquina 49
Common cuspidaria 39
Common cuttlefish 104
Common date mussel 180
Common distorsio 251
Common dove shell 157
Common egg shell 322
Common European tadpole snail 347
Common jingle shell 136
Common keyhole limpet 162
Common northern buccinum 16
Common nut clam 82
Common Pacific nerite 321
Common paper nautilus 304
Common purple sea snail 315
Common spirula 330
Common West Indian chiton 154
Common egg cockle 63
Cone-shaped hoof shell 313
Cone shells 11, 36, 158, 235, 238
Cone top shell 289
Conrad's false mussel 345

*Conus arenatus* 230
*Conus bandanus* 240
*Conus bellatus* 231
*Conus bengalensis* 35
*Conus brunneus* 159
*Conus californicus* 158
*Conus chaldaeus* 232
*Conus chelyoconus* 158
*Conus cleobula* 36
*Conus coccineus* 233
*Conus cylinder* 234
*Conus dauciconus* 235
*Conus daucus* 235
*Conus figulinus* 36
*Conus genuanus* 36
*Conus generalis* 238
*Conus geographus* 236
*Conus gloriamaris* 234
*Conus gradatus* 239
*Conus imperialis* 237
*Conus jaspideus* 238
*Conus leptoconus* 238
*Conus lithoconus* 239
*Conus litteratus* 239
*Conus lythoglyphys* 235
*Conus marmoreus* 240
*Conus mercator* 37
*Conus nussatella* 241
*Conus princeps* 159
*Conus purpurascens* 158
*Conus regius* 159
*Conus stephanoconus* 159
*Conus striatus* 242
*Conus textile* 234
*Conus vexillum* 243
Coquina shell 48
*Corbula gibba* 38
*Corculum cardissa* 244
Crenulate auger 293
*Crepidula fornicata* 145
*Crepidula moulinsi* 145
*Crepidulidae* 145
Crown cone 159
Crown shells 70
Crucified clausilia 341
*Cryptoplax larvaeformis* 160
Cup-and-saucer shells 145
Curly carrier shell 133
*Cuspidaria cuspidata* 39
*Cuspidaria rostrata* 40
*Cyclope meritaeus* 41
*Cymatium femorale* 42
*Cymatium lotorium* 161
*Cymatium rubeculum* 245

*Cymbiinae* 43
*Cymbiola* 246
*Cymbiola aulica* 246
*Cymbiola imperialis* 246
*Cymbiolacca peristicta* 44
*Cymbium glans* 43
*Cyphoma gibbosum* 328
*Cypraea pantherina* 247
*Cypraea tigris* 248
*Cypraecassis rufa* 249
*Cypraecassis testiculus* 250
*Cyrtopleura costata* 45

Damon's volute 222
Dealer's cone 37
Deep-water cuttlefish 105
Deer-horn murex 28
Deer toe 355
*Dentalium inaequicostatum* 46
*Diodora graeca* 162
Distorsio anus 251
*Distorsio clathrata* 47
*Donax variabilis* 48
*Donax variegatus* 49
*Dreissena polymorpha* 342
*Drupa morum* 252
Dull obovaria 346
Dwarf olive 85
Dwarf red ovula 324

Eben miter 302
*Echinius nodulosus* 163
Edible oyster 197
Eglantine cowrie 271
*Emarginula puncticulata* 164
*Emarginulinae* 164
Emerald nerite 329
English garden snail 339
Episcopal miter 273
*Epitonidae* 311
*Epitonium mellosum* 311
*Epitonium scalare* 311
*Erisoria lamarcki* 50
*Erosaria nebrites* 253
*Erosaria spurca acicularis* 165
*Eulima polita* 51
*Eulimidae* 51
Eyed auger 293
Eyed cowrie 266

False angel wing 88
False prickly winkle 163
Fan scallop 30
*Fasciolaria tulipa* 52

Fasciolariinae 52
Faucet Snail 337
Favartia cellulosa 166
Ficidae 53
Ficus communis 53
Ficus filosa 53
Fig shell 53
Fimbriate helmet 24
Fissurella nodosa 167
Flabellina affinis 312
Flame auger 294
Flamed astarte 58
Flat tree oyster 314
Florida rock shell 215
Fluted giant clam 298
Foliated thorn purpura 150
Folina costata 135
Food miter 302
Formosan Babylon 13
Frill-wing murex 96
Fulgoria clara 54
Fusiform miter 273
Fusinus longicaudatus 54

Gaping tun 67
Gari costulat 56
General cone 238
Geography cone 236
Germ murex 188
Ghost murex 29
Giant owl limpet 183
Giant tun 121
Gibbula fanulum 168
Gilchrist's volute 80
Girdled rock shell 215
Gleaming mactra 66
Glorious top shell 143
Glory-of-the-Sea 234
Glossodoris valenciennesi 169
Glossus humanus 57
Glycymeris pectiniformis 254
Gmelin's top shell 168
Gold-banded volute 61
Gold-ringed cowrie 275
Golden-capped risso 327
Golden cowrie 267
Golden moon shell 280
Golden Venus 116
Gonilia calliglypta 58
Graded cone 239
Gray auger 294
Great keyhole limpet 189
Green abalone 170
Greenish edible cockle 26

Groved auger 294
Guildfordia triumphans 59

Haliotis fulgens 170
Haliotis lamellosa 171
Haliotis refescens 172
Hand's peanut shell 340
Harpa costata 60
Harpa davidis 255
Harpa major 256
Harpulina arausiaca 61
Haustellum 276
Heart cockle 57, 244
Hebrew moon snail 75
Hemitoma octoradiata 164
Hexagonal murex 191
Hexaplex princeps (murican-
  thus) 173
Hiatella arctica 174
Hinia incrassata 175
Hipponix conicus 313
Hippopus hippopus 257
Hirase's cowrie 103
History cowrie 187
Homalocantha oxyacantha 62
Homalocantha scorpio 258
Horn-colored ram's horn 348
Horn shells 27, 283
Horn welk 142
Horses' hoof 257
Hydatina albocincta 259

Imbricariinae 260
Imperial cone 237
Imperial volute 246
Incomparable scallop 86
Incurved cap shell 147
Iniforis lifuana 123
Irus irus 176
Irus Venus 176
Isognomon alatus 314

Jackknife clam 110
Janthina janthina 315
Janthina nitens 316
Japanese frog shell 17
Jasper cone 238
Jeffrey's cadulus 18
Jenneria pustulata 261
Junonia 102

Knobby keyhole limpet 167
Kuroda's volute 269

Laciniated conch 287
*Laevicardium crassum* 63
Lake fingernail clam 344
Lamarck's cowrie 50
Lamarck's baby-ear 106
*Lambis* 262
*Lambis chiragra arthritica* 262
*Lambis crocata* 262
*Lambis violacea* 262
Lamellosa wentletrap 311
Lance auger 293
*Lanceolaria grayana* 343
Large cowries 186
Large harp 256
Large-neck clam (soft-shell clam; steamer) 72
Large-ribbed cardita 148
*Latiaxis pagodus* 263
*Latiaxis pilsbryi* 264
*Latirus infundibulum* 51
Leafed telline 292
Left-handed jewel box 206
Legume pharus 90
*Leiostraca subulata* 51
*Lemintina arenaria* 177
Letter cones 239
*Leucozonia nassa* 178
*Lioconcha castrensis* 265
*Lima lima* 179
Limpets 164
Line siphonalia 108
Linnes baby-bubble 2
Lion's paw 155
Lipped cask shell 89
Lister's conch 113
Lister's river snail 357
Lithograph cone 235
*Lithophaga lithophaga* 180
Little fox miter 302
Little frog triton 98
*Littorina saxatilis* 181
*Littorina ziczac* 182
*Loligo vulgaris* 317
Long-spined nerite 352
Long-tailed spindle 55
*Lopha cristagalli* 318
Lotorium triton 161
*Lottia gigantea* 183
*Lyncina reevei* 184
*Lyncina argus* 266
*Lyncina aurantium* 267
*Lyncina camelopardalis* 268
Lyrate cockle 77
Lyre-shaped volute 269

Lyre volutes 269
*Lyria* 269
*Lyria kurodai* 269
*Lyria lyraeformis* 269
*Lyromangelia taeniata* 185
*Lyrospectiin (chlamys nodosus)* 155

McMichael's volute 44
*Macoma balthica* 64
*Macoma melo* 65
*Macrocypraea cervinetta* 186
*Macrocypraea cervus* 186
*Macrocypraea* 186
*Mactra glauca* 66
Maculated top shell 299
Madras harp 255
*Magilus antiquus* 270
Magilus coral snail 270
Magnificent wentletrap 311
*Malea ringens* 67
*Malleus albus* 68
Many-shaped dreissena 342
Many-spotted moon shell 76
Map cowrie 272
Maple leaf 350
Marble cone 240
*Marchia* 97
*Marchia elongata* 97
Marginated cowrie 140
*Marginella goodalli* 69
*Marginella hematita* 69
*Marginella pseudofaba* 69
Marginellas 69
*Margenillidae* 69
Marlinspike 293
Martini's tibia 297
*Mauritia eglantina* 271
*Mauritia histrio* 187
*Mauritia mappa* 272
Maxwell murexes 188
*Maxwellia* 188
*Maxwellia gemma* 188
*Maxwellia santarosana* 188
Mediterranean abalone 171
Mediterranean flabellina 312
Mediterranean macoma 65
Mediterranean murex 276
Mediterranean mussel 192
Mediterranean purple sea snail 316
Mediterranean umbrella shell 217
Mediterranean worm shell 177

Megathura crenulata 189
Melo amphora 43
Melongena 70
Melongena corona 70
Melongenidae 70
Miniature triton trumpet 279
Miraculous thatcheria 117
Miter pyram 282
Miters 260, 273, 302
Mitra 273
Mitra barbadensis 273
Mitra fusiformis zonata 273
Mitra mitra 273
Mitra papalis 273
Modiolula phaseolina 71
Modiolus americanus 274
Modulus modulus 319
Monetaria 275
Monetaria annulus 275
Monetaria moneta 275
Money cowry 275
Monodonta turbinata 15, 190
Mouse cowrie 107
Mouse-eared marsh snail 198
Murex 276
Murex 276
Murex brandaris 276
Murex haustellum 276
Murex pecten 276
Muricanthus (hexaplex prin-
    ceps) 173
Muricopsis 191
Muricopsis aradasii 191
Muricopsis oxytatus 191
Musculium lacustre 344
Music volute 131
Mya arenaria 72
Myrtea spinifera 73
Mytilopsis leucophaeta 345
Mytilus galloprovincialis 192

Nassa serta 296
Natica canrena 74
Naticarius hebraeus 75
Naticarius millepunctatus 76
Nautilus pompilius 320
Nebrite cowrie 253
Needle cowrie 282
Nemocardium lyratum 77
Neocancilla papilio 260
Neotrigonia margaritacea 78
Neptune shells 79
Neptunea 79
Neptunea contraria 79

Neptunea lyrata decemcostata
    79
Neptuneopsis gilchristi 80
Nerita peloronta 193
Nerita scabricosta 194
Nerite mud-snail 41
Neritina communis 321
Neritina virginea 81
Noah's arc 137
Noble wentletrap 311
Northern rough periwinkle 181
Nucula nucleus 82
Nussatella cone 241

Obovaria retusa 346
Ocean quahog 9
Octopus vulgaris 195
Odontostomus pantagruelinus
    338
Old cardita 21
Old scallop 32
Oliva 83
Oliva bulbosa 277
Oliva incrassata 83
Oliva miniacea 278
Oliva porphyria 83
Oliva sayana 83
Olivancillaria urceus 84
Olive shells 83
Olivella 85
Olivella biplicata 85
Olivella voluntella 85
One-toothed turbin 190
Opeatostoma pseudodon 196
Oporrhais occidentalis 5
Orange spider conch 262
Orbign's helmet-bubble 99
Ostrea edulis 197
Otopleura mitralis 282
Ovatella myosotis 198
Ovula ovum 322

Pacific common olive 278
Pacific tiger lucine 229
Pagoda shell 33
Pagoda latiaxis 263
Pagodula (trophon vaginatus)
    125
Painted polymita 349
Painted topshell 144
Pallium incomparabilis 86
Panamaic vitularia 218
Panther cowrie 247
Papal miter 273

Papery rapa 326
Papilio miter 260
Parasitic snails 51
Patella caerula 199, 200
Patella cochlear 200
Patella laticostata 201
Patelloida nigrosulcata 201
Pearl-bearing trigonia 78
Pearl oyster 203
Pelican's foot 6
Pelicaria vermis 114
Penicillus australis 87
Peron's atlanta 305
Petricola lithophaga 202
Petricola pholadiformis 88
Phalium labiatum 89
Pharus legumen 90
Phasianella australis 323
Philippi's star shell 138
Physa fontinalis 347
Pilsbry's latiaxis 264
Pinctata imbricata 203
Pinna rudis 91
Pisania maculosa 204
Pisania pusio 279
Pitar lupanarius 92
Pitcher olive 84
Pitted murex 166
Plactopen (chlamys magellanicus) 31
Placuna sella 93
Planorbarius corneus 348
Pleurotomaria africana 94
Polinices aurantius 280
Polinices duplicatus 95
Precious wentletrap 311
Polymita picta 349
Prickly cockle 122
Prince cone 159
Prince murex 173
Prince thorny oyster 211
Propustularia surinamensis 205
Pseudochama gryphina 206
Pseudosimnia carnea 324
Pteria hirundo 325
Pteropurpura macroptera 96
Puperita pupa 207
Purple cone 158
Purple drupe 252
Purpurellus 97
Purpurellus gambiensis 97
Pustularia childreni 281, 284
Pustulate cowrie 261

Pyramidella acus 282
Pyramidellidae 282
Pyrams 282

Quadrula quadrula 350
Queen helmet 25
Queen miter 302
Queen viana 356

Ranella olearia 98
Rapa rapa 326
Rapana bezoar 208
Recurved cone shells 11
Red abalone 172
Red barley shell 306
Reeve's cowrie 184
Reticulated cowrie-helmet 250
Rhinoclavis 283
Rhinoclavis asper 283
Rhinoclavis fasciatus 283
Ribbed cockle 22
Ribbed harp 60
Ribbed sunset clam 56
Ringicula semistriata 99
Risso 327
Rissoa auriscalpium 327
Rissoa variabilis 327
Rissoa violacea 327
Rissoina bruguierei 209
Rissoinae 327
Rock-eating petricola 202
Rock shells 215, 296
Rooster-tail conch 112
Rostrate cuspidaria 40
Rotten amber snail 351
Rough horn 283
Rough-ribbed nerite 194
Ruby triton 245
Rude pen shell 91

Saddle jingle shell 93
St. Rosana murex 188
Sand-dusted cone 230
Scallop murex 276
Scalloplike bittersweet 254
Scaphander lignarius 100
Scapharca inaequivalvis 101
Scaphella junonia 102
Schilderia hirasei 103
Scorpion murex 258
Scutus unguis 163
Sea hares 303
Seed conch 286
Senegal auger 294

Sepia officinalis 104
Sepiola 105
Sertum rock shell 296
Shark eye 95
Sheath trophon 125
Showy pheasant 331
Siliquaria ponderosa 335
Siliquaridae 335
Silvery trochus 15
Simnia spelta 328
Simnia uniplacata 328
Simnias 328
Simniinae 328
Single-toothed simnia 328
Sinistral miniature horn shells 123
Sinum concavum 106
Siphocypraea mus 107
Siphonalia signum 108
Siphonaria sirius 210
Sirius false limpet 210
Slit worm shell 335
Smaragdia viridis 329
Smooth Atlantic tegula 214
Snail patella 200
Snipe's bill murex 276
Soft-shell clam (large-neck clam; steamer), 72
Solemya togata 109
Solen vagina 110
Southern cone shells 11
Southern Mediterranean nassa 10
Southern watering pot 87
Sowerby's typhus 120
Spider conchs 262
Spindle tibia 297
Spiny cockle 1
Spiny helmet 23
Spiny lima 179
Spiny myrtea 73
Spiny theora snail 353
Spirula spirula 330
Spondylus princeps 211
Spotted pisania 204
Spurred star shell 225
Squamose chiton 153
Staphylea cassiaui 284
Steamer (large-neck clam; soft-shell clam), 72
Stellaria solaris 111
Sthenorythis pernobilis 311
Stolid cowrie 226
Stomatella callosa 285

Stone cones 239
Stout tagelus 115
Strawberry top 228
Striated cone 242
Striped horn 283
Strombus gallus 112
Strombus listeri 113
Strombus pipus 286
Strombus sinuatus 287
Strombus tricornis 288
Struthiolaria populosa 114
Struthiolariid conchs 114
Struthiolariidae 114
Subcancilla 260
Subcylindrical truncatella 216
Succinea putris 351
Sun carrier shell 111
Sundial 7
Sun-and-moon scallop 3
Sunrise tellin 119
Surinam cowrie 205
Swollen olive 277
Syrinx aranus 70

Tagelus plebeius 115
Talparia cinerea 212
Tapes aureus 116
Tasmania Venus clam 14
Tatcheria mirabilis 117
Tectarius muricatus 213
Tectus conus 289
Tectus dentatus 290
Tectus niloticus 289, 291
Tegula fasciata 214
Tellina foliacea 292
Tellina pulchella 118
Tellina radiata 119
Tent cone (textile cone) 234
Terebellum conch 295
Terebellum terebellum 295
Terebra cinera 294
Terebra crenulata 293
Terebra dislocata 294
Terebra guttata 293
Terebra lanceata 293
Terebra maculata 293
Terebra senegalensis 294
Terebra strigata 294
Terebra taurinus 294
Terebra triseriata 293
Terebridae 293, 294
Textile cone (tent cone) 234
Thaidinae 296
Thais 215

Thais cingulifera 215
Thais haemostoma floridiana 215
Theodoxus longispina 352
Thiara amarula 353
Thorn latirus 196
Three-cornered conch 288
Three-toothed cavoline 310
Thyphinellus sowerby 129
Tibia 297
Tibia fusus 297
Tibis insulae-chorab 297
Tibia martini 297
Tibia conchs 297
Tiger cowrie 248
Tongue 328
Tonna galea 121
Tooth-mouthed bulimulus 338
Toothed top shell 290
Trachycardium egmontianum 122
Tricolia speciosa 331
Tridacna squamosa 298
Triphora perversa 123
Triphoridae 123
Triscriate augcr 203
Trisidos tortuosa 124
Triton's trumpet 151
Trivia adriatica 332
Trivia pediculus 333
Trochus maculatus 299
Tropidophora carinata 354
Trophon vaginatus (pagodula) 125
True spiny jewel box 8
Truncatella subcylindra 216
Truncilla truncata 355
Tube vase 301
Tulip mussel 274
Tulip shells 52
Turbinella 126
Turbinella angulata 126
Turbinella pyrum 126
Turbo canaliculatus 300
Turret shells 127, 128
Turrinae 127
Turris babylonia 127
Turris similis 127
Turritella acutangula 128
Turritella crocea 128
Turritella mediterranea 128
Turritella nivea 128
Turritellidae 335
Turritellinae 128

Twisted arc 124
Typhinellus sowerby 120

Umboniinae 129
Umbonium giganteum 129
Umbonium moniliferum 129
Umbraculum mediterraneum 217
Unequal arc 101
Unequal-ribbed tusk 46

Variable mussel 141
Variable risso 327
Vase shells 301
Vasum 301
Vasum ceramicum 301
Vasum muricatum 301
Vasum tubiferum 301
Venus verrucosa 130
Vermicularia spirata 335
Vermiculariinae 335
Vermiculated cone 232
Vexilla vexillum 296
Vexillinae 302
Vexillum cone 243
Vexillum ebenus 302
Vexillum regina 302
Vexillum rock shell 296
Vexillum trophonia 302
Vexillum vulpecula 302
Viana regina 356
Victorious turban 59
Violet risso 327
Virgin nerite 81
Viriola 123
Vitularia salebrosa 218
Viviparus contectus 357
Voluta musica 131
Volutes 43, 246
Volutoconus bednalli 132
Volva volva 328

Wagners 338
Warty Venus 130
Waved volute 222
Wentle traps 311
West Indian top shell 156
West Indian worm shell 335
Wheat simnia 328
Whelks 70
White-banded bubble 259
White bearded ark 139
White hammer oyster 68
Wide-ribbed patella 201

Wing murex 97
Wing oyster 325
Worm shells 335

*Xenophora crispa* 133
*Xenoturris cingulifera* 127

Zaplagius 338
*Zaplagius navicula* 338
Zebra nerite 207
Zebra periwinkle 182
Zigzag Venus 265
*Zonaria annettae* 219
*Zonaria pyrum* 220
*Zonaria spadicea* 221